Brita[n]

Encyclopædia Britannica, Inc., is a leader in reference and education publishing whose products can be found in many media, from the Internet to mobile phones to books. A pioneer in electronic publishing since the early 1980s, Britannica launched the first encyclopedia on the Internet in 1994. It also continues to publish and revise its famed print set, first released in Edinburgh, Scotland, in 1768. Encyclopædia Britannica's contributors include many of the greatest writers and scholars in the world, and more than 110 Nobel Prize winners have written for Britannica. A professional editorial staff ensures that Britannica's content is clear, current, and correct. This book is principally based on content from the encyclopedia and its contributors.

Introducer

Ziauddin Sardar is a writer, broadcaster, and academic. He was born in Northern Pakistan and grew up in Hackney, London. He is Visiting Professor at City University, London, a columnist in the *New Statesman* and contributes regularly to the *Observer*. He serves as a Commissioner on the UK's Equality and Human Rights Commission. He is the author of over 40 books, including *Balti Britain* (2008), *What do Muslims Believe?* (2006), and *Desperately Seeking Paradise: Journeys of a Sceptical Muslim* (2004).

ENCYCLOPÆDIA
THE Britannica® GUIDE TO

THE ISLAMIC WORLD

Religion, history,
and the future

Introduction by Ziauddin Sardar

ROBINSON

RUNNING PRESS
PHILADELPHIA · LONDON

Constable & Robinson Ltd
3 The Lanchesters
162 Fulham Palace Road
London W6 9ER
www.constablerobinson.com

Encyclopædia Britannica, Inc.
www.britannica.com

First published in the UK by Robinson,
an imprint of Constable & Robinson, 2009

A copy of the British Library Cataloguing in Publication
Data is available from the British Library

UK ISBN 978-1-84529-819-7
1 3 5 7 9 10 8 6 4 2

First published in the United States in 2009 by Running Press Book Publishers
All rights reserved under the Pan-American and International Copyright Conventions

US Library of Congress number: 2007938550
US ISBN 978-0-7624-3420-6

Running Press Book Publishers
2300 Chestnut Street
Philadelphia, PA 19103-4371

www.runningpress.com

Visit us on the web!

Printed and bound in the EU

CONTENTS

List of Illustrations   vii

Introduction   ix
Transition and Change in the Islāmic World
by Ziauddin Sardar

Part 1   What is Islām?
1 Who was Muḥammad?   3
2 The Foundations of Islām   24
3 Islāmic Thought, Beliefs, and Practice   38

Part 2   Islāmic World History
4 The Age of Muḥammad and the Caliphate   75
5 The Flowering of Islām   105
6 Expansion, Reform, and Renewal   138

Part 3   Islām in the Modern World
7 Islāmic Revivalism   175
8 Islāmist Fundamentalism   195
9 The Twenty-first Century   209

Part 4   The Islāmic Arts

10 Architecture   243
11 Visual and Decorative Arts   280
12 Literature   300

Part 5   Places – The Islāmic World Today   349
         Glossary   415

         Index   419

LIST OF ILLUSTRATIONS

1. Domes of a mosque silhouetted against the sky, Malaysia. *Comstock/Jupiterimages, courtesy of Encyclopædia Britannica, Inc.*

2. The Prophet's Mosque in Medina, Saudi Arabia. *Nabeel Turner – Stone/Getty Images, courtesy of Encyclopædia Britannica, Inc.*

3. Pilgrims in prayer at the Great Mosque in Mecca, Saudi Arabia. *Roger Viollet/Topfoto* (RV 9341-4).

4. The angels decorating the Ka'bah at the birth of Muhammad. Miniature by Lufti Abdullah, 1594. *Roger Viollet/Topfoto* (RV 8761-2).

5. The Great Mosque of Damascus, Syria. *Nasser Rabat, courtesy of Encyclopædia Britannica, Inc.*

6. Interior of the Blue Mosque of Ottoman sultan Ahmed I, designed by Mehmed Aġa, royal architect to the Ottoman court, 1609–16. *Roger Viollet/Topfoto* (RV 7754-13).

7. Ivory casket made for al-Mughīrah, son of 'Abd ar-Rahamān III (AD 891–961), the emir of Córdoba, Spain, dating from AD 968. *Musée du Louvre, Paris; photograph Mansell – Giraudon/Art Resource, New York, courtesy of Encyclopædia Britannica, Inc.*

8. An early nineteenth-century prayer rug from the town of Ghiordes, western Anatolia. *New York state private collection; photograph Otto E. Nelson, courtesy of Encyclopædia Britannica, Inc.*

9. Islāmic calligraphy. *TopFoto/ImageWorks* (imw 00900908).

10. The confrontation between radical Islāmic groups and government forces at Lal Masjid (Red Mosque) in Islambad, Pakistan, 2007. © *RIA Novosti / TopFoto* (RIA07-017660).

INTRODUCTION

Transition and change in the Islāmic World

Ziauddin Sardar

Making sense of the complexity of the Islāmic world is only possible by being alert to the multiplicities of its diversity. The Islāmic world refers to a swathe of nations, regions, and peoples whose defining feature is adherence to the religion of Islām. While shared religion is a unifying factor, the Islāmic world is far from being a composite whole and in many ways defies easy analysis. Indeed, depending upon the prism through which it is viewed, it can appear, almost disappear, or take on markedly different configurations. Shared faith does not create a monolith, rather it raises questions about the weight and balance to be given to the divergent, and at times contending, aspects of a complex reality.

To understand the Islāmic world today, as well as in the past, requires an appreciation of the multiple traits that constantly interact to create, temper, pull apart, and reconnect this protean entity. Elements that operate to unify have to be considered as they work through various forms of diversity: traditional, modern, ethnic, cultural, and linguistic, as well as religious. Tradition and modernity are less discrete alternate poles than compound elements in all aspects of the Islāmic world. The unity of the Islāmic world is impossible to conceive without its immense diversity, and this gives a distinctive character to how the potential and aspiration for unity is understood and expressed by different people in different places – geographic, intellectual, and social, as well as religious.

The complexity begins with the attempt to define the extent of the Islāmic world. Islām as a faith and significant communal bond is not contained within a collection of neatly bounded modern nation states. Allowing for the vagaries of census taking and national sensitivities, India has possibly the world's second largest Muslim population and has been a huge influence in the history and development of contemporary Muslim thought. Yet it does not consider itself to be part of the Islāmic world, nor is it included in the conventional meaning of the term. To think of the Islāmic world solely in terms of Muslim majority nations excludes not only geographically concentrated minority populations across its border in places like India and China, it also ignores the important influence of dispersed and distant minority populations – for example, the growing Diaspora of Muslims in Western nations which has considerable influence in the intellectual arena and makes significant contributions to all the ongoing debates throughout the Islāmic world.

How the Islāmic world relates to the concept of *ummah*, the Islāmic term for the worldwide community of believers, is no easy matter. At one level all Muslims acknowledge membership of the *ummah*, yet their membership raises complicated and subtle questions about the nature of plural identity. The *ummah* has always been a global concept; nationalism is a new development that overlays and often cross-cuts that sentiment with convoluted questions relating to the meaning of loyalty and belonging. The Islāmic world is a subset of the *ummah*. Neither the *ummah* nor the Islāmic world, in history or today, has ever been or is a fixed entity. However, the inability of the organization and structure of the modern world to accommodate the unifying trends based on Islām have been driving forces of much contemporary Muslim thought and action, both positive and negative.

The sheer diversity of the geographical regions, peoples, cultures, languages, and races embraced by the Islāmic world is remarkable. In general terms it extends from the western edge of Africa – from Morocco to Senegal – across continents to the eastern edge of the Indonesian archipelago. Its northern boundary arcs from the Balkans through the newly independent republics of Central Asia to the Muslim majority region of Western China. From the steppes of Central Asia it extends southwards through the Caucasus across the Anatolian peninsula to the Mediterranean region, through the Levant and Arabian Peninsula and down from the Horn of Africa along the eastern coast of the African continent to Tanzania and northern Mozambique.

This area is what is often termed 'the global middle belt' and includes the temperate climes of eastern Europe, vast stretches of desert and savannah lands as well as tropical and equatorial lands. The enormous range of environments that are home to and have been shaped by Islāmic history comprise a comparable range of cultures and ethnicities, nations and tribes, all of which have distinct antecedents as well as varied responses to and means of incorporating and expressing Islām in individual and social life.

It is also essential to recognize that the Islāmic world does not have one integrated history but many histories. Pre-Islāmic history gives way to the diverse eras and means by which Islām was introduced to specific regions. All of its component regions have a history of mutual contact and shared influences derived from their inclusion in the Islāmic world. In history this was an open, globalized world geared to long distance trade. It was a worldwide community structured around religious institutions such as *hajj*, the once-in-a-lifetime pilgrimage to Mecca, as well as a common system of religious and legal education which, from the earliest times, facilitated and encouraged travel and hence the transmission of ideas and knowledge.

What could be called the Islāmicate era gave way to the era of western colonization. Few parts of the Islāmic world escaped colonization. Even those parts of the Islāmic world not directly or indirectly colonized were drawn into the growing power of Western economic, military, diplomatic, and cultural influence. The history of colonization adds another layer of connections and discontinuities that affect perceptions of and relations to the wider Islāmic world. The colonial legacy continues to support discontinuities in matters such as language, systems of governance, modern legal code, and social organization.

The specific history of each country's process of decolonization has been a powerful influence on the formation of the contemporary nation states in which Muslims live, which range from autocratic monarchies to authoritarian one-party states to various degrees and forms of democratic government. The history of how the Islāmic world comes to be as it is today is not merely the story of various peoples' relationship to Islām but has been formed in the crucible of their varied relations with the non-Muslim world. The result is that while it is possible to talk of general trends affecting the Islāmic world, all generalizations must be balanced by the equally important realization that there is no such thing as a typical Muslim state. Each Muslim state, each Muslim community or population is conditioned by its distinctive histories, ancient and modern.

If this broad overview seems to imply the very concept of an Islāmic world is at best only a weak connection, it needs to be balanced by considering the countervailing principles of unity. Unity is a central principle of the worldview of Islām. The very idea of unity in diversity derives from the original source of Islām: the Qur'ān. The development of Islāmic law based on the Qur'ān accepted local cultural practise as a source of law. That which did not contradict the ethical and moral precepts of Islām in pre-existing cultural practise remained permissible and valid. It was also accepted that there were various ways to achieve the ethical and moral intent of Qur'ānic principles depending on context and circumstance, which again provided an authentic opening for diversity of practise within the bounds of unity.

The Qur'ān also provides a framework – a common core of concepts and a way of reasoning – which generates strong unifying trends. Indeed, the Qur'ān plays a central part in shaping the consciousness of each individual Muslim. It is the basis of prayer, education, and study. Its injunctions shape everything from dietary laws, marriage, and family affairs to social, economic, and political organization. And its powerful emphasis on the community of believers is a motive force of the idea of an Islāmic world.

Muslims learn about the implementation of the Qur'ān through the secondary source of Islāmic law: the example of the words and actions of the Prophet Muḥammad or the *sunnah*. This secondary source provides another set of unifying principles and experience. The *sunnah* pertains to details of intimate personal behaviour and presents an idealized personality profile that bears on all aspects of individual behaviour, as well as matters of communal and social organization. It has a strong affective hold on Muslim consciousness and is known from one end of the Islāmic world to the other. The common heritage of the Qur'ān and *sunnah* in effect permits Muslims travelling to a radically different part of the Islāmic world to orient themselves easily within a new setting.

The principles of brotherhood and fellowship are not abstract but are supported by shared forms of personal behaviour that straddle cultural differences. At its most basic, Islām is a religion of the home and its strong emphasis on unity is a powerful sentiment within each individual Muslim. The affective bonds of unity exist independently of and irrespective of the complications of history and modern nation states in the individual believer.

Traditionally, it was axiomatic that a Muslim, whatever his or her origin, was in some sense a citizen of any Muslim community where any Muslim stranger could lay valid claim to real rights, obligations, and resources. In the pre-modern era this made for ease of movement of people and hence ideas and knowledge around the Islāmic world. The life story of innumerable Muslim notables includes travelling from one end of the Islāmic world to the other by way of long working sojourns in different places along the way. The mosque provides a ubiquitous infrastructure where such fellowship and services can still be accessed by strangers.

The Qur'ān and *sunnah* provide the unifying basis of shared principles and example to all Muslims. They are the basis of law not because either source is definitively a literal legal code but because the moral and ethical principles and imperatives they contain impel the formal organization of social life and communal organization as the expression of religious faith and the fulfilment of a righteous life. The creation of Islāmic law, the Sharī'ah, follows as a logical consequence of the primary sources.

The construction of law was a work of interpretation by Muslims in history, however much succeeding generations have conflated the law with those primary sources. And however much Muslims may and do argue that one God, one Qur'ān and one *sunnah* can and should mean one law and one way for all, the formulation of law in ever-expanding and diversifying communities has produced distinct schools of thought, each with different interpretations and practises. The various schools of thought developed within the diversity of Muslim societies around the globe has produced numbers of what can be termed religious dominations.

Two main divisions are widely recognized within Islām: Sunni and Shī'a. Sunnis, 'the people of the path', emphasize the *sunnah* or the way of the Prophet Muḥammad; they constitute the majority of the Muslims. The Shī'as, who believe that only descendants of the family of the Prophet have a legitimate right to claim political authority, are largely concentrated in Iran and Iraq. Within this broad division, there are other schools of thought, various movements of interpretations, and supporters of liberal, modernist or traditionalist outlooks. There are also a variety of mystical traditions, generally termed Sufism, ranging from the Whirling Dervishes of Turkey to the Qawwali singers of the Indian subcontinent.

Diversity of religious interpretation and distinctions in the schools of thought and application of Islāmic law have been part of the historic development of the Islāmic world. But as with all other aspects of diversity, the significance of these differences needs to be weighed and balanced. A city such as Istanbul can contain mosques following many different schools of thought, denominational, sectarian, or spiritual traditions. The diversity is a legacy of the Ottoman practise of recognizing plurality of schools of law. Just as the Islāmic world as a whole is not homogeneous so there are few modern nations whose entire population follow only one tradition of Islām. Historically, the differences between schools of thought and practise have not precluded mutual recognition, interaction, and influence both at the level of scholarship and among ordinary followers. Individual or communal affiliation to one tradition or another can and does go hand in hand with the acknowledgement of a superior imperative for unity. The distinctions between the various traditions are less insurmountable in theological and practical terms than among and between the denominations of Christianity, for example. Yet it is also true that affiliation to different traditions can and has become a source of tension and communal divide.

The Islāmic world is defined by the adherence of its population to Islām, but what that adherence means and how it is expressed and practiced is not self-evident. Muslims claim Islām is a total way of life, containing a blueprint for the organization and operation of the entire spectrum of the life of a society. Yet this familiar definition is in many ways more rhetorical than real; more an aspiration than a lived reality in the modern nation states in which people actually live. The sense of disconnection between the ideal and the actual is not solely the product of colonization and modernity. The question of the legitimacy of governance begins in the early years of Islāmic history and has been a driving force of the perennial reform movements.

Diversity and difference have been always balanced by the search for authenticity and uniformity. Throughout history reform movements have sought to purge Islāmic society of its imperfections, which are defined as deviations from, and corruptions of, its religious ideals and their proper interpretation as the basis for social life. Therefore it would be wrong to see the Islāmic world as static and unchanging, although this is not an uncommon impression. The Islāmic world has always been in a state of flux and tradition is invoked to describe stasis as well as the urgent call for change. In the history of the

Islāmic world as much as in the present-day, tradition is a concept that requires careful examination and definition rather than being an obvious and self-evident condition. The battle of ideas and interpretation has been ongoing throughout Islāmic history and has always been compounded by the context of social, economic, and political circumstances. At times, the appeal of Islāmic tradition has been used to resist change. At other times, places, and circumstances, Islāmic tradition has been invoked as the authentic means to effect radical change.

The ability to appeal to Islām to justify both stasis and change should not be taken as another way of saying Muslims can make of Islām whatever they wish. It would be more appropriate to see the Islāmic world as engaged in a continuous dialogue within its own defined parameters, rhetoric, ideas, and ideals. The arguments and debates within the Islāmic world cannot be understood through simplistic or one-dimensional analysis. The complexities of the Islāmic world are simultaneous and coterminous. Tradition and modernity, stasis and change, diversity and unity, authenticity and lack of legitimacy, purity and corruption, coexist – they are features of the outlook of individuals as much as conditions of society and need to be balanced and weighted to develop a rounded picture of what is happening within the Islāmic world and how its future will be shaped.

The contemporary unrest and instability in the Islāmic world, as the section 'Islām in the Modern World' shows so well, is a legacy of the activism of Islāmic reform movements as well as the rise of 'Islāmic fundamentalism' which is usually taken to have become a predominant trend after the 1979 revolution in Iran. But the role that modernity has played both in the emergence of fundamentalism and militant traditionalism is not widely recognized. From the late 1940s through to the 1960s, the period during which Muslim countries obtained their independence, modernization – or more specifically development along Western patterns – was seen as a panacea for social and economic ills. Indeed, most Muslim countries whole-heartedly embarked on a rapid course of modernization. But the strategies for modernization were, on the whole, out of sync with the traditional societies they were attempting to change. Thus a rift developed between those who backed modernization and accompanying Westernization and those who were concerned about preserving the traditional culture, lifestyle, and outlook of Muslim societies. In most cases, the traditionalists tended to be romantics who saw tradition not as a changing and evolving phenomenon, but as an entity that was fixed and frozen in history.

The modernist leaders who took over from the departing colonial powers often maintained their hold on Muslim societies by resorting to excessive use of force and by ruthlessly persecuting the traditional leadership, abusing traditional thought and everything associated with it. What was traditional was seen as a historical heritage which was 'backward', which meant 'living in the past' and being incapable of change, and thus a serious obstacle to modernization. Most of these leaders were military dictators and despots who survived, and in some cases thrived, largely with the support of Western powers. The economic and development policies they pursued often ended in spectacular failure and accumulated national wealth in fewer and fewer hands. Fundamentalism emerged as a reaction to the excesses of modernity and political despotism.

The goal of global Muslim reformist movements, such as the Muslim Brotherhood of Egypt and Jamā'at-e Islāmī of Pakistan, was much more than simply a reassertion of cultural identity, formal religious observances and expression of

Islāmic values – though these were seen to be vital. Their ultimate aim was the creation of an 'Islāmic state' where the rule of the Sharī'ah, or Islāmic law, would be paramount.

In a sense, however, all Muslims are 'fundamentalist' in that they believe the Qur'ān to be the literal Word of God. Indeed, the very definition of a Muslim is someone who believes that the Qur'ān is the absolute and immutable Word of God. What made 'Islāmic fundamentalists' so fundamentalist was their unique vision of a centralized state that would rule all aspects of the lives of its citizens. A state where politics and religion, law and morality would be one and the same thing. In this framework, the integrated, holistic, and God-centred world-view of Islām is transformed into a totalitarian, theocratic world order and a persuasive moral God is replaced by a coercive, political one. Essential to this transmuted Islāmic fundamentalism, however, is a concept of the state which owes more to modern Western theory of state formation than anything based on or derived from Islāmic history.

The fundamentalism of Islāmic fundamentalists is a new phenomenon, a new fusion of a single interpretation of Islām, seen in essentialist terms as pure and unchanging, which invokes the formative era of Islāmic history as its model but understands this model according to the form, operation, power and instrumental rationality of a modern totalitarian state. It employs a romantic idealized notion of the perfection of the formative era of Islāmic history.

Yet for all its appeal to history, such fundamentalism is ahistorical: it sees Islām not as a religion interpreted in the lives and thoughts of people called Muslims, as something that unfolded in history with all its human strengths and weaknesses, but as a utopia that exists outside time. Hence it has no notion of progress, moral development, or human evolution. Moreover, it does not recognize, understand, or appreciate

other interpretations of Islām. Those with alternative interpretations are seen as weak Muslims at best, heretics and
apostates at worse. Thus the plurality and diversity of Islām
that has existed for the last 1,500 years is expunged.

The plight of the Islāmic world today is a product of
competing visions of the fundamentalists and the modernists:
Muslim societies are being squeezed, on the one hand by the
forces of aggressive modernity, and on the other by an emergent fundamentalism that purports to be the totality of traditionalism and can take a militant, aggressive form. The ensuing
struggles are evident in many countries and everywhere serve
to create a new and disturbing polarization. How the forces
are aligned varies from country to country. The circumstances
are different in Pakistan to those in Egypt for example, though
both countries are in a perilous and precarious condition.
Intense struggles, with different permutations and combina-
tions, are being acted out from Morocco to Saudi Arabia,
Algeria, the Sudan, Bangladesh, Malaysia and all the way to
Indonesia and the new Muslim republics of Central Asia.
Muslim societies are being pulled in different directions and
face the threat of rupture and fragmentation.

This struggle between modernists and traditionalists is not
likely to be resolved in the foreseeable future. Neither party has
shown itself capable of uplifting and bettering the lot of the
Islāmic world. Locked in contention they construct a permanent
impasse that forecloses the future potential of their societies in
an intractable set of unpalatable options that result in arrested
development. Both the Westernized model of modernity and
ossified traditionalism have failed Muslim societies. Resolving
the impasse requires genuine political and institutional change.
So where does the Islāmic world go next?

A viable future for the Islāmic world is hard to imagine
without consensual politics, more open societies, and a new,

contemporary interpretation of Islām and what it means to be a Muslim in the twenty-first century. Fortunately, the tools for adjusting to change and evolving a progressive outlook are at the very heart of Islām. Such fundamental concepts of Islām as *ijtihād* (reasoned innovation), *ijmā* (consensus) and *shūrā* (consultation) can be used to develop contemporary models of governance and social change that are based on the needs and aspirations of ordinary Muslims. And there is sufficient scholarly and pragmatic work underway to provide reasons for guarded optimism.

Beyond the headline issues of conflict and the remorseless attention given to fundamentalism, it is possible to miss the significant fact that the very idea of 'reform' has changed drastically. For the Islāmic movements, reform meant imposition of the Sharī'ah and transformation of the nation into an 'Islāmic state' – this is the course that was followed, for example, in Iran, which changed into a theocracy after the revolution. The last decade, however, has seen the emergence of a new approach focused on reform within Islām based not on accepting the Sharī'ah as a given, inherited and immutable historic body of law but as a work in progress that needs to be changed, rethought, remade, and updated to accommodate, and be relevant to, contemporary times. The new notion of reform has had significant success that needs to be acknowledged and appreciated.

The reformulation of the personal law aspects of the Sharī'ah in Morocco provide an example of what can be accomplished. The new Islāmic Family Law, or *Mudawwanah*, introduced on October 10 2003, sweeps away centuries of bigotry and blatant bias against women that has been accreted as the meaning and application of the Sharī'ah. It is a product of decades of agitation by women, activists, and progressive Muslim scholars. Most importantly it was produced with the full cooperation of the religious scholars as well as the active participation of women.

The changes it introduced are noteworthy. The traditional notion of the husband as head of the family has gone, the family becomes the joint responsibility of both spouses. The degrading and debasing language previously used in reference to women has been replaced with gender-sensitive terminology. Women's marriageable age has been raised from 15 to 18, bringing it on par with that of men. Women and men now have the right to contract their own marriage without the legal approval of a guardian. Women have the right to divorce and a man's right to unilateral divorce has been ditched. Verbal divorce has been outlawed. Men now require prior authorization from a court before they can obtain a divorce. Moreover, husbands are required to pay all monies owed to the wife and children in full before a divorce can be registered. Polygamy has been all but abolished. Men can take second wives only with the full consent of the first wife and only if they can prove, in a court of law, that they can treat them both with absolute justice – an impossible condition.

Moreover, women can now claim alimony and can be granted custody of their children even if they remarry. Indeed, a woman can even regain custody of her children if the courts initially ruled in favour of the husband but the husband failed to fulfil his responsibilities. There is also provision for the child to get suitable accommodation consistent with his or her living conditions prior to the parents' divorce. This requirement is separate from the other alimony obligations, which conventionally consisted of a paltry lump sum. The new law also protects the child's right to acknowledgement of paternity in cases where the marriage has not been officially registered or the child was born outside wedlock. The new law also requires that husbands and wives share the property acquired during marriage. Husbands and wives can have separate estates but the law makes it possible for the couple to agree, in a document other than the marriage contract, on how to manage and develop assets acquired during marriage.

The traditional tribal custom of favouring male heirs in the sharing of inherited land has also been dropped, making it possible for grandchildren on the daughter's side to inherit from their grandfather. The new Sharī'ah also assigns a key role to the judiciary. Public prosecutors must now be involved in every legal action involving family affairs. New family courts have been set up and a family mutual assistance fund has been established to ensure that the new code is effectively enforced. The reformulated Sharī'ah enshrines the principle that minorities should be allowed to follow their own laws. So Moroccan Jews can be governed by the provisions of the Hebraic Moroccan Family Law.

Morocco has demonstrated the Sharī'ah is not fixed in the way that most puritan Muslims believe it to be. It can be changed; and every change in the law can be justified with chapter and verse from the Qur'ān and the example and sayings of the Prophet Muḥammad. Furthermore, this change can have the consent and consensus of religious scholars. Not surprisingly, the new law has been welcomed not only by women's groups but also by the mainstream Islāmic parties. Where Morocco has led, other Muslim countries will follow. Indeed, similar efforts at reformulation of the Sharī'ah, or attempts at *ijtihād*, are on the agenda in Indonesia, Malaysia, India, and even in the Gulf States.

The relationship between Islām and politics is undergoing a parallel transformation. The conventional notion of Islāmic movements that politics should be geared to establishing an 'Islāmic state' has shifted. Increasingly, the politics of Islām are being focused on creating a democratically accountable civic society. Turkey is a leading example of this trend. The Justice and Development Party (AKP), which came to power in 2002, has deep Islāmic roots for which it has been challenged in the courts by its secular Kemalist opposition. But AKP's perception of Islāmic politics has nothing to do with a utopian Islāmic state.

Its leaders argue the Islāmic principle of *shūrā*, or consultation, means that politics in Islām has to be consensual and based on democratic principles. AKP introduced more liberal reforms than any other secular Turkish government in modern times: the death penalty was abolished and minorities were given more freedom including the right to their own minority language education. In pursuit of its stated objective of gaining admission to the European Union, various pieces of human rights legislation have been put on the statute books, including ending punishment for criticism of the armed forces.

Indeed, the AKP even tried to change the law to ensure the Turkish military cannot intervene in the democratic process, as it has done on numerous occasions in recent history. Economically, the AKP has provided efficient and effective management, making its administration one of the most successful in Turkish history by producing a dramatic turnaround in the country's fortunes. But more than anything else, AKP has demonstrated that Islāmic politics is much more than an ideology for the fanatics. It can be, and is, an effective instrument for mobilizing civic forces and establishing a stable functioning democracy in a society. Islām is not a threat to democracy or secularism.

Indonesia has achieved even more spectacular success in realigning Islāmic politics with democracy and civic institutions. The reformist agenda in Indonesia is led by two of the largest and most influential organizations in the country: Muhamadiyah and Nahdatul Ulama (NU). Established at the dawn of the twentieth century, these organizations command some 60 to 80 million followers spread across a vast network of mosques, schools, and universities throughout the country. Conventionally NU, which is essentially an organization of religious scholars, has been described as traditionalist; while Muhamadiyah, dominated by intellectuals and thinkers, has been seen as a modernist organization.

Since 9/11, however, these distinctions have become meaningless and the two organizations cooperate to promote a new concept of Islāmic politics focused on the creation of civic society. They campaign jointly against corruption in public life and for accountable, open democracy. The reform programme of Muhamadiyah, NU and Liberal Islām Network, a group of young, liberal writers, scholars, thinkers, and activists who publish on the internet, is described as 'deformalization'. Overemphasis on formality and symbolism, Indonesian thinkers argue, has drained Islām of vital elements; and Muslim societies need to move away from this obsession with formalism.

Deformalization has two objectives. First, it seeks to restore the missing ethical and humane aspects of Islām. Second, it seeks to separate the Sharī'ah from politics and to redefine Islāmic politics as the politics of civic society. Both politics and the Sharī'ah have to evolve from the grass roots to meet the demands of the twenty-first century. The programme has been so successful that virtually all mainstream Islāmic political parties in Indonesia now reject the formal implementation of the Sharī'ah as a state ideology.

Developments such as those taking place in Turkey and Indonesia are part of a growing debate in which Muslims around the world are acknowledging the need for fundamental change in their perception of Islām. There are indications of serious introspection; and conscious efforts are being made to move away from the medieval notions of Islāmic law and implement a vision of justice, equality, and beauty that is rooted in the Qur'ān.

From Morocco to Indonesia, efforts are being made to develop a more contemporary and humane interpretation of Islām. A new synthesis is emerging. Tradition is being redefined as a life enhancing force that is amenable to change, indeed, which must continually adapt to maintain itself. This redefined adaptive tradition can generate its own indigenous form of modernity as an expression of its core values and with respect for, and relevance to, the lifestyles of traditional cultures. The emerging synthesis is more evident on the periphery of the Islāmic world than at the centre – the Middle East. But throughout history, it has always been the periphery that has changed the centre and eventually the whole of the Islāmic world.

However, not all experiments have been successful. The Muslim majority region of northern Nigeria has long felt neglected and overlooked within the creaking and struggling politics of Africa's most populous nation. The endemic problems of corruption, mal- and mis-development in an oil-rich state have brought little improvement to the Muslim region. Activists argued that to change the circumstances of peoples' lives required a new ethos. Institutionalizing the Sharī'ah would provide this impetus by returning the population to their own code of cherished values. This would make exhortations to personal responsibility and mutual obligation more than rhetoric. It would provide a coherent vision of development and extended Islāmic values that people understood and to which they were committed across the whole spectrum of social life. It would mobilize and motivate popular support for genuine reform to deliver better living standards and social welfare for all.

When the campaign for Sharī'ah law succeeded, however, its proponents found they had to contend with the other face of tradition. Local Sharī'ah courts not only remained intact but acquired a significance they had not had in many decades. They were manned by old school *'ulama'*, the under-educated products of a system of Islāmic education that was neither reformed nor revitalized. The result was a spate of adultery cases which brought international attention focused on the prospect of a few unfortunate women being stoned for alleged adultery while their male partners went scot-free. It is not what the advocates of the extensive application of Islāmic principles and law to economic and social problems had envisaged.

But, as in so many other Muslim countries, personal and family law were the vestigial aspects of Islāmic law permitted to survive under colonial rule and in operating these areas of law judges made up with prurience what had been lost in autonomy. The local judges had not been engaged in new thinking, nor did they seem aware of the potential interpretations possible within the existing body of Sharī'ah law. The proponents of Sharī'ah had to console themselves with the knowledge that women found guilty in local courts would have their convictions overturned on appeal to higher courts – or if all else failed would be saved by the intervention of the Nigerian government, the very body whose shortcomings they sought to overcome by a return to Islāmic law.

In Northern Nigeria it was evident, as it has been in many other Muslim countries, that the potential for Islāmic reform requires preparation, the kind of preparing the way that cannot be provided by traditional Islāmic educational institutions. Without the critical mass of critical thinking and wholesale public participation in education and debate, Islāmic reform can be stillborn.

The Islāmic world is deeply traditional; and tradition will play an important part in its future. But what is meant by tradition, its content, application, and interpretation is the most important question. Invoking tradition does not mean the same thing to everyone. There are many and diverse meanings to tradition that jostle with each other across the Muslim world. The tradition of those highly educated in the modern Westernized system can be very different to the tradition of a landless farm worker in a rural backwater. Both have great attachment to tradition as a function of Islām and an inheritance of Islāmic history, but mutual consensus ends at the level of rhetoric. Educated urban elites are finding new confidence in arguing that tradition is not static, defined, and fixed as inherited from earlier ages.

There is increasing vigour and critical mass in the groups arguing that tradition becomes most truly tradition when it is constantly being reinvented, rethought, and changed while remaining true to and retaining its original spirit. Muslim identity is invested in Islāmic tradition, but finds it truncated, marginalized and much neglected as an irrelevance to the modern world. Taking a balanced view of the future potential of tradition requires more than bemoaning the failure of modern national governments and modernity in general. It demands undertaking a critical evaluation of Islāmic thought and ideas as they have been transmitted through history. It will require addressing the problems of history that encrust the Islāmic education and render it unfit for the purpose of serving an informed, open minded civic society that needs to think its way to relevant solutions to its contemporary problems. Belonging is more than strong sentimental affection, it requires becoming responsible for how tradition and affiliation meet the challenge of the times.

There is little point in eulogizing the virtues of traditional society if it cannot adapt to save its cherished values, ethos, and worldview from irrelevance to daily life in contemporary circumstances. The desire to be relevant has driven reform movements throughout history and across the extent of the Islāmic world. Reform has not always brought positive and beneficial change. It has created monsters, confusion, and often failed to enhance the capacities of Muslim society. The aspiration of Muslims to remain true to their identity defined by their affiliation to Islām has never been in doubt. The crucial question is whether, and how, the new critical reform dedicated to liberal interpretation and civic society can achieve the critical mass to effect meaningful change and deliver a vibrant future for the Islāmic world.

Traditional societies change slowly, at their own speed, within their own parameters, and towards their chosen direction. So change in the Islāmic world would be slow and painful, and sometimes minor; but even minor changes have the potential to generate major perturbations. The important thing to realize is that the Islāmic world is not static but dynamic. It is changing and will continue to change. Thus the future will be radically different from the past.

PART I

WHAT IS ISLĀM?

I

WHO WAS MUḤAMMAD?

Adherence to Islām is a global phenomenon: Muslims predominate in some 30 to 40 countries, from the Atlantic to
the Pacific and along a belt that stretches across northern
Africa into Central Asia and south to the northern regions of
the Indian subcontinent. The Islāmic faith continues to
expand, by some estimates faster than any other major
religion. In the early twenty-first century there were nearly
1.4 billion practising Muslims in more than 200 countries.
Islām is the world's second most populous religion after
Christianity (some 2.2 billion).

Islām was founded by the Prophet Muḥammad in Arabia in
the seventh century AD. The Arabic term *islām*, literally
"surrender", illuminates the fundamental religious idea of
Islām – that the believer (called a Muslim, from the active
particle of *islām*) accepts "surrender to the will of Allāh"
(Arabic for God). Allāh is viewed as the sole God – creator,
sustainer, and restorer of the world. The will of Allāh, to which
humanity must submit, is made known through the sacred
scriptures, the Qur'ān (Koran), which Allāh revealed to his

messenger, Muḥammad. In Islām Muḥammad is considered the last of a series of prophets (including Adam, Noah, Abraham, Moses, Jesus, and others), and his message simultaneously consummates and completes the "revelations" attributed to earlier prophets. Although many sectarian movements have arisen within Islām, all Muslims are bound by a common faith and a sense of belonging to a single community.

Muḥammad, in full Abū al-Qāsim Muḥammad ibn ʿAbd Allāh ibn ʿAbd al-Muṭṭalib ibn Hāshim, was born in Mecca, in Arabia (now in Saudi Arabia) in AD 570 and died in Medina on June 8 632. He is the only founder of a major world religion who lived in the full light of history and about whom there are numerous records in historical texts, although like other premodern historical figures not every detail of his life is known. Because Muḥammad is one of the most influential figures in history, his life, deeds, and thoughts have been debated by followers and opponents over the centuries.

Names and Titles of the Prophet

The most common name of Muḥammad, "the Glorified One", is part of the daily call to prayer (*adhān*); following the attestation to the oneness of God, the believer proclaims, "Verily, I bear witness that Muḥammad is the Messenger of God" (*Ashhadu anna Muḥammadan rasūl Allāh*). When this name is uttered among Muslims, it is always followed by the phrase *ṣalla Allāhu ʿalayhi wa sallam* ("may God's blessings and peace be upon him"), just as, whenever Muslims mention the name of other prophets such as Abraham, Moses, or Jesus, they recite the words *ʿalayhi al-salām* ("upon him be [God's] peace"). Muḥammad also became widely known in Europe by diverse forms of the name such as Mahon, Mahomés, Mahun, Mahum, and Mahumet (all French), Machmet (German), and Maúmet (Old Icelandic). Moreover, Muḥammad is the most popular male name in the Islāmic world, either by itself or in combination with other names such as 'Alī (Muḥammad's cousin and son-in-law) and Ḥusayn (Muḥammad's grandson and 'Alī's son).

Muḥammad, however, has many other names, including "sacred names", which Muslims believe were given to him by God and by which he is called in various contexts. Traditionally, 99 names for him are commonly used in litanies and prayers. Among the most often used and also central to the understanding of his nature is Aḥmad ("the Most Glorified"), which is considered an inner and celestial name for Muḥammad. Over the centuries Muslim authorities have believed that, when Christ spoke of the coming reign of the Paraclete, he was referring to Aḥmad. Also of great importance are the names that identify Muḥammad as the Prophet, including Nabī ("Prophet") and Rasūl Allāh ("the Messenger of God"). Other names of the Prophet are Ṭaha ("the Pure Purifier and Guide"), Yāsīn ("the Perfect Man"), Muṣṭafā ("the One Chosen"), 'Abd Allāh ("the Perfect Servant of God"), Ḥabīb Allāh ("the Beloved of God"), Dhikr Allāh ("the Remembrance of God"), Amīn ("the Trusted One"), Sirāj ("the Torch Lighting the True Path"), Munīr ("the Illuminator of the Universe"), Hudā ("the Guide to the Truth"), Ghiyāth ("the Helper"), and Ni 'mat Allāh ("the Gift of God"). These and his many other names play a major role in daily Muslim piety and in the practice of Sufism, or Islāmic mysticism (see Chapter 5, The Flowering of Islām).

The Early Life of Muḥammad

Both before the rise of Islām and during the Islāmic period, Arab tribes paid great attention to genealogy and guarded their knowledge of it with meticulous care, developing a whole science of genealogy (*'ilm al-ansāb*) that is of much historical significance. Muslims trace Muḥammad's ancestry to Isma'il (Ishmael) and hence to the prophet Abraham. According to traditional Islāmic sources, Muḥammad was born in Mecca in "the Year of the Elephant", which corresponds to the year AD 570. A single event gave the Year of the Elephant its name when Abrahah, the king of Abyssinia, sent an overwhelming force to Mecca to destroy the Ka'bah, the sanctuary which Muslims believe was built by Adam and reconstructed by Abraham, and which Abrahah viewed as a rival to his newly constructed temple in Sanaa in Yemen. According to tradition, the elephant that marched at the head of Abrahah's army knelt as it approached Mecca, refusing to go further. Soon the sky blackened with birds that pelted the army with pebbles, driving them off in disarray. Thus, the sanctuary that Muslims consider an earthly reflection of the celestial temple was saved, though at the time it served Arab tribes who (with the exception of the *ḥanīf*s, or primordialists) disregarded Abrahamic monotheism.

Soon after this momentous event, Muḥammad was born in Mecca. His father, 'Abd Allāh, and his mother, Āminah, belonged to the family of the Banū Hashīm, a branch of the powerful Quraysh, the ruling tribe of Mecca, that also guarded its most sacred shrine, the Ka'bah. Because 'Abd Allāh died before Muḥammad's birth, Āminah placed all her hopes in the newborn child. Without a father, Muḥammad experienced many hardships even though his grandfather 'Abd al-Muṭṭalib was a leader in the Meccan community. The emphasis in

Islāmic society on generosity to orphans is related to the childhood experiences of Muḥammad as well as to his subsequent love for orphans and the Qur'ānic injunctions concerning their treatment.

In order for Muḥammad to master Arabic in its pure form and become well acquainted with Arab traditions, Āminah sent him as a baby into the desert, as was the custom of all great Arab families at that time. In the desert, it was believed, one learned the qualities of self-discipline, nobility, and freedom. A sojourn in the desert also offered escape from the domination of time and the corruption of the city. Moreover, it provided the opportunity to become a better speaker through exposure to the eloquent Arabic spoken by the Bedouin. In this way the bond with the desert and its purity and sobriety was renewed for city dwellers in every generation. Āminah chose a poor woman named Ḥalīmah from the tribe of Banū Sa'd, a branch of the Hawāzin, to suckle and nurture her son. And so the young Muḥammad spent several years in the desert.

It was at this time that, according to tradition, two angels appeared to Muḥammad in the guise of men, opened his breast, and purified his heart with snow. This episode, which exemplifies the Islāmic belief that God purified his prophet and protected him from sin, was also described by Muḥammad: "There came unto me two men, clothed in white, with a gold basin full of snow. Then they laid upon me, and, splitting open my breast, they brought forth my heart. This likewise they split open and took from it a black clot which they cast away. Then they washed my heart and my breast with the snow." Muḥammad then repeated the verse, found in the Hadith (literally, "Report"; a collection of sayings attributed to the Prophet and members of the early Muslim community), "Satan toucheth every son of Adam the day his mother beareth him, save only Mary and her son." Amazed by this event and also noticing a mole on Muḥammad's back (later identified in the traditional sources as the sign of prophecy), Ḥalīmah and her husband, Ḥārith, took the boy back to Mecca.

Muḥammad's mother died when he was six years old. Now completely orphaned, he was brought up by his grandfather ʿAbd al-Muṭṭalib, who also died two years later. He was then placed in the care of Abū Ṭālib, Muḥammad's uncle and the father of ʿAlī, Muḥammad's cousin. Later in life Muḥammad would repay this kindness by taking ʿAlī into his household and giving his daughter Fāṭimah to him in marriage.

It is believed that Muḥammad grew into a young man of unusual physical beauty as well as generosity of character. His sense of fairness and justice were so revered that the people of Mecca often went to him for arbitration and knew him as al-Amīn, "the Trusted One". His striking appearance is the subject of countless poems in various Islāmic languages. Muḥammad, according to ʿAlī, was neither tall nor lanky nor short and stocky, but of medium height. His hair was neither crisply curled nor straight but moderately wavy. He was not overweight and his face was not plump. He had a round face. His complexion was white tinged with redness. He had big black eyes with long lashes. His brows were heavy and his shoulders broad. He had soft skin, with fine hair covering the line from mid-chest to navel. The palms of his hands and the soles of his feet were firmly padded. He walked with a firm gait, as if striding downhill. On his back between his shoulders lay the Seal of Prophethood (a mole), for he was the last of the prophets. Islāmic sources indicate that others recognized the mole as the sign of prophethood, including the Christian monk Baḥīrā, who met Muḥammad when the Prophet joined Abū Ṭālib on a caravan trip to Syria.

When he was 25 years old, Muḥammad received a marriage proposal from a wealthy Meccan woman, Khadījah bint al-Khuwaylid, whose affairs he was conducting. Despite the fact that she was 15 years older, Muhammad accepted the proposal. She bore him two sons, both of whom died young. It is from the first son, Qāsim, that one of the names of the Prophet, Abū' al-Qāsim ("the Father of Qāsim"), derives. Khadījah also bore him four daughters. Members of the Shī'ite branch of Islām are thought to be descendants of Muhammad, from the lineage of Fātimah, his youngest daughter, and 'Alī. Khadījah herself is considered one of the foremost female saints in Islām and, along with Fātimah, plays a very important role in Islāmic piety and in eschatological events connected with the souls of women.

By age 35, Muhammad had become a very respected figure in Mecca and had taken 'Alī into his household. When he was asked, according to Islāmic tradition, to arbitrate a dispute concerning which tribe should place the holy black stone in the corner of the newly built Ka'bah, Muhammad resolved the conflict by putting his cloak on the ground with the stone in the middle and having a representative of each tribe lift a corner of it until the stone reached the appropriate height to be set in the wall. His reputation stemmed, in part, from his deep religiosity and attention to prayer. He would often leave the city and retire to the desert for prayer and meditation. Moreover, before the advent of his prophecy, he received visions that he described as being like "the breaking of the light of dawn". It was during one of these periods of retreat, when he was 40 years old and meditating in a cave called al-Hirā' in the Mountain of Light (Jabal al-Nūr) near Mecca, that Muhammad experienced the presence of the archangel Gabriel and the process of the Qur'ānic revelation began.

The Advent of the Revelation
and the Meccan Period

In the month of Ramadan (the ninth month of the Islāmic calendar), in the year 610, the archangel Gabriel, in the form of a man, appeared to Muḥammad, asked him to "recite" (*iqra'*), then overwhelmed him with a very strong embrace. Muḥammad told the stranger that he was not a reciter. But the angel repeated his demand and embrace three times, before the verses of the Qur'ān, beginning with "Recite in the Name of thy Lord who created", were revealed. Muḥammad fled the cave thinking that he had become possessed by the *jinn*, or demons. When he heard a voice saying, "Thou art the messenger of God and I am Gabriel," Muḥammad ran down the mountain. Gazing upward, he saw the man who had spoken to him in his real form, an angel so immense that in whatever direction the Prophet looked the celestial figure covered the sky, which had turned green, the official colour of Islām to this day.

Muḥammad returned home and told Khadījah what had happened. She believed his account and sent for her blind cousin Waraqah, a Christian who possessed much religious wisdom. Having heard the account, Waraqah also confirmed the fact that Muḥammad had been chosen as God's prophet, and shortly afterwards Muḥammad received a second revelation. As the Prophet said later, the revelation would either come through the words of the archangel or be directly revealed to him in his heart. The revelation was accompanied by the sound of bell-like reverberations. According to Islāmic tradition, the process of the revelation of the Qur'ān lasted some 23 years and ended shortly before the Prophet's death.

Muḥammad first preached his message to the members of his family, then to a few friends, and finally, three years after the advent of the revelation, to the public at large. The first to accept Muḥammad's call to become Muslims were Khadījah, 'Alī, Zayd ibn al-Ḥārith, who was like a son to the Prophet, and Abū Bakr, a venerable member of the Meccan community who was a close friend. This small group was the centre from which Islām grew in ever-wider circles. Besides Muḥammad's family and friends, a number of prominent Meccans embraced Islām. However, most influential figures and families rejected his call, especially those prominent in trade. Even within his family there were sceptics. Although Muḥammad gained the support of many of the Banū Hāshim, his uncle Abū Lahab, a major leader of the Quraysh, remained adamantly opposed to Islām and Muḥammad's mission. These naysayers feared that the new religion, based on the oneness of God and unequivocally opposed to idolatry, would destroy the favoured position of the Ka'bah as the centre of the religious cults of various Arab tribes and hence jeopardize the commerce that accompanied the pilgrimage to Mecca to worship idols kept in or on the Ka'bah.

As Muḥammad's message spread, opposition to him grew and was led by 'Amr ibn Hishām, dubbed Abū Jahl ("Father of Ignorance") by the early Muslims. Abū Jahl even had some early converts tortured, which resulted in the death of one of them. Muḥammad then gave permission to a number of early disciples to migrate temporarily to Abyssinia, where the country's monarch, the negus, received them with kindness and generosity. They joined Muḥammad later in Medina. Meanwhile in Mecca, life for Muḥammad and the early Muslims was becoming ever more difficult and dangerous as the result of extreme pressure exerted upon them by the Quraysh rulers of the city.

In 619 Muḥammad was greatly saddened by the death of Khadījah and his uncle Abū Ṭālib. Not only was Khadījah his devoted wife of 25 years and the mother of his children, but she was also his friend and counsellor. (Only after her death did Muḥammad marry other women, mostly as a means of creating alliances with various families and tribes. The exception was the daughter of Abū Bakr, 'Ā'ishah, who was betrothed to the Prophet when she was very young and in whose arms he would die in Medina.) The death of Abū Ṭālib, Muḥammad's protector, created a much more difficult situation for him and for the young Islāmic community in Mecca. These deaths, combined with Muḥammad's lack of success in propagating the message of Islām in the city of Ṭā'if, severely tested his determination and resolve.

During this extremely difficult time Muḥammad underwent the supreme spiritual experience of his life. On one of his nightly visits to the Ka'bah, he fell asleep in the Ḥijr, an uncovered sanctuary attached to the north wall of the shrine, and experienced the Nocturnal Ascent (Isrā' or Mi'rāj), which is mentioned in the Qur'ān, numerous Hadith, and nearly every work of Islāmic sacred history. According to traditional accounts, Muḥammad was taken by the archangel Gabriel on the winged steed Burāq to Jerusalem. From the rock upon which Abraham offered to sacrifice his son (now the site of the Dome of the Rock, one of Islām's earliest and greatest mosques), they ascended through all the higher states of being to the Divine Presence itself. At one point Gabriel explained that he could go no further because, were he to do so, his wings would be burned; that is, Muḥammad had reached a state higher than that of the archangels. Muḥammad is said to have received the supreme treasury of knowledge while he stood and then prostrated himself before the divine throne. God also revealed to him the final form and number of the Islāmic daily prayers. In addition, it is said that, while going through the higher states of being symbolized by the heavenly spheres,

Muḥammad met earlier great prophets such as Moses and Jesus.

Traditional Muslims believe that the Mi'rāj of the Prophet was not only spiritual but also corporeal in the same way that Christ's Ascension was accomplished in both body and spirit, according to traditional Christian belief. Modern Western scholars usually consider Muḥammad's experience to be an inner vision or dream, while some modernized Muslims, responding to secularist and rationalistic objections, claim that the Mi'rāj was only spiritual. The Mi'rāj is the prototype of spiritual realization in Islām and signifies the final integration of the spiritual, psychic, and physical elements of the human state. Because of its central spiritual importance, the Mi'rāj has been the source of many major literary and metaphysical works in both prose and poetry, and figures as different as the philosophers Avicenna and Ibn al-Arabī have written of its inner meaning. The Mi'rāj is also one of the reasons why Muslims hold Jerusalem sacred.

The idea of spreading the message of Islām beyond Mecca grew in Muḥammad's mind despite the setback in Ṭā'if. In or around 621 a delegation from Yathrib, a city north of Mecca, contacted Muḥammad and, having heard of his sense of justice and power of leadership, invited him to go to their city and become their leader. At that time Yathrib endured a constant struggle between its two leading tribes, the 'Aws and the Khazraj, with a sizeable Jewish community constituting the third important social group of the city. After some deliberation by Muḥammad, a preliminary meeting was held in Al-'Aqabah (now in Jordan), and during the pilgrimage season of 622 a formal agreement was made with the people of Yathrib according to which Muḥammad and his followers would be protected by the people of that city. Upon finalizing the agreement, Muḥammad ordered his followers to leave Mecca in small groups, so as not to attract attention, and to await him in Yathrib.

Finally, he departed one evening with his friend Abū Bakr for Yathrib, using an indirect route after commanding 'Alī to sleep in the Prophet's bed. The Quraysh, who had decided to get rid of the Prophet once and for all, attacked the house but found 'Alī in Muḥammad's place. They then set out to find the Prophet. According to the traditional Islāmic version of the story, which is rejected by most modern Western historians, Muḥammad and Abū Bakr hid in a cave that was then camouflaged by spiders, which spun webs over its mouth, and birds, which placed their nests in front of the cave. Once the search party arrived at the mouth of the cave, they decided not to go in because the unbroken cobwebs and undisturbed nests seemed to indicate that no one could be inside. This story, mentioned in the ninth chapter of the Qur'ān, is of great symbolic importance and is also a popular part of Islāmic piety and Sufi literature.

On September 25 622, Muḥammad completed the Hijrah ("emigration") to Yathrib, which became known as Madīnat al-Nabī ("City of the Prophet"), or Medina. This momentous event led to the establishment of Islām as a religious and social order and became the starting point for the Islāmic calendar.

Muḥammad arrived in Qubā', on the outskirts of Medina, where he ordered the first mosque of Islām to be built. The people of the city came in large numbers to greet him, and each family wanted to take him to its own quarters. Therefore, he said that his camel, Qaṣwrā', should be allowed to go where it willed, and where it stopped, he would stay. A mosque, known later as the Mosque of the Prophet (Masjid al-Nabī), was built in the courtyard next to the house where the camel stopped and Muḥammad subsequently lived. Muḥammad's tomb is in the mosque.

The Medinan Period

When Muḥammad first settled in Medina, his most trusted followers were those who had migrated from Mecca. Soon, however, many Medinans embraced Islām, so the early Islāmic community came to consist of the emigrants (*al-muhājirūn*) and the Medinan helpers (*al-anṣār*). A few Medinan families and some prominent figures such as 'Abd Allāh ibn Ubayy held back, but gradually all the Arabs of Medina embraced Islām. Nevertheless, tribal divisions remained, along with a continued Jewish presence. Muḥammad hoped that they would come to embrace Islām and accept him as a prophet, but as he integrated the Medinan community into an Islāmic society, the enmity between Medina's Jewish community and the newly founded Islāmic order grew.

During the second year of the Hijrah, Muḥammad drew up the Constitution of Medina, defining relations between the various groups in the first Islāmic community. Later generations of Islāmic political thinkers have paid much attention to the constitution, for Muslims believe that Muḥammad created the ideal Islāmic society in Medina, providing a model for all later generations. It was a society in which the integration of tribal groups and various social and economic classes was based on social justice. According to Islāmic belief, that same year the *qiblah,* or the direction in which Muslims offered daily prayers, was changed by divine order from Jerusalem to Mecca, marking the clear crystallization of Islām as a distinct monotheistic religion. Jerusalem has continued to be revered as the first direction of the prayers chosen by God for Muslims, and, according to Islāmic eschatological teachings, the first *qiblah* will become one with the *qiblah* at Mecca at the end of time.

It was also in the year 622 that the message of Islām was explicitly defined as a return to the pure monotheism of

Abraham, or the primordial monotheism (*al-din al-ḥanīf*). From that time until his death, Muḥammad not only continued to be the channel for the revelation of the Qur'ān but also ruled the community of Muslims. He was also the judge and supreme interpreter of the law of Medinan society.

The Early Battles

The enmity between the Quraysh and Muḥammad remained very strong, in part because of the persecution, aggression, and confiscation of property the Muslims suffered at the hands of the Quraysh. On several occasions warriors from Medina intercepted caravans from Mecca going to or coming from Syria, but Muḥammad did not want to fight a battle against the Meccans until they marched against the nascent Medinan community and threatened the very future of Islām. At this time the following Qur'ānic verse was revealed: "Permission to fight is granted to those against whom war is made, because they have been wronged, and God indeed has the power to help them. They are those who have been driven out of their homes unjustly only because they affirmed: Our Lord is God" (22:39–40). Muslims saw this verse as a declaration of war by God against the idolatrous Quraysh.

In 624 an army of 1,000 men assembled by the Quraysh marched against Medina and met a much smaller force of 313 Muslims at a place called Badr on the seventeenth day of the month of Ramadan. Although the number of those involved was small, this event is seen by Muslims as the most momentous battle of Islāmic history. Muḥammad promised all those who were killed at Badr the death of a martyr and direct entry into paradise. Although heavily outnumbered, the Muslims achieved a remarkable victory. However, nine of the Companions of the Prophet (al-sahabah), the close associates of Muḥammad and the faithful who had personal contact with him, were killed. Muslims believe that the battle was won with the help of the angels, and to this day the whole episode remains etched deeply in the historical consciousness of Muslims.

The Quraysh, however, did not give up their quest to destroy the nascent Islāmic community. In 624–5 they dispatched an army of 3,000 men under the leader of Mecca, Abū Sufyan. Muḥammad led his forces to the side of a mountain near Medina called Uhud, and battle ensued. The Muslims had some success early in the engagement. However, after some Muslim soldiers deserted their posts to join in the looting of the Quraysh camp, Khalid ibn al-Walīd, a leading Meccan general and later one of the outstanding military figures of early Islāmic history, charged Muḥammad's left flank and defeated him.

The Jews of Medina, who allegedly plotted with the Quraysh, rejoiced in Muḥammad's defeat and in 626–7 urged the Quraysh to take over Medina. To this end the Quraysh helped raise an army of 10,000 men, which marched on Medina. Salman al-Farsi, the first Persian convert to Islām, whom Muḥammad had adopted as a member of his household, suggested that the Muslims dig a ditch around the city to protect it, a technique known to the Persians but not to the Arabs at that time. The Meccan army arrived and, unable to cross the ditch, laid siege to the city but without success. The invading army gradually began to disperse, leaving the Muslims victorious in the Battle of the Ditch (al-Khandaq).

When it was discovered that members of the Jewish tribe Qurayzah had been complicit with the enemy during the Battle of the Ditch, Muḥammad turned against them. The Qurayzah men were separated from the tribe's women and children and ordered by the Muslim general Sa'd ibn Mu'adh to be put to death; the women and children were enslaved. This tragic episode cast a shadow upon relations between the two communities for many centuries, even though the Jews, a "People of the Book" (that is, like Christians and Zoroastrians, as well as Muslims, possessors of a divinely revealed scripture), generally enjoyed the protection of their lives, property, and religion under Islāmic rule.

The Islāmic community had become more solidly established by 628, and in that year Muhammad decided to make the 'umrah ("lesser pilgrimage") to the Ka'bah. He set out for Mecca with a large entourage and many animals meant for sacrifice, but an armed Meccan contingent blocked his way. Because he had intended to perform a religious rite, he did not want to battle the Meccans at that time. So he camped at a site known as Al-Hudaybiyah and sent 'Uthmān ibn 'Affān, later the third caliph (khalīfah, "successor") of the Islāmic community, to Mecca to negotiate a peaceful visit. When 'Uthmān was delayed, Muhammad assembled his followers and had them make a pact of allegiance (al-bay'ah) to follow him under all conditions unto death, an act of great significance for later Islāmic history and Sufi belief and practice. Uthmān finally returned with Quraysh leaders who proposed as a compromise that Muhammad return to Medina but make a peaceful pilgrimage to Mecca the next year. In addition, a ten-year truce was signed with the Meccans.

In 628–9 Muhammad's first conquest was made when the Muslims captured Khaybar in a battle in which the valour of 'Alī played an important role. The Jews and Christians of Khaybar were allowed to live in peace, protected by the Muslims, but they were required to pay a religious tax called the jizyah. This became the model for the later treatment of People of the Book in Islāmic history.

It was also at this time that Muḥammad, according to Islāmic sources, sent letters inviting various leaders to accept Islām, including Muqawqis, the governor of Alexandria; the negus of Abyssinia; Heraclius, the emperor of Byzantinum; and Khosrow II, the king of Persia. He emphasized in these letters that there should be no compulsion for People of the Book to accept Islām.

In 628–9 Muḥammad finally made a pilgrimage to Mecca and reconciled members of his family and also many of his followers. During this pilgrimage a number of eminent Meccans – including two later major military and political figures, Khalid ibn Walīd and 'Amr ibn al-'Ās – accepted Islām, while Muhammad's uncle al-'Abbās, then the head of the Banū Hāshim family, was said to have secretly become a Muslim. Meanwhile, Islām continued to spread throughout Arabia.

In 628–9 the Quraysh broke the pact agreed upon at Al-Hudaybiyah, freeing Muḥammad to march on Mecca, which he did with a large group of the *al-ansār*, the *al-muhājirūn*, and Bedouins. The Quraysh pleaded for amnesty, which was granted. After many years of hardship and exile, in 630 Muḥammad entered Mecca triumphantly and directed his followers not to take revenge for the persecution many of them had endured. He went directly to the Ka'bah, where he ordered 'Alī and Bilal, the Abyssinian caller to prayer (*al-mu'adhdhin*), to remove all the idols and restore the original purity of the Ka'bah. All the Meccans then embraced Islām.

The Islāmization of Arabia, however, was not as yet complete. Muḥammad's army defeated the Hawāzin who had risen against him, but could not capture Tā'if, which surrendered of its own volition a year later. In 630–31 embassies from all over the Arabian Peninsula arrived in Medina to accept Islām, and by that time most of Arabia, save for the north, had united under the religion's banner. Muḥammad therefore marched with a large army north to Tabuk but did not engage the enemy. Nevertheless, the Jews and Christians of the region submitted to his authority, whereupon Muḥammad again guaranteed their personal safety and freedom to practise their religion as he did for the Zoroastrians of eastern Arabia. At that time too the pagan Arab tribes in the north, as well as in other regions, embraced Islām.

So by 631 Muḥammad had brought to a close "the age of ignorance" (al-jāhiliyyah), as Muslims called the pre-Islāmic epoch in Arabia. He broke the hold of tribal bonds as the ultimate links between an Arab and the society around him. Although tribal relations were not fully destroyed, they were now transcended by a more powerful bond based on religion.

Finally, in 632, Muḥammad made the first Islāmic pilgrimage to Mecca (al-ḥajj), which remains the model to this day for the millions of Muslims who make the hajj each year. This event marked the peak of Muḥammad's earthly life. At that time he delivered his celebrated farewell sermon, the Farewell Pilgrimage Address, and the last verse of the Qur'ān was revealed, completing the sacred text: "This day have I perfected for you your religion and fulfilled My favour unto you, and it hath been My good pleasure to choose Islām for you as your religion" (5:3). On the way back from Mecca, he and his entourage stopped at a pond called Ghadir Khumm where he appointed 'Alī as the executor of his last will and as his walī, a term that means "friend" or "saint" and also describes a person who possesses authority. This major event is seen by the Sunni branch of Islām as signifying a personal and family matter, while Shī'ites believe that at this time 'Alī received the formal investiture to succeed the Prophet.

Late in spring the same year Muḥammad, who had been considering another expedition to the north, suddenly fell ill and, according to tradition, died three days later on June 8. His legacy included the establishment of a new order that would transform and affect much of the world from the Atlantic to the China Sea; from France to India. According to Islāmic norms that he established, his body was washed by his family, especially by 'Alī, and buried in his house adjacent to the mosque of Medina. His tomb remains the holiest place in Islām after the Ka'bah; it is visited by millions of pilgrims annually.

Muḥammad and Islāmic Piety

One cannot understand Islāmic piety without comprehending the role of Muḥammad in it. His birthday is celebrated throughout the Islāmic world during the month of Rabī 'al-Awwal, not in the same way that Christians celebrate Christmas but as a major feast. Only in Saudi Arabia, dominated since the eighteenth century by the puritan Wahhābī movement, are these celebrations not encouraged publicly; there they are somewhat subdued. In the rest of the Islāmic world, the miracles associated with Muḥammad's life, such as his Nocturnal Ascent, are celebrated in numerous ways. Ordinary Muslims as well as the highly educated repeat the Qur'ānic dictum that Muḥammad was sent as "mercy unto all the worlds" (*rahmatan lī' al-'ālamīn*). People ask for his *shifā 'ah*, or intercession on the Day of Judgement, hoping to assemble that day under the green "flag of praise" (*liwā' al-ḥamd*) carried by him.

Muslims experience the Prophet as a living reality and believe that he has an ongoing relation not only with human beings but also with animals and plants. His relics are held sacred, and major edifices, such as the Jāmi' Mosque of Delhi, India, have been constructed around them. His own tomb is, after the Ka'bah in Mecca, the most important site of Islāmic pilgrimage, and all other pilgrimage sites – from Moulay Idrīs in Morocco to the Shī'ite places of pilgrimage in Iran and Iraq to the tomb of Mu 'īn al-Dīn Chishtī in Ajmer in India – are considered "extensions" of his mausoleum in Medina.

The benediction upon the Prophet punctuates daily Muslim life, and traditional Islāmic life reminds one at every turn of his ubiquitous presence. He even plays a major role in dreams. There are many prayers recited in order to be able to have a dream of the Prophet, who promised that the Devil could never appear in a dream in the form of Muḥammad. Not only for saints and mystics but also for many ordinary pious people, a simple dream of the Prophet has been able to transform a whole human life. One might say that the reality of the Prophet penetrates the life of Muslims on every level, from the external existence of the individual and of Islāmic society as a whole to the life of the psyche and the soul and finally to the life of the spirit.

During the 23-year period of his prophethood, Muḥammad accomplished what by any account must be considered among the most significant achievements of human history. First, he transmitted both the text of the Qur'ān and his own understanding of the Divine Word, which is the foundation of all later Qur'ānic commentaries. Second, he established a body of *sunnah* ("traditions") and Hadith (a collection of sayings attributed to him and to members of the early Muslim community) that are, after the Qur'ān, the most important sources for all things Islāmic. Third, he laid the foundation for a new religious and spiritual community, taught many disciples, and created the means for the continuity and transmission of the Islāmic tradition. Finally, he formed a new society, unifying Arabia in a sociopolitical structure based on the Qur'ān and establishing an empire of faith in the hearts and minds of his followers, who then took his message to the furthest confines of the Earth. It can therefore be argued that Muḥammad's mark was as profound and enduring as anything recorded in the pages of human history.

2

THE FOUNDATIONS OF ISLĀM

The Legacy of Muḥammad

From the very beginning of Islām, Muḥammad inculcated a sense of communal identity and a bond of faith among his followers that was intensified by their experiences of persecution as a nascent community in Mecca. During the early period at Medina, from 622, when the community-state of Islām emerged, Islām acquired its characteristic ethos as a religion uniting in itself both the spiritual and temporal aspects of life and seeking to regulate not only an individual's relationship to God (through that individual's conscience) but human relationships in a social setting as well. Thus, there is not only an Islāmic religious institution but also an Islāmic law, state, and other institutions governing society. Not until the twentieth century were the religious (private) and the secular (public) distinguished by some Muslim thinkers and separated formally, as in Turkey.

This dual religious and social character of Islām, expressing itself as a religious community commissioned by God to bring its own value system to the world through the *jihad* ("holy war" or "holy struggle"), explains much of the astonishing success of the early generations of Muslims. Within a century after the Prophet's death in 632 they had brought a large part of the globe – from Spain across Central Asia to India – under a new Arab Muslim empire. The period of Islāmic conquests and empire building marks the first phase of the expansion of Islām as a religion. Islām's essential egalitarianism within the community of the faithful and its official discrimination against the followers of other religions won rapid converts. Jews and Christians, as People of the Book, were assigned a special status and allowed religious autonomy, though they were required to pay the *jizyah* tax. Members of other faiths were required either to accept Islām or to die. The same status of People of the Book was later extended to Zoroastrians and Hindus, but many People of the Book eventually joined Islām in order to escape the disability of the *jizyah*.

A much more massive expansion of Islām after the twelfth century was inaugurated by the Sufis (Muslim mystics), who contributed significantly to the spread of Islām in India, Central Asia, Turkey, and sub-Saharan Africa. Besides the *jihad* and Sufi missionary activity, another factor in the spread of Islām was the far-ranging influence of Muslim traders, who not only introduced Islām quite early to the Indian east coast and south India but who proved also to be the main catalytic agents (besides the Sufis) in converting people to Islām in Indonesia, Malaya, and China. Islām was introduced to Indonesia in the fourteenth century, hardly having time to consolidate itself there politically before the country came under Dutch colonial domination.

The vast variety of cultures embraced by Islām has produced important internal differences. All segments of Muslim society, however, are bound by a common faith and a sense of belonging to a single religious community. Despite the loss of political power during the period of Western colonialism in the nineteenth and twentieth centuries, the concept of the Islāmic community (*ummah*) became stronger. Islām inspired various Muslim peoples in their struggles to gain political freedom in the mid-twentieth century, and the idealized unity of the community contributed to later attempts at political solidarity.

Sources of Islāmic Doctrinal and Social Views

Islāmic doctrine, law, and thinking in general are based on four sources, or fundamental principles (*usūl*): (1) the Qur'ān, (2) the *sunnah* ("traditions"), (3) *ijmā'* ("consensus"), and (4) *ijtihād* ("individual thought").

The Qur'ān ("Reading", or "Recitation") is regarded as the Word, or Speech, of God delivered to Muhammad by the archangel Gabriel and is the fundamental source of Islāmic teaching. The chapters revealed at Mecca during the earliest part of Muhammad's career are concerned with ethical and spiritual teachings and the Day of Judgement. The chapters revealed to the Prophet at Medina at a later period are concerned with social legislation, worship, and the politico-moral principles for constituting and ordering the community.

The word *sunnah* was used by pre-Islāmic Arabs to denote their tribal or common law; in Islām it came to mean the example of the Prophet – i.e. his words and deeds as recorded in compilations known as Hadith. Six Hadith collections, compiled in the ninth century, came to be regarded as especially authoritative by the largest branch of Islām, the Sunni. Another large branch, the Shī'ite, has its own Hadith collections, in which, in addition to the Prophet, the *imām*s (spiritual and temporal leaders) are of central importance.

The doctrine of *ijmā'*, or consensus, was introduced in the eighth century in order to standardize legal theory and practice and to overcome individual and regional differences of opinion. Though conceived as a "consensus of scholars", in actual practice *ijmā'* was a more fundamental operative factor. From the ninth century, points on which consensus was reached in practice were considered closed and further substantial questioning of them prohibited. Accepted interpretations of the Qur'ān and of the actual content of the *sunnah* all rest finally on the *ijmā'*.

Ijtihād, meaning "individual thought", was required to find the legal or doctrinal solution to a new problem. In the early period there was an abundance of conflicting and chaotic opinions. In the eighth century *ijtihād* was replaced by *qiyās* (reasoning by strict analogy), a formal procedure of deduction based on the texts of the Qur'ān and the Hadith. The transformation of *ijmā'* into a conservative mechanism and the acceptance of a definitive body of Hadith virtually closed the "gate of *ijtihād*" in the Sunni tradition. Nevertheless, certain outstanding Sunni thinkers (e.g. al-Ghazālī, d. 1111) and many Shī'ite jurists continued to claim the right of new *ijtihād* for themselves, and reformers of the eighteenth and nineteenth centuries, because of modern influences, caused this principle once more to receive wider acceptance.

Doctrines of the Qur'ān

God. The doctrine concerning God within the Qur'ān is rigorously monotheistic: God is one and unique; He has no partner and no equal. Muslims believe that there are no intermediaries between God and the creation that He brought into being by His sheer command: "Be." Although His

presence is believed to be everywhere, He does not inhere in
anything. He is the sole creator and the sole sustainer of the
universe, wherein every creature bears witness to His unity and
lordship. But He is also just and merciful: His justice ensures
order in His creation, in which nothing is believed to be out of
place, and his mercy is unbounded and encompasses everything. His creation and ordering of the universe is viewed as
the act of prime mercy for which all things sing His glories. The
God of the Qur'ān, while described as majestic and sovereign,
is also a personal God; whenever a person in need or distress
calls to Him, He responds. Above all, He is the God of
guidance and shows everything, particularly human beings,
the right way, "the straight path".

This picture of God – wherein the attributes of power,
justice, and mercy interpenetrate – is related to Judaism and
Christianity, whence it is derived with certain modifications,
and also to the concepts of pre-Islāmic Arabia, to which it
provided an effective answer. One traditional Arabic religious
belief held that humans were committed to a blind and
inexorable fate over which they had no control. For this
powerful but insensible fate the Qur'ān substituted a provident
and merciful God while rejecting idolatory and all divinities
that the Arabs worshipped in their sanctuaries, the most
prominent of which was the Ka'bah in Mecca itself.

The universe. In order to prove the unity of God, the Qur'ān
lays frequent stress on the design and order in the universe.
There are no gaps or dislocations in nature. Order is explained
by the fact that every created thing is endowed with a definite
and defined nature whereby it falls into a pattern. This nature,
though it allows every created thing to function as part of a
whole, sets limits and this idea of the limitedness of everything
is one of the fixed points in both the cosmology and theology
of the Qur'ān. The universe is viewed as autonomous, in the

sense that everything has its own inherent laws of behaviour, but not as autocratic, because the patterns of behaviour have been endowed by God and are strictly limited. Thus, every creature is limited and "measured out" and hence depends on God, who alone reigns unchallenged in the heavens and the earth, and is unlimited, independent, and self-sufficient.

The human condition. According to the Qur'ān, God created two apparently parallel species of creatures, humans and *jinn*, the one from clay and the other from fire. About the *jinn*, however, the Qur'ān says little, though it is implied that the *jinn* are endowed with reason and responsibility but are more prone to evil than humans. It is with the human being that the Qur'ān, which describes itself as a guide for the human race, is centrally concerned (e.g. 2:185). The Jewish and Christian story of the Fall of Adam (the first man) is accepted, but the Qur'ān states that God forgave Adam his act of disobedience, which is not viewed in the Qur'ān as original sin (20:122–3).

In the story of human creation, angels, who protested to God against such creation, lost in a competition of knowledge against Adam (2:30–34). The Qur'ān, therefore, declares humans to be the noblest creatures of all creation – those who bore the trust (of responsibility) that the rest of God's creation refused to accept. The Qur'ān thus reiterates that all nature has been made subservient to humans: nothing in all creation has been made without a purpose, and people themselves have not been created "in sport", their purpose being service and obedience to God's will.

Despite this lofty station, however, human nature is frail and faltering. Whereas everything in the universe has a limited nature, and every creature recognizes its limitation and insufficiency, humans are viewed as rebellious and full of pride, arrogating to themselves the attributes of self-sufficiency. Pride is thus viewed as the cardinal sin of humankind, because, by not recognizing its essential limitations, humankind becomes guilty of ascribing to itself partnership with God (a form of *shirk*, or associating a creature with the Creator) and of violating the unity of God. True faith (*imām*) thus consists in belief in the immaculate Divine Unity, and Islām consists in submission to the Divine Will.

Satan, sin, and repentance. The being who became Satan (Shayṭān, or Iblīs) had previously occupied a high station but fell from divine grace by his act of disobedience in refusing to honour Adam when he, along with other angels, was ordered to do so; his act of disobedience is construed by the Qur'ān as the sin of pride (2:34). Since then, his work has been to beguile humans into error and sin. Satan's machinations will cease only on the Last Day.

The whole universe is replete with signs of God; the human soul itself is viewed as a witness to the unity and grace of God. The messengers and prophets of God have, throughout history, been calling humankind back to God. Yet very few have accepted the truth; most have rejected it and have become disbelievers (*kāfir,* plural *kuffār*: "ungrateful" – i.e. to God). When a person thus becomes obdurate, his or her heart is sealed by God. Nevertheless, it is always possible for a sinner to repent (*tawbah*) and to achieve redemption by a genuine conversion to the truth. Genuine repentance has the effect of removing all sins and restoring people to the state of sinlessness in which they started their lives.

Prophecy. Prophets are specially elected by God to be His messengers. The Qur'ān requires recognition of all prophets without discrimination, yet they are not all equal, some of them being particularly outstanding in qualities of steadfastness and patience under trial. Abraham, Noah, Moses, and Jesus were such great prophets. As vindication of the truth of their mission, God often vested them with miracles: Abraham

was saved from fire, Noah from the deluge, and Moses from
the Pharaoh. Not only was Jesus born from the Virgin Mary
but, in Islāmic belief, God also saved him from crucifixion. All
prophets are human and never part of divinity; they are simply
recipients of revelation from God. God never speaks directly to
a human: He sends an angel messenger to him, makes him hear
a voice, or inspires him.

Muhammad is accepted as the last prophet in the series and
its greatest member. The archangel Gabriel brought the Qur'-
ān down to the Prophet's heart. Gabriel is represented by the
Qur'ān as a spirit, but the Prophet could sometimes see and
hear him. According to early traditions, the Prophet's revelations occurred in a state of trance. This phenomenon at the
same time was accompanied by an unshakeable conviction
that the message was from God, and the Qur'ān describes itself
as the transcript of a heavenly "Mother Book" (43:3–4)
written on a "Preserved Tablet" (85:21–2).

Eschatology. Because not all requital is meted out in this
life, a final judgement is necessary to bring it to completion.
On the Last Day, when the world will come to an end, the
dead will be resurrected and a judgement will be pronounced
on every person in accordance with his deeds. Although the
Qur'ān in the main speaks of a personal judgement, there are
several verses that speak of the resurrection of distinct
communities that will be judged according to "their own
book" (45:27–9). The actual evaluation, however, will be for
every individual, whatever the terms of reference of his or her
performance. Those condemned will burn in hellfire, and
those who are saved will enjoy the abiding pleasures of
paradise. As well as suffering in physical fire, the damned
will also experience fire "in their hearts"; similarly, the
blessed, besides physical enjoyment, will experience the greatest happiness of divine pleasure.

Social service. Because the purpose of human existence, as for every other creature, is submission to the Divine Will, God's role is that of commander. Whereas the rest of nature obeys God automatically, humans alone possess the choice to obey or disobey. With the deep-seated belief in Satan's existence, the human's fundamental role becomes one of moral struggle, which constitutes the essence of human endeavour. Recognition of the unity of God does not simply rest in the intellect but also entails consequences in terms of the moral struggle, which consists primarily in freeing oneself of narrowness of mind and smallness of heart. One must go outside of oneself and expend one's best possessions for the sake of others.

The doctrine of social service, in terms of alleviating suffering and helping the needy, constitutes an integral part of Islāmic teaching. Praying to God and other religious acts are deemed to be a mere facade in the absence of active welfare service to the needy. It is Satan who whispers into people's ears that by spending for others they will become poor. God, on the contrary, promises prosperity in exchange for such expenditure, which constitutes a credit with God and grows much more than money that is invested in usury. Hoarding of wealth without recognizing the rights of the poor invites the most dire punishment in the hereafter and is declared to be one of the main causes of the decay of societies in this world. The practice of usury is forbidden.

With this socio-economic doctrine cementing the bond of faith, the idea of a closely knit community of the faithful who are declared to be "brothers unto each other" emerges (49:10). Muslims are described as "the middle community bearing witness on mankind" (2:143), "the best community produced for mankind", whose function it is "to enjoin good and forbid evil" (3:110). Cooperation and "good advice" within the community are emphasized, and opponents from within the community are to be fought and reduced with armed force if issues cannot be settled by persuasion and arbitration.

Because the mission of the community is to "enjoin good and forbid evil" so that "there is no mischief and corruption" on earth, the doctrine of *jihad* is the logical outcome. For the early community it was a basic religious concept. The object of *jihad* is not the forced conversion of individuals to Islām but rather the gaining of political control over the collective affairs of societies, to run them in accordance with the principles of Islām. Individual conversions occur as a by-product of this process when the power structure passes into the hands of the Muslim community. In fact, according to strict Muslim doctrine, conversions "by force" are forbidden, and it is also strictly prohibited to wage wars for the sake of acquiring worldly glory, power, and rule. With the establishment of the Muslim empire, however, the doctrine of *jihad* was modified by the leaders of the community. Their main concern became the consolidation of the empire and its administration, and thus they interpreted the teaching in a defensive rather than in an expansive sense.

Distinction and privileges based on tribal rank or race were repudiated in the Qur'ān and in the celebrated "Farewell Pilgrimage Address" of the Prophet shortly before his death. All men are therein declared to be "equal children of Adam", and the only distinction recognized in the sight of God is said to be based on piety and good acts. The age-old Arab institution of inter-tribal revenge (*tha'r*) – whereby it was not necessarily the killer who was executed but a person equal in rank to the slain person – was rejected. The pre-Islāmic ethical ideal of manliness was modified and replaced by a more humane ideal of moral virtue and piety.

Fundamental Practices: The Five Pillars of Islām

During the earliest decades after the death of the Prophet, certain basic features of the religious and social organization of Islām were singled out to serve as anchoring points for the community's life. They were formulated as the "Pillars of Islām".

The first pillar is the *shahādah,* or profession of faith: "There is no god but God, and Muḥammad is the messenger of God", upon which depends membership of the community. The profession of faith must be recited at least once in one's lifetime, aloud, correctly, and purposively, with an under-standing of its meaning and with an assent from the heart. From this fundamental belief are derived beliefs in (1) angels (particularly Gabriel, the Angel of Revelation), (2) the revealed books (the Qur'ān and the sacred books of Jewish and Christian revelation described in the Qur'ān), (3) a series of prophets (among whom figures of the Jewish and Christian tradition are particularly eminent – although it is believed that God has sent messengers to every nation), and (4) the Last Day (Day of Judgement).

The second pillar consists of five daily prayers, *zalet,* per-formed facing toward the Ka'bah, a shrine within the Sacred Mosque in Mecca. These prayers may be offered individually if one is unable to go to the mosque. The first prayer is per-formed before sunrise, the second just after noon, the third later in the afternoon, the fourth immediately after sunset, and the fifth before retiring to bed. Before a prayer, ablutions, including the washing of hands, face, and feet, are performed. The noon prayer on Fridays is the chief congregational prayer.

The third pillar is the obligatory tax called *zakat* ("purifica-tion", indicating that such a payment makes the rest of one's wealth religiously and legally pure). This is the only permanent tax levied by the Qur'ān and is payable annually on food grains, cattle, and cash after one year's possession. *Zakat* is collectable by the state and is to be used primarily for the poor, but the Qur'ān mentions other purposes: ransoming Muslim war captives, redeeming chronic debts, paying tax collectors' fees, *jihad* (and, by extension, education and health), and creating facilities for travellers.

The obligation to fast (*zawm*) during the month of Ramadan, laid down in the Qur'ān (2:183–5), is the fourth pillar of the faith. Fasting begins at daybreak and ends at sunset, and during the day eating, drinking, and smoking are forbidden. The elderly and the incurably sick are exempted through the daily feeding of one poor person.

The fifth pillar is participation in the annual pilgrimage (*hajj*) to Mecca, prescribed for every Muslim once in a lifetime – "provided one can afford it" and provided there are enough provisions for the family in the pilgrim's absence. A special service is held in the Sacred Mosque on the seventh day of the month of Dhu al-Hijjah (the last month of the Muslim year). Pilgrimage activities begin by the eighth day and conclude on the twelfth or thirteenth. The principal activities consist of walking seven times around the Ka'bah, kissing and touching the Black Stone (Hajar al-Aswad), and ascending and running between Mount Zafa and Mount Marwa (which are now, however, mere elevations) seven times. At the second stage of the ritual, pilgrims proceed from Mecca to Mina, a few miles away; from there they go to 'Arafāt, where they must hear a sermon and spend one afternoon. The last rites consist of spending the night at Muzdalifah (between 'Arafāt and Mina) and offering sacrifice on the last day of *ihram,* which is the *'īd* ("festival") of sacrifice.

By the early twenty-first century the number of visitors to Mecca for the *hajj* was estimated to be about 2 million,

approximately half of them from non-Arab countries. All
Muslim countries send official delegations, a fact that is being
increasingly exploited for organizing religio-political con-
gresses. At other times in the year it is considered meritorious
to perform the lesser pilgrimage (*'umrah*), which is not, however, a substitute for the *hajj*.

Sacred Places and Days

The most sacred place for Muslims is the Sacred Mosque at
Mecca, which contains the Ka'bah, the object of the annual
pilgrimage and the site toward which Muslims direct their
daily prayers. It is much more than a mosque; it is believed to
be "God's Sacred House", where heavenly bliss and power
touch the Earth directly. The Prophet's mosque in Medina,
where Muḥammad and the first caliphs are buried, is the next
in sanctity. Jerusalem follows in third place as the first direction in which Muslims faced to offer prayers (*qiblah*) and as
the place from where Muḥammad, according to tradition,
made his ascent to heaven. For Shī'ites, Karbala' in Iraq (the
place of martyrdom of 'Alī's son, Husayn) and Meshed in Iran
(where Imām 'Alī ar-Rida is buried) constitute places of special
veneration and pilgrimage.

For Muslims in general, shrines of Sufi saints are particular
objects of reverence and even veneration. In Baghdad the tomb
of the most venerated Sufi saint, 'Abd al-Qādir al-Jilani, is
visited every year by large numbers of pilgrims from all over
the Muslim world. The shrine of Mu'in al-Din Chisti in Ajmer
(northern India) draws thousands of pilgrims annually, including Hindus and Christians as well as Muslims.

General religious life is centred around the mosque, and in
the days of the Prophet and early caliphs the mosque was the

centre of all community life. Small mosques are usually supervised by an *imām* who administers the prayer service, though sometimes also a *muezzin* (prayer-time announcer) is appointed. In larger mosques, where Friday prayers are offered, a *khaṭib* (one who gives the *khuṭbah*, or sermon) is appointed for Friday service. Many large mosques also function as religious schools and colleges.

The Muslim calendar (based on the lunar year) dates from the Hijrah (emigration) of the Prophet from Mecca to Medina in 622. The two feast days in the year are the *'īds*, 'Īd al-Fiṭr, celebrating the end of the month of Ramadan, and 'Īd al-Adḥā, marking the end of the pilgrimage. Other sacred times include the "Night of Determination" (Laylat al-Qadr, believed to be the night in which God makes decisions about the destiny of individuals and the world as a whole) and the night of the ascension of the Prophet to heaven (Laylat al-Isra' wa'l-Mi'raj). The Shī'ites observe the tenth of Muharram (the first month of the Muslim year) to mark the day of the martyrdom of Husayn at Karbala' (680). Muslims also celebrate the birth and death anniversaries of various saints in a festival called *mjlid* ("birthday"), or *'urs* ("nuptial ceremony"). The saints are believed to reach the zenith of their spiritual life on this occasion.

3

ISLĀMIC THOUGHT, BELIEFS, AND PRACTICE

Islāmic theology and philosophy are two traditions of learning developed by Muslim thinkers who were engaged, on the one hand, in the rational clarification and defence of the principles of the Islāmic religion and, on the other, in the pursuit of the ancient (Greco-Roman) sciences. These thinkers took a position that was intermediate between the traditionalists, who remained attached to the literal expressions of the primary sources of Islāmic doctrines (the Qur'ān and the Hadith) and who abhorred reasoning, and those whose reasoning led them to abandon the Islāmic community altogether.

Over the course of time, representatives of certain theological movements succeeded in converting rulers to their cause, made those rulers declare in favour of their movements, and even encouraged them to persecute their opponents. Thus there arose in some localities and periods a semblance of an official, or orthodox, doctrine.

Islāmic Theology

The beginnings of theology in the Islāmic tradition in the second half of the seventh century are not easily distinguishable from the beginnings of a number of other disciplines – Arabic philology, Qur'ānic interpretation, the collection of the sayings and deeds of the prophet Muḥammad, jurisprudence, and historiography. During the first half of the eighth century a number of questions centring on God's unity, justice, and other attributes, which were relevant to man's freedom, actions, and fate in the hereafter, formed the core of a more specialized discipline, which was called *kalām* ("speech"). The term *kalām* has come to include all matters directly or indirectly relevant to the establishment and definition of religious beliefs.

By the ninth century Islāmic theology had coined a vast number of technical terms and theologians had forged Arabic into a versatile language of science, Arabic philology had matured, and the religious sciences (jurisprudence, the study of the Qur'ān, Hadith, criticism, and history) had developed complex techniques of textual study and interpretation.

Despite the notion of a unified and consolidated community, immediately after the Prophet's death serious differences arose within the Muslim community over the succession, which led to a lasting division between the Shī'ites and the Sunni. According to the Sunnis, or traditionalist faction – who today constitute the majority of Islām – the Prophet had designated no successor. After some dispute with the Muslims at Medina, who had initially wanted to elect their own chief, the choice of the *ummah*, or Muslim community, fell upon Abū Bakr, father of the Prophet's favoured wife 'Ā'ishah.

According to the Shī'ites, or "Partisans", however, the Prophet had designated as his successor his cousin and son-in-law 'Alī, husband of his daughter Fāṭimah and father of his only surviving grandsons, Hasan and Husayn. Yet, while 'Alī and the Prophet's closest kinsmen were preparing the body for burial, Abū Bakr, 'Umar, and Abū 'Ubaydah, from Muḥammad's Companions in the Quraysh tribe, met with the leaders of the Medinans and agreed to elect the aging Abū Bakr as the successor (khalīfah, "caliph") of the Prophet. 'Alī and his kinsmen were dismayed but agreed – for the sake of unity and because 'Alī was still young – to accept the fait accompli. After the murder of 'Uthmen, the third caliph, following accusations of nepotism and misrule, 'Ali was invited by the rebels at Medina who had assassinated 'Uthmen to accept the caliphate. Thus 'Alī became the fourth caliph (reigned 656–61), but the disagreement over his right of succession brought about a major schism in Islām.

The rebels who had recognized 'Alī as ruler later fought against him, accusing him of having committed a grave sin in submitting his claim to the caliphate to arbitration. The basic doctrine of the Kharijites (from kharajū, "to withdraw") was that a person or a group who committed a grave error or sin and did not sincerely repent ceased to be Muslim. Mere profession of the faith did not make a person a Muslim; this faith had to be accompanied by righteous deeds. The second principle that flowed from their aggressive idealism was militancy, or jihad, which the Kharijites considered to be among the pillars of Islām.

Because the Kharijites believed that the basis of rule was righteous character and piety alone, any Muslim, irrespective of race, colour, or sex, could, in their view, become ruler. This was in contrast to the claims of the Shī'ites that the ruler must belong to the Prophet's family and tribe (the Quraysh) and that he must follow the sunnah ("traditions").

As a consequence of translations of Greek philosophical and scientific works into Arabic during the eighth and ninth centuries and controversies between Muslim thinkers and those adhering to Gnosticism, Manichaeism, Buddhism, or Christianity, a more powerful movement of rational theology emerged; its representatives are called the Mu'tazilah ("those who stand apart", a reference to the fact that they dissociated themselves from extreme views of faith and infidelity). On the question of the relationship of faith to works, the Mu'tazilah Kharijites taught that works were an essential part of faith but that a person guilty of a grave sin, unless he repented, was neither a Muslim nor yet a non-Muslim but occupied a "middle ground". They further defended the position, as a central part of their doctrine, that humans were free to choose and act and were, therefore, responsible for their actions. They claimed that human reason, independent of revelation, was capable of discovering what is good and what is evil, although revelation corroborated the findings of reason. Revelation had to be interpreted, therefore, in conformity with the dictates of rational ethics.

In the tenth century a reaction began against the Mu'tazilah that culminated in the formulation and subsequent general acceptance of another set of theological propositions that became Sunni, or orthodox, theology. The concept of the community so vigorously pronounced by the earliest doctrine of the Qur'ān gained both a new emphasis and a fresh context with the rise of Sunnism. An abundance of tradition (Hadith) came to be attributed to the Prophet to the effect that Muslims must follow the majority's way, that minority groups are all doomed to Hell, and that God's protective hand is always on (the majority of) the community, which can never be in error. Under the impact of the new Hadith, the community, which had been charged by the Qur'ān with a mission and com-manded to accept a challenge, now became transformed into a privileged one that was endowed with infallibility. The

dominant Sunni theological school, the Ash'arjya, displaced
the Mu'tazilah and successfully refuted key points of their
theology. As a result Sunni theology became identified with the
views that Muslim sinners remain Muslims, that good and evil
alike are from God but that humans nevertheless acquire
responsibility for their actions, that the Qur'ān is the uncreated
word of God, and that the qualities ascribed to God and the
hereafter by the Qur'ān are real – i.e. they cannot be reasoned
away as the Mu'tazilah argued.

At the same time, while condemning schisms and branding
dissent as heretical, Sunnism also developed the opposite trend
of accommodation, catholicity, and synthesis. A putative
tradition of the Prophet that says "differences of opinion
among my community are a blessing" was given wide cur-
rency. This principle of toleration ultimately made it possible
for diverse sects and schools of thought – notwithstanding a
wide range of differences in belief and practice – to recognize
and coexist with each other.

Besides the Sunni, the Shī'ite sect is the only important
surviving sect in Islām. Probably under Gnostic (esoteric,
dualistic, and speculative) and old Iranian (dualistic) influences, the figure of the political ruler, the *imām*, was transformed in Shī'ism into a metaphysical being, a manifestation of
God and the primordial light that sustains the universe and
bestows true knowledge on man. Through the *imām* alone the
hidden and true meaning of the Qur'ānic revelation could be
known, because the *imām* alone was infallible. The Shī'ites
thus developed a doctrine of esoteric knowledge that was also
adopted, in a modified form, by the Sufis, or Islāmic mystics.

The predominant Shī'ite community, the Ithnā 'Asharīyah
(Twelvers), recognizes 12 such *imām*s, the last having disap-
peared in the ninth century. Since that time, the *mujtahid*s
(Shī'ite jurists) have been able to interpret law and doctrine

under the putative guidance of the *imām*, who will return near the end of time to fill the world with truth and justice. On the basis of their doctrine of imamology, the Shī'ites emphasize their idealism and transcendentalism in conscious contrast with Sunni pragmatism. Thus, whereas the Sunnis believe in the *ijmā'* ("consensus") of the community as the source of decision-making and workable knowledge, the Shī'ites believe that knowledge derived from fallible sources is useless and that sure and true knowledge can come only through contact with the infallible *imām*.

Besides the main body of Twelver Shī'ites, Shī'ism has produced a variety of other sects, the most important of them being the Isma'ilis. Instead of recognizing Musa as the seventh *imām*, as did the main body of the Shī'ites, the Isma'ilis upheld the claims of his elder brother Isma'il. One group of Isma'ilis, called Sab'iyah (Seveners), considered Isma'il the seventh and last of the *imām*s. The majority of Isma'ilis, however, believed that the imamate continued in the line of Isma'il's descendants. The Isma'ili teaching spread during the ninth century from North Africa to Sind, in India, and the Isma'ili Fatimid dynasty succeeded in establishing a prosperous empire in Egypt.

In Isma'ilite theology, the universe is viewed as a cyclic process, and the unfolding of each cycle is marked by the advent of seven "speakers" – messengers of God with scriptures – each of whom is succeeded by seven "silents" – messengers without revealed scriptures; the last speaker (the Prophet Muhammad) is followed by seven *imām*s who interpret the will of God to man and are, in a sense, higher than the Prophet because they draw their knowledge directly from God and not from the Angel of Revelation.

During the tenth century certain Isma'ili intellectuals formed a secret society called the Brethren of Purity, which issued a philosophical encyclopedia, *The Epistles of the Brethren of*

Purity, aiming at the liquidation of the particular religions in favour of a universalist spirituality. Islāmic mysticism, or Sufism, emerged out of early ascetic reactions on the part of certain religiously sensitive personalities against the general worldliness that had overtaken the Muslim community and the purely "externalist" expressions of Islām in law and theology. These persons stressed the Muslim qualities of moral motivation, contrition against excessive worldliness, and "the state of the heart" as opposed to the legalist formulations of Islām.

During a nineteenth-century anticlerical movement in Iran, a certain 'Alī Muḥammad of Shiraz appeared, declaring himself to be the Bab ("Gate"; i.e. to God). At that time the climate in Iran was generally favourable to messianic ideas. He was, however, bitterly opposed by the Shī'ite *'ulama'* ("the learned") and was executed in 1850. After his death, his two disciples, Sobh-e Azal and Baha' Ullah, broke and went in different directions. Baha' Ullah eventually declared his religion – stressing a humanitarian pacifism and universalism – to be independent of and outside Islām. The Baha'i faith won a considerable number of converts in North America during the early twentieth century.

Islāmic Philosophy

The origin and inspiration of Islāmic philosophy are quite different from those of Islāmic theology. Philosophy developed out of and around the non-religious practical and theoretical sciences, it recognized no theoretical limits other than those of human reason itself, and it assumed that the truth found by unaided reason does not disagree with the truth of Islām when both are properly understood.

The first major Muslim philosopher, al-Kindī, who flourished in the first half of the ninth century, was a diligent student of Greek and Hellenistic authors in philosophy, and his conscious, open, and unashamed acknowledgement of earlier contributions to scientific inquiry was foreign to the spirit, method, and purpose of the theologians of the time. Al-Kindī was particularly concerned with the relation between corporeal things – which are changeable, in constant flux, and as such unknowable – on the one hand and the permanent world of forms (spiritual or secondary substances) – which are not subject to flux yet to which man has no access except through things of the senses – on the other. He insisted that a purely human knowledge of all things is possible through the use of various scientific devices, the study of mathematics and logic, and the assimilation of the contributions of earlier thinkers.

The existence of a supernatural way to this knowledge in which all these requirements can be dispensed with was acknowledged by al-Kindī: God may choose to impart it to His prophets by cleansing and illuminating their souls and by giving them His aid, right guidance, and inspiration; and they, in turn, communicate it to ordinary men in an admirably clear, concise, and comprehensible style. This is the prophets' "divine" knowledge, characterized by a special mode of access and style of exposition. In principle, however, this very same knowledge is accessible to human beings without divine aid, even though "human" knowledge may lack the completeness and consummate logic of the prophets' divine message.

Reflection on the two kinds of knowledge – the human knowledge bequeathed by the ancients and the revealed knowledge expressed in the Qur'ān – led al-Kindī to pose a number of themes that became central in Islāmic philosophy: the rational-metaphorical exegesis of the Qur'ān and the

Hadith, the identification of God with the first being and the first cause, creation as the giving of being and as a kind of causation distinct from natural causation and Neoplatonic emanation, and the immortality of the individual soul.

The philosopher whose principal concerns, method, and opposition to authority were inspired by the extreme Mu'tazilah was the physician Abū Bakr ar-Razi (ninth–tenth century). He was intent on developing a rationally defensible theory of creation that would not require any change in God or attribute to Him responsibility for the imperfection and evil prevalent in the created world. To this end, he expounded the view that there are five eternal principles – God; Soul; prime matter; infinite, or absolute, space; and unlimited, or absolute, time – and explained creation as the result of the unexpected and sudden turn of events (*faltah*). *Faltah* occurred when Soul, in her ignorance, desired matter and the good God eased her misery by allowing her to satisfy her desire and to experience the suffering of the material world, then giving her reason to make her realize her mistake and to be delivered from her union with matter, the cause of her suffering and of all evil.

Al-Fārābī (ninth–tenth century) saw that theology and the juridical study of the law were derivative phenomena that function within a framework set by the Prophet as lawgiver and founder of a human community. In this community, revelation defines the opinions that the members of the community must hold and the actions that they must perform if they are to attain the earthly happiness of this world and the supreme happiness of the other world. Philosophy could not understand this framework of religion as long as it concerned itself almost exclusively with its truth content and confined the study of practical science to individualistic ethics and personal salvation.

Al-Fārābi recast philosophy in a new framework analogous to that of the Islāmic religion. The sciences were organized within this philosophical framework so that logic, physics, mathematics, and metaphysics culminated in a political science whose subject matter was the investigation of happiness and how it could be realized in cities and nations. Philosophical cosmology, psychology, and politics were blended by al-Fārābī into a political theology whose aim was to clarify the foundations of the Islāmic community and to defend its reform in a direction that would promote scientific inquiry and encourage philosophers to play an active role in practical affairs.

In al-Fārābī's lifetime the fate of the Islāmic world was in the balance. The Sunni caliphate's power extended hardly beyond Baghdad, and it appeared quite likely that the various Shī'ite sects, especially the Isma'ilis, would finally overpower it and establish a new political order. Isma'ilism's Neoplatonic cosmology, revolutionary background, and general expectation that divine laws were about to become superfluous with the appearance of the *qe'im* (the *imām* of the "resurrection") all militated against the development of a coherent political theory to meet the practical demands of political life and present a viable alternative to the Sunni caliphate. Al-Fārābī's writings underlined this basic weakness in Isma'ilism and, under the Feeimids in Egypt (969–1171), Isma'ili theology modified its cosmology in the direction suggested by al-Fārābī. It returned to the view that the community must continue to live under the divine law and postponed the prospect of the abolition of divine laws and the appearance of the *qe'im* to an indefinite point in the future.

Al-Fārābī's writings also influenced Avicenna (died 1037), who shaped philosophy into a powerful force that gradually penetrated Islāmic theology and mysticism and Persian poetry in eastern Islām. Following al-Fārābī, Avicenna initiated a fully-fledged inquiry into the question of being, in which he distinguished between essence and existence. He argued that the fact of existence cannot be inferred from or accounted for by the essence of existing things and that form and matter by themselves cannot interact and originate the movement of the universe or the progressive actualization of existing things. Existence must, therefore, be due to an agent-cause that necessitates, imparts, gives, or adds existence to essence. To do so, the cause must be an existing thing and must coexist with its effect. The universe consists of a chain of actual beings, each giving existence to the one below it and responsible for the existence of the rest of the chain below it. Because an actual infinite is deemed impossible by Avicenna, this chain as a whole must terminate in a being that is wholly simple and one whose essence is its very existence, and who is therefore self-sufficient and not in need of something else to give it existence.

By the twelfth century the writings of al-Fārābī, Avicenna, and al-Ghazālī, a Sufi theologian who offered a critical account of the theories of Avicenna and other Muslim philosophers, had found their way to the West. A philosophical tradition emerged, based primarily on the study of al-Fārābī.

Ibn Bajjah (died 1138/9) initiated this tradition with a radical interpretation of al-Fārābī's political philosophy that emphasized the virtues of the perfect but non-existent city and the vices prevalent in all existing cities. He concluded that the philosopher must order his own life as a solitary individual, shun the company of non-philosophers, reject their opinions and ways of life, and concentrate on reaching his own final goal by pursuing the theoretical sciences and achieving intuitive knowledge through contact with the Active Intelligence. The multitude lives in a dark cave and sees only dim shadows. The philosopher's duty is to seek the light of the sun (the intellect). To do so, he must leave the cave, see all colours as they truly are and see light itself, and finally become transformed into that light. Philosophy, he claimed, is the only way to the truly blessed state, which can be achieved only by going through theoretical science, even though philosophy is higher than theoretical science.

To Ibn Rushd (Averroës; d. 1198) belongs the distinction of presenting a solution to the problem of the relation between philosophy and the Islāmic community in the West. The intention of the divine law, he argued, is to assure the happiness of all members of the community. This requires everyone to profess belief in the basic principles of religion as enunciated in the Qur'ān, the Hadith, and the *ijmā*' ("consensus") of the learned, and to perform all obligatory acts of worship. Beyond this, the only just requirement is to demand that each pursue knowledge as far as his natural capacity and make-up permit. The divine law directly authorizes philosophers to pursue its interpretation according to the best – i.e. demonstrative or scientific – method, and theologians have no authority to interfere with the conduct of this activity or to judge its conclusions. Thus, theology must remain under the constant control of philosophy and the supervision of the divine law, so as not to drift into taking positions that cannot be demonstrated philosophically or that are contrary to the intention of the divine law.

These philosophical developments were in time met with a resurgent traditionalism, which found effective defenders in men such as Ibn Taymiyah (thirteenth–fourteenth century), who called for a return to the beliefs and practices of the pious ancestors. Philosophy was driven underground for a period, only to re-emerge in a new garb. Contributing to this development was the success of al-Ghazālī's integration of theology, philosophy, and mysticism into a new kind of philosophy called wisdom (*hikma*). It consisted of a critical review of the philosophy of Avicenna, preserving its main external features (its logical, physical, and, in part, metaphysical structure and

terminology) and introducing principles of explanation for the
universe and its relation to God based on personal experience
and direct vision.

The critique of Aristotle that had begun in Mu'tazili circles
and had found a prominent champion in Abū Bakr al-Rāzī was
provided with a far more solid foundation in the tenth and
eleventh centuries by the Christian theologians and philosophers of Baghdad, who translated the writings of the Hellenistic critics of Aristotle (e.g. John Philoponus) and made use
of their arguments both in commenting on Aristotle and in
independent theological and philosophical works. In the
twelfth century their theologically based anti-Aristotelianism
spread among Jewish and Muslim students of philosophy,
such as Abū al-Barakāt al-Baghdādī (died c. 1175) and Fakhr
ad-Din al-Rāzī. They suggested that a thorough examination
of Aristotle had revealed to them, on philosophical grounds,
that the fundamental disagreements between Aristotle and the
theologies based on the revealed religions represented open
options, and that Aristotle's view of the universe was in need of
explanatory principles that could be readily supplied by theology. This critique provided the framework for the integration
of philosophy into theology from the thirteenth century onward.

Although it made use of such theological criticisms of philosophy, the new wisdom took the position that theology did
not offer a positive substitute for, and was incapable of solving,
the difficulties of Aristotelian philosophy. It did not question the
need to have recourse to the Qur'ān and the Hadith to find the
right answers; it did, however, insist (on the authority of a long-
standing mystical tradition) that theology concern itself only
with the external expressions of this divine source of knowledge. The inner core was reserved for the adepts of the mystic
path, whose journey leads to the experience of the highest

reality in dreams and visions. Only the mystical adepts are in possession of the one true wisdom, the ground of both the external expressions of the divine law and the phenomenal world of human experience and thought.

As-Suhrawardi (twelfth century), the first master of the new wisdom, called it the "Wisdom of Illumination". He concentrated on the concepts of being and non-being, which he called light and darkness, and explained the gradation of beings according to the strength, or perfection, of their light. This gradation forms a single continuum that culminates in pure light, self-luminosity, self-awareness, self-manifestation, or self-knowledge, which is God, the light of lights, the true One. The stability and eternity of this single continuum result from every higher light overpowering and subjugating the lower, and movement and change along the continuum result from each of the lower lights desiring and loving the higher.

As-Suhrawardi's doctrine claims to be the inner truth behind the exoteric (external) teachings of both Islām and Zoroastrianism, as well as the wisdom of all ancient sages, especially Iranians and Greeks, and of the revealed religions as well. This neutral yet positive attitude toward the diversity of religions was to become one of the hallmarks of the new wisdom. Different religions were seen as different manifestations of the same truth, their essential agreement was emphasized, and various attempts were made to combine them into a single harmonious religion meant for all humankind.

The impact of Ibn al-'Arabi (twelfth–thirteenth century) on the subsequent development of the new wisdom was especially significant for his central doctrine of the "unity of being" and his distinction between the absolute One – which is undefinable truth (*haqq*) – and his self-manifestation (*zuhul*), or creation (*khalq*), which is ever new (*jadid*) and in perpetual movement – a movement that unites the whole of creation in constant renewal. At the very core of this dynamic edifice stands nature, the "dark cloud" ('*ama*') or "mist" (*bukhar*), as the ultimate principle of things and forms: intelligence, heavenly bodies, and elements and their mixtures that culminate in the perfect man. This primordial nature is the "breath" of the merciful God in His aspect as Lord. It flows throughout the universe and manifests truth in all its parts. It is the first mother through which truth manifests itself to itself and generates the universe. And it is the universal natural body that gives birth to the translucent bodies of the spheres, to the elements, and to their mixtures, all of which are related to that primary source as daughters to their mother.

After Ibn al-'Arabi, the new wisdom developed rapidly in intellectual circles in eastern Islām. Commentators began the process of harmonizing and integrating the views of the masters. Great poets made them part of every educated man's literary culture. Mystical fraternities became the custodians of such works, spreading them into Central Asia and the Indian subcontinent and transmitting them from one generation to another.

Following the Mongol khan Hülagü's entry into Baghdad (1258), the Twelver Shī'ites were encouraged by the Il Khanid Tatars and Nazir ad-Din at-Tusi (the philosopher and theologian who accompanied Hülagü as his vizier) to abandon their hostility to mysticism. Mu'tazili doctrines were retained in their theology. Theology, however, was downgraded to "formal" learning that must be supplemented by higher things, the latter including philosophy and mysticism, both of earlier Shī'ite (including Isma'ili) origin and of later Sunni provenance. Al-Ghazālī, As-Suhrawardi, al-'Arabi, and Avicenna were then eagerly studied and (except for their doctrine of the imamate) embraced with little or no reservation.

This movement in Shī'ite thought gathered momentum

when the leaders of a mystical fraternity established themselves as the Safavid dynasty (1501–1732) in Iran, where they championed Twelver Shī'ism as the official doctrine of the new monarchy. During the seventeenth century Iran experienced a cultural and scientific renaissance that included a revival of philosophical studies. There, Islāmic philosophy found its last creative exponents. The new wisdom as expounded by the masters of the school of Esfahan radiated throughout Eastern Islām and continued as a vital tradition until modern times.

The new wisdom lived on during the eighteenth and nineteenth centuries, conserving much of its vitality and strength but not cultivating new ground. It attracted able thinkers such as Shah Wali Allāh of Delhi and Hadi Sabzevari, and became a regular part of higher education in the Ottoman Empire, Iran, and the Indian subcontinent, a status never achieved by the earlier tradition of Islāmic philosophy. In collaboration with its close ally Persian mystical poetry, the new wisdom determined the intellectual outlook and spiritual mood of educated Muslims in the regions where Persian had become the dominant literary language. Attempts to reject the new wisdom in the name of simple, robust, and more practical piety or a return to an older, more orthodox form of mysticism remained isolated and were either ignored or reintegrated into the mainstream until the coming of the modern reformers.

In the nineteenth and twentieth centuries Jamal ad-Din al-Afghani, Muḥammad 'Abduh, and Muḥammad Iqbal advocated radical reforms. The modernists attacked the new wisdom's social and political norms, its individualistic ethics, and its inability to speak intelligently about social, cultural, and political problems generated by a long period of intellectual isolation and domination by the European powers.

None of the reformers was a great political philosopher.

They were concerned with reviving their nations' latent
energies, urging them to free themselves from foreign domination, and impressing on them the need to reform their social
and educational institutions. They also saw that all this
required a total reorientation, which could not take place
so long as the new wisdom remained not only the highest
aim of a few solitary individuals but also a social and popular
ideal. As late as 1917, Iqbal found that "the present-day
Muslim prefers to roam about aimlessly in the valley of
Hellenic–Persian mysticism, which teaches us to shut our eyes
to the hard reality around, and to fix our gaze on what is
described as 'illumination'." His reaction was harsh: "To me
this self-mystification, this nihilism, i.e. seeking reality where it
does not exist, is a physiological symptom, giving me a clue to
the decadence of the Muslim world."

The modern reformers advocated a return to the movements
and masters of Islāmic theology and philosophy antedating the
new wisdom. They argued that these, rather than the "Persian
incrustation of Islām", represented Islām's original and creative impulse. The modernists were attracted in particular to the
views of the Mu'tazilah: affirmation of God's unity and denial
of all similarity between Him and created things, reliance on
human reason, emphasis on human freedom, faith in the
human ability to distinguish between good and bad, and
insistence on the human responsibility to do good and fight
against evil in private and public places. They were also
impressed by the traditionalists' devotion to the original,
uncomplicated forms of Islām and by their fighting spirit,
as well as by the Ithnā 'Asharīyahs' view of faith as an affair
of the heart and their spirited defence of the Muslim community from extreme expressions of rationalism and sectarianism
alike.

In viewing the scientific and philosophical tradition of

Eastern and Western Islām prior to the Tatar and Mongol invasions, the modernists saw an irrefutable proof that true Islām stands for the liberation of human spirit, promotes critical thought, and provides both the impetus to grapple with the temporal and the demonstration of how to set it in order. These ideas initiated what was to become a vast effort to recover, edit, and translate into the Muslim national languages works of earlier theologians and philosophers, which had been long neglected or known only indirectly through later accounts.

The modern reformers insisted that Muslims must be taught to understand modern science and philosophy, including modern social and political philosophies. Initially, this challenge became the task of the new universities in the Muslim world. In the latter part of the twentieth century, however, the originally wide gap between the various programmes of theological and philosophical studies in religious colleges and in modern universities narrowed considerably.

Education

Muslim educational activity began in the eighth century, primarily in order to disseminate the teaching of the Qur'ān and the *sunnah* of the Prophet. The first task was to record oral traditions and collect written manuscripts. By the time of the ninth and early tenth centuries the Arab sciences of tradition, history, and literature had been established.

When the introduction of the Greek sciences – philosophy, medicine, and mathematics – created a formidable body of lay knowledge, its reaction with the traditional religious base resulted in the rationalist theological movement of the Mu'tazilah. In reaction to this, from the ninth to the twelfth centuries,

Sunni scripturalists formulated a religious dogma and began to draw a sharp distinction between religious and secular sciences. The custodians of the Sharīʿah (Islāmic law) developed an unsympathetic attitude toward the secular disciplines and excluded them from the curriculum of the *madrasah* (college) system. This exclusion proved fatal, not only for those disciplines but, in the long run, for religious thought in general because of the lack of intellectual challenge and stimulation. A typical *madrasah* curriculum included logic, Arabic literature, law, Hadith, Qur'ān commentary, and theology. Despite sporadic criticism from certain quarters, the *madrasah* system remained impervious to change. In contrast to the Sunnis, the Shīʿites continued seriously to cultivate philosophy, which developed a strong religious character.

One important feature of Muslim education was that primary education (which consisted of Qur'ān reading, writing, and rudimentary arithmetic) did not feed candidates to institutions of higher education, and the two remained separate. In higher education, emphasis was on books rather than subjects and on commentaries rather than original works. This, coupled with the habit of learning by rote (which was developed from a tradition that encouraged learning more than thinking), impoverished intellectual creativity still further. Despite these grave shortcomings, however, the *madrasah* produced one important advantage. Through the uniformity of its religio-legal content, it gave the *ʿulama* ("the learned") the opportunity to effect that overall cohesiveness and unity of thought and purpose that, despite great variations in local Muslim cultures, has become a palpable feature of the world Muslim community.

When higher learning in the form of tradition grew in the eighth and ninth centuries, it was centred around learned men to whom students travelled from far and near and from whom they obtained a certificate to teach what they had learned. Women were excluded from *madrasah*s, but in urban areas they had access to learning at mosques. Women in scholarly families sometimes became renowned teachers, especially of Hadith. Through the munificence of rulers, princes, and even wealthy female patrons, large private and public libraries were built, and schools and colleges arose.

In the early ninth century a significant incentive to learning came from translations of scientific and philosophical works from the Greek (and partly Sanskrit) at the famous *bayt al-hikmah* ("house of wisdom") at Baghdad. The Fatimid caliph al-Hakim set up a *dar alhikmah* ("hall of wisdom") in Cairo in the tenth–eleventh century. With the advent of the Seljuq Turks, the famous vizier Nizam al-Mulk created an important college at Baghdad, devoted to Sunni learning, in the latter half of the eleventh century. In Turkey a new style of *madrasah* came into existence; it had four wings, for the teaching of the four schools of Sunni law. Professorial chairs were endowed in large colleges by princes and governments, and residential students were supported by college endowment funds. Myriad smaller centres of learning were endowed by private donations.

One of the world's oldest surviving universities, al-Azhar at Cairo, was originally established by the Fatimids. After ousting the Fatimids in the twelfth century, Saladin, the founder of the Ayyubid dynasty, consecrated the university to Sunni learning. Throughout subsequent centuries, colleges and quasi-universities arose throughout the Muslim world from Spain (whence Islāmic philosophy and science were transmitted to the Latin West) across Central Asia to India.

Today, al-Azhar remains the chief centre of Islāmic and Arabic learning in the world. The basic programme of studies was, and still is, Islāmic law, theology, and the Arabic language. Late in the European Middle Ages philosophy and medicine were added to the curriculum, but, because original and independent thinking was suspect in orthodox scholarly circles, these subjects were soon eliminated. Only in the nineteenth century was philosophy reinstated. Twentieth-century efforts at modernization resulted in the addition of social sciences at al-Azhar's new supplementary campus at Nasr City.

There are 14 subject faculties for men and 5 for women in Cairo, as well as regional faculties. Women have been admitted since 1962. Also important is Aligarh Muslim University (founded 1875), south-east of Delhi. A number of educational foundations, such as Al-Maktoum and Al-Haramain, are also significant in spreading Islām through education.

The Family

A basic social teaching of Islām is the encouragement of marriage, and the Qur'ān regards celibacy as something to be resorted to only under economic stringency. Many Sufis, on the other hand, prefer celibacy, and some even regard women as an evil distraction from piety, although marriage also remains the normal practice with Sufis.

Polygamy is permitted by the Qur'ān, which, however, limits the number of simultaneous wives to four, and this permission is made dependent on the condition that justice be done among co-wives (4:3). Medieval law and society regarded this "justice" to be primarily a private matter between a husband and his wives, although the law did provide redress in cases of gross neglect of a wife. The right to divorce was also vested basically in the husband, who could unilaterally repudiate his wife, although the woman could also sue her husband for divorce before a court on certain grounds.

The virtue of chastity is regarded as of prime importance by Islām. The Qur'ān advances its universal recommendation of marriage as a means to ensure a state of chastity (*ihsan*), which is held to be induced by a single free wife. The Qur'ān states that those guilty of adultery are to be severely punished with 100 lashes (24:2). Tradition has intensified this injunction and has prescribed this punishment for unmarried persons, while married adulterers are to be stoned to death. A false accusation of adultery is punishable by 80 lashes.

The general ethic of the Qur'ān considers the marital bond to rest on "mutual love and mercy". The detailed laws of inheritance prescribed by the Qur'ān also tend to confirm the idea of a central family – husband, wife, and children, along with the husband's parents (4:7–12). In recent times most Muslim countries have enacted legislation to tighten marital relationships. The right of parents to good treatment is stressed in Islām, and the Qur'ān extols filial piety, particularly tenderness to the mother, as an important virtue (46:15–17). So strong is the patriarchal family group ethos that in most Muslim societies daughters are not given the inheritance share prescribed by the sacred law in order to prevent disintegration of the joint family's patrimony.

For some women, modernization since the twentieth century has been especially problematic. Urged on the one hand to be liberated from Islām and thereby become modern, they are told by others to be liberated from being Western through being self-consciously Muslim.

There is little information on the situation of ordinary women in premodern Islāmdom, but evidence from the modern period underscores the enormous variety of settings in which Muslim women live and work, as well as the inability of the stereotype of meek, submissive, veiled passivity to reflect the quality of their lives. As always, Muslim women live in cities, towns, villages, and among migratory pastoral tribes; some work outside the home, some inside, some not at all; some wear concealing clothing in public, most do not; for some, movement outside the home is restricted, for most not; and, for many, public modesty is common, as it is for many Muslim men. For many, the private home and the public bath continue to be the centres of social interaction; for others, the world of employment and city life is an option. As always, few live in polygamous families. Strict adherence to the Sharī'ah's provision for women to hold their property in their own right has produced Muslim women of great wealth, in the past as well as today.

Cultural Diversity

The world of Islām harbours a tremendous diversity of cultures, and in different areas it has assimilated native practices into its own. Because Islām draws no absolute distinction between the religious and the temporal, the Muslim state is by definition religious.

The expansion of Islām can be divided into two broad periods. In the first period of the Arab conquests the assimilative activity of the conquering religion was far-reaching. Although Persia resurrected its own language and a measure of its national culture after the first three centuries of Islām, its culture and language had come under heavy Arab influence. Only after Safavid rule installed Shī'ism as a distinctive creed in the sixteenth century did Persia regain a kind of religious autonomy. The language of religion and thought, however, continued to be Arabic.

In the second period, the spread of Islām was largely the work of Sufi missionaries, who compromised with local customs and beliefs and left a great deal of the pre-Islāmic legacy in every region intact. Thus, among the Central Asian Turks, shamanistic practices were absorbed, while in Africa the holy man and his *barakah* (an influence supposedly causing material and spiritual well-being) survive. In India there are large areas geographically distant from the Muslim religio-political centre of power in which customs are still Hindu and even pre-Hindu. The custom of *sati*, in which a widow burned herself alive along with her dead husband, persisted in India even among some Muslims until late into the Mughal period. The eighteenth- and nineteenth-century reform movements strove to "purify" Islām of these accretions and superstitions.

Caste developed among Muslims in India and Pakistan as a result of the proximity of Hindu culture and the fact that in most South Asian societies Muslims had converted from Hinduism. Hindus gave the Muslim ruling class its own status. In South Asian Muslim societies a distinction is made between the *ashrāf* ("noblemen"), descendants of Muslim Arab immigrants, and the non-*ashrāf* Hindu converts. The *ashrāf* group is further divided into four subgroups: (1) *sayyid*s, descendants of Muḥammad through his daughter Fāṭimah and son-in-law 'Alī, (2) *shaykh*s (Arabic: "chiefs"), descendants of Arab or Persian immigrants but including some Rajputs, (3) Pashtuns, members of Pashto-speaking tribes in Afghanistan and north-western Pakistan, and (4) Mughals. The non-*ashrāf* Muslim castes have three levels: at the top, converts from high Hindu castes, mainly Rajputs, insofar as they have not been absorbed into the *shaykh* castes; next, artisan caste groups, such as the Julehes, originally weavers; and lowest, the converted Dalits or Harijans (formerly called "untouchables"), who have continued their old occupations.

In Indonesia, Islām arrived late and soon came under the influence of European colonialism. Indonesian society, therefore, has kept its customary law (called *adat*) at the expense of the Sharīʻah; many of its tribes are still matriarchal, and culturally the Hindu epics Ramayana and Mahabarata hold a high position in national life. Since the nineteenth century, however, orthodox Islām has gained steadily in strength because of fresh contacts with the Middle East.

Apart from regional diversity, the main internal division within Islāmic society is between urban and village life. Islām originated in the two cities of Mecca and Medina, and, as it expanded, its peculiar ethos appears to have developed mainly in urban areas. Culturally, it came under a heavy Persian influence in Iraq, where the Arabs learned the ways and style of life of their conquered people. The custom of veiling women (the *purdah*), for example, was acquired in Iraq. In general, Islām came to appropriate a strong feudal ethic from the peoples it conquered. Also, because the Muslims generally represented the administrative and military aristocracy and because the learned class (the *'ulama'*) was an essential arm of the state, the higher culture of Islām became urban-based.

This city orientation explains and also underlines the traditional cleavage between the orthodox Islām of the *'ulama'* and the folk Islām espoused by the Sufi orders of the countryside. In the modern period, the advent of education and rapid industrialization threatened to make this cleavage still wider. Since the advent of a strong and widespread fundamentalist movement in the second half of the twentieth century, this dichotomy has decreased.

Religious Dress

Islām attaches less importance to liturgical vestments than do most religions, but the social emphasis of the Islāmic faith finds expression in the universal application of the regulations governing dress. Because Islām recognizes no priesthood, "clerical" functions are discharged by the 'ulama', whose insignia is the 'imamah (a scarf or turban).

In the western part of the Muslim world, "clerical" dress has tended to become standardized according to the Azhar (Egyptian) pattern: a long, wide-sleeved gown (*jubbah*) reaching to the feet and buttoned halfway down its total length over a striped garment (caftan); the headgear consists of a soft collapsible cap (*qalansuwah*) of red felt around which is wound a white muslin 'imamah. In Syria a hard *tarbush* of the same red shade replaces the *qalansuwah*. Both the *qalansuwah* and the *tarbush* are provided with a blue tassel. The *jubbah* is usually a sober shade of blue, grey, or brown, and seldom black. Among the Sunnis – from Iraq eastward – the *jubbah* is worn in association with an 'aba' (a long, full garment), traditionally of camel's hair and brown or black in colour. This is sometimes secured by a *hijam,* or cummerbund. In this second regional variant, the 'imamah becomes a full turban replacing the cap, or fez. A green turban usually denotes a *sharīf,* or descendant of the Prophet Muḥammad, and among the Shī'ites the entire garb is black, as a symbol of mourning for the death of Husayn ibn 'Alī at Karbala' (680).

For all Muslim males, the wearing of gold or silk is forbidden in consequence of a prescription (*hadith*) of the Prophet, whereby the wearing of either was rendered "*haram* [forbidden] for the males of my nation". Footwear must be removed on entering a mosque for fear of defiling the interior with ritually impure substances that may have adhered to the sole of the shoe. This rule applies also to entering a grave; thus, gravediggers and stonemasons must be unshod on such occasions. A head covering should properly be worn in the mosque and even when praying outside the mosque as a mark of respect.

When a Muslim purposes to visit the holy city of Mecca at the time of the major pilgrimage (*hajj*), he enters on a state of consecration and robes himself in two white seamless garments (*ihram*), the guise of a beggar, which may not be exchanged for normal dress until he deconsecrates himself after the conclusion of the pilgrimage ceremonies. To these two garments women may add a veil.

Many of the mystical dervish orders (*turuq*) wear distinctive robes, frequently with hierarchical differences. In Turkey, headstones are carved in the shape of the headdress distinctive of the order to which the deceased belonged and are tinctured in the appropriate colours. Particularly interesting are the ceremonial robes of the Mawlawiyah order (popularly known in the West as the Whirling or Dancing Dervishes), in which the symbolism of the robes is central to the mysteries of the order. The dervishes wear over all other garments a black robe (*khirqah*), which symbolizes the grave; the tall camel's hair hat (*sikke*) represents the headstone. Underneath are the white "dancing" robes consisting of a very wide, pleated frock (*tannur*), over which fits a short jacket (*destegül*). On arising to participate in the ritual dance, the dervish casts off the blackness of the grave and appears radiant in the white shroud of resurrection. The head of the order wears a green scarf of office wound around the base of his *sikke*.

For all Muslims of whatever sect, the standard graveclothes are the threefold linen shroud, or *kafan*; the *izar*, or lower garment; the *rida'*, or upper garment; and the *lifafah*, or overall shroud. Martyrs, however, are buried in the clothes in which they die, without their bodies or their garments being washed, because the blood and the dirt are viewed as evidences of their state of glory.

The tradition for women to cover themselves from head to toe and veil their faces when they go out in public is an old one, predating Islām in Persia, Syria, and Anatolia. The Qur'ān provides instructions giving guidance on this matter but not a strict ruling. The enveloping cloaks worn by women for this purpose are similar to one another and often incorporate a mesh panel through which women may peer at the world outside. The most common names for this garment are chador, *chādar*, *chadri*, *çarsaf*, and *tcharchaf*.

Dietary Laws

Islāmic dietary laws – as spelled out in the Qur'ān – illustrate the establishment of a sense of social identity and separateness in the early Islāmic community. Many of the dietary regulations in the Qur'ān are explicit in establishing distinctions between Arabs and Jews and borrow heavily from Mosaic Law.

Muḥammad proscribed for Muslims the flesh of animals that are found dead, blood, swine's flesh, and food that had been offered or sacrificed to idols. The most radical departure of Qur'ānic from Mosaic dietary laws was in connection with intoxicating liquor. Though Jews frown upon alcoholic beverages, they do not forbid them; however Muḥammad absolutely forbade alcohol.

Islām represents a more fundamental removal from all other major religions: what is polluting, forbidden, and enjoined for one person in Islām applies equally to all. Islām's sharpest contrast in this regard is to the religions of India. This difference is highlighted by the fact that Muslims of all social statuses in an Indian village eat freely with each other, worship in the same mosques, and participate in ceremonies together.

Religion and the Arts

Artistic works in the Islāmic world borrowed from Persia and Byzantine traditions but were Islāmized in a manner that fused them into a homogeneous spiritual-aesthetic complex. The most important principle governing art was the religious prohibition of figurization and representation of living creatures. Underlying this prohibition is the assumption that God is the sole author of life and that a person who produces a likeness of a living being seeks to rival God. Hence, in Islāmic aniconism two considerations are brought together: rejection of such images that might become idols (these may be images of anything) and rejection of figures of living things.

This basic principle has, however, undergone modifications. First, pictures were tolerated if they were confined to private apartments and harems of palaces. This was the case with some members of the Umayyad and 'Abbāsid dynasties, Turks, and Persians – in particular with the Shī'ites, who have produced an abundance of pictorial representations of the holy family and of Muḥammad himself. Second, animal and human figures in pictures are combined with other ornamental designs such as geometrical patterns and arabesques – stressing their ornamental nature rather than representative function. Third, for the same reason, in sculptural art they appear in low relief. In other regions of the Muslim world – in North Africa, Egypt, and India (except for Mughal palaces) – representational art was strictly forbidden.

Instrumental music was forbidden by the orthodox in the formative stages of Islām. As for vocal music, its place was largely taken by a sophisticated and artistic form of the recitation of the Qur'ān known as *tajwid*. Nevertheless, the Muslim princely courts generously patronized and cultivated music. Among the religious circles, the Sufis introduced both vocal and instrumental music as part of their spiritual practices. The *sama'*, as this music was called, was opposed by the orthodox at the beginning, but the Sufis persisted in its use, which slowly won general recognition. The great Sufi poet Jalal ad-Din ar-Rumi (died 1273) – revered equally by the orthodox and the Sufis – heard the divine voice in his stringed musical instrument when he said "Its head, its veins [strings] and its skin are all dry and dead; whence comes to me the voice of the Friend?"

In literature, drama and pure fiction were not allowed – drama because it was a representational art and fiction because it was akin to lying. Similar constraints operated against the elaboration of mythology. Story literature was tolerated, and the great story works of Indian origin – *The Thousand and One Nights* and *Kalilah wa Dimnah* – were translated from the Persian, introducing secular prose into Arabic. Didactic and pious stories were used and even invented by popular preachers. Much of this folklore found its way back into enlarged editions of *The Thousand and One Nights* and, through it, has even influenced later history writing.

Because of the ban on fictional literature, there grew a strong tendency in later literary compositions – in both poetry and prose – toward hyperbole (*mubalaghah*), a literary device to satisfy the need to get away from what is starkly real without committing literal falsehood, thus often resulting in the caricature and the grotesque. Poetry lent itself particularly well to this device, which was freely used in panegyrics, satires, and lyrics. Poetry also afforded an especially suitable vehicle for a type of mystic poetry in which it is sometimes impossible to determine whether the poet is talking of earthly love or spiritual love. For the same reason, poetry proved an effective haven for thinly veiled deviations from and even attacks on the literalist religion of the orthodox.

Islāmic Myth and Legend

The strict monotheism of Islām does not allow for much mythological embellishment, and only reluctantly were the scriptural revelations of the Qur'ān elaborated and enlarged by commentators and popular preachers. Thus, in the first three centuries, a number of ideas from the ancient Middle East and from Hellenistic and especially from Judaeo–Christian traditions were absorbed into Islām and given at least partial sanction by the theologians. At the same time, legends were woven around the Prophet Muḥammad and the members of his family. Though inconsistent with historical reality, these legends formed for the masses the main sources of inspiration about the famous figures of the past.

Since early times Islāmic theologians have sought to disregard the Qur'ānic interpretation of both storytellers and mystics. The *qussa*s, or storytellers, made the Qur'ānic revelation more understandable to the masses by filling in the short texts with detailed descriptions that were not found in scripture. Though the mystics tried to maintain the purity of the divine word, they also attempted a spiritualization of both the Qur'ān and the popular legends that developed around it. Their way of giving to the Qur'ānic words a deeper meaning, however, and discovering layer after layer of meaning in them, sometimes led to new quasi-mythological forms. Later Islāmic mystical thinkers built up closed systems that can be called almost mythological (e.g. the angelology – theory of angels – of Suhrawardi al-Maqtul, [died 1191]).

The sources of Islāmic mythology are first of all the Qur'ānic revelations. Since the ninth century, commentators on the Qur'ān have been by far the most important witnesses for Islāmic "mythology". They wove into their explanations various strands of Persian and ancient oriental lore and relied heavily on Jewish tradition. Traditions about the life and sayings of the Prophet grew larger and larger and adopted foreign mythological material. While the classical mythology of Islām, as far as it can be properly called so, is spread over the whole area of Islām, the miracles and legends around a particular Muslim saint are found chiefly in the area of his special influence (especially where his order is most popular).

From the eleventh century onward, the biographies of the mystics often show interesting migrations of legendary motifs from one culture to another. The *Tazkerat ol-Owliya'* ("Memoirs of the Saints") of Farīd od-Dīn 'Attār (died *c.* 1220), for instance, has become the storehouse of legendary material about the early Sufi mystics for the Persian-speaking countries. Muslim historians interested in world history often began their works with mythological tales; central Asian traditions were added in Iran during the Il-Khanid Dynasty (1256–1335). Folk poetry, in the different languages spoken by Muslims, provides a popular representation of traditional material, whether in Arabic, Persian, Turkish, the Indian and Pakistani languages (e.g. Urdu, Bengali, Sindhi, Panjabi, and Baluchi), or the African languages; in all of them allusions to myth and legend are found down to the level of riddles and lullabies. Typical of the legendary tradition of the Shī'ites are the *ta'ziyas* ("passion-plays") in Iran, commemorating the death of Husayn (680), and the *marsiyehs* (threnodies or elegies for the dead), which form an important branch of the Urdu poetry of India and Pakistan.

Myths covering the cosmology and eschatology of the Muslim world vary from its creation out of nothing by God's word *kun* ("Be") and the questioning of the dead by two terrible angels (thus the reciting of the profession of faith to the dying), to the announcement of the end of the world by the coming of the *mahdī* ("divinely guided one") – a messianic figure who will appear in the last days; he is not found in the Qur'ān but developed out of Shī'ite speculations and is sometimes identified with Jesus.

Muḥammad, whose only miracle, according to his own words, was the bringing of the Qur'ān, is credited with innumerable miracles and associated with a variety of miraculous occurrences: his finger split the moon; the cooked poisoned meat warned him not to touch it; the palm trunk sighed; the gazelle spoke for him; he cast no shadow; from his perspiration the rose was created. Muḥammad-mysticism proper was developed in the late ninth century; he is shown as the one who precedes creation, his light is pre-eternal, and he is the reason for and the goal of creation. He becomes the perfect man, uniting the divine and the human sphere as dawn unites night and day.

Muḥammad's cousin and son-in-law 'Alī has also been surrounded by legends, and 'Alī's son Husayn is the subject of innumerable poems that concern the day of his final fight in Karbala'. Almost every figure mentioned in the Qur'ān has become the centre of a circle of legends, be it Yusuf, the symbol of overwhelming beauty, or Jesus with the life-giving breath, the model of poverty and asceticism. The great religious personalities have become legendary, especially the martyr-mystic Hallaj (died 922). His words *ana al-Haqq*, "I am the Creative Truth", became the motto of many later mystics. His death on the gallows in Baghdad is the model for the suffering of lovers. The founders of mystical orders were credited by their followers with a variety of miracles, such as riding on lions, healing the sick, and walking on water.

A feature of Islāmic mythology is the transformation of unreligious stories into vehicles of religious experience. The old hero of romantic love in Arabic literature, Majnun, "the demented one", became a symbol of the soul longing for identification with God, and in the Indus Valley the tales of Sassui and Sohni, the girls who perish for their love, and other romantic figures, have been understood as symbols of the soul longing for union with God through suffering and death.

Many Muslim tales, legends, and traditional sayings are built upon the mystical value of numbers, such as the threefold or sevenfold repetition of a certain rite. This is largely explained by examples from the life of a saintly or pious person, often the Prophet himself. The number 40, found in the Qur'ān (as also in the Bible) as the length of a period of repentance, suffering, preparation, and steadfastness, is connected in Islām with the 40 days' preparation and meditation, or fasting, of the novice in the mystical brotherhood. To each number, as well as to each day of the week, special qualities are attributed through the authority of both actual and alleged statements of the Prophet.

The importance given to the letters of the Arabic alphabet is peculiar to Muslim pious thought. Letters of the alphabet were assigned numerical values: the straight *alif* (numerical value one), the first letter of the alphabet, becomes a symbol of the uniqueness and unity of Allāh; the *b* (numerical value two), the first letter of the Qur'ān, represents to many mystics the creative power by which everything came into existence; the *h* (numerical value five) is the symbol of *huwa*, He, the formula for God's absolute transcendence; the *m* (numerical value 40) is the "shawl of humanity" by which God, the One (al-Ahad), is separated from Aḥmad (Muḥammad). *M* is the letter of human nature and hints at the 40 degrees between humanity and God. The sect of the Hurufis developed these cabalistic interpretations of letters, but they are quite common in the whole Islāmic world and form almost a substitute for mythology.

Today, mythology proper has only a very small place in official Islām. Reformers tried to purge Islām of all non-Qur'ānic ideas and picturesque elaborations of the texts, whereas the mystics tried to spiritualize them as far as possible. Modern Muslim exegesis attempts to interpret many of the mythological strands of the Qur'ān in the light of modern science; to some interpreters, *jinn* (demons) and angels are spiritual forces; to others, *jinn* are microbes or the like. Nevertheless, popular legends surrounding the Prophet and the saints are still found among the masses; while they are tending to disappear under the influence of historical research, many have formed models for the behaviour and spiritual life of the Muslim believer.

PART 2

ISLĀMIC
WORLD HISTORY

4

THE AGE OF MUḤAMMAD AND THE CALIPHATE

Pre-Muḥammadan Society

When Muḥammad was born in 570, the potential for pan-Arab unification seemed nil; but after he died, in 632, the first generation of his followers were able not only to maintain pan-Arab unification but to expand far beyond the Arabian Peninsula. The potential for Muslim empire building had been established with the rise of the earliest civilizations in western Asia and was refined with the emergence and spread of what have been called the region's Axial Age religions – Abrahamic, centred on the Hebrew patriarch Abraham, and Mazdean, focused on the Iranian deity Ahura Mazdah – and their later relative, Christianity. It was facilitated by the expansion of trade from eastern Asia to the Mediterranean and by the political changes thus effected.

In the seventh century AD a coalition of Arab groups inside and outside the Arabian Peninsula, some sedentary and some migratory, seized political and fiscal control in western Asia. The factors that surrounded and directed their

accomplishment had begun to coalesce long before, with the
emergence of agrarian-based societies and the founding of
cities and the consequent increase in agricultural production
and intercity trading. A few individuals were able to establish
territorial monarchies and foster religious institutions with
wider appeal.

By the middle of the first millennium BC the settled world
had crystallized into four cultural core areas: Mediterranean,
Nile-to-Oxus, Indic, and East Asian. The Nile-to-Oxus, the
future core of Islāmdom, was the least cohesive of these, with
Irano–Semitic languages of several sorts. Yet, located at the
crossroads of the trans-Asian trade and blessed with numerous
natural transit points, the region offered special social and
economic prominence to its merchants.

During the period from 800 to 200 BC, the Axial Age, the
world's first religions of salvation developed, and from these
traditions – including Judaism, Mazdeism, Buddhism, and
Confucianism – derived all later forms of high religion, including Christianity and Islām. In the Nile-to-Oxus region two
major traditions arose: the Abrahamic in the west and the
Mazdean in the east. Because they required exclusive allegiance through an individual confession of faith in a just and
judging deity, they are called confessional religions. The god of
these religions was a unique, all-powerful creator who remained active in history, and each event in the life of every
individual was meaningful in terms of the judgement of God at
the end of time. The traditions reflected the mercantile environment in which they were formed in their special concern for
fairness, honesty, covenant keeping, moderation, law and
order, accountability, and the rights of ordinary human
beings.

Although modern Western historiography has projected an
East–West dichotomy on to ancient times, Afro-Eurasian

continuities and interactions were well established throughout premodern times. Through the conquests of Alexander the Great in the fourth century BC the Irano-Semitic cultures of the Nile-to-Oxus region were permanently overlaid with Hellenistic elements, and a link was forged between the Indian subcontinent and Iran.

From the beginning of the first century AD the major occupants of the habitable parts of the arid central zone of the Arabian Peninsula were known as Arabs. They were Semitic-speaking tribes of settled, semi-settled, and fully migratory peoples who drew their name and apparently their identity from what the camel-herding Bedouin pastoralists among them called themselves: 'arab. To the north lay the irrigated agricultural areas of Syria and Iraq. Until the beginning of the third century AD the greatest economic and political power in the peninsula was in the Yemen, which had evolved an exceptionally long and profitable trade route from East Africa across the Red Sea and from India across the Indian Ocean up through the peninsula into Iraq and Syria, where it joined older Phoenician routes across the Mediterranean and into the Iberian Peninsula.

By the third century, however, the Sasanian Empire, founded by Ardashir I in 226, was at war with Rome, a conflict that was to continue up to Islāmic times. The reorganization of the Roman Empire under Constantine the Great (280–337) and the adoption of Christianity as the Roman state religion exacerbated the competition with the Sasanian Empire and resulted in the spreading of Christianity into Egypt and Abyssinia and the encouraging of missionizing in Arabia itself. By the beginning of the fourth century the rulers of Abyssinia and Ptolemaic Egypt were carrying their aggression into the Yemen. In the first quarter of the sixth century the proselytizing efforts of a Jewish Yemeni ruler resulted in a massacre of

Christians in Najran, provoking Abyssinian Christian reprisal and occupation and control of the Yemen. In conflict with the Byzantines, the Zoroastrian–Mazdean Sasanians invaded the Yemen toward the end of the sixth century, further expanding the religious and cultural horizons of Arabia, where membership in a religious community could not be apolitical and could even have international ramifications. Such connection between communal affiliation and political orientations would be expressed in the early Islāmic community.

Paradoxically, the long-term result of Arabia's entry into international politics was to enhance the power of the tribal Arabs. The settled powers needed their hinterlands enough to foster client states: the Byzantines oversaw the Ghassanid kingdom, the Persians oversaw the Lakhmid, and the Yemenis (prior to the Abyssinian invasion) had Kindah. Arab cultural activity increased, and the prosperity of the fifth and sixth centuries, as well as the intensification of imperial rivalries in the late sixth century, seems to have brought the Arabs of the interior permanently into the wider network of communication that fostered the rise of the Islāmic community at Mecca and Medina.

Although the sixth-century client states were the largest Arab polities of their day, it was among independent Arabs living in Mecca in the Hejaz (al-Hijaz) that a permanently significant Arab state arose. Around the year AD 400 Mecca had come under the control of the Quraysh Arabs, and, during the generations before Muhammad's birth, they used their trading connections and their relationships with their Bedouin cousins to make their town a regional centre whose influence radiated in many directions. They designated Mecca as a quarterly safe haven from the inter-tribal warfare and raiding that was endemic among the Bedouin. Thus Mecca became an attractive site for large trade fairs that coincided with pilgrimage (*hajj*) to a local shrine, the Ka'bah. The Ka'bah housed the deities of visitors as well as the Meccans' supra-tribal creator and covenant-guaranteeing deity, called Allāh. Most Arabs probably viewed this deity as one among many, possessing powers not specific to a particular tribe; others may have identified this figure with the God of the Jews and Christians.

The building activities of the Quraysh threatened one non-Arab power enough to invite direct interference: the Abyssinians are said to have invaded Mecca in the year of Muḥammad's birth. But the Byzantines and Sasanians were distracted by internal reorganization and renewed conflict, and the Yemeni kingdoms were declining. With their weakening, Mecca became an attractive new focus for supra-tribal organization.

Meccan society was markedly diverse, including non-Arabs as well as Arabs, slave as well as free, and so a hierarchy based on wealth developed there. Meccans needed to act in their own interest and to minimize conflict by institutionalizing new, broader social alliances and interrelationships. Very little in the Arabian environment, however, favoured the formation of stable, large-scale states, and Meccan efforts at centralization and unification might well have been transient. But the rise of the Meccan system also coincided with the spread of the confessional religions and, eventually, in Mecca and elsewhere a few individuals came to envision the possibility of effecting supra-tribal association through a leadership role common to the confessional religions – that is, prophethood or messengership. The only such individual who succeeded in effecting broad social changes was a member of the Hāshim (Hashem) clan of Quraysh: Abū Al-Qāsim Muḥammad ibn 'Abd Allāh ibn 'Abd al-Muṭṭalib ibn Hāshim – the Prophet Muḥammad. One of their own, he accomplished what the Quraysh had started, first by working against them; later by working with them.

Muḥammad and his Community

It was Muḥammad's individual genius to articulate an ideol-ogy capable of appealing to multiple constituencies and form-ing them into a single community. He was particularly well placed to lead such a social movement. Although he was a member of a high-status tribe, he belonged to one of its less well-placed clans. He was fatherless at birth; his mother and grandfather died when he was young, leaving him under the protection of an uncle. Although he possessed certain admir-able personality traits to an unusual degree, his commercial success derived not from his own status but from his marriage to a much older woman, a wealthy widow named Khadījah.

A few individuals, including Khadījah, immediately recog-nized Muḥammad's vision of the archangel Gabriel as that of a messenger of God, but adherence of the surrounding Arabs to his beliefs came more slowly. Because Muḥammad's utter-ances seemed similar to those of the *kahin*s (religious specia-lists who delivered oracles in ecstatic rhymed prose [*saj'*] and read omens), many of his hearers assumed that he was another one of them. But by eschewing any source other than the one supreme being, whom he identified as Allāh ("God") and whose message he regarded as cosmically significant and binding, Muḥammad was gradually able to distinguish himself from all other intermediaries.

In 622, by the time of Muḥammad's emigration to Medina (see Chapter 1 for an account of his life), a new label had begun to appear in his recitations to describe his followers: in addition to being described in terms of their faithfulness (*iman*) to God and his messenger, they were also described in terms of their undivided attention, that is, as *muslim*s, individuals who assumed the right relationship to God by surrendering (*islām*) to His will. As an autonomous community *muslim*s might have become a tribal unit like those with whom they had affiliated, yet under Muḥammad's leadership they developed a social organization that could absorb or challenge everyone around them. They became Muḥammad's *ummah* ("community") because they had recognized and supported God's emissary (*rasul Allāh*). The *ummah*'s members differed from one another not by wealth or genealogical superiority but by the degree of their faith and piety, and membership in the community was itself an expression of faith. Anyone could join, regardless of origin, by following Muḥammad's lead, and the nature of members' support could vary. In the concept of *ummah*, Muḥammad supplied the missing ingredient in the Meccan system: a powerful abstract principle for defining, justifying, and stimulating membership in a single community.

Muḥammad made the concept of *ummah* work by expanding his role as arbiter so as to become the sole spokesman for all residents of Medina. He also used his outstanding knowledge of tribal relations to act as a great tribal leader and developed a network of alliances between his *ummah* and neighbouring tribes. He managed and distributed the booty from raiding, keeping one-fifth for the *ummah*'s overall needs and distributing the rest among its members. In return, members gave a portion of their wealth as *zakat* ("purification"), to help the needy and to demonstrate their awareness of their dependence on God for all of their material benefits.

During this period, Muḥammad led campaigns against non-supporters in Medina, against the Quraysh in Mecca, and against surrounding tribes. Activism in the name of God, both non-military as well as military, would become a permanent strand in Muslim piety. After the Muslims occupied Mecca in 630, Muḥammad began to receive deputations from many parts of Arabia. By his death in 632 he was ruler of virtually all of it. The Meccan Quraysh quickly became assimilated.

Ironically, in defeat they accomplished much more than they would have had they achieved victory: the centralization of all of Arabia around their polity and their shrine, the Ka'bah, which had been emptied of its idols to be filled with an infinitely greater invisible power.

The broader solidarity that Muḥammad had begun to build was stabilized only after his death in 632. In the next two years one of his most significant legacies became apparent: the willingness and ability of his closest supporters to sustain the ideal and the reality of one Muslim community under one leader, even in the face of significant opposition. When Muḥammad died, two vital sources of his authority ended – ongoing revelation and his unique ability to exemplify his messages on a daily basis. The *al-ansār* ("helpers"), his early supporters in Medina, moved to elect their own leader, leaving the *al-muhājirūn* ("emigrants", his fellow emigrants to Medina) to choose theirs; but a small number of *al-muhājirūn* managed to impose one of their own over the whole. That man was Abū Bakr, one of Muḥammad's earliest followers and the father of his favoured wife 'Ā'ishah. The title Abū Bakr took, *khalīfah* (caliph; deputy or successor), echoed revealed references to those who assist major leaders and even God himself. To *khalīfah* he appended *rasūl Allāh*, so that his authority was based on his assistance to Muḥammad as messenger of God.

Abū Bakr's Succession

Abū Bakr soon confronted two new threats: the secession of many of the tribes that had joined the *ummah* after 630 and the appearance among them of other prophet figures who claimed continuing guidance from God. Abū Bakr put an end to revelation with a combination of military force and coherent rhetoric. He defined withdrawal from Muḥammad's coalition as ingratitude to or denial of God (the concept of *kufr*); thus he gave secession (*riddah*) cosmic significance as an act of apostasy punishable, according to God's revealed messages to Muḥammad, by death. He declared that the secessionists had become Muslims, and thus servants of God, by joining Muḥammad; they were not free *not* to be Muslims, nor could they be Muslims, and thus loyal to God, under any leader whose legitimacy did not derive from Muḥammad. Finally, he declared Muḥammad to be the last prophet God would send, relying on a reference to Muhammad in one of the revealed messages as *khatm al-anbīyā'* ("Seal of the Prophets"). In his ability to interpret the events of his reign from the perspective of Islām, Abū Bakr demonstrated the power of the new conceptual vocabulary Muḥammad had introduced.

To provide an adequate fiscal base, Abū Bakr enlarged impulses present in pre-Islāmic Mecca and in the *ummah*. At his death he was beginning to turn his followers to raiding non-Muslims in the only direction where that was possible: Syria and Iraq in the north. The ability of the Medinan state to absorb random action into a relatively centralized movement of expansion testifies to the strength of the new ideological and administrative patterns inherent in the concept of *ummah*. This fusion of two once-separable phenomena, membership in Muḥammad's community and faith in Islām – the mundane and the spiritual – would become one of Islām's most distinctive features. Becoming and being Muslim always involved *doing* more than it involved *believing*. Muslims were not to be asked to choose between religion and politics, or church and state, but between living in the world the right way or the wrong way.

Conversion and Crystallization

Between 634 and 870, through conquest, Islām was transformed from the badge of a small Arab ruling class to the
dominant faith of a vast empire that stretched from the western
Mediterranean into Central Asia. As a result, Arab cultures
intermingled with the indigenous cultures of the conquered
peoples to produce Islām's fundamental orientations and
identities, and the Arabic language became a vehicle for the
transmission of high culture, even though the Arabs remained
a minority. Trade and taxation replaced booty as the fiscal
basis of the Muslim state, a non-tribal army replaced a tribal
one, and a centralized empire became a nominal confederation.

When the Muslim conquests began, the Byzantines and
Sasanians had been in conflict for a century; in the most recent
exchanges, the Sasanians had established direct rule in the
town of al-Ḥīrah, further exposing its many Arabs to their
administration. When the Arab conquests began, representatives of Byzantine and Sasanian rule on Arabia's northern
borders were not strong enough to resist.

Abū Bakr's successor in Medina, 'Umar I (ruled 634–44),
had not so much to stimulate conquest as to organize and
channel it. As leaders he chose skilful managers experienced in
trade and commerce as well as warfare and imbued with an
ideology that provided their activities with a cosmic significance. The total numbers involved in the initial conquests may
have been relatively small, perhaps less than 50,000, divided
into numerous shifting groups. Yet few actions took place
without any sanction from the Medinan government or one of
its appointed commanders.

'Umar defined the *ummah* as a continually expansive polity
managed by a new ruling elite, and even after the conquests

ended, this sense of expansiveness continued to be expressed in the way Muslims divided the world into their own zone, the Dar al-Islām, and the zone into which they could and should expand, the Dar al-Harb, the abode of war. Muhammad's revelations from God and his *sunnah* ("traditions") defined the cultic and personal practices that distinguished Muslims from others: prayer, fasting, pilgrimage, charity, avoidance of pork and intoxicants, membership in one community centred at Mecca, and activism (*jihad*) in the community's behalf.

'Umar symbolized this conception of the *ummah* in two ways. He assumed an additional title, *amīr al-mu'minīn* ("commander of the faithful"), which linked organized acti-vism with faithfulness (*īmān*), the earliest defining feature of the Muslim. He also adopted a lunar calendar that began with the Hijrah (emigration), the moment at which a group of individual followers of Muhammad had become an active social presence. Because booty was the *ummah*'s major re-source, 'Umar concentrated on ways to distribute and sustain it. After the government's fifth-share, the rest was distributed according to the *dīwān*, a register of the ruling elite and the conquering forces, in order of entry into the *ummah*.

The fighters, or *muqātilah*, he stationed as an occupying army in garrisons (*amsār*) constructed in locations strategic to further conquest: al-Fustāt in Egypt, Damascus in Syria, and Kūfah and Basra in Iraq. The garrisons attracted members of the indigenous population; initiated population shifts, such as that from northern to southern Iraq; and also inaugurated the rudiments of an "Islāmic" daily life: each garrison was com-manded by a caliphal appointee, responsible for setting aside an area for prayer, a mosque (*masjid*), named for the prostra-tions (*sujūd*) that had become a characteristic element in the five daily worship sessions (*salāt*s). There the fighters could hear God's revelations to Muhammad recited by men trained in that emerging art. There, too, the Friday midday *ṣalāt* could be performed communally, accompanied by an important educational device, the sermon (*khuṭbah*), through which the fighters could be instructed in the principles of the faith. The mosque fused the practical and the spiritual in a special way: because the Friday prayer included an expression of loyalty to the ruler, it could also provide an opportunity to declare rebellion.

The series of ongoing conquests that fuelled this system had their most extensive phase under 'Umar and his successor, 'Uthmān ibn 'Affān (ruled 644–56). Within 25 years, Muslim Arab forces created the first empire permanently to link western Asia with the Mediterranean. Within another century, Muslim conquerors surpassed the achievement of Alexander the Great, not only in the durability of their accomplishment but also in its scope, reaching from the Iberian Peninsula to Central Asia. After al-Ḥīrah fell in 633, a large Byzantine force was defeated in Syria, opening the way to the final conquest of Damascus in 636 and the taking of Jerusalem in 638. By 640, Roman control in Syria was over; by 646 Egypt had come under Islāmic control. In 651 the defeat and assassination of the last Sasanian emperor, Yazdegerd III, marked the end of the 400-year-old Sasanian Empire.

This phase of conquest ended under 'Uthmān and ramified widely – by the end of the seventh century Arab Muslims were trading in China – but the fiscal strain of such expansion and the growing independence of Arabs outside the peninsula gave rise to discontent toward the end of 'Uthmān's reign. Into a society organized along family lines, 'Uthmān had introduced the supremacy of trans-kinship ties. He had established the power of Medina over some of the Quraysh families at Mecca and local notables outside Arabia. He was now accused of nepotism for relying on his own family. His call for the production of a single standard collection of Muḥammad's messages from God, known simply as the Qur'ān ("Reading", or "Recitation"), and the destruction of the collections of other local communities, was also resented.

Above all, 'Uthmān was the natural target of anyone dissatisfied with the distribution of the conquest's wealth, since he represented and defended a system that defined all income as Medina's to distribute. He had granted privileges to the earliest and most intensely devoted followers of his cause and to wealthy high-placed Meccans, assigning a lower status to indigenous inhabitants who joined the cause later, though he felt they had made an equal contribution. Other tensions resulted from conditions in the conquered lands: the initial isolation of Arab Muslims, and even Arab Christians who fought with them, from the indigenous non-Arab population; the discouragement of non-Arab converts, except as clients (*mawālī*) of Arab tribes; the administrative dependence of peninsular Arabs on local Arabs and non-Arabs; and the development of a tax system that discriminated against non-Muslims.

The ensuing conflicts were played out in a series of intra-Muslim disputes that began with 'Uthmān's assassination and continued until 870. The importance of kinship ties persisted, but they were gradually replaced by the identities of a new social order. Because the *ummah*, unified under one leader, was seen as an earthly expression of God's favour, and because God was seen as the controller of all aspects of human existence, the identities formed in the course of the *ummah*'s early history fused the religious, social, political, and economic dimensions. The meaningfulness of the new identities expanded as non-Muslims contributed to Islām's formation, through opposition or through conversion. In spite of, and perhaps because of, Muslims' willingness to engage in continuing internal conflicts, the faith of Islām thus became one of the most unified religious traditions in human history.

The First and Second *fitnah*s

By the end of the period of conversion and crystallization, Muslim historians would retrospectively identify four discrete periods of conflict and label them *fitnah*s, trials or temptations to test the unity of the *ummah*. This retrospective interpretation may be anachronistic and misleading: the entire period between 656 and the last quarter of the ninth century was conflict ridden, yet the most striking characteristic of the period was the pursuit of unity.

In the first two *fitnah*s, claimants to the caliphate relied on their high standing among the Quraysh and their local support in either Arabia, Iraq, or Syria. The first *fitnah*, occurring between 'Uthmān's assassination in 656 and the accession of his kinsman Mu'āwiyah I in 661, included the caliphate of 'Alī, the cousin and son-in-law of Muhammad. It involved a three-way contest between 'Alī's party in Iraq; a coalition of important Quraysh families in Mecca, including Muhammad's wife 'Ā'ishah and Talhah and Zubayr; and the party of Mu'āwiyah, the governor of Syria and a member of 'Uthmān's clan, the Banū Umayyah. Ostensibly the conflict focused on whether 'Uthmān had been assassinated justly, whether 'Alī had been involved, and whether 'Uthmān's death should be avenged by Mu'āwiyah or by the leading Meccans. 'Alī and his party (*shī'ah*) at first gained power, then lost it permanently to Mu'āwiyah. Disappointed at the Battle of Siffin (657) with 'Alī's failure to insist on his right to rule, a segment of his partisans withdrew, calling themselves Khāwarijism (Kharijites; "seceders", see Chapter 3). Their spiritual heirs would come to recognize any pious Muslim as leader. Meanwhile, another segment of 'Alī's party intensified their loyalty to him as a just and heroic leader who was one of Muḥammad's dearest intimates and the father of his only male descendants.

The second *fitnah* followed Muʿāwiyah's caliphate (661–80), and coincided with the caliphates of Muʿāwiyah's son Yazīd I (ruled 680–83), whom he designated as successor, and Yazīd's three successors. Once again, different regions supported different claimants, as new tribal divisions emerged in the garrison towns; and once again, representatives of the Syrian Umayyads prevailed. In the Hejaz, the Marwānid branch of the Umayyads, descendants of Marwān I, who claimed the caliphate in 685, fought against 'Abd Allāh ibn az-Zubayr for years; by the time they defeated him, they had lost most of Arabia to Kharijite rebels.

During the period of the first two *fitnah*s, resistance to Muslim rule was an added source of conflict. Some of this resistance took the form of syncretic or anti-Islāmic religious movements. In other areas it took the form of large-scale military hostility. In the 660s the Umayyads had expanded their conflict with the Byzantine Empire by competing for bases in coastal North Africa; it soon became clear, however, that only a full fledged occupation would serve their purposes. That occupation was begun by 'Uqbah ibn Nāfiʿ, the founder of al-Qayrawan (Kairouan, in modern Tunisia) and, as Sidi (Saint) 'Uqbah, the first of many Maghribi Muslim saints. It eventually resulted in the incorporation of large numbers of pagan or Christianized Berber tribes.

During the caliphate of 'Abd al-Malik ibn Marwān (ruled 685–705), and under his successors during the next four decades, the problematic consequences of the conquests became much more visible. While the Marwān id caliphs nominally ruled the various religious communities, they allowed

the communities' own appointed or elected officials to admin-
ister most internal affairs. Yet now the right of religious
communities to live in this fashion was justified by the Qur'ān
and *sunnah*; as peoples with revealed books (*ahl al-kitāb*), they
deserved protection (*dhimmah*) in return for a payment. The
Arabs also formed a single religious community whose right to
rule over the non-Arab protected communities the Marwān ids
sought to maintain.

To signify this supremacy, 'Abd al-Malik ordered the
construction of the Dome of the Rock, a monumental
mosque, in Jerusalem, a major centre of non-Muslim population. The site chosen was sacred to Jews and Christians
because of its associations with biblical history; it held added
meaning for Muslims, who believed it to be the starting point
for Muhammad's Mi'rāj, or Nocturnal Ascent to heaven.
Although this and other early mosques resembled contemporary Christian churches, gradually an Islāmic aesthetic
emerged: a dome on a geometrical base, accompanied by
a minaret from which to deliver the call to prayer; and an
emphasis on surface decoration that combined arabesque and
geometrical design with calligraphic representations of God's
Word.

'Abd al-Malik took other steps to mark the distinctiveness of
Islāmic rule: for example, he encouraged the use of Arabic as
the language of government and had Islāmized coins minted.
During the Marwān id period, the Muslim community was
further consolidated by the regularization of public worship
and the crystallization of a set of five minimal duties (the
Pillars of Islām). Yet the Marwān ids also depended heavily on
the help of non-Arab administrative personnel (*kuttāb*; singular, *kātib*) and on administrative practices (e.g. a set of
government bureaus) inherited from Byzantine and, in particular, late Sasanian practice.

Gradually, most of the subject population was incorporated into the *ummah*. As the conquests slowed, it became more and more difficult to keep Arabs garrisoned, and the sedentation of Arabs outside the peninsula grew. As the tribal links that had so dominated Umayyad politics began to break down, the meaningfulness of tying non-Arab converts to Arab tribes as clients was diluted. Simultaneously, the growing prestige and elaboration of things Arabic and Islāmic made them more attractive, to non-Arab Muslims and to non-Muslims alike.

The more the Muslim rulers succeeded, the more prestige their customs, norms, and habits acquired. Heirs to the considerable agricultural and commercial resources of the Nile-to-Oxus region, they increased its prosperity and widened its horizons by extending its control far to the east and west. Arabic now became a valuable lingua franca. Many Muslims cultivated reports, which came to be known as Hadith, of what Muḥammad had said and done, in order to develop a clearer and fuller picture of his *sunnah*. These materials were sometimes gathered into accounts of his campaigns, called *maghāzi*.

The emulation of Muḥammad's *sunnah* was a major factor in the development of recognizably "Muslim" styles of personal piety and public decision-making. As differences in the garrisons needed to be settled according to "Islāmic" principles, the caliphs appointed arbitrating judges, *qāḍī*s, who were knowledgeable in Qur'ān and *sunnah*. The pursuit of legal knowledge, *fiqh*, was taken up in many locales and informed by local pre-Islāmic custom and Islāmic resources. These special forms of knowledge began to be known as *'ulūm* (singular, *'ilm*); the persons who pursued them, as *'ulama'* (singular, *'ālim*), a role that provided new sources of prestige and influence, especially for recent converts or sons of converts.

Muslims outside Arabia were also affected by interacting with members of the religious communities over which they

ruled. When protected non-Muslims converted, they brought
new expectations and habits with them; unconverted protected
groups (*dhimmī*s) were equally influential. This interaction
had special consequences in the areas of prophethood and
revelation, where major shifts and accommodations occurred
among Jews, Christians, Mazdeans, and Muslims during the
first two centuries of their coexistence. Muslims attempted to
establish Muḥammad's legitimacy as an heir to Jewish and
Christian prophethood, while non-Muslims tried to distinguish their prophets and scriptures from Muḥammad and
the Qur'ān.

With the *dhimmī* system, Muslim rulers formalized and
probably intensified pre-Islāmic tendencies toward religious
communalization. Furthermore, the greater formality of the
new system could protect the subject communities from each
other as well as from the dominant minority. One of the most
significant aspects of many Muslim societies was the insepar-
ability of "religious" affiliation and group membership. In the
central caliphal lands of the early eighth century, membership
of the Muslim community offered the best chance for social
and physical mobility, regardless of a certain degree of discrimination against non-Arabs.

The Marwān id Maghrib illustrates a kind of conversion
more like that of the peninsular Arabs. After the defeat of
initial Berber resistance movements, the Arab conquerors of
the Maghrib quickly incorporated the Berber tribes en masse
into the Muslim community, turning them immediately to
further conquests. In 710 an Arab-Berber army set out and
conquered the Iberian Peninsula, which they called al-Andalus,
and ruled in the name of the Umayyad caliph. From there, the
Andalusian Muslims conducted seasonal raiding along the
southern French coast for many years, though they never
had serious goals across the Pyrenees. Muslim presence in

Andalusia was different in form from that in the Middle East, however: it may never have become a majority, and non-Muslims entered into the Muslim realm as Mozarabs, Christians who had adopted the language and manners, rather than the faith, of the Arabs.

The Berbers who remained in the Maghrib had no sooner joined the Muslim community than they rebelled again, but this time an Islāmic identity, Khārijism, provided the justification. Kharijite ideas had been carried to the Maghrib by refugees from the numerous revolts against the Marwān ids. Kharijite egalitarianism suited the economic and social grievances of the Berbers as non-Arab Muslims under Arab rule. The revolts outlasted the Marwān ids; they resulted in the first independent Maghribi dynasty, the Rustamid, founded by Muslims of Persian descent. The direct influence of the revolts was felt as late as the tenth century and survives among small communities in Tunisia and Algeria.

The Third *fitnah*

Meanwhile, in the central caliphal lands, growing discontent and opposition to the Marwān ids culminated in the third *fitnah* (744–50) and the establishment of a new and final dynasty of caliphs, the 'Abbāsids. Ever since the second *fitnah*, a number of Muslims had begun to raise serious questions about the proper Muslim life and the Marwān ids' ability to exemplify it. Pious Muslims tried to define a good Muslim and to decide whether a bad Muslim should be excluded from the community, or a bad caliph from office. They also considered God's role in determining a person's sinfulness and final dispensation. The proper relationship between Arab and non-Arab Muslims, and between Muslims and *dhimmī*s, was another important focus. The willingness of non-Arabs to join the *ummah* was growing, but fiscal stability seemed to depend on continuing to discourage conversion. In the positions taken in these debates lay the germs of Muslim theology: rejecting the history of the community by demanding rule by Muḥammad's family; rejecting the history of the community by following any pious Muslim and excluding any sinner; or accepting the history of the community, its leaders, and most of its members.

In the course of these debates the Marwān id caliphs began to seem severely deficient. Al-Ḥasan al-Baṣrī, a pious ascetic and a model for the early Sufis, called on the Marwān ids to rule as good Muslims and on good Muslims to be suspicious of worldly power. To the pious, the ideal ruler, or *imām* (the word also for a Muslim who led the *ṣalāt*), should, like Muḥammad, possess special learning and knowledge. The first four caliphs, they argued, had been *imām*s in this sense, but under the Umayyads the caliphate had been reduced to a military and administrative office devoid of *imām ah*, or true legitimacy. This piety-minded opposition to the Umayyads, as it has been aptly dubbed, now began to talk about a new dispensation. Some found special learning and knowledge only in Muḥammad's family. Some defined Muḥammad's family broadly to include any Hashimite; others, more narrowly, to include only descendants of 'Alī.

In the late Marwān id period, the piety-minded opposition found expression in a movement organized in Khorāsān (Khurasan) by Abū Muslim, a semi-secret operative of one particularly ambitious Hashimite family, the 'Abbāsids. The 'Abbāsids, who were kin but not descendants of Muḥammad, claimed also to have inherited, a generation earlier, the authority of one of 'Alī's actual descendants, Abū Hāshim. Publicly Abū Muslim called for any qualified member of Muḥammad's family to become caliph; but privately he allowed the partisans (*shī'ah*) of 'Alī to assume that he meant them. Abū Muslim ultimately succeeded because he managed to link the concerns of the piety-minded in Syria and Iraq with Khorāsānian discontent.

When in 750 the army organized and led by Abū Muslim succeeded in defeating the last Marwān id ruler, his caliph-designate represented only one segment of this broad coalition. He was the head of the 'Abbāsid family, Abū al-'Abbās as-Saffāḥ, who now subordinated the claims of the party of 'Alī to those of his own family, and who promised to restore the unity of the *ummah*, or *jamā'ah*. The party of 'Alī refused to accept this compromise, isolating them and causing them to define themselves in terms of more radical points of view. Those who accepted the early 'Abbāsids came to be known as the People of the Sunnah and Jamā'ah. They accepted the cumulative historical reality of the *ummah*'s first century: all of the decisions of the community, and all of the caliphs it had accepted, had been legitimate, as would be any subsequent caliph who could unite the community. The concept of *fitnah* acquired a fully historicist meaning: if internal discord were a trial sent by God, then any unifying victor must be God's choice.

Sunnis and Shī'ites

The historicists came to be known as Sunnis and their main opponents as Shī'ites. While both groups relied on the *sunnah*, they emphasized different elements: for the Sunnis (more properly, the Jama'i-Sunnis), the principle of solidarity was essential to the *sunnah*, while the Shī'ites argued that the fundamental element of the *sunnah* was Muḥammad's devotion to his family and his wish that they succeed him through 'Alī.

When the 'Abbāsids denied the special claims of the family of 'Alī, they prompted the Shī'ites to define themselves as a permanent opposition to the status quo. The crystallization of Shī'ism into a movement of protest received its greatest impetus during and just after the lifetime of one of the most influential Shī'ite leaders of the early 'Abbāsid period, Ja'far aṣ-Ṣādiq. Ja'far's vision and leadership allowed the Shī'ites to understand their chaotic history as a meaningful series of efforts by truly pious and suffering Muslims to right the wrongs of the majority. The leaders of the minority had occupied the office of *imām*, the central Shī'ite institution, which had been passed on from the first *imām*, 'Alī, by designation down to Ja'far, the sixth. To protect his followers from increasing Sunni hostility to the views of radical Shī'ites, known as the *ghulāt* ("extremists"), who claimed prophethood for 'Alī, Ja'far made a distinction that both protected the uniqueness of prophethood and established the superiority of the role of *imām*. Since prophethood had ended, its true intent would die without the *imām*s, whose protection from error allowed them to carry out their indispensable task.

Although Ja'far did develop an ideology that invited Sunni toleration, he did not unify all Shī'ites. Differences continued to be expressed through loyalty to various of his relatives. During Ja'far's lifetime, his uncle Zayd revolted in Kūfah (740), founding the branch of the Shī'ism known as the *zaydīyah* (Zaydis), or Fivers (for their allegiance to the fifth *imām*), who became particularly important in southern Arabia.

The Shī'ite majority followed Ja'far's son Mūsā al-Kāzim and *imām*s in his line through the twelfth, who disappeared in 873. Those loyal to the 12 *imām*s became known as the Imaiis or Ithnā 'Asharīyah (Twelvers). They adopted a quietistic stance toward the status quo government of the 'Abbāsids and prepared to wait until the twelfth *imām* should return as the messiah to avenge injustices against Shī'ites and to restore justice before the Last Day (or Day of Judgement).

Some of Ja'far's followers, however, remained loyal to Isma'il, Ja'far's eldest son, who predeceased his father after being designated. These became the Isma'iliyah (Isma'ilis) or Sab'iyah (Seveners), and they soon became a source of continuing revolution in the name of Isma'il's son Muḥammad at-Tamm, who was believed to have disappeared. Challenges to the 'Abbāsids were not long in coming; of particular significance was the establishment, in 789, of the first independent Shī'ite dynasty, in present-day Morocco, by Idris ibn 'Abd Allāh ibn Hasan II, who had fled after participating in an unsuccessful uprising near Mecca.

The 'Abbāsids

The 'Abbāsid claim to legitimacy, as with many premodern societies, was fragile, and their early actions undermined the unitive potential of their office. Having alienated the Shī'ites, they liquidated the Umayyad family, one of whom, 'Abd ar-Raḥmān I, escaped and founded his own state in Andalusia. The 'Abbāsids' move to Iraq and their execution of Abū Muslim (whose power and popularity they had begun to fear) disappointed the Khorāsānian troops who had supported them. The non-Muslim majority often rebelled, too. Bih'āfrīd ibn Farwardīn claimed to be a prophet capable of incorporating both Mazdaism and Islām into a new faith. Hāshim ibn Ḥākim, called al-Muqanna' (the "Veiled One"), around 759 declared himself a prophet and then a god, heir to all previous prophets, to numerous followers of 'Alī, and to Abū Muslim himself.

The 'Abbāsids symbolized their connection with their pre-Islāmic predecessors by founding a new capital, Baghdad, near the old Sasanian capital. They also continued to elaborate the Sasanian-like structure begun by the Marwān id governors in Iraq. Their court life became more and more elaborate, the bureaucracy fuller, and the palace fuller than ever with slaves and concubines as well as with the retinues of the caliph's four legal wives. By the time of Hārūn ar-Rashīd (ruled 786–809), Europe had nothing to compare with Baghdad, not even the court of his contemporary Charlemagne (742–814). But problems surfaced, too. Slaves' sons fathered by Muslims were not slaves and so could compete for the succession. Despite the 'Abbāsids' defence of Islām, unconverted Jews and Christians could be influential at court. The head (vizier or *wazir*) of the financial bureaucracy sometimes became the effective head of government by taking over the chancery as well.

Like all absolute rulers, the 'Abbāsid caliphs soon confronted the insoluble dilemma of absolutism: the monarch cannot be absolute unless he depends on helpers, but his dependence on helpers undermines his absolutism. Having drawn into his service prominent members of a family of Buddhist converts, the Barmakids, Hārūn ar-Rashīd found them such rivals that he liquidated them within a matter of years. It was also during Hārūn's reign that Ibrāhīm ibn al-Aghlab, a trusted governor in Tunis, founded a dynasty that gradually became independent, as did the Tahirids, the 'Abbāsid governors in Khorāsān, two decades later.

The 'Abbāsids' ability to rival their pre-Islāmic predecessors was enhanced by their generous patronage of artists and artisans. The great 7,000-mile Silk Road from Ch'ang-an (now Sian, China) to Baghdad (then the two largest cities in the world) helped provide the wealth. The ensuing literary florescence, promoted by the capture of a group of Chinese papermakers at the Battle of Talas in 751, gave rise to a literary genre called *adab* (literally, "norm of conduct") that fused pre-Islāmic and Islāmic concerns in excellent Arabic style. The 'Abbāsids encouraged translation from pre-Islāmic languages, particularly Middle Persian, Greek, and Syriac. Al-Khwarizmi, from whose name the word *algorithm* is derived, creatively combined Hellenistic and Sanskritic concepts; the word *algebra* derives from the title of his major work, *Kitab al-jabr wa al-muqābalah* ("The Book of Integration and Equation"). Movements such as *falsafah* (a combination of the positive sciences with logic and metaphysics) and *kalām* (systematic theological discourse) applied Hellenistic thought to new questions.

Despite such integration of pre-Islāmic and Islāmic influences, the 'Abbāsids, having encouraged conversion, tried to "purify" the Muslim community of what they perceived to be socially dangerous and alien ideas. Al-Mahdī (ruled 775–85) actively persecuted the Manichaeans, whom he defined as heretics so as to deny them status as a protected community. Even though the 'Abbāsids continued to maintain administrative courts, not accessible to the *qādī*s, they also promoted the study of *'ilm* and the status of those who pursued it. In so doing they fostered the emergence of an independent body of law, Sharī'ah, which Muslims could use to evaluate and circumvent caliphal rule itself.

Sharī'ah

A key figure in the development of Sharī'ah was Abū 'Abd Allāh ash-Shafi'i, who died in 820. By his time Islāmic law was extensive but uncoordinated, reflecting differing local needs and tastes. Schools had begun to form around various recognized masters, such as al-Awza'i in Syria, Abū Hanifah in Iraq, and Malik ibn Anas, all of whom used some combination of local custom, personal reasoning, Qur'ān, and Hadith. Like most other *faqih*s (students of jurisprudence, or *fiqh*), ash-Shafi'i viewed Muhammad's community as a social ideal and his first four successors as rightly guided. So that this exemplary time could provide the basis for Islāmic law, he constructed a hierarchy of legal sources: Qur'ān; Hadith, clearly traceable to Muhammad and in some cases to his companions; *ijmā'* ("consensus"); and *qiyās* (analogical reasoning as applied to the first three).

The way in which Islāmic law had developed had allowed many pre-Islāmic customs, such as the veiling and seclusion of women, to receive a sanction not given to them in the Qur'ān or the Hadith. Ash-Shafi'i did not change that entirely. Law continued to be pursued in different centres, and several major "ways" (*madhhab*s) began to coalesce among Sunnis and Shī'ites alike. Among Sunnis, four schools came to be preeminent, Shafi'iyah (Shafiites), Malikiyah (Malikites), Hanafiyah (Hanafites), and Hanabilah (Hanbalites), and each individual Muslim was expected to restrict himself to only one. Furthermore, the notion that the gate of *ijtihād* ("individual thought") closed in the ninth century was not firmly established until the twelfth century. However, ash-Shafi'i's system was widely influential in controlling divergence and in limiting undisciplined forms of personal reasoning. It also stimulated the collecting and testing of *hadith* for their unbroken traceability to Muhammad or a companion. The need to verify *hadith* stimulated a characteristic form of premodern Muslim intellectual and literary activity, the collecting of biographical materials into compendiums (*tabaqāt*).

The Sharī'ah came to be a supremely authoritative, comprehensive set of norms and rules covering every aspect of life, from worship to personal hygiene. It applied equally to all Muslims, including the ruler, whom Sharī'ah-minded Muslims came to view as its protector, not its administrator or developer. According to the Sharī'ah, a Muslim order was one in which the ruler was Muslim and the Sharī'ah was enshrined as a potential guide to all; Muslims were one confessional community among many, each of which would have its own laws that would apply except in disputes between members of different communities. The Sharī'ah regulated relations and inequities among different segments of society, freeborn Muslim, slave, and protected non-Muslim. Many ultra-pious Muslims came to view the law as a divine rather than human creation.

The Fourth *fitnah*

During the reign of al-Ma'mun (813–33) the implications of all this *'ilm*-based activity for caliphal authority began to become clear. Al-Ma'mun came to the caliphate as the result of the fourth *fitnah*. Al-Ma'mun's father, Hārūn ar-Rashīd, had provided for the empire to be divided between his two sons upon his death, but al-Ma'mun successfully fought his brother Al-Amin from his provincial seat at Merv in Khorāsān, from which he controlled the less-significant eastern sector, for rule of the capital and all the western domains.

During his reign, which probably represents the high point of caliphal absolutism, the court intervened in an unprecedented manner in the intellectual life of its Muslim subjects, who for the next generation engaged in the first major intra-Muslim conflict that focused on belief as well as practice. The argument centred on the Qur'ān and its created or uncreated nature. Al-Ma'mun, as well as his brother and successor al-

Mu'tasim, was attracted to the Mu'tazilah (Mutazilites; see "Islāmic Theology", Chapter 3). If the Qur'ān were eternal along with God, His unity would, for the Mu'tazilah, be violated. They especially sought to avoid literal exegesis of the Qur'ān, which in their view discouraged free will and produced embarrassing inconsistencies and anthropomorphisms. By arguing that the Qur'ān was created in time, they could justify metaphorical and changing interpretation. By implication, Muhammad's position as deliverer of revelation was undermined because the Hadith was made less authoritative.

The opponents of the Mu'tazilah, and therefore of the official position, coalesced around the figure of Ahmad ibn Hanbal. A leading master of Hadith, he was able to mobilize large public demonstrations against the doctrine of the created Qur'ān. Ibn Hanbal argued for an eternal Qur'ān and emphasized the importance of Muhammad's *sunnah* to the understanding of it. By his time, major literary works had established a coherent image of the indispensability of Muhammad's prophethood.

These were not merely dogmatic issues. The Qur'ān for the Muslims was somehow part of God; Hadith-mindedness and emulation of Muhammad's *sunnah* had become such an essential part of the daily life of ordinary people that the Mu'tazilite position, as intellectually consistent and attractive as it was, was unmarketable. In a series of forcible inquiries called *mihnah*, al-Ma'mun and al-Mu'tasim actively persecuted those who, like Ibn Hanbal, would not conform; but popular sentiment triumphed, and after al-Mu'tasim's death the caliph al-Mutawakkil was forced to reverse the stand of his predecessors.

This caliphal failure to achieve doctrinal unity coincided with other crises. By al-Mu'tasim's reign the tribal troops were becoming unreliable and the Tahirid governors of Khorāsān more independent. Al-Mu'tasim expanded his use of military slaves, finding them more loyal, and housed them at Samarra', a new capital north of Baghdad, where the caliphate remained until 892. For most of this period, the caliphs were actually under the control of their slave soldiery; and even though they periodically reasserted their authority, rebellions continued. Many were anti-Muslim, like that of the Iranian Babak (whose 20-year-long revolt was crushed in 837); but increasingly they were intra-Muslim, like the Kharijite-led revolt of black agricultural slaves (Zanj) in southern Iraq (868–83).

By 870, the Baghdad–Samarra' caliphate had become one polity among many; its real rulers had no ideological legitimacy. At Córdoba the Umayyads had declared their independence, and the Maghrib was divided among several dynasties of differing persuasions: the Shī'ite Idrisids, the Kharijite Rustamids, and the Jama'i-Sunni Aghlabids. The former governors of the 'Abbāsids, the Tulunids, ruled Egypt and parts of Arabia; Iran was divided between the Saffarids, governors of the 'Abbāsids in the south, and the Persian Samanids in the north.

Nevertheless, the ideal of the caliphate continued to be a source of unity after the reality waned; among all the new states, no alternative to the caliphate could replace it. Muslim worship and belief remained remarkably uniform. The annual pilgrimage to Mecca helped reinforce this underlying unity by bringing disparate Muslims together in a common rite. The pilgrimage, as well as the rise of prosperous regional urban centres, enhanced the trade that traversed Islāmdom. A network of credit and banking, caravanserais, and inter-city mercantile alliances tied far-flung regions together. Central was the caravan, then the world's most effective form of transport. Across Islāmdom, mosque-market complexes sprang up in most towns; because municipal institutions were rare, political stability so unpredictable, and government intervention kept to a minimum, the Sharī'ah and the learned men who carried it became a mainstay of everyday life and social intercourse.

No one can say exactly when the majority of Islāmdom's population became Muslim. Older scholarship looks to the end of the first quarter of the ninth century; newer scholarship to the beginning of the third quarter. In 870 a man died whose life's work symbolized the consolidation of Islām in everyday life: al-Bukhari, who produced one of the six collections of *hadith* recognized as authoritative by Jama'i-Sunni Muslims. His fellow collector of *hadith*, Muslim ibn al-Hajjaj, died about four years later. About the same time, classical thinkers in other areas of Islāmicate civilization died, among them the great author of *adab*, al-Jahiz (868/9), the great early ecstatic Sufis Abū'l Fayd Dhu'n-Nun al-Misri (861) and Abū Yazīd Bistami (874), the philosopher Ya'qub ibn Ishaq as-Sabah al-Kindī (870), and the historian of the conquests al-Baladhuri (*c.* 892). Men of different religious and ethnic heritages, they signified, by the last quarter of the ninth century, the full and varied range of intellectual activities of a civilization that had come of age.

5

THE FLOWERING OF ISLĀM

Premodern Islāmic Society

Premodern Islāmicate societies were characterized by a high degree of fluidity, occasionalism, and voluntarism in the structuring of associations, organizations, loyalties, and occupations, and the maintenance of social boundaries and order. In Muslim cities, the only official officeholders were appointees of the central government, such as the governor; the *muhtasib*, a transformed Byzantine *agoranomos* who was monitor of public morality as well as of fair-market practice; or the *sahib ash-shurtah*, head of the police. In the absence of an organized church or ordained clergy, those whose influence derived from piety or learning were influential because they were recognized as such, not because they were appointed; and men of very different degrees of learning might earn the designation of *'ālim*. Although the ruler was expected to contribute to the maintenance of public services, neither he nor anyone else was obligated to do so. Though the ruler might maintain prisons for those whose behaviour he disapproved of, the local *qāḍī*s had need of none, relying generally on persuasion or negotiation and borrowing the caliphal police on the relatively rare occasion on which someone needed to be brought before them by force.

There was no formalized mode of succession for any of the dynasties of the time. Competition, sometimes armed, was relied upon to produce the most qualified candidate. Patronage was an important basis of social organization. The family served as a premodern welfare agency; where it was absent, minimal public institutions, such as hospitals, provided. One of the most important funding mechanisms for public services was a private one, the *waqf*, through which an individual could circumvent the Sharī'ah's requirement that an individual's estate be divided among many heirs, and endow an institution or group with all or part of his estate. In addition to patronage, many other overlapping ties bound individual Muslims together: loyalties to an occupation, a town or neighbourhood, to a form of piety, or to persons to whom one made an oath for a specific purpose; and ties to patron or to family.

The Qur'ān and Sharī'ah discouraged corporate responsibility in favour of individual action, yet the unstable political realities of the Islāmic world sometimes called for corporate action, as when a city came to terms with a new ruler or invader. In those cases, a vaguely defined group of notables, known usually as *a'yān*, might temporarily come together to represent their city in negotiations, to be disbanded when more functional small-group loyalties could safely be resumed. Within this shifting frame of individuals and groups, the ruler was expected to maintain a workable, if not equitable, balance. More often than not the real ruler was a local *amir* of some sort, the de facto system of rule that emerged during this period sometimes being referred to as the *a'yān-āmir*.

The city's physical and social organization reflected this complex relationship between public and private, individual and group: physically separated quarters; multiple markets and mosques; mazelike patterns of narrow streets and alleys with dwellings oriented toward an inner courtyard; an absence of public meeting places other than bath, market, and mosque; and the concentration of social life in private residences.

The Rise of Competitive Regions

In the period from 870 to 1041 the unifying forces of the previous era persisted but the caliphal lands in Iraq became less central. Though Baghdad remained pre-eminent, important initiatives were being taken in surrounding areas: Andalusia; the Maghrib and sub-Saharan Africa; Egypt, Syria, and the holy cities (Mecca and Medina); Iraq; Iran, Afghanistan, Transoxania; and, toward the end of the period, northern India. Regional courts could compete with the 'Abbāsids; conflicts were often couched in terms of local identities, and although the 'Abbāsid caliphate was still a focus of concern and debate, other forms of leadership became important. Just as being Muslim no longer meant being Arab, being cultured no longer meant speaking and writing exclusively in Arabic. Certain Muslims began to cultivate a second language of high culture, New Persian. Ethnic differences were blurred by the effects of peripatetic education and shared languages.

Economic changes also promoted regional strengths. Although Baghdad continued to profit from its central location, caliphal neglect of Iraq's irrigation system and southerly shifts in trans-Asian trade promoted the fortunes of Egypt; the opening of the Sahara to Maghribi Muslims provided a new source of slaves, salt, and minerals; and Egyptian expansion into the Mediterranean opened a major channel for Islámicate influence on medieval Europe. Islámdom continued to expand, sometimes as the result of aggression on the part of frontier warriors (*ghāzī*s), but more often as the result of trade.

Andalusia illustrates the extent of 'Abbāsid prestige and the assertion of local creativity. In the beginning of the period, Islámicate rule was represented by the Umayyads at Córdoba. At first the Córdoban Umayyads styled themselves *amir*s, the title also used by caliphal governors and other local rulers, and continued to mention the 'Abbāsids in the Friday worship session. But in 929, 'Abd ar-Rahmān III (ruled 912–61) adopted the title of caliph and began having the Friday prayer recited in the name of his own house. The Umayyad state continued to be the major Muslim presence in the peninsula until 1010, after which time it became, until 1031, but one of many independent city-states. The Umayyad rulers patronized some of Andalusia's most brilliant Islámicate culture.

In 870 the Maghrib, to the south, was divided among several dynasties, all but one of foreign origin, and only one of which, the Aghlabids, nominally represented the 'Abbāsids. The Muslim Arabs, unlike their predecessors, who had restricted themselves to coastal settlements, came inland to compete more effectively with the Byzantines, and there they tried to incorporate the Berbers. One branch of the Berbers, the Sanhajah, extended far into the Sahara, across which they had established a caravan trade with blacks in the Sudanic belt. At some time in the tenth century the Sanhajah nominally converted to Islám, and their towns in the Sahara began to assume Muslim characteristics. Around 990 a black kingdom in the Sudan, Ghana, extended itself as far as Audaghost, the Sanhajah centre in the Sahara. Thus was black Africa first brought into contact with the Muslim Mediterranean.

In the late ninth century the Maghrib was unified and freed from outside control for the first time. Driven underground by 'Abbāsid intolerance and a maturing ideology of covert re-volutionism, the Isma'ili Shī'ites had developed mechanisms to maintain solidarity and undertake political action. These mechanisms can be subsumed under the term *da'wah*, the same word that had been used for the movement that brought the 'Abbāsids to power. The *da'wah*'s ability to communicate rapidly over a large area rested on its travelling operatives as well as on a network of local cells. In the late ninth century an Isma'ili movement, nicknamed the Qaramitah (Qarmatians), had unsuccessfully threatened the 'Abbāsids in Syria, Iraq, and Bahrain. Seeking other outlets, a Yemeni operative known as Abū 'Abd Allāh ash-Shī'i made contact, on the occasion of the *hajj*, with representatives of a Berber tribe that had a history of Kharijite hostility to caliphal control.

In 901 Abū 'Abd Allāh arrived in Little Kabylia (in present-day Algeria); for eight years he prepared for an *imām*, preach-ing of a millennial restoration of justice after an era of foreign oppression. After conquering the Aghlabid capital al-Qayra-wan (in present-day Tunisia), he helped free from a Sijilmassa prison his *imām*, 'Ubayd Allāh, who declared himself the *mahdī* ("divinely guided one"). Such a word was applied differently by different constituencies: some Muslims applied it to any justice-restoring divinely guided figure; others, in-cluding many Jama'i-Sunnis, to the apocalyptic figure ex-pected to usher in the millennium before the Last Judgement; and still others, including most Shī'ites, to a returned or restored *imām*.

Abū 'Abd Allāh's followers may have differed in their expectations, but the *mahdī* himself was unequivocal: he was a descendant of 'Alī and Fāṭimah through Isma'il's dis-appeared son and therefore was a continuation of the line of the true *imām*. He symbolized his victory by founding a new capital named after himself, al-Mahdīyah (in present-day Tunisia). During the next half-century the "Fatimids" tried with limited success to expand westward into the Maghrib and north into the Mediterranean, but their major goal was Egypt, nominally under 'Abbāsid control. From Egypt they would challenge the 'Abbāsid caliphate itself. In 969 the Fatimid army conquered the Nile Valley and advanced into Palestine and southern Syria as well.

The Fatimids established a new and glorious city, al-Qahir-ah ("The Victorious"; Cairo), to rival 'Abbāsid Baghdad. They then adopted the title of caliph, laying claim to be the legit-imate rulers of all Muslims as well as head of all Isma'ilis. Now three caliphs reigned in Islāmdom, where there was supposed to be only one. In Cairo the Fatimids founded a great mosque–school complex, al-Azhar. They fostered local handicraft production and revitalized the Red Sea route from India to the Mediterranean. They built up a navy to trade as well as to challenge the Byzantines and underscore the 'Abbāsid caliph's failure to defend and extend the frontiers.

Fatimid occupation of the holy cities of Mecca and Medina, complete by the end of the tenth century, had economic as well as spiritual significance: it reinforced the caliph's claim to leadership of all Muslims; provided wealth; and helped him keep watch on the western Arabian coast, from the Hejaz to the Yemen, where a sympathetic Zaydi Shī'ite dynasty had ruled since 897. Fatimid presence in the Indian Ocean was even strong enough to establish an Isma'ili missionary in Sind. The Fatimids patronized the arts: Fatimid glass and ceramics were some of Islāmdom's most brilliant. As in other regions, imported styles and tastes were transformed by or supplemen-ted with local artistic impulses, especially in architecture, the most characteristic form of Islāmicate art.

The reign of one of the most unusual Fatimid caliphs, al-Hakim, from 996 to 1021, again demonstrated the interregional character of the Isma'ili movement. Historians describe al-Hakim's religious values as inconsistent with official Isma'ili teachings, tending toward the Jama'i-Sunni majority. After he vanished under mysterious circumstances, his religious revisionism was not pursued by his successors or by the Isma'ili establishment in Egypt, but in Syria it inspired a peasant revolt that produced the Druze, who still await al-Hakim's return.

When the Fatimids expanded into southern Syria, another Shī'ite dynasty, the Hamdanid, of Bedouin origin, had been ruling northern Syria from Mosul since 905. In 944 a branch of the family had taken Aleppo, from where they ruled until they were absorbed by the Fatimids after 1004. At their court some of Islāmdom's most lastingly illustrious writers found patronage, including the poet al-Mutanabbi (915–65) and al-Fārābī, who tried to reconcile reason and revelation. Al-Fārābī contributed to the ongoing Islāmization of Hellenistic thought. The *falsafah*, the Arabic cognate for the Greek *philosophia*, included metaphysics and logic, as well as the positive sciences such as mathematics, music, astronomy, and anatomy. Exponents questioned the relationship of revelation to real truth and shared the principle of concealment with the Shī'ites, believeing that inner truth was accessible to only a very few.

The Flourishing of Iraq

By the late ninth and early tenth centuries the last remnant of the caliphal state was Iraq, under control of the Turkic soldiery. Despite its political decline and instability, this period contained some of the most striking and lastingly important creative figures in all of early Islāmicate civilization. Among them are the historian and Qur'ānic exegete at-Ṭabarī (c. 839–923), the theologian Abū al-Hasan al-Ash'arī (c. 873–c. 935), and the ecstatic mystic al-Hallāj (c. 858–922).

At-Ṭabarī (Abū Ja'far Muḥammad ibn Jarir) was born in Tabaristan, south of the Caspian Sea, and as a young man travelled to Baghdad. At-Ṭabarī said that he produced 40 leaves a day for 40 years; his works, which include a commentary on the Qur'ān and a universal history, testify to the accuracy of his claim. His method involved the careful selection, organization, and juxtaposition of separate and often contradictory accounts cast in the form of *hadith*. This technique celebrated the *ummah*'s collective memory and established a range of acceptable disagreement.

Al-Ash'arī made his contribution to systematic theological discourse (*kalām*). Attracted early to a leading Mu'tazilite teacher, he broke away at the age of 40 but went on to use Mu'tazilite methods of reasoning to defend popular ideas such as the eternality and literal truth of the Qur'ān and the centrality of Muḥammad's *sunnah* as conveyed by the Hadith. Where his approach yielded objectionable results, such as an anthropomorphic rendering of God or a potentially polytheistic understanding of his attributes, al-Ash'ari resorted to the principle of *bila kayfah* ("without regard to the how"), whereby a person of faith accepts that certain fundamentals are true without regard to how they are true, and that divine intention is not always accessible to human intelligence. Al-Ash'arī's harmonization also produced a simple creed, which expressed faith in God, his angels, and his books, and affirmed belief in Muḥammad as God's last messenger and in the reality of death, physical resurrection, the Last Judgment, and heaven and hell. Taken together, at-Ṭabarī's historiography and al-Ash'ari's theology symbolize the consolidation of Jama'i-Sunni, Sharī'ah thought and piety.

The most visible and powerful tenth-century exponent of Sufism was al-Ḥallāj. By his day, Sufism had grown far beyond its early forms, which were represented by al-Ḥasan al-Baṣrī (died 728), who practiced *zuhd*, or rejection of the world, and by Rabi'ah al-'Adawiyah (died 801), who formulated the Sufi ideal of a disinterested love of God. The mystics Abū Yazīd Bistami (died 874) and al-Junayd (died 910) had begun to pursue the experience of unity with God, first by being "drunk" with his love and with love of him, and then by acquiring life-transforming self-possession and control. Masters (called *shaykh*s or *pir*s) were beginning to attract disciples (*murid*s) to their way. Like other Muslims who tried to go "beyond" the Sharī'ah to inner truth, the Sufis practiced concealment of inner awareness (*taqiyah*). Al-Ḥallāj, one of al-Junayd's disciples, began to travel and preach publicly, however. His success was disturbing enough for the authorities in Baghdad to have him arrested and condemned to death. Yet his career had shown the power of Sufism, which would by the twelfth century become an institutionalized form of Islāmic piety.

Long before, in 945, control over the caliphs at Baghdad passed from their Turkish soldiery to a dynasty known as the Buyids or Buwayhids. The Buyids, who came from Daylam, near the southern coast of the Caspian Sea, identified with Imami Shī'ism. By about 930, three sons of a fisherman named Buyeh had emerged as leaders. One of them conquered Baghdad, not replacing the caliph but ruling in his name. The fact that they were Shī'ite, as were the Idrisids, Fatimids, and Hamdanids, led scholars to refer to the period from the mid-tenth to mid-eleventh century as the Shī'ite century.

Like other contemporary rulers, the Buyids were patrons of culture, especially of speculative thought (Shī'ism, Mu'tazilism, *kalām*, and *falsafah*). Buyid attempts to maintain the cultural brilliance of the court at Baghdad were, however, limited by a decline in revenue occasioned partly by a shift in trade routes to Fatimid Egypt and partly by long-term neglect of Iraq's irrigation works. The caliphs had occasionally made land assignments (*iqta's*) to soldiers in lieu of paying salaries; now the Buyids extended the practice to other individuals and thus removed an important source of revenue from central control. After 983, Buyid territories were split among members of the family, and pressure was applied to their borders from both the west (by Hamdanids and Fatimids) and the east (by Samanids, Ghaznavids, and Seljuqs).

The economic difficulties of Buyid Iraq promoted urban unrest, including raiding, looting, and assault, directed most often toward the wealthy or the military. For some of the Islāmicate "gangs" or "clubs", thuggery may have been the norm; for others, the figure of the fourth caliph and first *imām*, 'Alī, seems to have provided an exemplar. Even though Shī'ites had become a separate group with a distinctive interpretation of 'Alī's significance, a more generalized affection for the family of the Prophet, and especially for 'Alī, was widespread among Jama'i-Sunnis. 'Alī had come to be recognized as the archetypal young male (*fata*); a related word, *futuwah*, signified groups of young men who pursued such virtues as courage, aiding the weak, generosity, endurance of suffering, love of truth, and hospitality.

The Samanids and the Ghaznavids

In the middle of the "Shī'ite century" a major Sunni revival occurred in eastern Islāmdom in connection with the emergence of the second major language of Islāmicate high culture, New Persian. This double revival was accomplished by two

Iranian dynasties, the Samanids and the Ghaznavids; Ghaznavid zeal even spilled over into India.

The Samanid Dynasty (819–999) stemmed from a local family appointed by the 'Abbāsids to govern at Bukhara and Samarkand. Gradually the Samanids had absorbed the domains of the rebellious Tahirids and Saffarids in northeastern Iran and reduced the Saffarids to a small state in Sistan. The Samanids, relying on Turkic slave troops, also managed to contain the migratory pastoralist Turkic tribes who continually pressed on Iran from across the Oxus River. In the 950s they even managed to convert some of these Turkic tribes to Islām.

The Samanid court at Bukhara attracted leading scholars, such as the philosophers Abū Bakr al-Rāzī (died 925) and Avicenna (980–1037), who later worked for the Buyids; and the poet Ferdowsi (died c. 1020). Though not Shī'ites, the Samanids expressed an interest in Shī'ite thought, especially in its Isma'ili form. The Samanids also fostered the development of New Persian, which combined the grammatical structure and vocabulary of spoken Persian with vocabulary from Arabic. A landmark of this "Persianizing" of Iran was Ferdowsi's epic poem *Shāh-nāmeh* ("Book of Kings"), covering several thousand years of detailed mythic Iranian history and Iran's ancient heroic lore.

The Ghaznavid Dynasty originated with Sebüktigin (ruled 977–97), a Samanid Turkic slave governor in Ghazna (now Ghazni) in the Afghan mountains, who had made himself independent of his masters as their central power declined. His eldest son, Mahmud, expanded into Buyid territory in western Iran, identifying himself staunchly with Sunni Islām. Presenting himself as a frontier warrior against the pagans, Mahmud invaded and plundered north-western India, establishing a permanent rule in the Punjab; but it was through ruling Iran, which gave a Muslim ruler true prestige, that Mahmud sought to establish himself. He declared his loyalty to the 'Abbāsid caliph, whose "investiture" he sought, and expressed his intention to defend Sunni Islām against the Shī'ite Buyids.

Although he and his regime were proud of their Turkic descent, Mahmud encouraged the use of New Persian, with its echoes of pre-Islāmic Iranian glory, for administration and for prose as well as poetry. The first major prose work in New Persian, a remarkable history of the Ghaznavids, was written by Bu'l-Fazl-i Bayhaqi (995–1077), who worked in the Ghaznavid chancery. Mahmud also brought to his court writers and artisans including the scholar al-Biruni (973–c. 1050), whose works included studies of astronomy (he even suggested a heliocentric universe); his most famous book, inspired by accompanying Mahmud on his Indian campaigns, is a survey of Indian life, language, religion, and culture.

Like most other rulers of the day, Mahmud styled himself *amir* and emphasized his loyalty to the caliph in Baghdad; but he and later Ghaznavid rulers also called themselves by the Arabic word *sultan* (sultan). Over the next five centuries the office of sultan would become an alternative to caliph. The Ghaznavid state presaged other changes as well, especially by stressing the cleavage between ruler and ruled and by drawing into the ruling class not only the military but also the bureaucracy and the learned establishment. Ghaznavid "political theory" shared with other states the concept of the circle of justice, or circle of power – i.e. that justice is best preserved by an absolute monarch completely outside society; that such a ruler needs an absolutely loyal army; and that maintaining such an army requires prosperity, which in turn depends on the good management of an absolute ruler.

In the reign of Mahmud's son, Mas'ud I, the weaknesses in the system had already become glaringly apparent. At the

Battle of Dandanqan (1040), Mas'ud lost control of Khorāsān, his main holding in Iran, to the pastoralist Seljuq Turks; he then decided to withdraw to Lahore in his Indian domains, from which his successors ruled until overtaken by the Ghurids in 1186.

By the end of Mas'ud's reign, government in Islāmdom had become government by *amir*. Caliphal centralization had lasted 200 years, and even after the caliphal empire became too large and complex to be ruled from a single centre, the separate emirates that replaced it all defined their legitimacy in relation to it. As the Ghaznavids were ruling in Iran, the Baghdadi legal scholar al-Mawardi, who produced the caliphate's first systematic description and justification, had defended the caliph as the ultimate source of legitimacy and the guardian of pan-Islāmic concerns, while relegating day-to-day government to his "appointees". Al-Mawardi may have hoped that the Ghaznavids would expand far enough to be "invited" by the caliph to replace the uninvited Shī'ite Buyids. This replacement did occur; however, it was not the Ghaznavids who appeared in Baghdad but rather the migratory pastoralist Turks who had meanwhile replaced them. The Seljuqs joined many other migrating groups to produce the next phase of Islāmicate history.

The Seljuq Turks

When the Ghaznavid state lost control of its eastern Iranian domains to the Seljuq Turks, Islāmdom's second era of tribal expansion was inaugurated. During the period from 1041 to 1405, which ends with the death of Timur (Tamerlane), the last great tribal conqueror, the tense yet creative relationship between sedentary and migratory peoples emerged as one of the great themes of Islāmicate history, played out as it was in the centre of the great arid zone of Eurasia.

For almost 400 years a succession of Turkic peoples entered eastern Islāmdom from Central Asia. These nearly continuous migrations can be divided into three phases: Seljuqs (1055–92), Mongols (1256–1411), and neo-Mongols (1369–1405). The Seljuqs were a family among the Oguz Turks, migratory pastoralists of the Syrdarya-Oxus basin. Their name has come to stand for the group of Oguz families led into Ghaznavid Khorāsān after they had been converted to Sunni Islām, probably by Sufi missionaries after the beginning of the eleventh century. In 1040 the Seljuqs' defeat of the Ghaznavid sultan allowed them to proclaim themselves rulers of Khorāsān. Having expanded into western Iran as well, Toghrïl Beg, also using the title "sultan", was able to occupy Baghdad (1055) after "petitioning" the 'Abbāsid caliph for permission. The Seljuqs quickly took the remaining Buyid territory and began to occupy Syria, whereupon they encountered Byzantine resistance in the Armenian highlands. In 1071 a Seljuq army under Alp-Arslan defeated the Byzantines at Manzikert north of Lake Van; while the main Seljuq army replaced the Fatimids in Syria, large independent tribal bands occupied Anatolia, coming closer to the Byzantine capital than had any other Muslim force.

The Seljuqs derived their legitimacy from investiture by the caliph and from "helping" him reunite the *ummah*; yet their governing style prefigured the emergence of true alternatives to the caliphate. Some of their Iranian advisers urged them to restore centralized absolutism as it had existed in pre-Islāmic times and in the period of Marwān id–'Abbāsid strength. The best known proponent was Nizam al-Mulk, chief minister to the second and third Seljuq sultans, Alp-Arslan and Malik-Shah. Nizam al-Mulk explained his plans in his *Seyasat-nameh*, one of the best known manuals of Islāmicate political theory and administration. He was unable, however, to persuade the Seljuq sultans to assert enough power over other tribal leaders. Eventually the Seljuq sultans alienated their tribal supporters and resorted to the costly alternative of a Turkic slave core, whose leading members were appointed to tutor and train young princes of the Seljuq family to compete for rule on the death of the reigning sultan. The tutors were known as *atabeg*s; more often than not, they became the actual rulers of the domains assigned to their young charges, cooperating with urban notables (*a'yae*) in day-to-day administration.

Although Nizam al-Mulk was not immediately successful, he did contribute to long-term change. He encouraged the establishment of state-supported schools (*madrasah*s); those he personally patronized were called Nizamiyahs, the most important of which was founded in Baghdad in 1067. Systematic and broad instruction in Jama'i-Sunni learning would counteract the disruptive influences of non-Sunni or anti-Sunni thought and activity, particularly the continuing agitation of Isma'ili Muslims.

In 1090 a group of Isma'ilis established themselves in a mountain fortress at Alamut in the mountains of Daylam. From there they began to coordinate revolts all over Seljuq domains. Nominally loyal to the Fatimid caliph in Cairo, the eastern Isma'ilis confirmed their growing independence and radicalism by supporting a failed contender for the Fatimid caliphate, Nizar. For that act they were known as the Nizari Isma'ilis. They were led by Hasan-e Sabbah and were dubbed by their detractors the *hashishiyah* (assassins) because they practiced political murder while they were allegedly under the influence of hashish.

Nizam al-Mulk's *madrasah* system enhanced the prestige and solidarity of the Jama'i-Sunni *'ulama'* without actually drawing them into the bureaucracy or combating anti-Sunni agitation, but it also undermined their autonomy. It established the connection between state-supported education and office holding, and it subordinated the spiritual power and prestige of the *'ulama'* to the indispensable physical force of the military *amirs*. Yet Nizam al-Mulk unintentionally encouraged the independence of these *amirs* by extending the *iqta'* system beyond Buyid practice; he regularly assigned land revenues to individual military officers, assuming that he could keep them under bureaucratic control. When that failed, his system increased the *amirs'* independence and drained the central treasury.

The *madrasah* system had other unpredictable results that can be illustrated by al-Ghazālī, who was born in 1058 at Tus and in 1091 was made head of the Baghdad Nizamiyah. He was to undertake a radically sceptical re-examination of all of the paths available to the pious Muslim, culminating in an incorporation of the active, immediate, and inspired experience of the Sufis into the Sharī'ah-ordered piety of public worship. He thus became viewed as a renewer (*mujaddid*), a role expected by many Muslims to be filled by at least one figure at the turn of every Muslim century.

In the twelfth century Muslims began to group themselves into *ṭarīqah*, fellowships organized around and named for the *ṭarīqah* ("way" or "path") of given masters. Al-Ghazālī may have had such a following himself. One of the first large-scale orders, the Qādiriyah, formed around the teachings of 'Abd al-Qādir al-Jilani of Baghdad. The activities of a *ṭarīqah* often centred around assembly halls (called *khānqāh or zāwiyah* or *tekke*) that could serve as places of retreat or accommodate special spiritual exercises.

Thousands of *ṭarīqah* sprang up over the centuries, and it is possible that by the eighteenth century most adult Muslim males had some connection with one or more. The structure of the *ṭarīqah* ensued from the charismatic authority of the master, who, though not a prophet, replicated the direct intimacy that the prophets had shared with God. This quality he passed on to his disciples through a hierarchically ordered network that could extend over thousands of miles. The *ṭarīqah* thus became powerful centripetal forces among societies in which formal organizations were rare.

Long before these developments could combine to produce stable alternatives to the caliphal system, Seljuq power had begun to decline, only to be replaced for a century and a half with a plethora of small military states. When the Frankish crusaders arrived in the Holy Land in 1099, no one could prevent them from quickly establishing themselves along the eastern Mediterranean coast.

The Crusades

At the Council of Clermont in 1095 Pope Urban II responded to an appeal from the Byzantine emperor for help against the Seljuq Turks, who had expanded into western Anatolia. The First Crusade, begun the next year, brought about the conquest of Jerusalem in 1099. The Christian Reconquista (reconquest) of Spain was already under way, having scored its first great victory at Toledo in 1085. In the four centuries between the fall of Toledo and the fall of Granada (1492), Spanish Christians replaced Muslim rulers throughout the Iberian Peninsula, although Muslims remained as a minority under Christian rule until the early seventeenth century. In the 200 years from the fall of Jerusalem to the end of the Eighth Crusade (1291), western European crusaders failed to halt the Turkish advance or to establish a permanent presence in the Holy Land. By 1187 local

Muslims had managed to retake Jerusalem and thereby contain Christian ambitions permanently. By the time of the Fourth Crusade (1202–04) the crusading movement had been turned inward against Christian heretics.

The direct impact of the Crusades on Islāmdom was limited largely to Syria. The crusaders had arrived in Syria at one of the most factionalized periods in its history. Seljuq control, never strong, was then insignificant; local Muslim rule was anarchic; the Seljuq regime in Baghdad was competing with the Fatimid regime in Egypt; and all parties in Syria were the target of the Nizari Isma'ili movement at Alamut. The crusaders soon found it difficult to operate as more than just another faction.

The crusaders' situation encouraged interaction with the local population and even assimilation. They needed the food, supplies, and services available in the Muslim towns. Like their Christian counterparts in Spain, they took advantage of the enemy's superior skills, in medicine and hygiene, for example. Because warfare was seasonal and occasional, they spent much of their time in peaceful interaction with their non-Christian counterparts. Some early-generation crusaders intermarried with Arab Muslims or Arab Christians and adopted their personal habits and tastes.

Although the crusaders never formed a united front against the Muslims, Syrian Muslims did eventually form a united front against them, largely through the efforts of the family of the *amir* Zangi, a Turkic slave officer appointed Seljuq representative in Mosul in 1127. After Zangi had extended his control through northern Syria, one of his sons and successors, Nureddin (Nur ad-Din), based at Aleppo, was able to associate Zangi's movement with the frontier warrior (*ghāzī*) spirit. This he used to draw together urban and military support for a *jihad* against the Christians.

After taking Damascus, Nureddin established a second base in Egypt. He offered help to the failing Fatimid regime in return for being allowed to place one of his own lieutenants, Saladin (Salah ad-Din Yusuf ibn Ayyub), as chief minister to the Fatimid caliph, thus warding off a crusader alliance with the Fatimids. This action gave Nureddin two fronts from which to counteract the superior seaborne and naval support the crusaders were receiving from western Europe and the Italian city-states. Three years before Nureddin's death in 1174, Saladin substituted himself for the Fatimid caliph he theoretically served, thus ending more than 200 years of Fatimid rule in Egypt. When Nureddin died, Saladin succeeded him as head of the whole movement. When Saladin died in 1193, he had recaptured Jerusalem (1187) and begun the reunification of Egypt and Syria; his successors were known, after his patronymic, as the Ayyubids.

The Ayyubids ruled in Egypt and Syria until 1250, when they were replaced first in Egypt and later in Syria by the leaders of their own slave-soldier corps, the Mamluks. It was they who expelled the remaining crusaders from Syria, subdued the remaining Nizari Isma'ilis there, and consolidated Ayyubid holdings into a centralized state. That state became strong enough in its first decade to do what no other Muslim power could: in 1260 at 'Ayn Jālūt, south of Damascus, the Mamluk army defeated the recently arrived Mongols and expelled them from Syria.

The Mongols

The Mongols were pagan, horse-riding tribes of the northeastern steppes of Central Asia. In the early thirteenth century, under the leadership of Genghis Khan, they formed, led, and gave their name to a confederation of Turkic tribes that they channelled into a movement of global expansion, spreading east into China, north into Russia, and west into Islãmdom. Like other migratory peoples before them – Arabs, Berbers, and Turks – they had come to be involved in citied life through their role in the caravan trade. Unlike others, however, they did not convert to Islãm before their arrival. Furthermore, they brought a greater hostility to sedentary civilization, a more ferocious military force, a more cumbersome material culture, a more complicated and hierarchical social structure, and a more coherent sense of tribal law.

The first Mongol incursions into Islãmdom in 1220 were a response to a challenge from the Khwarezm-Shah 'Ala' ad-Din Muḥammad, the aggressive reigning leader of a dynasty formed in the Oxus Delta by a local governor who had rebelled against the Seljuq regime in Khorãsãn. Under Genghis Khan's leadership, Mongol forces destroyed numerous cities in Transoxania and Khorãsãn in an unprecedented display of terror and annihilation. By the time of Genghis Khan's death in 1227, his empire stretched from the Caspian Sea to the Sea of Japan.

A later successor, Möngke, decided to extend the empire in two new directions. From the Mongol capital of Karakorum, he simultaneously dispatched Kublai Khan to southern China (where Islãm subsequently began to expand inland) and Hülegü to Iran (1256). Hülegü had already received Sunni ambassadors who encouraged him to destroy the Isma'ili state at Alamut; this he did and more, reaching Baghdad in 1258, where he terminated and replaced the caliphate. The 'Abbãsid line continued, however, until 1517; the Mamluk sultan Baybars I, shortly after his defeat of the Mongols, invited a member of the 'Abbãsid house to "invest" him and to live in Cairo as spiritual head of all Muslims.

The Mongol regimes in Islāmdom quickly became rivals. The Il-Khans controlled the Tigris-Euphrates valley and Iran; the Chagatai dominated the Syrdarya and Oxus basins, the Kabul mountains, and eventually the Punjab; and the Golden Horde was concentrated in the Volga basin. The Il-Khans ruled in the territories where Islām was most firmly established. They patronized learning of all types and scholars from all parts of the vast Mongol empire, especially China. Evincing a special interest in nature, they built a major observatory in Azerbaijan. Just as enthusiastically as they had destroyed citied life, they now rebuilt it.

The writings of 'Ata Malek Joveynī, who was appointed Mongol governor in Baghdad in 1259, describe the type of rule the Mongols sought to impose. It has been called the "military patronage state" because it involved a reciprocal relationship between the foreign tribal military conquerors and their subjects. The entire state was defined as a single mobile military force connected to the household of the monarch. All non-Turkic state workers, bureaucratic or religious, even though not military specialists, were defined as part of the army (*asker*); the rest of the subject population as the herds (*ra'īyah*). The leading tribal families could dispose of the wealth of the conquered populations as they wished, except that their natural superiority obligated them to reciprocate by patronizing whatever of excellence the cities could produce.

What the Ghaznavids and Seljuqs had begun, the Mongols now accomplished. The self-confidence and superiority of the leading families were bolstered by a fairly elaborate set of tribal laws, inherited from Genghis Khan and known as the Yasa, which served to regulate personal status and criminal liability among the Mongol elite. In Il-Khanid hands, this dynastic law merely coexisted but did not compete with Sharī'ah; but in later Turkic regimes a reconciliation was achieved that extended the power of the rulers beyond the limitations of an autonomous Sharī'ah.

For a time the Il-Khans tolerated and patronized all religious persuasions, but in 1295 a Buddhist named Mahmud Ghazan became Khan and declared himself Muslim, compelling other Mongol notables to follow suit. His patronage of Islāmicate learning fostered such brilliant writers as Rashid ad-Din, the physician and scholar who authored one of the most famous Persian universal histories of all time. The Mongols, like other Islāmicate dynasties swept into power by a tribal confedera- tion, were able to unify their domains for only a few genera- tions. By the 1330s their rule had begun to be fragmented among myriad local leaders. Meanwhile, on both Mongol flanks, other Turkic Muslim powers were increasing in strength.

To the east the Delhi Sultanate of Turkic slave soldiers withstood Mongol pressure, benefited from the presence of scholars and administrators fleeing Mongol destruction, and gradually began to extend Muslim control south into India, a feat that was virtually accomplished under Muhammad ibn Tughluq. Not possessing the kind of dynastic legitimacy the pastoralist Mongols had asserted, he tied his legitimacy to his support for the Sharī'ah, and he even sought to have himself invested by the 'Abbāsid "caliph" whom the Mamluks had taken to Cairo. His concern with the Sharī'ah coincided with the growing popularity of Sufism, especially as represented by the massive Chishti *tarīqah*. In India, Sufism, which inherently undermined communalism, was bringing members of different religious communities together in ways very rare in the more westerly parts of Islāmdom.

To the west, the similarly constituted Mamluk state con- tinued to resist Mongol expansion. Its sultans were chosen, on a non-hereditary basis, from among a group of freed slaves who acted as the leaders of the various slave corps. These leaders formed an oligarchy that exercised control over the sultan. Despite the political instability that this produced, the sultans actively encouraged trade and building, and Mamluk Cairo became a place of splendour, filled with numerous architectural monuments. While the Persian language was becoming the language of administration and high culture over much of Islāmdom, Arabic alone continued to be cultivated in Mamluk domains, to the benefit of a diversified intellectual life. Ibn an-Nafis (died 1288), a physician, wrote about pulmonary circulation 300 years before it was "discovered" in Europe; al-Qalqashandi composed a comprehensive encyclopaedia; and Ibn Khallikan composed one of the most important Islāmicate biographical works, a dictionary of eminent men. Sharī'ah-minded studies were elaborated: the *'ulama'* worked out a political theory that tried to make sense of the sultanate, and they also explored the possibility of enlarging on the Sharī'ah by reference to *falsafah* and Sufism.

However, Ibn Taymiyah, a great legal and religious reformer living in Damascus in the late thirteenth and early fourteenth century, cautioned against such extra-legal practices and pursuits. He insisted that the Sharī'ah was complete in and of itself and could be adapted to every age by any *faqih* who could analogize according to the principle of human advantage (*maslahah*). A member of the Hanabilah school himself, Ibn Taymiyah became as popular as his school's founder, Ahmad ibn Hanbal. Like him, Ibn Taymiyah attacked all practices that undermined what he felt to be the fundamentals of Islām, including all forms of Shī'ite thought as well as aspects of Jama'i-Sunni piety that stressed knowledge of God over service to Him. Ibn Taymiyah's programme and popularity so threatened the Mamluk authorities that they put him in prison, where he died. His movement did not survive, but when his ideas surfaced, in the revolutionary movement of the Wahhā-bīyah in the late eighteenth century, their lingering power became dramatically evident.

Further west, the Rum Seljuqs at Konya submitted to the Mongols in 1243 but survived intact. They continued to cultivate the Islāmicate arts, in particular architecture. The most famous Muslim ever to live at Konya, Jalal ad-Din ar-Rumi, who was attracted to Sufi activities, attached himself to the master Shams ad-Din. The poetry inspired by their association is unparalleled in Persian literature. Its recitation, along with music and movement, was a key element in the devotional activities of Jalal ad-Din's followers, who came to be organized into a Sufi *tarīqah* named the Mevleviyah (Mawlawiyah) after their title of respect for him, Mevlana ("Our Master").

It was not from the Rum Seljuqs, however, that lasting Muslim power in Anatolia was to come, but rather from one of the warrior states on the Byzantine frontier. The successive waves of Turkic migrations had driven unrelated individuals and groups across central Islāmdom into Anatolia. Avoiding the Konya state, they gravitated toward an open frontier to the west, where they began to constitute themselves into quasi-tribal states that depended on raiding each other and Byzantine territory and shipping. One of these, the Osmanlis, or Ottomans, named for their founder, Osman I (ruled 1281–1324), was located not on the coast, where raiding had its limits, but in Bithynia just facing Constantinople. In 1326 they won the town of Bursa and made it their first capital. From Anatolia they crossed over into Thrace in the service of rival factions at Constantinople, then began to occupy Byzantine territory, establishing their second capital at Edirne on the European side.

Their sense of legitimacy was complex. They were militantly Muslim, bound by the *ghāzī* spirit, spurred on in their intolerance of local Christians by Greek converts and travelling Sufis who gravitated to their domains. At the same time, *'ulama'* from more settled Islāmic lands to the east encouraged them to abide by the Sharī'ah and tolerate the Christians as protected non-Muslims. The Ottomans also cast themselves as deputies of the Rum Seljuqs, who were themselves originally "deputized" by the 'Abbāsid caliph. Finally they claimed descent from the leading Oguz Turk families, who were natural rulers over sedentary populations.

Under Murad I (ruled *c.* 1360–89) the state began to downplay its warrior fervour in favour of more conventional Islāmicate administration. Instead of relying on volunteer warriors, Murad established a regular cavalry, which he supported with land assignments, as well as a specially trained infantry force called the "new troops", Janissaries, drawn from converted captives. Expanding first through western Anatolia and Thrace, the Ottomans under Bayezid I (ruled 1389–1403) turned their eyes toward eastern and southern Anatolia; just as they had incorporated the whole, they encountered a neo-Mongol conqueror expanding into Anatolia from the east who utterly defeated their entire army in a single campaign (1402).

Timur (Tamerlane) was a Turk, not a Mongol, but he aimed to restore Mongol power. He was born a Muslim in the Syrdarya valley and served local pagan Mongol warriors and finally the Chagatai heir-apparent, but he rebelled and made himself ruler in Khwarezm in 1380. He planned to restore Mongol supremacy under a thoroughly Islāmic programme. He surpassed the Mongols in terror, constructing towers out of the heads of his victims. Having established himself in Iran, he moved first on India and then on Ottoman

Anatolia and Mamluk Syria; but before he could consolidate his realm, he died.

His impact was twofold: his defeat of the Ottomans inspired a comeback that would produce one of the greatest Islāmicate empires of all time, and one of the Central Asian heirs to his tradition of conquest would found another great Islāmicate empire in India. These later empires managed to find the combination of Turkic and Islāmic legitimacy that could produce the stable centralized absolutism that had eluded all previous Turkic conquerors.

The Arabs and the Berbers

When the Fatimids conquered Egypt in 969, they left a governor named Ziri in the Maghrib. By 1041 the dynasty founded by Ziri declared its independence from the Fatimids, but it too was challenged by breakaways such as the Zanatah in Morocco and the Hammadids in Algeria. Gradually the Zirids were restricted to the eastern Maghrib. There they were invaded from Egypt by two Bedouin Arab tribes, the Banū Halil and the Banū Sulaym, at the instigation (1052) of the Fatimid ruler in Cairo. This mass migration of warriors as well as wives and children is known as the Hilalian invasion. Though initially disruptive, the Hilalian invasion had an important cultural impact: it resulted in a much greater spread of the Arabic language than had occurred in the seventh century and inaugurated the real Arabization of the Maghrib.

When the Arab conquerors arrived in the Maghrib in the seventh century, the indigenous peoples they met were the Berbers, a group of predominantly but not entirely migratory tribes who could be found from present-day Morocco to present-day Algeria, and from the Mediterranean to the

Sahara. The Arabs quickly converted them and enlisted their aid in further conquests. At first only Berbers nearer the coast were involved, but by the eleventh century Muslim affiliation had begun to spread far into the Sahara.

The western Saharan Berber confederation, the Sanhajah, was responsible for the first Berber-directed effort to control the Maghrib. The Sanhajah were camel herders who traded mined salt for gold with the black kingdoms of the south. By the eleventh century their power in the western Sahara was being threatened by expansion both from other Berber tribes and from the Soninke state at Ghana to the south, which had actually captured their capital of Audaghost in 990.

The Sanhajah had been in contact with Islām since the ninth century, but their distance from major centres of Muslim life had kept their knowledge of the faith minimal. In 1035, however, Yahya ibn Ibrahim, a chief from one of their tribes, the Gudalah, went on *hajj*. For the Maghribi pilgrim, the cultural impact of the *hajj* was experienced not only in Mecca and Medina but also on the many stops along the 3,000-mile overland route. When Yahya returned, he was accompanied by a teacher from Nafis (in present-day Libya), 'Abd Allāh ibn Yasin, who would instruct the Berbers in Islām.

Having met with little initial success, the two are said to have retired to a *ribāt*, a fortified place of seclusion, perhaps as far south as an island in the Sénégal River, to pursue a purer religious life. The followers they attracted to that *ribāt* were known as *al-murabitun* ("the people of the retreat"), and the dynasty they founded came to be known by the same name – the Almoravids in Anglicized form. In 1042 Ibn Yasin declared a *jihad* against the Sanhajah tribes, including his own, as people who had embraced Islām but then failed to practise it properly. By his death in 1059, the Sanhajah confederation had been restored under an Islāmic ideology, and the conquest of Morocco, which lacked strong leadership, was under way.

Ibn Yasin's spiritual role was taken by a consultative body of *'ulama'*. His successor as military commander was Abū Bakr ibn 'Umar, who, while pursuing a campaign against Morocco, was supplanted by his cousin Yusuf ibn Tashufin, whom he had left in control as his deputy. Under Ibn Tashufin's leadership, by 1082, Almoravid control extended as far as Algiers. In 1086 Ibn Tashufin responded to a request for help from the Andalusian party kings, unable to defend themselves against the Christian kingdoms in the north. By 1110 all Muslim states in Andalusia had come under Almoravid control.

Like most other Jama'i-Sunni rulers of his time, Ibn Tashufin had himself "appointed" deputy by the caliph in Baghdad. He also based his authority on the claim to bring correct Islām to peoples who had strayed from it. For him "correct" Islām meant the Sharī'ah as developed by the Maliki *faqih*s, who played a key role in the Almoravid state by working out the application of the Sharī'ah to everyday problems.

A second major Berber movement originated in a revolt begun against Almoravid rule in 1125 by Ibn Tumart, a settled Masmudah Berber from the Atlas Mountains. Like Ibn Yasin, Ibn Tumart had been inspired by the *hajj*, which he used as an opportunity to study in Baghdad, Cairo, and Jerusalem, acquainting himself with all current schools of Islāmic thought and becoming a disciple of the ideas of the recently deceased al-Ghazālī. Emulating his social activism, Ibn Tumart was inspired to act on the familiar Muslim dictum, "Command the good and forbid the reprehensible." His early attempts took two forms, disputations with the scholars of the Almoravid court and public chastisement of Muslims who in his view contradicted the rules of Islām; he went so far as to throw the

Almoravid ruler's sister off her horse because she was unveiled in public. His activities aroused hostility and he fled to the safety of his own people. There, like Muḥammad, he grew from teacher of a personal following to leader of a social movement.

Like many subsequent reformers, Ibn Tumart used Muḥammad's career as a model. He interpreted the Prophet's rejection and retreat as an emigration (Hijrah) that enabled him to build a community, and he divided his followers into *muhājirūn* ("fellow emigrants") and *ansār* ("helpers"). He preached the idea of surrender to God to a people who had strayed from it. Thus could Muḥammad's ability to bring about radical change through renewal be invoked without actually claiming the prophethood that he had sealed forever. Ibn Tumart further based his legitimacy on his claim to be a *sharīf* (descendant of Muḥammad) and the *mahdī*, not in the Shī'ite sense but in the more general sense of a human sent to restore pure faith. In his view Almoravid students of legal knowledge were so concerned with pursuing the technicalities of the law that they had lost the purifying fervour of their own founder, Ibn Yasin, and even failed to maintain proper Muslim behaviour. Ibn Tumart decried the way in which the law had taken on a life of its own, and he called upon Muslims to rely on the original and only reliable sources, the Qur'ān and the Hadith.

Although he opposed irresponsible rationalism in the law, in matters of theological discourse he leaned toward the limited rationalism of the Ash'arite school, which was becoming so popular in the eastern Muslim lands. Like the Ash'arites, he viewed the unity of God as one of Islām's fundamental principles and denounced any reading of the Qur'ān that led to anthropomorphism. Because he focused on attesting the unity of God (*tawhid*), he called his followers al-Muwah-hidun (Almohads), "those who attest the unity of God".

By 1147, 17 years after Ibn Tumart's death, Almohads had replaced Almoravids in all their Maghribi and Andalusian territories. In Andalusia their arrival slowed the progress of the Christian Reconquista. There, as in the Maghrib, arts and letters were encouraged: an example is an important movement of *falsafah* that included Ibn Tufayl, Ibn al-'Arabi, and Ibn Rushd (Averroës), the Andalusian *qāḍī* and physician whose interpretations of Aristotle became so important for medieval European Christianity. During the late Almohad period in Andalusia the intercommunal nature of Islāmicate civilization became especially noticeable in the work of non-Muslim thinkers, such as Moses Maimonides.

By the early thirteenth century, Almohad power began to decline; a defeat in 1212 at Las Navas de Tolosa by the Christian kings of the north forced a retreat to the Maghrib. But the impact of Almohad cultural patronage on Andalusia long outlasted Almohad political power; successor dynasties in surviving Muslim states were responsible for some of the highest achievements of Andalusian Muslims, among them the Alhambra palace in Granada. Furthermore, the 400-year southward movement of the Christian–Muslim frontier resulted, ironically, in some of the most intense Christian–Muslim interaction in Andalusian history. Muslims, as Mudejars, could live under Christian rule and contribute to its culture; Jews could translate Arabic and Hebrew texts into Castilian.

Almohads were replaced in the Maghrib as well, through a revolt by their own governors: the Hafsids in Tunis and the Marinid Berber dynasty in Fès. There too, however, Almohad influence outlasted their political presence: both towns became centres, in distinctively Maghribi form, of Islāmicate culture and Islāmic piety.

Continued Spread of Islāmic Influence

As the Maghrib became firmly and distinctively Muslim, Islām moved south. The spread of Muslim identity into the Sahara and the involvement of Muslim peoples, especially the Tuareg, in trans-Saharan trade provided several natural channels of influence. By the time of the Marinids, Hafsids, and Mamluks, several major trade routes had established criss-crossing lines of communication: from Cairo to Timbuktu, from Tripoli to Bornu and Lake Chad, from Tunis to Timbuktu at the bend of the Niger River, and from Fès and Tafilalt through major Saharan entrepôts into Ghana and Mali. The rise at Timbuktu of Mali, the first great western Sudanic empire with a Muslim ruler, attested the growing incorporation of sub-Saharan Africa into the North African orbit. The reign of Mansa Musa, who even went on pilgrimage, demonstrated the influence of Islām on at least the upper echelons of African society.

The best picture of Islāmdom in the fourteenth century appears in the work of a remarkable Maghribi *qāḍī* and traveller, Ibn Baṭṭūṭah (1304–68/77). In 1325, the year that Mansa Musa went on pilgrimage, Ibn Battutah also left for Mecca, from his home town of Tangiers. He was away for almost 30 years, visiting most of Islāmdom including Andalusia, all of the Maghrib, Mali, Syria, Arabia, Iran, India, the Maldive Islands, and, he claimed, China. He described the unity within diversity that was one of Islāmdom's most prominent features. Although local customs often seemed at variance with his notion of pure Islāmic practice, he felt at home everywhere; a Muslim could attend the Friday worship session in any Muslim town in the world and feel comfortable.

By the time of Ibn Baṭṭūṭah's death, Islāmdom comprised the most far-flung yet interconnected set of societies in the world. By 1405, Islām had begun to spread not only into sub-Saharan

Africa but also into the southern seas with the establishment of a Muslim presence in the Strait of Malacca. Conversion to Islām across its newer frontiers was at first limited to a small elite, who supplemented local religious practices with Muslim ones. Islām could offer not only a unifying religious system but also social techniques, including alphabetic literacy, a legal system applicable to daily life, a set of administrative institutions, and a body of science and technology – all capable of enhancing the power of ruling elements and of tying them into a vast and lucrative trading network.

The period of migration and renewal exposed, however, both the potential and the limitations of government by tribal peoples. This great problem of Islāmicate history received its most sophisticated analysis from a Maghribi Muslim named Ibn Khaldun (1332–1406), a *faylasuf* (philosopher) and a *qāḍī*. In his *Muqaddimah* (the introduction to his multi-volume world history) he used his training in *falsafah* to discern patterns in history. Whereas Muslim historians conventionally subscribed to the view that God passed sovereignty and hegemony (*dawlah*) from one dynasty to another through His divine wisdom, Ibn Khaldun explained it in terms of a cycle of natural and inevitable stages.

By Ibn Khaldun's day it had become apparent that tribally organized migratory peoples could easily acquire military superiority over settled peoples if they could capitalize on the inherently stronger group feeling (*'aṣabīyyah*) that kinship provides. Once in power, a small number of "builders" among the conquerors bring renewed vitality to their conquered lands. As the family disperses itself among sedentary peoples and ceases to live the hard life of migration, it begins to degenerate. Then internal rivalries and jealousies force one member of the family to become a king who must rely on mercenary troops and undermine his own prosperity by paying for them. In the end, the ruling dynasty falls prey to a new tribal group with fresh group feeling. Thus did Ibn Khaldun call attention to the unavoidable instability of all premodern Muslim dynasties, caused by their lack of the regularized patterns of succession that were beginning to develop in European dynasties.

6

EXPANSION, REFORM, AND RENEWAL

After the death of Timur in 1405, power began to shift from migrating peoples to sedentary populations living in large centralized empires. After about 1683, when the last Ottoman campaign against Vienna failed, the great empires for which this period is so famous began to shrink and weaken, just as western Europeans first began to show their potential for worldwide expansion and domination. When the period began, Muslim lands had begun to recover from the devastating effects of the Black Death (1346–8), and many were prospering. Muslims had the best opportunity in history to unite the settled world, but by the end of the seventeenth century they had been replaced by Europeans as the leading contenders for this role.

In the period from 1405 to 1683, Muslims formed the cultural patterns that they brought into modern times, and adherence to Islām expanded to approximately its current distribution. The unity of several regions was expressed through the creation of three of the greatest empires in world history – the Ottomans in south-eastern Europe, Anatolia, the eastern Maghrib, Egypt, and Syria; the Safavids in Iran and Iraq; and the Indo-Timurids (Mughals) in India. In these empires, Sunni and Shī'ite became identities on a much larger scale than ever before, expressing competition between large populations; simultaneously, Shī'ism acquired a permanent base from which to generate international opposition.

Elsewhere, less formal and often commercial ties bound Muslims from distant locales; growing commercial and political links between Morocco and the western Sudan produced a trans-Saharan Maghribi Islām; Egyptian Islām influenced the central and eastern Sudan; and steady contacts between East Africa, South Arabia, southern Iran, south-west India, and the southern seas promoted a recognizable Indian Ocean Islām, with Persian as its lingua franca. The expansion and natur-alization of Islām also fostered a number of local languages into vehicles for Islāmicate administration and high culture – Ottoman, Chagatai, Swahili, Urdu, and Malay. Everywhere Muslims were confronting adherents of other religions, and new converts often practised Islām without abandoning their previous practices. This was to be a period of major realign-ments and expansion.

The Ottoman Empire

After the Ottoman state's devastating defeat by Timur, its leaders had to retain the vitality of the warrior spirit and the validation of the Sharī'ah (without its confining independ-ence). In 1453, Mehmed II the Conqueror defeated Con-stantinople (soon to be known as Istanbul), putting an end to the Byzantine Empire and subjugating the local Christian and Jewish populations. Except for those forcibly converted, the rest of the non-Muslim population was protected for payment according to the Sharī'ah and the preference of the *ulema* (the Turkish spelling of '*ulama*'), and organized into self-governing communities known as *millet*s.

The sultans also began to claim the caliphate because they met two of its traditional qualifications: they ruled justly, in principle according to the Sharī'ah, and they defended and extended the frontiers, as in their conquest of Mamluk Egypt, Syria, and the holy cities in 1516–17. Meanwhile, they built on Seljuq and Mongol practice of the *ulema*: they promoted state-supported training of *ulema*, they defined and paid holders of religious offices as part of the military, and they aggressively asserted the validity of dynastic law alongside Sharī'ah. Simultaneously, they emphasized their inheritance of Byzantine legitimacy by transforming Byzantine symbols, such as Hagia Sophia (Church of the Divine Wisdom), into symbols for Islām, and by favouring their empire's European part, called, significantly, Rum.

The classical Ottoman system crystallized during the reign of Süleyman I the Lawgiver (ruled 1520–66). He also pushed the empire's borders almost to their furthest limits, to the walls of Vienna in the north-west, up to Morocco in the south-west, into Iraq to the east, and to the Yemen in the south-east. In theory, Süleyman presided over a balanced four-part structure: the palace household, the bureaucracy (chancery and treasury), the armed forces, and the religious establishment. Yet, important positions in the army and bureaucracy went to the cream of the *devsirme* – Christian youths converted to Islām and put through special training to be the sultan's personal "slaves". *Ulema* who acquired government posts had undergone systematic training at the major *madrasah*s and so in the Ottoman state were more integrated than were their counterparts in other states; yet they were freeborn Muslims, not brought into the system as slaves of the sultan.

Ottoman control had already begun to relax by the first quarter of the seventeenth century as the state treasury had passed, through land grants, into the hands of local *a'yān* (notables), and they gradually became the real rulers. Discontinuance of the *devsirme* and the rise of hereditary succession to imperial offices further weakened the empire. Sultan Murad IV tried to restore Ottoman efficiency and central control, and his efforts were continued by subsequent sultans. However, during a war with Austria and Poland from 1682 to 1699, the Ottomans suffered their first serious losses to an enemy and signed two treaties, at Carlowitz in 1699 and at Passarowitz in 1718, that signified their inferiority to the Habsburgs and established the defensive posture they would maintain into the twentieth century.

The Safavid State

The Safavid state began from a local Sufi *tarīqah* of Ardabil in Azerbaijan, named after its founder, Shaykh Safi od-Din (1252/3–1334), a local holy man. During the fifteenth century Shaykh Safi's successors transformed their local *tarīqah* into an inter-regional movement by translating 'Alīd loyalism into full-fledged Imami Shī'ism. They attracted support from Turkic tribal disciples (known as the Kizilbash, or "Red Heads", because of their symbolic 12-fold red headgear) and, outside Iran, in eastern Anatolia (where the anti-Ottoman Imami Bektashi *tarīqah* was strong), Syria, the Caucasus, and Transoxania.

By 1501 the Safavids were able to defeat the Ak Koyunlu rulers of northern Iran, whereupon their teenage leader Isma'il I (ruled 1501–24) had himself proclaimed shah, using that pre-Islāmic title for the first time in almost 900 years and thereby invoking the glory of ancient Iran. The Safavids thus asserted a multivalent legitimacy that flew in the face of Ottoman claims to have restored caliphal authority for all Muslims. Eventually, irritant became threat: by 1510, when Isma'il had conquered all of Iran (to approximately its present frontiers) as well as the Fertile Crescent, he began pushing against the Uzbeks in the east and the Ottomans in the west. Having to fight on two fronts was the most difficult military problem any Muslim empire could face, since the army was attached to the household of the ruler and moved with him at all times. After dealing with his eastern front, Isma'il turned west. At Chaldiran (1514) in north-western Iraq, Isma'il suffered defeat at Ottoman hands; yet, through the war of words waged between Isma'il and the Ottoman sultan Selim I and invasions from both fronts over the next 60 years, the Safavid state survived and prospered.

The Safavid state first set out to convert its predominantly Jama'i-Sunni population to Imami Shī'ism through the state-appointed leader of the religious community, the *sadr*. Gradually, forms of piety emerged that were specific to Safavid Shī'ism; they centred on pilgrimage to key sites connected with the *imām*s, as well as on the annual remembering and re-enacting of the key event in Shī'ite history, the caliph Yazīd I's destruction of Husayn at Karbala' in 680.

The state also survived because Isma'il's successors moved, like the Ottomans, toward a type of legitimation different from the one that had brought them to power. This development began in the reign of Tahmasp (1524–76) and culminated in the reign of the greatest Safavid shah, 'Abbās I (ruled 1588–1629). Since Isma'il's time, the tribes had begun to lose faith in the Safavid monarch as spiritual leader; now 'Abbās appealed for support more as absolute monarch and less as the charismatic Sufi master or incarnated *imām*. At the same time he freed himself from his unruly tribal *amir*s by depending more and more on a paid army of converted Circassian, Georgian, and Armenian Christian captives. He continued to rely on a large bureaucracy headed by a chief minister but, unlike the Ottomans, he distanced members of the religious community from state involvement while allowing them a source of support in their administration of the *waqf* system (which enabled individuals to donate to institutions and groups). 'Abbās' policies were probably not unpopular with the Shī'ite *'ulama'*, who had a tradition of independence, but they eventually undermined his state's legitimacy. By the end of the seventeenth century, it was the religious leaders, the *mujtahid*s, who would claim to be the spokesmen for the hidden *imām*, while the Safavid became more civilized and secular. The long-term consequences of this breach between government and the religious institution were extensive, culminating in the establishment of the Islāmic Republic of Iran in 1979.

'Abbās expressed his new role by moving his capital in about 1597–8 to Esfahan in Fars, the central province of the ancient pre-Islāmic Iranian empires and symbolically more Persian than Turkic. It became one of the most beautiful cities in the world and the centre of a major cultural flowering, containing myriad palaces, gardens, parks, and mosques, including the famed Masjed-e Shah. It was here that 'Abbās received diplomatic and commercial visits from Europeans, whom he hoped to use as sources of firearms and military technology or as pawns in his economic warfare against the Ottomans. Like other Shī'ite dynasties before them, the Safavids encouraged the development of *falsafah* as a companion to Shī'ite esotericism and cosmology.

None of 'Abbās' successors was his equal, though his state, ever weaker, survived for a century. The last effective shah, Husayn I (1694–1722), could defend himself neither from tribal raiding in the capital nor from interfering *mujtahid*s led by Mohammad Baqir Majlisi (whose writings later would be important in the Islāmic Republic of Iran). In 1722, when Mahmud of Qandahar led an Afghan tribal raid into Iran from the east, he easily took Esfahan and destroyed what was left of central authority.

The Mughals

Although the Mongol-Timurid legacy influenced the Ottoman and Safavid states, it had its most direct impact on Babur (1483–1530), son of one of many Timurid princes and founder of the third major empire of the period. In his youth Babur dreamed of capturing Samarkand as a base for reconstructing Timur's empire. For a year after the Safavid defeat of the Uzbek Muhammad Shaybani Khan, Babur and his Chagatai followers did hold Samarkand, as Safavid vassals, but lost it when the Safavids were in turn defeated. From Kabul, where he had been forced to retreat, barred from moving north or west, Babur took the Timurid legacy south, to northern India, where he defeated the much larger army of the Lodi sultans in 1526 at Panipat. By his death just four years later, he had laid the foundation for the Mughal (i.e. Mongol) empire.

By the time of the death of his grandson, Akbar (ruled 1556–1605), the Mughals ruled all of present-day India north of the Deccan Plateau and Gondwana and more: one diagonal of the empire extended from the Hindu Kush to the Bay of Bengal; the other from the Himalayas to the Arabian Sea. Like its contemporaries, this state endured because of a regularized and equitable tax system that provided the central treasury with funds to support the ruler's extensive building projects as well as his *mansabdar*s, the imperial military and bureaucratic officers, who were largely foreigners trained especially for his service.

In Akbar's empire, unlike Süleyman's and 'Abbās', Islām was much more recently established and Muslims were not in the majority but coexisted, interacted, and came into conflict with Jacobites (members of the Monophysite Syrian Church), Sufis, Isma'ili Shī'ites, Zoroastrians, Jains, Jesuits, Jews, and Hindus. Akbar's response was to ban intolerance and even the special tax on non-Muslims. To keep the 'ulama' from objecting, he tried to tie them to the state financially.

With the help of Abū'l-Fazl, his Sufi adviser and biographer, he established a kind of salon for religious discussion. A very small circle of personal disciples seems to have emulated Akbar's own brand of tawhid-i ilahi ("divine oneness"), which appears to have been a general monotheism akin to what the ḥanīfs (primordialists) of Mecca, and Muḥammad himself, had once practised. Akbar combined toleration for all religions with condemnation of practices that seemed to him humanly objectionable, such as enslavement and the immolation of widows.

For half a century, Akbar's first two successors, Jahangir and Shah Jahan, continued his policies. A rebuilt capital at Delhi was added to the old capitals of Fatehpur Sikri and Agra. The mingling of Hindu and Muslim traditions was expressed in all the arts. Shah Jahan's son, Dara Shikoh (1615–59), was a Sufi thinker and writer who tried to establish a common ground for Muslims and Hindus. In response to such attempts, a Sharī'ah-minded movement of strict communalism arose, connected with a leader of the Naqshbandi ṭarīqah named Shaykh Ahmad Sirhindi. With the accession of Aurangzeb (ruled 1659–1707) there arose a stricter communalism that imposed penalties on protected non-Muslims and stressed the shah's role as leader of the Muslim community by virtue of his enforcing the Sharī'ah. The empire continued to expand up to the beginning of the eighteenth century but began to disintegrate shortly after the end of Aurangzeb's reign.

Trans-Saharan Islām

In Morocco it was an old legitimacy proven to be especially powerful in Africa, that of the *sharīf*s, descendants of Muhammad, that motivated a formation of the state. It was the Sufi Sidi Barakat who legitimated the Sa'di family of *sharīf*s as leaders of a *jihad* that expelled the aggressively Christian Portuguese and established an independent state (1511– 1603) strong enough to expand far to the south. In 1591, when the greatest Muslim kingdom of the Sudan, Songhai, expanded northward and took growing control of major trade routes into Morocco, it was invaded by Morocco, becoming the latter's vassal for 40 years. After a period of political confusion and instability, Morocco was reunited in 1668 by the 'Alawite *sharīf*s.

Like the Sa'dis, the 'Alawite *sharīf*s were legitimated in two ways: by the recognition of leading Sufis and by the special spiritual quality (*barakah*) presumed to have passed to them by virtue of their descent from the Prophet through 'Alī. Although they were not Shī'ites, they cultivated charismatic leadership that undermined the power of the *'ulama'* to use the Sharī'ah against them. They also recognized the limits of their authority as absolute monarchs, dividing their realm into the area of authority and the area of no authority (where many of the Berber tribes lived).

Meanwhile Islām had come to a number of small states in the Sudanic region – Senegambia, Songhai, Aïr, Mossi, Nupe, Hausa, Kanem-Bornu, Darfur, and Funj – along trade and pilgrimage routes. By the sixteenth century these were in contact not only with the major Muslim centres of the Maghrib and Egypt but also with each other through an emerging trans-Sudanic pilgrimage route. Furthermore, Islām had by then become well-enough established to provoke efforts at purification. Some of these were gradualist and primarily educational, as was the case with the enormously influential Egyptian scholar as-Suyuti (1445–1505), whose works dealt with numerous subjects, including the coming of the *mahdī* to restore justice and strengthen Islām. He also wrote letters to Muslim scholars and rulers in West Africa explaining the Sharī'ah and encouraging its careful observance.

Others were more militant. Rulers might forcibly insist on an end to certain non-Muslim practices, as did Muḥammad Rumfa (ruled 1463–99) in the Hausa city-state of Kano, and Muḥammad I Askia, the greatest ruler of Songhai (ruled 1493–1528). To the east in Ethiopia, a *jihad* was carried out by Aḥmad Grañ (*c*. 1506–43), and a conquest of Christian Nubia by Arab tribes of Upper Egypt resulted in the conversion of the pagan Funj to Islām and the creation of a major Muslim kingdom there. Although most indigenous West African scholars looked to foreigners for inspiration, by the late seventeenth century Muslims in the Sudanic belt were being steadily influenced by North African Islām as well as developing distinctive traditions of their own.

Indian Ocean Islām

A similar relationship was simultaneously developing across the Indian Ocean, which tied South and South-east Asian Muslims to East African and southern Arabian Muslims. But here Muslims had to cope with the Portuguese threat and face Hindus and

Buddhists, sophisticated and refined religious traditions that possessed written literatures and considerable political power.

The first major Muslim state in South-east Asia, Aceh, was established about 1524 in northern and western Sumatra in response to more than a decade of Portuguese advance. Under Sultan Iskandar Muda (ruled 1608–37), Aceh reached the height of its prosperity and importance in the Indian Ocean trade, encouraging Muslim learning and expanding Muslim adherence. By the end of the seventeenth century, Aceh's Muslims were in touch with major intellectual centres to the west, particularly in India and Arabia. After studying in Arabia from about 1640 to 1661, 'Abd ar-Ra'uf of Singkel made the first "translation" of the Qur'ān into Malay. In China, Liu Chih, a scholar born about 1650 in Nanking, created serious Islāmicate literature in Chinese.

In the early seventeenth century another Muslim commercial power emerged when its ruler, the prince of Tallo, converted: Macassar (now Makassar) became an active centre for Muslim competition with the Dutch into the third quarter of the seventeenth century. A serious Islāmic presence also developed in Java, and by the early seventeenth century the first inland Muslim state in South-east Asia, Mataram, was established. Javanese Muslims, however, would have to struggle for centuries to negotiate the confrontation between Hindu and Muslim cultures.

Pre-colonial Reform and Experimentation (1683–1818)

In the eighteenth century, activism and revival were present throughout Islāmdom, but the three major Muslim empires also experienced a decline compared with the rising powers in

Europe. Population increased, as it did almost everywhere in the eighteenth-century world, just as inflation and expensive reform reduced the income of central governments. European explorers had built on and surpassed Muslim seafaring technology to compete in the southern seas and discover new sea routes – and, accidentally, a new source of wealth in the Americas. In Islāmdom, the power of merchants had been inhibited by imperial over-taxation of local private enterprise, appropriation of the benefits of trade, and the privileging of foreign traders through agreements known as the Capitulations. In some areas, Muslims were largely unaware of the rise of Europe; in others, such as India, Sumatra, and Java, the eighteenth century actually brought European control.

Some leaders attempted to revive existing political systems. In Iran, for example, attempts at restoration combined military and religious reform. In about 1730 a Turk from Khorāsān named Nader Qoli Beg reorganized the Safavid army and, in 1736, replaced the Safavid Shah with himself. Nader Shah extended the borders of the Safavid state, defeated the Ottomans, and may even have been aspiring to be the leader of all Muslims. To this end he made overtures to neighbouring rulers, seeking their recognition by trying to represent Iranian Shī'ism as a *madhhab* ("way") alongside the Sunni *madhhab*s. After he was killed in 1747, however, his reforms did not survive and his house disintegrated. Karim Khan Zand, a general from Shiraz, ruled in the name of the Safavids but did not restore real power to the shah. By the time the Qajars (1779–1925) managed to re-secure Iran's borders, reviving Safavid legitimacy was impossible.

In the Ottoman Empire, from 1718 to 1730, experimentation with European manners and tastes was matched by reinvigorating the military, the key to earlier Ottoman success, using European technology and Christian-European advice.

After Nader Shah's defeat of the Ottoman army, this first phase of absolutist restoration ended, but the pursuit of European fashion had become a permanent element in Ottoman life. Central power, however, continued to weaken, especially in the area of international commerce. Foreign nationals and non-Muslim Ottoman subjects, both groups given certificates of protection under the Capitulation arrangements, were integrated into the Ottoman state, which was further weakened by the recognition, in the disastrous Treaty of Kücük Kaynarca (1774), of the Russian tsar as protector of the Ottoman's Greek Orthodox *millet*. A second stage of absolutist restoration occurred under Selim III (ruled 1789–1807), whose military and political reforms, referred to as the New Order (Nizam-i Cedid), included replacing the Janissaries with European-trained troops.

In other areas, leaders envisioned or created new social orders that were self-consciously Islāmic. The growing popularity of Westernization and a decreasing reliance on Islām as a source of public values was counterbalanced by Islāmic activism ranging from educational reform to *jihad*. Sufism in the form of renovated *ṭarīqah*s could also support reform and stimulate pan-Islāmic awareness, sometimes promoting an indigenous form of social organization that could even lead to the founding of a dynasty, as in the case of the Libyan monarchy. Sufis often encouraged the study of the Hadith so as to establish the Prophet Muḥammad as a model for spiritual and moral reconstruction and to invalidate many unacceptable traditional or customary Islāmic practices.

Sufism could also be condemned as a source of degeneracy. The most famous and influential militant anti-Sufi movement arose in the Arabian Peninsula and came to be known as Wahhābīyah, after its founder, Muḥammad ibn 'Abd al-Wahhab (1703–92). Inspired by the legal and religious reformer Ibn Taymiyah, Ibn al-Wahhab argued that the Qur'-ān and *sunnah* could provide the basis for a reconstruction of Islāmic society out of the degenerate form in which it had come to be practised. The Wahhābis refuted blind imitation (*taqlīd*), arguing instead for reform and making the pious personal effort or individual thought (*ijtihād*) necessary to understand the fundamentals. The Wahhābī movement attracted the support of a tribe in the Najd led by Muḥammad ibn Sa'ud. Although the first state produced by this alliance did not last, it laid the foundations for the existing Saudi state in Arabia, officially proclaimed in 1932, and inspired similar activism elsewhere down to the present day.

In West Africa a series of activist movements appeared from the eighteenth century into the nineteenth. There, as in Arabia, Islāmic activism was directed less at non-Muslims than at Muslims who had gone astray. As in many of Islāmdom's outlying areas, emergent groups of indigenous educated, observant Muslims, such as the Tukulor, were finding the casual, syncretistic, opportunistic nature of official Islām to be increasingly intolerable. Such Muslims were inspired by reformist scholars such as al-Ghazālī, as-Suyuti, and Maghili; by a theory of *jihad* comparable to that of the Wahhābīs; and by expectations of a *mujaddid* (renewer) as the Islāmic century turned in AH (Latin: *anno Hegirae*) 1200 (AD 1785). In what is now northern Nigeria, the discontent of the 1780s and 1790s erupted in 1804, when Usman dan Fodio declared a *jihad* against the Hausa rulers. Others followed, among them Muḥammad al-Jaylani in Aïr, Shehuh Ahmadu Lobbo in Macina, al-Hajj 'Umar Tal (a member of the reformist Tijani *tarīqah*) in Fouta Djallon, and Samory in the Malinke (Mandingo) states. *Jihad* activity continued for a century, as the need to resist against European occupation became more urgent.

In the Indian Ocean area, Islāmic activism was more often intellectual and educational. Its best exemplar was Shah Wali Allāh of Delhi (1702–62), the spiritual ancestor of many later Indian Muslim reform movements. During his lifetime the collapse of Muslim political power was painfully evident. He tried to unite the Muslims of India, not around Sufism as Akbar had tried to do but around the Sharī'ah. Once again, the study of the Hadith inspired a positive spirit of social reconstruction akin to that of the Prophet Muḥammad.

Dependency and Resistance

The many efforts to revive Islām and resist Western colonialism were largely unsuccessful. By 1818, British hegemony over India was complete, and many other colonies and mandates followed between then and the aftermath of the First World War. Not all Muslim territories were colonized, but nearly all experienced some kind of dependency. The Saudi régime was perhaps the exception to this, but even there oil exploration, begun in the 1930s, brought European interference. In the nineteenth century Westernization and Islāmic activism coexisted and competed. By the turn of the twentieth century secular ethnic nationalism had become the most common mode of protest in Islāmdom; but the spirit of Islāmic reconstruction was also kept alive, either in conjunction with secular nationalism or in opposition to it.

In the nineteenth-century Ottoman Empire, selective Westernization coexisted with a reconsideration of Islām. The program of reform known as the Tanzimat, in effect from 1839 to 1876, aimed to emulate European law and administration by giving all Ottoman subjects, regardless of religious confession, equal legal standing and by limiting the powers of the monarch. In the 1860s the Young Ottomans tried to identify the basic principles of European liberalism and even love of nation with Islām itself. In Iran, the Qajar shahs brought in a special "Cossack Brigade", trained and led by Russians, while at the same time the Shī'ite *mujtahids* viewed the decisions of their spiritual leader as binding on all Iranian Shī'ites and declared themselves to be independent of the shah. (One Shī'ite revolt, that of the Bab [died 1850], led to a new religion, Baha'i.) Like the Young Ottomans, Shī'ite religious leaders came to identify with constitutionalism in opposition to the ruler.

Islāmic protest often took the form of *jihad* against the Europeans: by South-east Asians against the Dutch, by the Sanusi *ṭarīqah* over Italian control in Libya; by the Mahdist movement in the Sudan, or by the Salihi *ṭarīqah* in Somalia. Sometimes religious leaders, like those of the Shī'ites in Iran, took part in constitutional revolutions (1905–11). Underlying much of this activity was a pan-Islāmic sentiment that drew on very old conceptions of the *ummah* as the ultimate solidarity group for Muslims.

Three of the most prominent Islāmic reconstructionists were Jamal ad-Din al-Afghani, his Egyptian disciple Muḥammad 'Abduh, and the Indian poet Sir Muḥammad Iqbal. All warned against blind pursuit of Westernization, arguing that the blame for the weaknesses of Muslims lay not with Islām but rather with Muslims themselves, because they had lost touch with the progressive spirit of social, moral, and intellectual reconstruction of early Islāmicate civilization. Although al-Afghani acknowledged that organization by nationality might be necessary, he viewed it as inferior to Muslim identity.

Like al-Afghani, Iqbal assumed that without Islām Muslims could never regain the strength they had possessed when they were a vital force in the world, united in a single international community and unaffected by differences of language or ethnos. This aggressive recovery of the past became a permanent theme of Islāmic reconstruction. In many regions of Islāmdom the movement known as Salafiyah also identified with an ideal time in history, that of the "pious ancestors" (*salaf*) in the early Muslim state of Muḥammad and his companions, and advocated past-oriented change to bring present-day Muslims up to the progressive standards of an earlier ideal.

In addition to clearly Islāmic thinkers, there were others, such as the Egyptian Mustafa Kamil, whose nationalism was not simply secular. Kamil saw Egypt as simultaneously European, Ottoman, and Muslim. The Young Turk Revolution of 1908 was followed by a period in which similarly complex views of national identity were discussed in the Ottoman Empire.

Secular Nationalism in the Twentieth Century

The need to throw off European control promoted the fortunes of secular nationalism and other narrower forms of loyalty. Especially after Japan's defeat of Russia in 1905, nationalist fervour increased. Sometimes it was associated with related ideologies, such as pan-Arabism, pan-Turkism, or Arab socialism. Often accepting European assessments of traditional religion as a barrier to modernization, many nationalists sought an identity in the pre-Islāmic past.

In Iran, Reza Shah Pahlavi argued that the Islāmic period was but an accidental interlude in the continuous history, since Achaemenid times, of Iran as a unified entity. The Egyptian Taha Hussein connected his country's national identity with Pharaonic times and with Mediterranean-European culture;

Christians were thus as much Egyptians as were Muslims, and the development of a standard literary Arabic, *fuṣḥā*, emphasized the unity of all Arabs.

Kemal Atatürk looked to the Turkic past in Central Asia and Anatolia to transform Ottomanism into a Turkish identity not dependent on Islām. In a 1928 constitutional amendment, Islām was removed as the official state religion. "Islāmic" dress was discouraged. Muslim males, who prayed with covered heads, were now asked to replace the fez, which could be kept on during prayer, with the brimmed hat, which could not. Arabic script, too closely associated with Islām, was replaced with the Roman alphabet. Populism mobilized popular support from the top through such characteristic devices as the People's Houses (1931–51), which spread the new concept of a national culture in provincial towns, and the village institutes, which performed the same educational and proselytizing role in the countryside. The creation of a sense of nationalism was encouraged by changes in school curricula, the rewriting of history to glorify the Turkish past, the "purification" of the language by a reduction of the number of words of foreign origin, and the renunciation of pan-Islāmic, pan-Turkish, and pan-Ottoman goals in foreign policy.

Secularism included the reform of law, involving the abolition of religious courts and schools (1924) and the adoption of a purely secular system of family law; the adoption (1925) of the Gregorian calendar, which had been jointly used with the Muslim (Hijri) calendar since 1917; the replacement of Friday by Sunday as the weekly holiday (1935); and the adoption of surnames (1934). The wearing of clerical garb outside places of worship was forbidden in 1934. These changes, coupled with the abolition of the caliphate and the elimination of the dervish (Sufi) orders after a Kurdish revolt in 1925, dealt a tremendous blow to Islām's position in social life, completing

the process begun in the Tanzimat reforms under the Ottomans. With secularism there came a steady improvement in the
status of women, who were given the right to vote and to sit in
parliament.

During the 1950s, religious influence on social policies in
Turkey revived: religious instruction in schools was extended
and the organization of religious schools permitted, Arabic
was reinstated for the call to prayer, and radio readings of the
Qur'ān were allowed. By the last quarter of the twentieth
century pro-Islāmic political movements had grown in influence. The most striking feature of the 1995 election was the
extent of support for the Welfare Party (WP), an Islāmic party,
which emerged as the largest single party, with about one-fifth
of the vote. It stood for a greater role for Islām in public life
and a turning away from Europe and the West toward the
Islāmic countries of the Middle East. Its political success
reflected the increasing role of Islām in Turkish life during
the 1980s and 1990s, as evidenced by changes in dress and
appearance, segregation of the sexes, the growth of Islāmic
schools and banks, and support for Sufi orders.

Islāmic Nationalism

While secular approaches required all religious communities to
partake of a single legal and societal system, other nationalists
made more of Islām. In Saudi Arabia and Pakistan, for example, Islām played a primary role in the formation of a
national identity. It had been the alliance of the reformer 'Abd
al-Wahhab and Muḥammad ibn Sa'ud in the mid-eighteenth
century that led to the formation of first Saudi state. In 1745
people flocked to Al-Dir'iyyah, in Arabia, the seat of the
prince, to hear the teaching of the reformer. The alliance of

theologian and prince, duly sealed by mutual oaths of loyalty, soon began to prosper in terms of military success and expansion. By 1765, when Muḥammad ibn Sa'ud died, only a few parts of central and eastern Arabia had fallen under Wahhābī rule, but his son and successor, 'Abd al-'Azīz I (reigned 1765–1803), continued the extension of his father's realm. Conflict with the Ottomans and then the Egyptians followed, and in 1818 the Wahhābīs were roundly defeated.

The Wahhābī empire ceased to exist, but the faith lived on in the desert and in the towns of central Arabia in defiance of the new rulers of the land. The dynasty was restored and the second Saudi state begun in 1824 when Turki (1823–34), a grandson of Muḥammad ibn Sa'ud, succeeded in capturing Riyadh and expelling the Egyptian garrison. Further conflict with the Rashidi emirs of Jabal Shammar ensued, and at the Battle of Al-Mulaydah (in Al-Qāsim) in 1891, the Wahhābī state seemed to be completely destroyed for the second time in 70 years. In 1902, with a select body of only 15 warriors, 'Abd al-'Azīz (known commonly as Ibn Sa'ud) scaled the walls of Riyadh, surprised and defeated the Rashidi governor and his escort before the gate of the fort of Mismak (Musmak), and was hailed by the populace as the new ruler.

The following years witnessed the development of the struggle by the third Saudi state to expand its control once again over most of the Arabian Peninsula. In 1926, Ibn Sa'ud, who had adopted the title sultan of Najd in 1921, was proclaimed king of the Hejaz in the Great Mosque of Mecca. In 1927, in the Treaty of Jiddah, the British fully acknowledged Saudi independence. A series of Muslim conferences legitimized their presence as rulers. In 1932, the dual kingdom of the Hejaz and Najd with its dependencies, administered since 1927 as two separate units, was unified under the name of the Kingdom of Saudi Arabia. Above all, the king was concerned to assert and maintain the complete independence of his country and in it the exclusive supremacy of Islām.

In Pakistan Islāmic nationalism provided, according to the statesman Mohammed 'Alī Jinnah, an alternative for Muslims who would otherwise have to share in an identity defined by a Hindu majority. In many Arab countries, especially in the Maghrib, secular nationalism's downgrading of Islām was muted by a qualified acceptance of Islām as one, but not the only, important source of loyalty. At the same time there were Muslims who opposed nationalism altogether. In India, Mawlana Abū'l-'Alā' Mawdūdī, who was the founder of the Jama'at-i Islāmi, opposed both secular and religious nationalism and argued for the Islāmization of society and an Islāmic alternative to nationalism. In Egypt, Sayyid Qutb and Hasan al-Banna', who were the mentors of the Muslim Brotherhood, fought for the educational, moral, and social reform of an Islāmic Egypt and indeed of all Islāmdom.

Creating National Identities

Only a few existing states where Muslims predominate, such as Turkey and Saudi Arabia, had no colonial interval; most became independent after the Second World War. An even larger number of countries have Muslim minorities. Many of them are not nation-states – that is, states established by a group of people who decided that they belonged together and therefore went about acquiring sovereignty over a territory – but rather are state-nations, composed of groups of people who acquired or were given sovereignty over a territory and then had to develop a sense of nationality.

The most obvious state-nations are Syria, Iraq, Lebanon, and Jordan. All resulted from the interaction of intra-European rivalry and diplomacy with the aspirations of a prominent Ottoman-Hashimite sharifian family in Mecca to create a single Arab state in the East. Instead of a single state, however, three monarchies emerged: the kingdom of Husayn ibn 'Alī in the Hejaz (to be replaced by the Saudis; see above), the kingdom of Faysal I in Iraq (because he had to be compensated for being ousted from Syria), and the kingdom of Abdullah in Transjordan. Lebanon was carved from French Syria with borders that would establish a bare Christian majority loyal to the French.

Many Muslim countries were united by negative nationalism, aimed at ejecting a common enemy, but turning negative into positive has been difficult. Rarely have the groups that achieved independence survived. Often, as in Libya, Iraq, or Egypt, further revolutions have occurred, in many cases led by the military, whose role as a vehicle for modernization cannot be underestimated. Subsequent governments have had to deal with the social and economic problems that plague all developing countries, as well as with regional rivalries and conflicts.

Arab Palestine

In the last years of the nineteenth century and the early years of the twentieth, the Palestinian Arabs shared in a general Arab renaissance. Arab nationalism and opposition to Zionism were strong among some sections of the intelligentsia even before the First World War. The Arabs sought an end to Jewish immigration and to land purchases by Zionists.

The population of Palestine was about 690,000 in 1914 (535,000 Muslims; 70,000 Christians, most of whom were Arabs; and 85,000 Jews). Palestinian Arabs believed that Britain had promised them independence in return for their support against the Ottomans during the First World War. Yet by May 1916 Britain, France, and Russia had reached an agreement (the Sykes–Picot Agreement) according to which, inter alia, the bulk of Palestine was to be internationalized, while the the Balfour Declaration of November 1917 expressed sympathy for the establishment in Palestine of a national home for the Jewish people on the understanding that "nothing shall be done which may prejudice the civil and religious rights of existing non-Jewish communities in Palestine."

At the war's end, Britain, which had set up a military administration in Palestine, was faced with the problem of having to secure international sanction for the continued occupation of the country in a manner consistent with its ambiguous, seemingly conflicting wartime commitments. On March 20 1920, delegates from Palestine attended a general Syrian congress at Damascus, which passed a resolution rejecting the Balfour Declaration and elected Faysal I – son of Husayn ibn 'Alī, who ruled the Hejaz – king of a united Syria (including Palestine). In April 1920, however, at a peace conference held in San Remo, Italy, the Allies divided the former territories of the defeated Ottoman Empire: in the Syrian region, the northern portion (Syria and Lebanon) was mandated to France, and the southern portion (Palestine) was mandated to Britain. By July 1920 the French had forced Faysal to give up his newly founded kingdom of Syria. The hope of founding an Arab Palestine within a federated Syrian state collapsed and with it any prospect of independence.

Following the confirmation of the mandate at San Remo, the British replaced the military administration with a civilian administration in July 1920. The new administration proceeded to implement the Balfour Declaration, announcing in August a quota of 16,500 Jewish immigrants for the first year. In December 1920, Palestinian Arabs at a congress in Haifa established the Arab Executive to act as the representative of the Arabs. It was never formally recognized by the British and was dissolved in 1934. However, the platform of the Haifa Congress, which set out the position that Palestine was an autonomous Arab entity and totally rejected any rights of the Jews to Palestine, remained the basic policy of the Palestinian Arabs until 1948.

The arrival of more than 18,000 Jewish immigrants between 1919 and 1921 and land purchases in 1921 by the Jewish National Fund (established in 1901), which led to the eviction of Arab peasants (*fellahin*), further aroused Arab opposition and anti-Zionist riots broke out. An Arab delegation of notables visited London in August–November 1921, demanding that the Balfour Declaration be repudiated and proposing the creation of a national government with a parliament democratically elected by the country's Muslims, Christians, and Jews. The British government issued a White Paper in June 1922 declaring that Britain did "not contemplate that Palestine as a whole should be converted into a Jewish National Home, but that such a Home should be founded in Palestine" and that immigration would not exceed the economic absorptive capacity of the country, but these proposals were rejected.

In July 1922 the Council of the League of Nations approved the mandate instrument for Palestine, including its preamble incorporating the Balfour Declaration and stressing the Jewish historical connection with Palestine. Palestine was a distinct political entity for the first time in centuries, but at the end of the mandate period the region's future would be determined by size of population and ownership of land. Conflict over Jewish immigration and land purchases often escalated into violence, and the British were forced to take action. Several Arab organizations in the 1920s opposed Jewish immigration, including the Palestine Arab Congress, Muslim–Christian associations, and the Arab Executive.

In 1921 the British high commissioner appointed Amin al-Husayni to be the (grand) mufti of Jerusalem and made him president of the newly formed Supreme Muslim Council, which controlled the Muslim courts and schools and a considerable portion of the funds raised by religious charitable endowments. Amin al-Husayni used this religious position to transform himself into the most powerful political figure among the Arabs. The World Zionist Organization (founded 1897) was regarded as the de facto Jewish Agency stipulated in the mandate, although its president, Chaim Weizmann, remained in London, close to the British government; the Polish-born émigré David Ben-Gurion became the leader of a standing executive in Palestine.

There was little political cooperation between Arabs and Jews in Palestine. While the Jewish national home continued to consolidate itself in terms of urban, agricultural, social, cultural, and industrial development, Arab unease escalated. In August 1929, a dispute in Jerusalem concerning religious practices at the Western Wall flared up into communal clashes, killing 250. In response to two royal commissions of inquiry, which underlined Arab fears of Jewish domination and the lack of land available for agricultural settlement by new immigrants, the Passfield White Paper was issued. This called for a halt to Jewish immigration, recommending that land be sold only to landless Arabs and that the determination of "economic absorptive capacity" be based on levels of Arab as well as Jewish unemployment. This was seen by the Zionists as cutting at the root of their programme, for, if the right of the Arab resident were to gain priority over that of the Jewish immigrant, development of the Jewish national home would come to a standstill. In response to protests from Palestinian

Jews and London Zionists, the British prime minister, Ramsay MacDonald, in February 1931 wrote to Chaim Weizmann nullifying the Passfield White Paper. This letter convinced the Arabs that recommendations in their favour made in Palestine could be annulled by Zionist influence at the centre of power in London. In December 1931 a Muslim congress at Jerusalem was attended by delegates from 22 countries to warn against the danger of Zionism.

With the rise of Nazism in Europe from the early 1930s, Jewish immigration rose; by 1936 the Jewish population of Palestine had reached almost 400,000, or one-third of the total. In November 1935 the Arab political parties collectively demanded that Jewish immigration cease, land transfer be prohibited, and democratic institutions be established. A boycott of Zionist and British goods was proclaimed. In December the British administration offered to set up a legislative council, in which the Arabs (both Muslim and Christian) would have a majority. Though Arab leaders favoured the proposal, London rejected it. This, together with the example of rising nationalism in neighbouring Egypt and Syria, increasing unemployment in Palestine, and a poor citrus harvest, touched off a long-smouldering Arab rebellion.

The Arab Revolt of 1936–9 was the first sustained violent uprising of Palestinian Arabs in more than a century. The British shipped more than 20,000 troops into Palestine, and by 1939 the Zionists had armed more than 15,000 Jews in their own nationalist movement. The revolt began with spontaneous acts of violence. The Arab High Committee, formed by the Arab political parties, then called for a general strike and Arab rebels, joined by volunteers from neighbouring Arab countries, attacked Jewish settlements and British installations. By the end of the year, the movement had assumed the dimensions of a national revolt, the mainstay of which was the Arab peasantry. Armed rebellion, arson, bombings, and assassinations continued.

In 1937, the Peel Commission reported that the revolt was caused by Arab desire for independence and fear of the Jewish national home and recommended that the region be partitioned. For the first time a British official body explicitly spoke of a Jewish state. The Arabs were horrified by the idea of dismembering the region and particularly by the suggestion that they be forcibly transferred (to Transjordan). As a result, the momentum of the revolt increased during 1937 and 1938.

In September 1937 the British were forced to declare martial law. The Arab High Committee was dissolved, and many officials of the Supreme Muslim Council and other organizations were arrested. Although the Arab Revolt continued well into 1939, high casualty rates and firm British measures gradually eroded its strength. However, the prospect of war in Europe alarmed the British government and caused it to reassess its policy in Palestine. In November 1938 the Woodhead Commission, set up to examine the practicality of partition, put forward alternative proposals drastically reducing the area of the Jewish state and limiting the sovereignty of the proposed states. This was unacceptable to both Arabs and Jews.

Following an unsuccessful round-table conference in London in early 1939, in May the British government issued a White Paper which essentially yielded to Arab demands. It stated that the Jewish national home should be established within an independent Palestinian state. During the next five years 75,000 Jews would be allowed into the country; thereafter Jewish immigration would be subject to Arab "acquiescence". Land transfer to Jews would be allowed only in certain areas in Palestine, and an independent Palestinian state would be considered within ten years. The Arabs, although in favour of the new policy, rejected the White Paper, largely because they mistrusted the British government and opposed a provision contained in the paper for extending the mandate beyond the ten-year period. The Zionists were shocked and enraged by the paper, which they considered a death blow to their programme and to Jews who desperately sought refuge in Palestine from the growing persecution they were enduring in Europe. The 1939 White Paper marked the end of the Anglo–Zionist entente.

With the outbreak of the Second World War in September 1939, Zionist and British policies came into direct conflict. Throughout the war Zionists sought with growing urgency to increase Jewish immigration to Palestine, while the British sought to prevent such immigration, regarding it as illegal and a threat to the stability of a region essential to the war effort. During the war years the Jewish community's moderate wing supported the British. The Arabs of Palestine remained largely quiescent throughout the war; the majority supported the Allies.

The Allied discovery of the Nazi extermination camps at the end of the Second World War and the undecided future of Holocaust survivors led to an increasing number of pro-Zionist statements from U.S. politicians. The question of Palestine, now linked with the fate of Holocaust survivors, became once again the focus of international attention. In October 1944 Arab heads of state issued the Alexandria Protocol, setting out the Arab position. It stated that the issue of European Jewish survivors ought not to be confused with Zionism and that solving the problem of European Jewry should not be achieved by inflicting injustice on Palestinian Arabs. The covenant of the League of Arab States, or Arab League, formed in March 1945, contained an annex emphasizing the Arab character of Palestine. The Arab League appointed an Arab Higher Executive for Palestine (the Arab

Higher Committee), which included a broad spectrum of Palestinian leaders, to speak for the Palestinian Arabs.

The major issue between 1945 and 1948 was, as it had been throughout the mandate, Jewish immigration to Palestine. The Yishuv (the Jewish community in Palestine) was determined to remove all restrictions to Jewish immigration and to establish a Jewish state. The Arabs were determined that no more Jews should arrive and that Palestine should achieve independence as an Arab state. The primary goal of British policy following the Second World War was to secure British strategic interests in the Middle East and Asia. Because the cooperation of the Arab states was considered essential to this goal, British Foreign Secretary Ernest Bevin opposed Jewish immigration and the foundation of an independent Jewish state in Palestine. The U.S. State Department basically supported the British position, but Truman was determined to ensure that Jews displaced by the war were permitted to enter Palestine. The issue was resolved in 1948 when the British mandate collapsed under the pressure of force and diplomacy.

A plan of provincial autonomy for Arabs and Jews was worked out in an Anglo-American conference in 1946 and became the basis for discussions in London between Britain and the representatives of Arabs and Zionists. On the Arab side, a meeting of the Arab states took place in June 1946 at Bludan, Syria, at which secret resolutions were adopted threatening British and American interests in the Middle East if Arab rights were disregarded. In Palestine the followers of Amin al-Husayni consolidated their power, despite widespread mistrust of the mufti, who now resided in Egypt.

While Zionists pressed ahead with immigration and attacks on the government and while Arab states mobilized in response, British resolve to remain in the Middle East was collapsing, and in February 1947 Britain referred the Palestine question to the United Nations (UN). On August 31 a majority report of the UN Special Committee on Palestine (UNSCOP) recommended that the region be partitioned into an Arab and a Jewish state, which, however, should retain an economic union. These recommendations were substantially adopted by the UN General Assembly in a resolution dated November 29 1947. The Zionists welcomed the partition proposal, both because it recognized a Jewish state and because it allotted slightly more than half of (west-of-Jordan) Palestine to it. The Arabs fiercely opposed it both in principle and because nearly half of the population of the Jewish state would be Arab. May 15 1948 was set as the date for ending the mandate.

Soon after the UN resolution, fighting broke out in Palestine. Haifa and Jaffa fell to the Zionists, while Arab offensives faltered and their efforts to prevent partition collapsed. On May 14 the last British high commissioner, General Sir Alan Cunningham, left Palestine. On the same day the State of Israel was declared and within a few hours won de facto recognition from the United States and de jure recognition from the Soviet Union. Early on May 15 units of the regular armies of Syria, Transjordan, Iraq, and Egypt crossed the frontiers of Palestine. In a series of campaigns alternating with truces between May and December 1948, the Arab units were routed, and by the summer of 1949 Israel had concluded armistices with its neighbours. It had also been recognized by more than 50 governments throughout the world, joined the United Nations, and established its sovereignty over about 8,000 square miles (21,000 square km) of formerly mandated Palestine west of the Jordan River. The remaining 2,000 square miles (5,200 square km) were divided between Transjordan and Egypt. In 1949 the name of the former country was changed to the Hashimite Kingdom of Jordan. Egypt retained control of, but did not annex, a small area on the Mediterranean coast that became known as the Gaza Strip. The Palestinian Arab community ceased to exist as a cohesive social and political entity.

If one chief theme in the post-1948 pattern was embattled Israel and a second the hostility of its Arab neighbours, a third was the plight of the huge number of Arab refugees. The violent birth of Israel led to a major displacement of the Arab population. In 1950 the United Nations Relief and Works Agency for Palestine Refugees in the Near East (UNRWA) would establish a total of 53 refugee "camps" on both sides of the Jordan River and in the Gaza Strip, Lebanon, and Syria to assist the 650,000 or more Arab refugees it calculated needed help. More than 400 Arab villages disappeared, and Arab life in the coastal cities (especially Jaffa and Haifa) virtually disintegrated. The centre of Palestinian life shifted to the Arab towns of the hilly eastern portion of the region – which was immediately west of the Jordan River and came to be called the West Bank.

Of those displaced, some 276,000 moved to the West Bank; by 1949 more than half the pre-war Arab population of Palestine lived in the West Bank (from 400,000 in 1947 to more than 700,000). Between 160,000 and 190,000 fled to the Gaza Strip. More than one-fifth of Palestinian Arabs left Palestine altogether. About 100,000 of these went to Lebanon, 100,000 to Jordan, between 75,000 and 90,000 to Syria, 7,000 to 10,000 to Egypt, and 4,000 to Iraq. After 1948 – and even more so after 1967, when the Gaza Strip was lost by Egypt to Israel (see Chapter 7) – for Palestinians themselves the term Palestine came to signify not only a place of origin but, more importantly, a sense of a shared past and future in the form of a Palestinian state.

During the 20 years the Gaza Strip was under Egyptian control (1948–67), Palestinians were denied citizenship, which rendered them stateless, and they were allowed little real control over local administration. The Gaza Strip became one of the most densely populated areas of the world, with more than four-fifths of its population urban. Poverty and social misery became characteristic of life in the region.

The events of 1948 and the experience of exile shaped Palestinian political and cultural activity for the next generation. By the 1960s, a new Palestinian leadership had emerged from the schools UNRWA had established and from among those who had moved to various Middle Eastern states and to the West. A new sense of identity was generated based on a pan-Arabism inspired by Nasser, the cultivated memory of a lost paradise (Palestine), and an emerging pan-Islāmic movement. In 1964 the Palestine Liberation Organization (PLO) was formed. A political umbrella organization of several Palestinian groups, the PLO thereafter consistently claimed to be the sole representative of all Palestinian people. It supported the right to an independent state, the total liberation of Palestine, and the destruction of the State of Israel. In 1969 Yāsir 'Arafāt, leader of the Palestine National Liberation Movement (Fatah), became chairman of the PLO's executive committee and thus the chief of the Palestinian national movement. Both the PLO and Fatah trained guerrilla units for raids on Israel. Their opposition would culminate in the bombing of Lebanon by Israel in 1982 and continued retaliation from both sides throughout the 1980s (see Chapter 7). However, in September 1993 a peace agreement between the PLO and Israel established Palestinian self-rule in Israeli-occupied territory.

Modern Islām's Unifying Forces

Given the multi-communal structure of premodern Muslim societies, nationalism has frequently led to competition and rivalry among new nations' religious communities. Many countries inherited a relatively simple form of this problem: the people within their borders were primarily of one faith, Islām, and of one form of that faith, the Sunni. That majority adherence could in some way be associated with or bolster the national identity, while discomfiting only a small number of people. Turkey, Iran, Jordan, Indonesia, Yemen, and all the states of North Africa and the Arabian Peninsula fall into this category. Elsewhere, self-consciously Islāmic governments have introduced a religious intolerance. For example, in Iran, intolerance discouraged by the Sharī'ah is encouraged by local sentiment as well as by the staunch nationalism Iran shares with secular states. The leaders of the Islāmic Republic of Iran have associated being Iranian with being Muslim.

Further from the centre of Islāmdom, Islām plays various roles as a minority religion. Among Turks in the Central Asian states, for example, Islām is an important source of identity. Muslims living in western Europe and the Americas are generally able to form communities and practise their religion as they will: in Canada, for example, Isma'ili Muslims, under the guidance of Aga Khan IV, form a cohesive group that promotes the economic and cultural development of its members. In the United States, tenets of Islām were embraced by the founders of the American Muslim Mission (originally called Nation of Islām) in the early 1930s. As the community has developed, its leaders have increasingly emphasized the Qur'ān and Muḥammad's example as sources of authority.

Although Islāmic activism never disappeared during the years in which Muslim countries were becoming independent, other ideological orientations seemed more important between the end of the Second World War and the declaration of the Islāmic Republic of Iran in 1979. Many Westerners or Westernized Muslims expected religion to recede as modernization progressed. In the 1950s, however, the Muslim Brotherhood in Egypt called for an exclusively Islāmic state in place of the secular multi-communal state that Gamal Abdel Nasser had founded. In the early 1960s new circumstances were beginning to foster increased Islāmic activity; some popular, some supported by official institutions. In these years critics of Mohammad Reza Shah Pahlavi began to rally around the exiled Ayatollah Ruhollah Khomeini; the writings of 'Alī Shari'ati began to influence Muslims inside and outside Iran; and two great pan-Islāmic organizations were formed, the Muslim World League (1962) and the Organization of the Islāmic Conference (1971). All these developments occurred in the wake of the formation of the Organization of Petroleum Exporting Countries in 1961 and culminated in Egypt's success in its war with Israel in 1973.

The resurgence of economic and military power was not the only factor that could foster those who had maintained an interest in Islām all along. In a few parts of the Muslim world, petroleum-based prosperity promoted increased international influence and pride; elsewhere, modernization was producing widespread educational and economic cleavages and populations with very low median ages. As dissatisfaction with the material failures of secular modernization grew, so did disenchantment with the Western ideologies that had undergirded it. Eventually these forces would bring forth the Islāmic revivalism and fundamentalism that would dominate the late twentieth and early twenty-first centuries.

PART 3

ISLĀM IN THE MODERN WORLD

7

ISLĀMIC REVIVALISM

Islāmic revivalism builds on a considerable legacy of activism and reform. A common theme was the need to purify Islām through the suppression of foreign (un-Islāmic) practices and to return to the fundamentals of Islām – the Qur'ān and the model of Muḥammad and the early Muslim community. In the first half of the twentieth century the Muslim Brotherhood in Egypt and the Jama'at-i-Islāmi (Islāmic Society) in South Asia became prototypes of present-day Islāmic movements. Their legacy included the belief that Islām affects public policy as much as it does private worship, and the objective of establishing effective organizations to implement an Islāmic system of government and law.

During the 1970s contemporary Islāmic revivalism emerged. The personal aspect was reflected in increased emphasis upon religious observances (mosque attendance, Ramadan fast, outlawing of alcohol and gambling), the proliferation of religious literature, and the birth of new associations or movements that sought to "Islāmize" the population.

At the same time, Islām dramatically re-emerged in public life. Throughout the Islāmic world Islāmic symbols, slogans, ideology, and actors became prominent fixtures in politics. Religion was used both by incumbent governments and by opposition movements to reinforce their legitimacy and mobilize popular support. Instances of Islām reasserting itself were seen in Libyan leader Muammar al-Qaddafi's *Green Book* of Islāmic socialism; Zia ul-Haq's 1977 coup d'état in Pakistan and his call for the establishment of an Islāmic system of government; Ayatollah Khomeini's Iranian Revolution of 1978–9; the seizure of the Grand Mosque in Mecca by militants in 1979; President Anwar el-Sadat's appeal to Islām in Egyptian politics, his legitimation of the 1973 war with Israel as a *jihad*, and his assassination in 1981 by religious extremists; and the Afghan resistance (by *mujahideen*, or holy warriors) to the Soviet invasion and occupation throughout the 1980s.

The Arab–Israeli Wars

During the Arab–Israeli Wars the forces of Islāmism and Arab nationalism coalesced. The war of 1967 was preceded by a series of military conflicts between Israeli and various Arab forces, most notably in 1948–9 and 1956, and was followed by the Yom Kippur War in 1973 and the Israeli invasion of Lebanon in 1982.

The first war immediately followed Israel's proclamation of statehood on May 14 1948. In an effort to forestall the creation of a Jewish state in Palestine, Arab forces from Egypt, Transjordan (Jordan), Iraq, Syria, and Lebanon occupied the areas in southern and eastern Palestine not apportioned to the Jews by the United Nations (UN) partition of Palestine and then captured east Jerusalem. The Israelis, meanwhile, won control of the main road to Jerusalem through the Yehuda Mountains ("Hills of Judaea") and successfully repulsed repeated Arab attacks. By early 1949 the Israelis had managed to occupy all of the Negev up to the former Egypt–Palestine frontier, except for the Gaza Strip. Between February and July 1949, as a result of separate armistice agreements between Israel and each of the Arab states, a temporary frontier was fixed between Israel and its neighbours.

Tensions mounted again with the rise to power of Egyptian President Gamal Abdel Nasser, a staunch pan-Arab nationalist. In 1956 Nasser nationalized the Suez Canal, a vital waterway connecting Europe and Asia that was largely owned by French and British concerns. France and Britain responded by striking a deal with Israel – whose ships were barred from using the canal and whose southern port of Elat had been blockaded by Egypt – whereby Israel would invade Egypt; France and Britain would then intervene, ostensibly as peacemakers, and take control of the canal. In October 1956 Israel invaded Egypt's Sinai Peninsula. In five days the Israeli army captured Gaza, Rafah, and Al-'Arīsh and occupied most of the peninsula east of the Suez Canal. The Israelis were then in a position to open sea communications through the Gulf of Aqaba. In December, after the joint Anglo-French intervention, a UN Emergency Force was stationed in the area, and Israeli forces withdrew in March 1957. Though Egyptian forces had been defeated on all fronts, the Suez Crisis, as it is sometimes known, was seen by Arabs as an Egyptian victory. Egypt dropped the blockade of Elat. A UN buffer force was placed in the Sinai Peninsula.

Arab and Israeli forces clashed for the third time in June 5–10 1967, in what came to be called the Six-Day War (or June War). In early 1967 Syria intensified its bombardment of

Israeli villages from positions in the Golan Heights. When the
Israeli Air Force shot down six Syrian fighter jets in reprisal,
Nasser mobilized his forces near the Sinai border, dismissing
the UN force there, and again sought to blockade Elat. In May
1967 Egypt signed a mutual defence pact with Jordan.

In reaction, on June 5, Israeli planes destroyed the Egyptian
air force on the ground in a pre-emptive strike that began the
total rout of all Egyptian, Jordanian, and Syrian forces. Israeli
troops captured huge quantities of arms and took many
prisoners. Six days later, Israeli troops stood victorious along
the Suez Canal, having overrun the Sinai Peninsula; on the
banks of the Jordan River, after occupying the entire West
Bank; and atop the Golan Heights, after driving the Syrians
from that strategic position. Most significant to all involved,
Israel had captured the remaining sections of Jerusalem not
already under its control, including the Old City and the
Western Wall.

Israel's victory gave rise to another exodus of Palestinians,
with more than 250,000 people fleeing to the eastern bank of
the Jordan River. However, roughly 600,000 Palestinians
remained in the West Bank and 300,000 in Gaza. Thus the
3 million Israeli Jews came to rule some 1.2 million Arabs
(including the 300,000 already living in the State of Israel).
Moreover, a movement developed among Israelis who advocated settling the occupied territories – particularly the West
Bank – as part of the Jewish patrimony in the Holy Land.
Several thousand Israeli Jews settled in the territories in the
decade following the war.

It was not clear, however, how military victory could be
turned into peace. Israeli Prime Minister Levi Eshkol's secret
offer to trade much of the newly won territory for peace
agreements with Egypt, Jordan, and Syria was rejected by
Nasser, who, supported by an emergency resupply of Soviet

arms, led the Arabs at the Khartoum Arab Summit in The Sudan in August 1967 in a refusal to negotiate directly with Israel. The UN Security Council responded by passing Resolution 242 in November, demanding that Israel withdraw from "occupied territories" and that all parties in the dispute recognize the right of residents of each state to live within "secure and recognized borders". The wording of this statement became crucial to peace negotiations for years to come. By not stating "all the occupied territories" in the English version – the only one accepted by Israel – the resolution left room for the Israelis to negotiate. The Palestinians, the residents of these territories, were mentioned only as refugees, it being presumed that Jordan would represent them. Nearly two years of fruitless mediation ensued while Israel held the occupied territories with a minimum of force.

The Egypt–Israel War and its Consequences

The sporadic fighting that followed the Six-Day War again developed into full-scale war in 1973. On October 6, the Jewish holy day of Yom Kippur (thus "Yom Kippur War"), Israel was attacked by Egypt across the Suez Canal and by Syria on the Golan Heights. Washington's initial reluctance to help Israel changed rapidly when the Soviet Union launched its own resupply effort to Egypt and Syria. The Israeli army reversed early losses, pushed its way into Syrian territory, and encircled the Egyptian Third Army by crossing the Suez Canal and establishing forces on its west bank.

A ceasefire was secured by the United States while Egyptian troops remained east of the Suez Canal and Israeli forces had crossed over to its western side, and Israel and Egypt signed peace agreements on January 18 1974. The accords provided for Israeli withdrawal into the Sinai west of the Mitla and Gidi passes, while Egypt was to reduce the size of its forces on the east bank of the canal. A UN peacekeeping force was established between the two armies. This agreement was supplemented by another, signed on September 4 1975. On May 31 1974, Israel and Syria signed a ceasefire agreement that also covered separation of their forces by a UN buffer zone and the exchange of prisoners of war.

The initial successes in October 1973 had enabled Egyptian President Anwar Sadat to pronounce the war an Egyptian victory and to seek an honourable peace. When Israeli inflexibility and Arab resistance combined to slow events, Sadat made a dramatic journey to Jerusalem on November 19 1977, to address the Israeli Knesset (parliament). Tortuous negotiations between Egypt and Israel ensued. The climactic meeting in September 1978 of Sadat, Israeli Prime Minister Menachem Begin, and U.S. President Jimmy Carter at Camp David in Maryland produced a pair of agreements known as the Camp David Accords. Both Sadat and Begin were awarded the 1978 Nobel Prize for Peace for these negotiations, and on March 26 1979, the two leaders signed the Israeli–Egyptian peace treaty formally ending the state of war that had existed between the two countries for 30 years. Under the terms of the treaty, Israel returned the entire Sinai Peninsula to Egypt, and, in return, Egypt recognized Israel's right to exist. The two countries subsequently established normal diplomatic relations.

The Sadat peace with Israel was not without its costs, however. As the narrowness of the Israeli interpretation of Palestinian autonomy under the Camp David agreement became clear, Sadat could not convince the Arab world that the accords would ensure legitimate Palestinian rights. Egypt lost the financial support of the Arab states and, shortly after signing the peace treaty, was expelled from the Arab League.

A new Egyptian constitution promulgated in 1971 demo-cratized the political process, but, as Egypt entered the 1980s, the failure to resolve the Palestinian issue and to relieve mass economic hardships undermined Sadat's legitimacy. During the 1970s Muslim activists – many of them radicalized by imprisonment by Nasser and by Sayyid Qutb's writings on *jihad* and the apostasy of modern Muslim culture – were given wide latitude to proselytize, while members of the Muslim Brotherhood were released from prison and allowed to operate with relative freedom. The group al-Takfir wa al-Hijrah (roughly, "Identification of Unbelief and Flight from Evil") engaged in several terrorist attacks, and Islāmic Jihad (al-Jihad al-Islāmi) and the Islāmic Group (al-Jamā'a al-Islāmiyah) were formed with the goal of overthrowing Egypt's secular state. On October 6 1981, Sadat was assassinated by Egyptian soldiers associated with Islāmic Jihad. Hosni (Husni) Mubarak was elected as Sadat's successor with a mandate for cautious change. Mubarak released Sadat's political prisoners while prosecuting vigorously the Islāmic militants who had plotted the late president's assassination.

When Israel invaded Lebanon in June 1982, only five weeks after the Jewish state's final withdrawal from the Sinai Penin-sula, the invasion was perceived in Egypt as an Israeli attempt to destroy Palestinian nationalism. Official relations with Israel were severely strained until Israel initiated its partial withdrawal from Lebanon in 1985. However, Mubarak's cautious policies enabled Egypt to repair its relationships with most of the moderate Arab states. At an Arab League summit in 1987, each government was authorized to restore diplo-matic relations with Egypt, and Egypt resumed membership in the league two years later.

Mubarak continued in power throughout the 1980s and 1990s. Unrest continued, however, and the government adopted several measures aimed at curbing a determined drive by Islāmic extremists to destabilize the regime. During a period of economic hardship, as falling oil prices hit the economy in the late 1980s, the poorest Egyptians often looked to Islāmist groups such as the Muslim Brotherhood for assistance. Some Muslim extremists, however, including Islāmic Jihad and the Islāmic Group, continued to resort to terrorism, assassinating several government ministers and gunning down tourists near Egypt's most famous monuments.

Although the press was initially freer under Mubarak than under his predecessors, in the twentieth and early twenty-first centuries the Islāmic courts and the rector of al-Azhar University censored freedom of speech and the press. The Islāmist leader Ayman al-Zawahiri fled to Afghanistan, where he and members of Islāmic Jihad joined the Islāmic terrorist organization al-Qaeda. Domestic terrorism remained a threat to Egypt's stability in the early twenty-first century.

Palestine and the Rise of the PLO

The Israeli bombing of Beirut and southern Lebanon on June 5 1982 was an assault on the Palestine Liberation Organization (PLO), which had a number of strongholds there. Throughout the 1970s and 1980s the PLO, dominated by Fatah, had acted as a state in the making, launching frequent military attacks on Israel. It had intensified its activities and emerged as an element of major importance in the Middle East. The Arab–Israeli war had discredited Nasser's pan-Arabism, and Fatah quickly permeated and mobilized the reunited Palestinian population, providing social services and organizations. Guerrilla attacks on Israeli occupation forces and terror attacks on Israeli civilians (defended by the PLO until they were renounced by 'Arafāt in 1988) became a key element in the struggle against Israel.

In Jordan, tensions between the Jordanian army loyal to King Hussein and the Palestinian guerrillas erupted in a brief but bloody civil war in September 1970 that became known as "Black September". Driven from Jordan, the PLO intensified its activities in Lebanon. The presence of more than 235,000 Palestinians there was a source of tension and conflict: Palestinians had few rights, and most worked for low wages in poor conditions.

The PLO made important gains in its international relations during the 1970s. By the end of the decade the organization had representatives in more than 80 countries. On September 22 1974, the UN General Assembly, overriding strong Israeli objections, included on its agenda for the first time the "Palestine question". On November 13 the assembly heard 'Arafāt plead for the Palestinian people's national rights.

International recognition of the PLO had important repercussions within the Arab camp. At an Arab summit conference held in Rabat, Morocco, on October 26–28 1974, King Hussein accepted a resolution stating that any "liberated" Palestinian territory "should revert to its legitimate Palestinian owners under the leadership of the PLO". The Rabat decision was denounced by the more radical "rejection front", composed of the militant Popular Front for the Liberation of Palestine (PFLP), the independent faction PFLP-General Command (PFLP-GC), the pro-Iraq Arab Liberation Front, and the Front for the Popular Palestinian Struggle, which sought to regain all of Palestine.

Palestinian guerrilla activity against Israel in 1975 was largely confined to the southern Lebanese border area but was overshadowed by the civil war between the militias of Lebanon's Christians and Muslims, which eventually killed more than 100,000 people. The civil war proved disastrous for the Palestinians in Lebanon.

The PLO initially tried to stay out of the fighting, but by the end of 1975 groups within the overall organization, particularly those in the "rejection front", were being drawn into an alliance with Muslim and leftist groups fighting against the Christians. A peace agreement was negotiated in October 1976. The settlement provided for the creation of a 30,000-member Arab Deterrent Force (ADF), a ceasefire throughout the country, the withdrawal of forces to positions held before April 1975, and the implementation of a 1969 agreement limiting Palestinian guerrilla operations in Lebanon.

Although the Palestinian guerrillas suffered heavy losses in the Lebanese civil war, they continued to mount attacks against Israel in the late 1970s, and Israel again responded with raids into southern Lebanon. On March 19 1978 the UN Security Council passed resolution 425, calling for Israel to withdraw and establishing the UN Interim Force in Lebanon (UNIFIL). The Israelis withdrew their forces only partially and continued to occupy a strip of Lebanese territory along the southern frontier.

In the late 1970s and early 1980s, Israel's settlements in the West Bank grew dramatically, accompanied by an increase in Israeli control. As this occupation solidified, many local Palestinian leaders turned to building social organizations, labour unions, and religious, educational, and political institutions. The PLO responded by making its presence increasingly felt, and by the early 1980s it had set up an extensive bureaucratic structure that provided health, housing, educational, legal, media, and labour services for Palestinians both inside and outside the camps. Active opposition to Israeli control in the West Bank spread, while frequent demonstrations, strikes, and other incidents occurred, particularly among students.

The late 1970s was a period of more active negotiation on Arab–Israeli disputes within the framework of the 1978 Camp David Accords and the Egyptian–Israeli peace treaty in 1979. The Soviet Union during the time of the peace negotiations recognized the PLO as the sole legitimate representative of the Palestinians and in 1981 extended formal diplomatic recognition. The nations of western Europe announced their support of PLO participation in peace negotiations in June 1980. The PLO continued to seek diplomatic recognition from the United States, but the Carter administration honoured a secret commitment to Israel, made by former U.S. Secretary of State Henry Kissinger, not to deal with the PLO so long as it declined to renounce terrorism and to recognize Israel's right to exist.

The Likud Party government of Israel viewed the possibility of peace and compromise with suspicion. On the grounds that it intended to end attacks on its territory, in June 1982 Israel invaded Lebanon. PLO and Syrian forces were defeated by Israeli troops, and by June 14 Israeli land forces had encircled Beirut. The Israeli government then agreed to halt its advance and begin negotiations with the PLO. After much delay and massive Israeli shelling of west Beirut, the PLO evacuated the city under the supervision of a multinational force. Although not all PLO guerrillas were forced to leave Lebanon, the PLO infrastructure in the southern part of the country was destroyed, and 'Arafāt's departure from Beirut to northern Lebanon marked the effective end of the PLO's military and political presence in the country. Ultimately, the new government of Lebanon came under the sway of Syria.

The dispersal of the PLO from Lebanon significantly weakened the organization's military strength and political militancy. After having established himself near Tunis, Tunisia, 'Arafāt turned once again to diplomatic initiatives. He sought

Egyptian and Jordanian support against Syria. He also looked to King Hussein as an intermediary for negotiations with the United States and Israel that might lead to a Palestinian mini-state on the West Bank within a Jordan–Palestine confederation – an idea that had been favoured by the dominant factions in the PLO since the early 1980s.

Palestinian demonstrations and riots continued in the following years and took on the character of a mass popular rebellion (known as the *intifāda*, or "shaking off") directed against continued Israeli occupation of the West Bank and the Gaza Strip. The persistent disturbances, initially spontaneous, before long came under the leadership of the Unified National Command of the Uprising, which had links to the PLO. The PLO soon incorporated the Unified Command, but not before the local leaders had pushed 'Arafāt to abandon formally his commitment to armed struggle and to accept Israel and the notion of a two-state solution to the conflict. One group, Hamas (see Chapter 8) – whose name, meaning "zeal" in Arabic, is an acronym of Harakat al-Muqawamah al-Islāmiyyah ("Islāmic Resistance Movement") – challenged the authority of the secular nationalist movement, especially inside Gaza, and sought to take over the leadership of the *intifāda*, also rejecting any accommodation with Israel.

'Arafāt sought to establish himself as the only leader who could unite and speak for the Palestinians, and in mid-1988 he took the diplomatic initiative. At the nineteenth session of the Palestine National Council (PNC), held near Algiers on November 12–15 1988, he succeeded in having the council issue a declaration of independence for a state of Palestine in the West Bank and Gaza Strip. 'Arafāt proclaimed the state (without defining its borders) on November 15. Within days more than 25 countries (including the Soviet Union and Egypt but excluding the United States and Israel) had extended recognition to the government-in-exile.

In December 'Arafāt announced that the PNC recognized Israel as a state in the region and condemned and rejected terrorism in all its forms. He addressed a special meeting of the UN General Assembly convened at Geneva and proposed an international peace conference under UN auspices. He publicly accepted UN resolutions 242 (1967), which encapsulated the principle of land for peace, and 338 (1973), which called for direct negotiations, thereby recognizing, at least implicitly, the State of Israel. Although Israeli Prime Minister Yitzhak Shamir stated that he was still not prepared to negotiate with the PLO, the U.S. government announced that it would open dialogue with the organization.

The approaching end of the Cold War left the Palestinians diplomatically isolated, as did PLO support for Iraqi President Saddam Hussein, who had invaded Kuwait in August 1990 but was defeated by a U.S.-led alliance in the Persian Gulf War (1990–91). Funds from Saudi Arabia, Kuwait, and the Persian Gulf states dried up. However, prospects for a settlement of the outstanding issues between the Palestinians and Israel became significantly altered by several factors: the convening of an international peace conference between Israeli and Arab delegates (including Palestinians from the occupied territories as part of a joint Jordanian-Palestinian delegation) at Madrid in October 1991, sponsored by the United States and the Soviet Union (after December 1991, Russia); the dissolution of the Soviet Union in December; and the replacement, in the Israeli general elections of June 1992, of Shamir and the Likud-bloc government with a Labour Party government that was committed to implementing Palestinian autonomy within a year.

Although progress at the Madrid peace conference was discouraging, secret meetings held in Norway from January

1993 between PLO and Israeli officials produced an under-standing, known as the Oslo Accords, that involved mutual recognition and envisaged the gradual implementation of Palestinian self-government in the West Bank and Gaza Strip before a permanent peace settlement.

Despite continuing acts of violence by extremist groups on both sides, the Israelis completed their withdrawal from the West Bank town of Jericho and parts of the Gaza Strip, and on July 1 1994 'Arafāt entered Gaza in triumph. Four days later he swore in members of the Palestinian Authority (PA) in Jericho, which by the end of the year had assumed control of education and culture, social welfare, health, tourism, and taxation. On September 28 1995, 'Arafāt, Israeli Prime Min-ister Yitzhak Rabin, and Foreign Minister Shimon Peres signed an agreement in Washington providing for the expansion of Palestinian self-rule in the West Bank and for elections of a chairman and a legislative council of the PA. Reaffirming the commitment made in the 1993 peace accord, permanent-status negotiations were to be concluded by 1999.

The process was fraught with difficulty, however. After a decade of negotiating, less than one-fifth of the West Bank (in 15 isolated segments) and about two-thirds of the Gaza Strip had reverted to full Palestinian control. The number of Israelis living in West Bank settlements (which now exceeded 150) had grown by some 80,000. Accusations were widespread of corruption within the PA and of human rights abuses by its leaders. An Israeli-Palestinian summit meeting sponsored by the United States in July 2000 failed to resolve outstanding issues, and a second *intifāda* erupted. Violence would continue to ebb and flow in the early twenty-first century, sometimes reaching the level of full-scale war, and the victory of Hamas in elections for the Palestinian Legislative Council in 2006 would cause a major political upheaval.

The Iranian Revolution, 1978–9

In little more than a generation, under the Shah, Iran changed from a traditional, conservative, and rural society to one that was industrial, modern, and urban. There was a sense, however, that too much had been attempted too soon and that the government, either through corruption or incompetence, had failed to deliver all that was promised, and this provoked demonstrations against the regime in 1978.

The resistance gathered around the figure of Ayattolah Ruhollah Khomeini, a Shī'ite cleric who was to lead the revolution that overthrew Mohammad Reza Shah Pahlavi in 1979 and become Iran's religious and political authority for the next ten years. His denunciations of Western influences and his uncompromising advocacy of Islāmic purity had won him his initial following in Iran, and by the early 1960s he had received the title of grand ayatollah, thereby making him one of the supreme religious leaders of the Shī'ite community in the country. In 1962–3 Khomeini spoke out against the Shah's reduction of religious estates in a land-reform programme and against the emancipation of women. His ensuing arrest sparked anti-government riots, and, after a year's imprisonment, Khomeini was forcibly exiled from Iran. He first settled in the Shī'ite holy city of Al-Najaf, Iraq, from where he continued to call for the Shah's overthrow and the establishment of an Islāmic republic in Iran.

Forced to leave Iraq, he moved to Neauphle-le-Château, a suburb of Paris. From there his supporters relayed his tape-recorded messages to an increasingly aroused Iranian populace. In January 1978, incensed by what they considered to be slanderous remarks made against Khomeini in a Tehran newspaper, thousands of young *madrasah* students took to the streets. They were followed by thousands more Iranian youths

who began protesting the regime's excesses. The Shah, weakened by cancer and stunned by the sudden outpouring of
hostility against him, vacillated, assuming the protests to be
part of an international conspiracy against him. Many people
were killed by government forces in the ensuing chaos, serving
only to fuel the violence in a Shī'ite country where martyrdom
played a fundamental role in religious expression.

In January 1979, in what was officially described as a
"vacation", the Shah and his family fled Iran; he died the
following year in Cairo. The Regency Council established to
run the country during the Shah's absence proved unable to
function, and Prime Minister Shahpur Bakhtiar, hastily appointed by the Shah before his departure, was incapable of
effecting compromise with either his former National Front
colleagues or Khomeini. Crowds in excess of one million
demonstrated in Tehran, proving the wide appeal of Khomeini, who arrived in Iran amid wild rejoicing on February 1. Ten
days later Bakhtiar went into hiding, eventually to find exile in
France, where he was assassinated in 1991.

On April 1, following overwhelming support in a national
referendum, Khomeini declared Iran an Islāmic republic. Elements within the clergy promptly moved to exclude their
former left-wing, nationalist, and intellectual allies from any
positions of power in the new regime, and a return to conservative social values was enforced. The Family Protection
Act, which had provided guarantees and rights to women in
marriage, was declared void, and mosque-based revolutionary
bands known as *komiteh*s (Persian: "committees") patrolled
the streets enforcing Islāmic codes of dress and behaviour and
dispatching impromptu justice to perceived enemies of the
revolution. Throughout most of 1979 the Revolutionary
Guards, then an informal religious militia formed by Khomeini
to forestall another CIA-backed coup – such as the one that

deposed Mohammed Mosaddeq and restored the Shah to power in 1953 – engaged in similar activity, which was aimed at intimidating and repressing political groups not under control of the ruling Revolutionary Council and its sister Islāmic Republican Party (both clerical organizations loyal to Khomeini). The violence and brutality often exceeded that of SAVAK, the Shah's secret police.

The main thrust of Khomeini's foreign policy was the complete abandonment of the Shah's pro-Western orientation and the adoption of an attitude of unrelenting hostility towards both the United States and the Soviet Union. The militias and the clerics made every effort to suppress Western cultural influence – e.g. Western music and alcohol were banned – and punishments prescribed by Islāmic law were reinstated. Facing persecution and violence, many of the Western-educated elite fled the country.

This anti-Western sentiment eventually manifested itself in the November 1979 seizure of the U.S. embassy by a group of Iranian protesters demanding the extradition of the Shah, who at the time was undergoing medical treatment in the United States. Through the embassy takeover, Khomeini's supporters could claim to be as "anti-imperialist" as the political left. This ultimately gave them the ability to suppress most of the regime's left-wing and moderate opponents. The Assembly of Experts (Majles-e Khobregan), overwhelmingly dominated by clergy, ratified a new constitution the following month.

The taking of 66 U.S. hostages at the embassy, however, highlighted the fractures that had begun to occur within the revolutionary regime. Moderates, such as provisional Prime Minister Mehdi Bazargan and the republic's first president, Abolhasan Bani-Sadr, who opposed holding the hostages, were steadily forced from power by conservatives within the government who questioned their revolutionary zeal. Iran also tried to export its brand of Islãmic revivalism to neighbouring Muslim countries. Khomeini refused to countenance a peaceful solution to the Iran–Iraq War, which had begun in 1980 and which he insisted on prolonging in the hope of overthrowing Saddam Hussein. Khomeini finally approved a ceasefire in 1988 that effectively ended the war.

Iran's course of economic development foundered under Khomeini's rule, and his pursuit of victory in the Iran–Iraq War ultimately proved futile. Khomeini, however, was able to retain his charismatic hold over Iran's Shī'ite masses. His gold-domed tomb in Tehran's Behesht-e Zahra' cemetery has since become a shrine for his supporters. Ideologically, he is best remembered for having developed the concept of *vilayat-e faqih* ("guardianship of the jurist") in which he argued for the establishment of a theocratic government administered by Islãmic jurists in place of corrupt secular regimes. The Iranian constitution of 1979 embodies articles upholding this concept of juristic authority.

Khomeini's death in June 1989 was followed by a period of reform. The Assembly of Experts appointed President 'Alī Khamenei *rahbar*, or leader, but the election of Hojatoleslam 'Alī Akbar Hashemi Rafsanjani brought a policy of economic liberalization, privatization of industry, and rapprochement with the West that would encourage much-needed foreign investment.

In the mid-1990s, the philosopher Abdolkarim Soroush attracted thousands of Iranians to his lectures, in which he advocated a type of reformist Islãm that went beyond most liberal Muslim thinkers of the twentieth century. He called for a re-examination of all tenets of Islãm, insisting on the need to maintain the religion's original spirit of social justice and its emphasis on caring for other people. In 1997 his supporter Mohammad Khatami was elected as Rafsanjani's successor.

Khatami had campaigned on a platform of curbing censorship, fighting religious excess, and allowing greater tolerance.

Less than one year later some 900 new newspapers and journals had received authorization to publish, adding their voices to earlier reformist publications such as *Zanan* and *Kiyan*. However, Iran's leader, Ayatollah Khamenei, continued to exercise sweeping executive powers, which he did not hesitate to use to thwart Khatami's reforms. Reformist newspapers were accused of offending Islãmic principles and shut down, and agents of the Iranian intelligence services assassinated six prominent intellectuals, including secular nationalist leader Dariyush Farouhar and his wife Parvaneh Eskandari.

In the 1999 elections for roughly 200,000 seats on village, town, and city councils, reformers once again won overwhelmingly, electing many women to office in rural areas. Vigorously debated was the anti-democratic nature of the office of the *rahbar*, and calls for its removal from the constitution now began to appear in the press. In July 1999 student protests at Tehran University against the closing of the *Salam* newspaper and restrictions on the press provoked retaliation by police and a vigilante group known as Ansar-e Hezbollah; four students were reported killed, and hundreds more were injured or detained. On the day after the attack, 25,000 students staged a sit-in at the university, and within 48 hours demonstrations demanding justice for the murders had erupted in at least 18 major cities. Demonstators called for freedom of the press, an increase in personal liberty, an end to vigilante attacks on universities, and the release of 13 Iranian Jews who had been arrested by the government on allegations they were spying for Israel. This was the first major student demonstration since the 1979 revolution, and it lasted for five days.

In 2001 President Khatami was re-elected by an overwhelming majority, but successive elections in the early twenty-first century would see a return to revolutionary Islāmic values and hard-line conservatism, including enforcement of the dress code, limited recognition of human rights, continued restrictions on the media, and antagonism toward the West.

8

ISLĀMIST FUNDAMENTALISM

Islāmic fundamentalism came to worldwide attention in the West after the Iranian Revolution of 1978–9 and especially after the 2001 September 11 attacks on the United States by al-Qaeda, an international Islāmist terrorist network. Islāmic fundamentalism has swept across much of the Muslim world, from North Africa to South-east Asia. Contemporary Islāmic fundamentalism has manifested itself in personal and political life, from greater emphasis on religious observances such as prayer, fasting, and Islāmic dress, and on family values, to the reassertion of Islām in politics.

Islāmist fundamentalists generally believe that they are engaged in a holy war, or *jihad*, against their evil enemies. Messianism, which plays an important role in Shī'ite Islāmic fundamentalism, is less important in the fundamentalism of the Sunni branch of Islām.

Islāmism has as its goal the reordering of government and society in accordance with the law of Islām. Islāmist parties can be found in nations throughout the Muslim world, including Algeria, Egypt, Pakistan, Afghanistan, and Turkey.

Although there are regional differences among the various Islāmist groups, there are a number of common traits, especially the belief that Islām is a comprehensive ideology that offers a blueprint for social and political order. Islāmism is primarily an urban phenomenon and one brought on by the urbanization of the Muslim world. It is not, however, motivated by the discontent of the poor or of displaced peasants but is rather a movement of lower-middle- and middle-class professionals. Many Islāmists are university graduates, some with degrees from Western institutions. Among the ranks of the Islāmist parties are doctors, educators, engineers, lawyers, and scientists. There are also 'ulama' ("the learned", or religious teachers) in the leadership, and all Islāmists possess at least some knowledge of the holy texts.

Islāmism is characterized by a number of shared values. The most important trait is a rejection of Western models of government and economics, both capitalism and communism. Islāmists tend to believe that Muslim society has been corrupted by the secularism, consumerism, and materialism of the West. As a consequence, Islāmists generally advocate a new Hijrah (emigration), a flight from the corrupting influence of an alien, Western culture. Islāmism is not a completely negative ideology, however, and the Hijrah itself can be seen as a flight toward a better Muslim society. Islāmists look back to the golden age of Islām, before the arrival of the Westerners, and hope to restore the traditional values and social relations that characterized that period.

It is Islām itself that holds the key to societal reform, because it is not just a collection of beliefs and rituals, but an all-embracing ideology to guide public and private life. Islāmists, therefore, look to the teachings of Islām and, especially, to Islāmic law (Sharī'ah) as the key to the creation of a better social order.

Among the economically and politically disaffected populations of the Islāmic world a radical Islāmism has emerged.
The more well-known radical groups include Hamas in
Palestine, Hezbollah in Lebanon, and the Taliban in Afghanistan. Lesser-known organisations include Egypt's al-Jamā'a
al-Islāmiya (Islāmic Group), which battles the government
and attacks and kills Coptic Christians and foreign tourists,
and Saudi Arabia's Sunni Islāmist Committee for the Defence
of Legitimate Rights (CDLR), which organized mass Islāmist
demonstrations and was connected to bombings; subsequently outlawed by the Sa'ud family, whose legitimacy it
threatened, it thereafter operated in London, until it broke
apart in 1996. Although these groups have been accused of
terrorist acts, however, Islāmism itself is not intrinsically
violent and can be a movement of peaceful social and
political reform.

Origins of Contemporary Fundamentalism

Muslim belief and history have provided the sources for the
world view of Islāmic activists. A Muslim's duty is obedience
and submission (*islām*) to the will of God. However, the
submission incumbent upon the Muslim is not mere passivity
or acceptance of a set of dogmas or rituals; rather, it is
submission to the divine command, to strive (*jihad*) to actively
realize God's will in history. Thus, the Qur'ān declares that
Muslims are God's vicegerents, or representatives, on earth;
that God has given creation to humankind as a divine trust;
and that realization of God's will leads to eternal reward or
punishment. Islāmic activists believe that religion is integral to
every aspect of life: prayer, fasting, politics, law, and society.
This belief is reflected not only in Islām's doctrine of *tawhid*

(oneness of God, or monotheism) but also in the development
of the Islāmic state and Shar'iah.

The resurgence of Islām has many and varied causes. Widespread failures (the 1967 Arab–Israeli war, Malay–Chinese
riots in 1969, Bangladesh's war of succession from Pakistan
in 1971, and the Lebanese civil war in the mid-1970s) served as
catalysts. As a result of such events, Muslims experienced a
sense of impotence and loss of self-esteem, as well as disillu-
sionment with the West and with governments that failed to
respond to the needs of their societies. The 1973 Arab–Israeli
war and Arab oil embargo and the Iranian revolution of 1978–9
produced a newfound sense of pride and power.

The negative effects of modernization are equally important
in understanding the Islāmic resurgence. They include massive
migration from villages and rapid urbanization of over-
crowded cities; the breakdown of traditional family, religious,
and social values; and the adoption of a Western lifestyle,
enthusiastically pursued as a symbol of modernity but also
criticized as a source of moral decline and spiritual malaise,
corruption, unemployment, and maldistribution of wealth.

For the vast majority of Muslims, the resurgence of Islām is
a reassertion of cultural identity, formal religious observance,
family values, and morality. The establishment of an Islāmic
society is seen as requiring a personal and social transformation that is a prerequisite for true Islāmic government. Effective
change is to come from below through a gradual social
transformation brought about by implementation of Islāmic
law.

On the other hand, a significant minority views the societies
and governments in Muslim countries as hopelessly corrupt.
They believe that un-Islāmic societies and their leaders are no
better than infidels and that the religious establishment has
been co-opted by the government. Such critics believe that

both established political and religious elites must be over-thrown and a new Islāmically committed leadership chosen and Islāmic law imposed. These radical revolutionary groups, though relatively small in membership, have proved effective in political agitation, disruption, and assassination. They have not, however, been successful in mobilizing the masses.

By the late 1980s and early 1990s, a number of diverse Islāmic movements were evident. A minority of radical extremists, with names like Islāmic Jihad, Hezbollah, the Islāmic Liberation Front, and the Islāmic Group, existed in many parts of the Muslim world. Islāmically inspired organizations also ran schools, clinics, hospitals, banks, and publishing houses and offered a wide array of social welfare services.

Where governments opened up their political systems, Islāmic organizations participated in elections and emerged as the leading opposition, as in Egypt, Tunisia, and Jordan. In Algeria the Islāmic Salvation Front swept municipal and parliamentary elections in the early 1990s and seemed poised to come to power when the Algerian military intervened. The successes of Islāmic movements in electoral politics led governments such as those in Algeria, Tunisia, and Egypt to engage in political repression, charging that religious extremists threaten to "hijack democracy" – that is, to use the political system to come to power and then impose their will and undermine the stability of society. Iran and The Sudan are often cited to support concerns about democracy and pluralism, in particular as governments that deny the rights of minorities and women.

Islāmist movements have been politically significant in most Muslim countries primarily because they articulate political and social grievances better than do the established secular parties, some of which (the leftist parties) were discredited following the collapse of communism in eastern Europe and the Soviet Union in 1990–91. Although the governments of Saudi Arabia and other oil-producing countries of the Persian Gulf region have represented themselves as conforming strictly to Islāmic law, they continue to face internal opposition from Islāmist movements for their pro-Western political and economic policies, the extreme concentration of their countries' wealth in the hands of the ruling families, and, in the Islāmists' view, the rulers' immoral lifestyles.

To some extent, the Islāmists' hostility toward the West is symptomatic of the rejection of modernity. But another important factor is the Islāmists' resentment of Western political and economic domination of the Middle East. This is well illustrated by the writings of Osama bin Laden, the founder and leader of al-Qaeda, which repeatedly condemn the United States for enabling the dispossession of the Palestinians, for orchestrating international sanctions on Iraq that contributed to the deaths of hundreds of thousands of Iraqi citizens in the 1990s, and for maintaining a military "occupation" of Saudi Arabia during the Persian Gulf War (1990–91). Bin Laden also condemned the Saudi regime and most other governments of the Middle East for serving the interests of the United States rather than those of the Islāmic world. Thus, the fundamentalist dimension of bin Laden's world view is interwoven with resentment of Western domination.

Hamas

Among the Islāmist movements that have attracted the most attention in the West is the militant Palestinian movement Hamas, which is formally dedicated to the destruction of Israel and the creation of an Islāmic state in Palestine. This position brought it into conflict with the PLO, which in 1988 recognized Israel's right to exist. There is clearly a nationalist dimension to this movement, though it is also committed to the creation of a strictly Islāmic state.

Hamas opposed the idea of a Palestinian state in the West Bank and Gaza and insisted on fighting a *jihad* to expel the Israelis from all of Palestine – from the Jordan River to the Mediterranean and from Lebanon to Egypt. It justified its terrorist attacks on Israelis as legitimate acts of war against an occupying power. Like some other Islāmist movements in the Middle East, Hamas provides basic social services – including schools, clinics, and food for the unemployed – that are not provided, or are inadequately provided, by local authorities. These charitable activities are an important source of its appeal among the Palestinian population.

From the late 1970s, Islāmic activists connected with the pan-Islāmic Muslim Brotherhood (see below) established a network of charities, clinics, and schools and became active in the Gaza Strip and West Bank territories occupied by Israel after the 1967 Six-Day War. The Muslim Brotherhood's activities in these areas were generally non-violent, but a number of small groups in the occupied territories began to call for *jihad*, or holy war, against Israel. In December 1987, at the beginning of the Palestinian *intifāda* against Israeli occupation, Hamas was established by members of the Muslim Brotherhood and religious factions of the PLO, and the new organization quickly acquired a broad following.

Hamas's armed wing, the 'Izz al-Dīn al-Qassam Forces, began a campaign of terrorism against Israel. Israel responded by imprisoning the founder of Hamas, Shaykh Aḥmad Yasin, in 1991 and arresting and deporting hundreds of Hamas activists. Hamas denounced the 1993 peace agreement between Israel and the PLO and, along with Islāmic Jihad, subsequently intensified its terror campaign using suicide bombers. The

PLO and Israel responded with harsh security and punitive measures, although PLO chairman Yāsir 'Arafāt, seeking to include Hamas in the political process, appointed Hamas members to leadership positions in the Palestinian Authority (PA). The collapse of peace talks between Israelis and Palestinians in September 2000 led to an increase in violence that came to be known as the Aqsa *intifāda*. That conflict was marked by a degree of violence unseen in the first *intifāda*, and Hamas activists further escalated their attacks on Israelis and engaged in a number of suicide bombings in Israel itself.

In early 2005 Mahmoud Abbas, president of the PA, and Israeli Prime Minister Ariel Sharon announced a suspension of hostilities as Israel prepared to withdraw troops from some Palestinian territories. After much negotiation, Hamas agreed to the ceasefire, although sporadic violence continued. In the 2006 elections for the Palestinian Legislative Council, Hamas won a surprise victory over the moderate Fatah, capturing the majority of seats. The two groups eventually formed a coalition government, though clashes between Hamas and Fatah forces in the Gaza Strip intensified, prompting Abbas to dissolve the Hamas-led government and declare a state of emergency in June 2007. A new Palestine–Israel peace initiative was launched, the negotiating process aimed at reaching a final peace deal by the end of 2008. Throughout 2007, however, Hamas persisted in its refusal to recognize Israel, and on September 19 Israel declared Gaza an "enemy entity".

Muslim Brotherhood

The Muslim Brotherhood (Al-ikhwan Al-muslimun) was founded in 1928 at Isma'iliyah, Egypt, by Hasan al-Banna'. It advocated a return to the Qur'ān and the Hadith as guidelines for a healthy, modern Islāmic society. The brother-hood spread rapidly throughout Egypt, the Sudan, Syria, Palestine, Lebanon, and North Africa.

After 1938 the Muslim Brotherhood began to politicize its outlook. It demanded purity of the Islāmic world and rejected Westernization, secularization, and modernization. The brotherhood organized a terrorist arm, and when the Egyptian government seemed to weaken in the mid-1940s, the brother-hood posed a threat to the monarchy and the ruling Wafd Party. With the advent of the revolutionary regime in Egypt in 1952, the brotherhood retreated underground. An attempt to assas-sinate Egyptian president Gamal Abdel Nasser in Alexandria on October 26 1954 led to the Muslim Brotherhood's forcible suppression. Six of its leaders were tried and executed for treason, and many others were imprisoned. In the 1960s and 1970s the brotherhood's activities remained largely clandestine.

In the 1980s the Muslim Brotherhood experienced a renew-al as part of the general upsurge of religious activity in Islāmic countries. Its new adherents aimed to reorganize society and government according to Islāmic doctrines, and they were vehemently anti-Western. An uprising by the Muslim Brother-hood in the Syrian city of Hamah in February 1982 was crushed by the government of Hafiz al-Assad at a cost of thousands of lives. The Brotherhood revived in Egypt and Jordan in the same period and, beginning in the late 1980s, its political arm, the Political Action Front, emerged to compete in legislative elections in those countries.

Hezbollah

Hezbollah (Hizb Allāh; "Party of God") is a militia group and political party that first emerged as a faction in Lebanon following the Israeli invasion of that country in 1982. Shīʿite Muslims, traditionally the weakest religious group in Lebanon, first found their voice in the moderate, and largely secular, Amal movement. Following the Islāmic Revolution in Shīʿite Iran in 1979 and the Israeli invasion in 1982, a group of Lebanese Shīʿite clerics formed Hezbollah with the goal of driving Israel from Lebanon and establishing an Islāmic state there. Based in the predominately Shīʿite areas of the Biqaʾ Valley, southern Lebanon, and southern Beirut, Hezbollah coordinated its efforts closely with Iran, whence it acquired substantial logistical support, and drew its manpower largely from disaffected younger and more radical members of Amal.

Throughout the 1980s Hezbollah engaged in increasingly sophisticated attacks against Israel and fought in Lebanon's civil war (1975–90), during which it repeatedly came to blows with Amal. Although Hezbollah allegedly engaged in terrorist attacks, including kidnappings and car bombings, directed predominantly against Westerners, it also established a comprehensive social-services network for its supporters. Hezbollah was one of the few militia groups not disarmed by the Syrians at the end of the civil war, and it continued to fight a sustained guerrilla campaign against Israel in southern Lebanon until Israel's withdrawal in 2000. Hezbollah emerged as a leading political party in post-civil-war Lebanon.

On July 12 2006, Hezbollah, in an attempt to pressure Israel into releasing three Lebanese jailed in Israeli prisons, launched a military operation against Israel, killing a number of Israeli soldiers and abducting two as prisoners of war. This action prompted Israel to launch a major military offensive against Hezbollah. The 34-day war between Hezbollah and Israel resulted in the deaths of 1,000 Lebanese and the displacement of some one million. Fighting the vaunted Israeli Defence Forces to a standstill – a feat no other Arab militia had accomplished – Hezbollah and its leader, Hassan Nasrallah, emerged as heroes throughout much of the Arab world. Within Lebanon, Hezbollah used its prestige to attempt to topple the government, with Hezbollah's members (along with those of the Amal militia) resigning from the cabinet in the months following the war.

Al-Qaeda

Al-Qaeda ("the Base"), a broad-based Islãmic terrorist organization founded by Osama bin Laden, began as a logistical network to support Muslims fighting against the Soviet occupation of Afghanistan; members were recruited throughout the Islãmic world. Like thousands of other Muslims, bin Laden, one of more than 50 children of one of Saudi Arabia's wealthiest families, joined the Afghan resistance shortly after the Soviet Union invaded Afghanistan in 1979, viewing it as his Muslim duty to repel the occupation. After the Soviet withdrawal in 1989, he returned home as a hero, but he was quickly disappointed with what he perceived as the corruption of the Saudi government and of his own family. His objection to the presence of U.S. troops in Saudi Arabia during the Persian Gulf War led to a growing rift with his country's leaders.

By 1993 bin Laden had purportedly formed the early al-Qaeda network, which consisted largely of militant Muslims he had met in Afghanistan. The group continued to oppose what its leaders considered corrupt Islãmic regimes and foreign (particularly U.S.) presence in Islãmic lands. With active members and sympathizers in dozens of countries, the group eventually re-established its headquarters in Afghanistan (c. 1996), where it received the patronage of the country's

Taliban government and merged with other Islāmic extremist organizations, including Egypt's Islāmic Jihad and the Islāmic Group. Aided by bin Laden's considerable wealth, al-Qaeda established training camps for Muslim militants from throughout the world and funded and organized several attacks in the 1990s, including truck-bombings of American targets in Saudi Arabia (1996), the killing of tourists in Egypt (1997), the simultaneous bombings of the U.S. embassies in Nairobi, Kenya, and Dar es Salaam, Tanzania (1998), and a suicide bomb attack against the U.S. warship *Cole* in Aden, Yemen (2000).

In 1996–8 bin Laden, a self-styled scholar, issued a series of *fatwa*s ("religious opinions") declaring a *jihad* against the United States, which he accused, among other things, of looting the natural resources of the Muslim world and aiding and abetting the enemies of Islām. Bin Laden's apparent goal was to draw the United States into a large-scale war in the Islāmic world that would eventually lead to the overthrow of moderate Islāmic governments and the re-establishment of the Caliphate.

In 2001, 19 militants associated with al-Qaeda staged the September 11 attacks against the United States (see Chapter 9). In response, the United States led an international military coalition that attacked Taliban and al-Qaeda forces in Afghanistan, overthrowing the Taliban government, killing and capturing thousands of militants, and driving the remainder and their leaders (including bin Laden) into hiding. Despite the subsequent capture of several key al-Qaeda members (including the militant who allegedly planned and organized the September 11 attacks), the organization and its sympathizers purportedly continued to stage acts of terrorism throughout the world.

The Taliban

The Taliban (Persian: *Taleban*, "Students") is an ultra-conservative political and religious faction that emerged in Afghanistan in the mid-1990s following the withdrawal of Soviet troops, the collapse of Afghanistan's communist regime, and the subsequent breakdown in civil order. The group took its name from its membership, which consisted largely of students trained in *madrasah*s (religious schools) that were established for Afghan refugees in the 1980s in northern Pakistan. In a short time the students were joined by others, including members of the *mujahideen* and fighters formerly associated with the communists – many of whom were induced to switch sides by generous payments funded by the government of Saudi Arabia, then a major Taliban supporter.

The Taliban emerged as a force for social order in 1994 in the southern Afghan province of Kandahar and quickly subdued the local warlords who controlled the south of the country. The movement's spiritual and political leader was a former *mujahideen* fighter, Mullah Mohammad Omar, who was best known for his displays of piety and participation in the fight against the Soviet occupation.

By late 1996 popular support for the Taliban among Afghanistan's southern Pashtun ethnic group, as well as assistance from conservative Islāmic elements abroad, particularly from Pakistan, enabled the faction to seize the capital, Kabul, and gain effective control of the country. Resistance to the Taliban continued, however, particularly among non-Pashtun ethnic groups – namely the Tajik, Uzbek, and Hazara – in the north, west, and central parts of the country, who saw the power of the predominantly Pashtun Taliban as a continuation of the traditional Pashtun hegemony of the country. By 2001 the

Taliban controlled all but a small section of northern Afghanistan.

Pakistan, Saudi Arabia, and the United Arab Emirates gave formal recognition to the Taliban government, but the movement was denied Afghanistan's seat at the UN. World opinion largely disapproved of the Taliban's social policies – including the near-total exclusion of women from public life (including employment and education), the systematic destruction of non-Islāmic artistic relics (as occurred in the town of Bamian), and the implementation of harsh criminal punishments. More significant was the fact that the Taliban allowed Afghanistan to become a haven for Islāmic militants from throughout the world, including Osama bin Laden, the leader of al-Qaeda. The Taliban's refusal to extradite bin Laden to the United States following the 2001 September 11 attacks prompted a military confrontation with the United States and allied powers as described above (see also Chapter 9). The Taliban was subsequently driven from power. In the early twenty-first century, however, Taliban resistance would increase, with growing support particularly in the Pashtun tribal areas, and there would be an upsurge in targeted attacks and suicide bombings in Kabul and across the country.

9

THE TWENTY-FIRST CENTURY

September 11 Attacks and Their Aftermath

During the late twentieth century the radical Islāmic fundamentalism that had swept across much of the Muslim world
erupted in militancy and terrorism against the West. While
many fundamentalists maintained their fight for peaceful,
albeit radical, reform, Islāmist terrorist networks used violent
means. Perhaps the most extreme example was the 2001
September 11 attacks by al-Qaeda on the World Trade Center
and the Pentagon in the United States, which shocked the
world. These attacks initiated a flood of events that affected all
aspects of life in all corners of the world. Yet seven years later,
in 2008, Osama bin Laden, the leader of al-Qaeda and the man
held responsible for the September 11 attacks, remained at
large, his Taliban supporters in Afghanistan were still active,
and many of the issues between Islāmist extremists and Western democracies were unresolved.

On September 11 2001, groups of attackers boarded four
domestic aircraft at three East Coast airports in the United

States and, soon after take-off, disabled the crews and took control of the planes. The hijackers, most of whom were from Saudi Arabia, had previously established themselves in the United States, many well in advance of the attacks. The air-craft, all large and bound for the West Coast, had full loads of fuel. At 8.46 a.m. (local time) the terrorists piloted the first plane, which had originated from Boston, into the north tower of the World Trade Center in New York City. A second plane, also from Boston, struck the south tower roughly 15 minutes later. Each structure was badly damaged by the impact and erupted into flames. A third plane, from the Washington, D.C. area, struck the south-west side of the Pentagon just outside the city at 9.40, touching off a fire in that section of the structure. Within the next hour the fourth aircraft (from Newark, New Jersey) crashed in the Pennsylvania countryside after its passengers – informed of events via cellular phone – attempted to overpower their assailants.

At 9.59 the World Trade Center's heavily damaged south tower collapsed; the north tower fell about half an hour later. A number of other buildings adjacent to the twin towers suffered serious damage, and several subsequently fell. Rescue operations began almost immediately, as the country and the world sought to come to grips with the enormity of the losses. Some 2,750 people were killed in New York, 184 at the Pentagon, and 40 in Pennsylvania; all 19 terrorists died; more than 400 police officers and fire-fighters were killed.

The emotional distress caused by the attacks – particularly the collapse of the twin towers, New York City's most visible landmark – was overwhelming. Hundreds of thousands of people witnessed the attacks first-hand, and millions watched the tragedy unfold on television. World markets were badly shaken; the towers were at the heart of New York's financial

Domes of a mosque silhouetted against the sky, Malaysia.

The Prophet's Mosque in Medina, Saudi Arabia, contains the tomb of
Muḥammad and is one of the three holiest places of Islām.

(*above*) Nearly one million pilgrims in prayer at the Great Mosque in Mecca, Saudi Arabia. The Ka'bah is a small shrine located near the centre of the Great Mosque and is considered by Muslims everywhere to be the most sacred spot on Earth. Muslims orient themselves towards this shrine during the five daily prayers, bury their dead facing its meridian, and cherish the ambition of visiting it on pilgrimage, or *hajj*.

(*left*) The angels decorating the Ka'bah at the birth of Muhammad. This miniature is by Lufti Abdullah, master painter at the court of the sultan Murat III (1546–95), and dates from 1594.

The Great Mosque of Damascus, Syria, also known as the Umayyad Mosque. It is the earliest surviving stone mosque, built between AD 705 and 715 by the Umayyad Caliph al-Walid I. The mosque was destroyed by Timur in 1401, rebuilt by the Arabs, and damaged by fire in 1893. Although it could not be restored to its original splendour, the mosque is still an impressive architectural monument.

(*above*) Interior of the Blue Mosque of Ottoman sultan Ahmed I, designed and built by Mehmed Aġa, royal architect to the Ottoman court, between 1609 and 1616. Probably the most well known of all the mosques in Istanbul, it has six minarets instead of the customary four.

(*left*) Ivory casket (15 cm in height) made for al-Mughīrah, son of ʿAbd al-Rahmān III (AD 891–961), the emir of Córdoba, Spain, dating from AD 968. Now in the Louvre, Paris, it is a fine example of early Islāmic decorative art.

An early nineteenth-century prayer rug from the town of Ghiordes (Gördes), western Anatolia (now in Turkey). Prayer rugs are used by Muslims primarily to cover the bare ground or floor while they pray and are characterized by the prayer niche, or *mihrab*, an arch-shaped design at one end of the carpet. The *mihrab* must point toward Mecca while the rug is in use.

An example of Islāmic calligraphy. Because representation of living beings is prohibited in Islām, the centre of the Islāmic artistic tradition lies in work like this, and the word as the medium of divine revelation is a distinguishing feature of Islāmic culture.

The confrontation between radical Islāmic groups and government forces at Lal Masjid (Red Mosque) in Islambad, Pakistan, 2007.

district, and damage to Lower Manhattan's infrastructure, combined with fears of stock market panic, kept New York markets closed for four trading days. Markets afterwards suffered record losses.

Countries allied with the United States rallied to its support. Evidence gathered by the United States soon convinced most governments that al-Qaeda was responsible for the attacks. The group had been implicated in previous terrorist strikes against Americans, and its leader, Osama bin Laden, had made numerous anti-American statements. Al-Qaeda was headquartered in Afghanistan and had forged a close relationship with that country's ruling Taliban militia, which subsequently refused U.S. demands to extradite bin Laden and to terminate al-Qaeda activity there. In early October, U.S. and allied military forces launched an attack that, within months, killed or captured thousands of militants and drove Taliban and al-Qaeda leaders into hiding (see below).

Other nations rushed to America's side, offering condolences and active assistance. The North Atlantic Treaty Organization (NATO) invoked Article 5 of its founding treaty, declaring that the terrorist actions constituted an attack against all NATO members, which would respond – as required by the treaty – as if they had been attacked themselves. Article 5 had never before been invoked. President Putin of Russia phoned the U.S. president and pledged his country's cooperation in a war against terrorism. As a demonstration of support, Australia invoked the Australia–New Zealand–United States (ANZUS) Treaty, putting elements of its armed forces on a higher state of readiness in case they were called upon to assist the United States. On September 19 the Organization of American States agreed by acclamation to invoke the Rio Treaty, a mutual defence pact.

The near unanimity of support for America among political leaders was not so evident on the streets of the world's cities, towns, and villages. Within hours of the attacks, cameras caught Palestinians on the West Bank exulting over the terrorists' successes. Posters carrying the likeness of Osama bin Laden blossomed throughout the Muslim world. Public opinion polls and questioning reporters found that citizens of many lands felt sympathy for the terrorists and antipathy for the United States. In China, government officials censored Internet discussions that included much cheering for a blow struck against American arrogance. A poll taken in Bolivia found that bin Laden was the most admired man in that Andean nation.

Anti-Americanism was nothing new, of course, but this latest strain had special characteristics related to America's overwhelming power and the way it had been used and perceived through the 1990s. By 2001 the new U.S. administration under President George W. Bush was infuriating allies and rivals alike with its unilateral approach to international affairs and its reluctance to join other countries in collective action.

Bush spent most of the first days after the attacks speaking and meeting with foreign leaders, building what he called a new global coalition against terrorism. On September 24 the House of Representatives voted to release $582 million of the $819 million in dues that the United States had been withholding from the United Nations. Concerns that just before September 11 dominated American policy suddenly disappeared. So, for example, Uzbekistan, with its corrupt and authoritarian regime that had been held at arm's length by the United States before September 11, became an important ally and a base for American military operations soon afterwards.

The United States declared a "war on terrorism" and promptly focused on al-Qaeda and its Taliban protectors in Afghanistan. At home, security measures were tightened at such places as airports, government buildings, and sports venues. In 2002, President Bush signed into law the Homeland Security Act, which created the Department of Homeland Security, merging the functions of 22 existing agencies, including the U.S. Coast Guard, the Secret Service, and the Border Patrol. In January 2002 Bush secretly authorized the National Security Agency (NSA) to monitor the international telephone calls and e-mail messages of American citizens and others in the United States without first obtaining an order from the Foreign Intelligence Surveillance Court, as required by the Foreign Intelligence Surveillance Act of 1978. When the spying programme was revealed in news reports in December 2005, the administration insisted that it was justified by a September 2001 joint Congressional resolution that authorized the president to use "all necessary and appropriate force" against those responsible for the September 11 attacks.

In September 2002 Bush announced a new National Security Strategy of the United States of America. It was notable for its declaration that the United States would act "preemptively", using military force if necessary, to forestall or prevent threats to its security by terrorists or "rogue states" possessing biological, chemical, or nuclear weapons – so-called weapons of mass destruction.

Several other states also began taking tough measures to eradicate terrorist groups. Following a mass hostage-taking incident in Moscow in October 2002, the Kremlin announced that it was prepared to strike pre-emptively across international borders in order to stop terrorist actions. Australian Prime Minister John Howard put Australia's security forces on high alert after a terrorist bombing in Bali, Indonesia in which nearly 200 people, including 90 Australian citizens, were killed, and in December 2002 he announced that he was prepared to order pre-emptive strikes against terrorists anywhere in the region.

Afghanistan: Operation Enduring Freedom

Blaming bin Laden for the September 11 attacks, the U.S. turned its military wrath against the Taliban for continuing to protect him. On September 19 2001, the U.S. dispatched more than 100 combat and support aircraft to various bases in the Middle East and the Indian Ocean. A large naval task force was sent to join what was first called Operation Infinite Justice but was later renamed Operation Enduring Freedom, after complaints were received from Muslims. The anti-terrorist coalition constituted for the U.S. war on terrorism included contributions from Germany and Japan, countries that were largely able to overcome their post-Second World War reluctance to deploy armed forces abroad.

Allied air strikes by U.S. and British forces in Afghanistan, aimed at Taliban military targets, began on October 7. Later, U.S. special forces launched ground raids inside the country. The United States enlisted as an ally the anti-Taliban Northern Alliance, the principal remaining opposition to the Taliban in Afghanistan, relying on them to provide the bulk of ground troops for the campaign. The northern city of Mazar-e Sharif fell one month later, and on November 13 the Northern Alliance entered Kabul as Taliban forces fled the capital.

On December 9, with the fall of the Taliban's principal city of Kandahar imminent, American B-52s began carpet bombing a network of caves in the Tora Bora mountains of eastern Afghanistan, the last stronghold of forces loyal to Osama bin Laden and the Taliban. Many Taliban disappeared into the countryside, fled to Pakistan, or shifted their allegiance. On December 15 anti-Taliban Afghan troops, backed by British and American commandos, surrounded a cave where bin Laden and a dwindling force of al-Qaeda fighters were thought to be hiding, but bin Laden was not found.

Afghanistan's Interim Administration 2001–03

International moves to solve the resulting political crisis focused on avoiding the chaos and destruction that had followed the *mujahideen* takeover from the communist government of Mohammad Najibullah in 1992. On November 27 a UN-sponsored conference in Bonn, Germany, convened to settle on an interim government to replace the Taliban. The largest share of delegates represented the Northern Alliance. Supporters of former king Zahir Shah also participated. It was agreed that Hamid Karzai, a Pashtun tribal leader and supporter of the former king, would lead an interim administration for six months, when a *loya jirga*, a traditional Afghan assembly of notables, would choose a new government.

Warlordism and ethnic rivalry were prominent in Afghanistan throughout 2002, yet important steps were taken toward building a stable, democratic social structure based on traditional Afghan values. Karzai sought to maintain balance among the country's ethnic and tribal groups while laying a foundation for national institutions. Security in Kabul was maintained by an International Security Assistance Force (ISAF) of 4,000 to 5,000 troops contributed by 31 countries whose command was rotated among them. U.S. troops did not participate in the ISAF, but they operated throughout the country in an attempt to root out fighters loyal to the ousted Taliban regime or al-Qaeda. Meanwhile, growing numbers of Afghan civilian casualties from American military activity provoked criticism from those who opposed Karzai's friendly relations with the United States.

In March Karzai took initial steps toward the creation of a national army not dependent on tribal or ethnic loyalties. Its projected strength was 50,000, but only a few hundred recruits could be found. Beyond Kabul, Karzai's government depended for support on Tajik militias, led by Karzai's defence minister, Muhammad Qāsim Fahim; tough Uzbek fighters in northern Afghanistan; and the powerful governor of Herat, Ismail Khan, also a Tajik. In the southern and eastern provinces, Pashtun tribes from which the Taliban had drawn the core of its strength, and who constituted more than half of the country's population, expressed dissatisfaction with their share in the government.

In June the country's former king, Mohammad Zahir Shah, returned to Kabul and officially opened an emergency *loya jirga*, as prescribed by the Bonn agreement. The body's most important task was to choose a president of the Transitional Authority that, according to the Bonn agreement, should replace the Interim Authority. Challenges from former president Burhaneddin Rabbani, a Tajik, and from supporters of the former king were avoided when both men withdrew in a demonstration of national unity, and Karzai was elected. His administration included four vice presidents, one each from Afghanistan's Pashtun, Tajik, Uzbek, and Hazara ethnic groups. However, persistent violence, including the assassination of the Pashtun vice president, Haji Abdul Qadir, a bombing in Kabul killing more than two dozen Afghans, and an attempted shooting of Karzai in

Kandahar, demonstrated the government's continued vulner-ability to breakdowns in public security.

In 2003, preparations began to register Afghans for a general election in June 2004, when a fully representative government was to be formed under the Bonn agreement timetable. In November the government announced the draft of a new constitution that was submitted to a special *loya jirga*. Some Afghans criticized the government for having invited public debate only after the constitution was drafted, and many advocated strict accordance with Sharī'ah.

In the meantime, Kabul experienced a boom with the in-crease of reconstruction projects paid for with international assistance. Much of the $4.5 billion previously pledged to Afghanistan's reconstruction, however, had not arrived or had already been used for humanitarian aid. In the summer the United States said it would increase its reconstruction aid by $900 million. More than 2.5 million refugees and internally displaced persons had returned to their homes, but many were faced with food shortages and an increased cost of living. When the country's school system reopened in March, five million students, boys and girls, enrolled.

The most serious worry to those working for a stable, democratic Afghanistan was the general deterioration of sec-urity in parts of the country beyond the reach of the central government. U.S. Defense Secretary Donald Rumsfeld visited Kabul in May and declared that major combat activity by U.S. forces there was over. Still, a U.S.-led coalition of 12,500 soldiers battled against terrorist and Taliban opposition throughout the remainder of the year.

The ISAF, for whom responsibility passed to NATO in August 2003, was the security guarantor for areas directly under the control of the central government. In October the UN Security Council authorized NATO to send ISAF troops anywhere in Afghanistan. This was intended as support for President Karzai. Tension had grown between Pakistan and Afghanistan after exchanges of fire between Pakistani troops and Afghans on the Afghan border and the ransacking of Pakistan's embassy in Kabul. Reports of raids and bomb attacks by Taliban fighters also increased. In the summer the Taliban reportedly set up a new command structure for southern Afghanistan, its traditional base of support, and weeks later the establishment of another Taliban command for northern Afghanistan was claimed. Lack of countrywide security caused some, including UN special representative Lakhdar Brahimi, to doubt the possibility of conducting fair elections on schedule. Despite these concerns and continuing instability, a new constitution was ratified on January 4 2004. Nine months later, in October, democratic elections were held in which women were granted the right to vote, and Karzai was elected president.

The Iraq War

The conflict in Iraq consisted of two phases. The first was a brief, conventionally fought war (March–April 2003), in which a combined force of troops from the United States and Britain (with smaller contingents from several other countries) invaded Iraq and rapidly defeated Iraqi military and paramilitary forces. It was followed by a longer second phase in which a U.S.-led occupation of Iraq was opposed by an increasingly intensive armed insurgency. The war was preceded by repeated statements by leaders of the United States and the United Kingdom that Iraq was manufacturing and stockpiling weapons of mass destruction and that it was lending support to terrorist groups, including al-Qaeda.

Although no weapons of mass destruction were found in Iraq, the perceived threat of such weapons falling into the wrong hands was enough to create confrontations between the international community and both Iran and North Korea and to inspire the creation of a new multinational partnership to combat proliferation of such weapons. Bush's decision to start the Iraq War remains controversial.

After Iraq's defeat by a U.S.-led coalition in the Persian Gulf War (1990–91), the Iraqi Ba'th Party, headed by Saddam Hussein, managed to retain power by harshly suppressing uprisings of the country's minority Kurds and its majority Shī'ite Arabs. To stem the exodus of Kurds from Iraq, the allies established a "safe haven" in northern Iraq's predominantly Kurdish regions, and allied warplanes patrolled Iraqi aircraft "no-fly" zones. To restrain future Iraqi aggression, the United Nations (UN) also implemented economic sanctions against Iraq in order to, among other things, hinder the progress of its most lethal arms programmes. UN inspections during the mid-1990s uncovered a variety of proscribed weapons and technology. In 1998 U.S. President Bill Clinton ordered the bombing of several Iraqi military installations (Operation Desert Fox). After the bombing, however, Iraq refused to allow inspectors to re-enter the country.

In November 2002 the Bush administration successfully lobbied for a new Security Council resolution providing for the return of weapons inspectors to Iraq. Although Iraq appeared to comply, Bush soon declared that the country had offered less than full compliance and that it continued to possess weapons of mass destruction. For several weeks, the United States and Britain tried to secure support from other Security Council members for a second resolution explicitly authorizing the use of force against Iraq (though officials of both countries insisted that earlier resolutions provided sufficient legal justification for military action). In response, France and Russia, while agreeing that Iraq had failed to cooperate fully with weapons inspectors, argued that the inspections regime should be continued and strengthened and that a second resolution, which they did not support, would be necessary to justify military action under international law.

As part of the administration's diplomatic campaign, Bush and other officials frequently warned that Iraq possessed weapons of mass destruction, that it was attempting to acquire nuclear weapons, and that it had longstanding ties to al-Qaeda and other terrorist organizations. In his State of the Union address in January 2003, Bush announced that Iraq had attempted to purchase enriched uranium from Niger for use in nuclear weapons. The subsequent determination that some intelligence reports of the purchase had relied on forged documents complicated the administration's diplomatic efforts in the United Nations. Meanwhile, massive anti-war demonstrations took place in several major cities around the world.

Finally, Bush announced the end of U.S. diplomacy. On March 17 he issued an ultimatum to Hussein, giving him and his immediate family 48 hours to leave Iraq or face removal by force; he also indicated that, even if Hussein relinquished power, U.S. military forces would enter the country to search for weapons of mass destruction and to stabilize the new government. After Hussein's public refusal to leave and as the 48-hour deadline approached, Bush ordered the invasion of Iraq, called Operation Iraqi Freedom, to begin on March 20 (local time).

The assault began when U.S. aircraft dropped several precision-guided bombs on a bunker complex in which the Iraqi president was believed to be meeting with senior staff. This was followed by a series of air strikes directed against government and military installations. U.S. and British ground forces then invaded from Kuwait. In southern Iraq the greatest resistance to U.S. forces as they advanced northward was from irregular groups of Ba'th Party supporters, known as Saddam's Fedayeen. British forces – which had deployed around the southern city of Basra – faced similar resistance from paramilitary and irregular fighters. In central Iraq units of the Republican Guard – a heavily armed paramilitary group connected with the ruling party – were deployed to defend the capital of Baghdad.

Baghdad fell to U.S. troops on April 9, and the focus of action then moved to northern Iraq, where U.S.-backed Kurdish forces took control of Kirkuk and Mosul before Hussein's home town of Tikrit fell to U.S. forces on April 14. Bush declared an end to "major combat operations" on May 1. Iraqi leaders fled into hiding and were the object of an intense search by U.S. forces. Saddam Hussein was captured on December 13 2003, and was turned over to Iraqi authorities in June 2004 to stand trial for various crimes; he was subsequently convicted of crimes against humanity and was executed on December 30 2006.

In the wake of the invasion, hundreds of sites suspected of producing or housing weapons of mass destruction within Iraq were investigated. As the search continued without success into the following year, Bush's critics accused him of having misled the country into war by exaggerating the threat posed by Iraq. In 2004 the Iraq Survey Group, a fact-finding mission comprising American and British experts, concluded that Iraq did not possess weapons of mass destruction or the capacity to produce them at the time of the invasion, though it found evidence that Hussein planned to reconstitute programmes for producing such weapons once UN sanctions were lifted. In the same year the bipartisan 9/11 Commission (the National

Commission on Terrorist Attacks Upon the United States) reported that there was no evidence of a "collaborative operational relationship" between Iraq and al-Qaeda.

Iraq Government and Insurgency, 2004–08

As occupying powers, the United States and the United Kingdom established the Coalition Provisional Authority (CPA). Its primary goal was to maintain security and rebuild Iraq's badly damaged and deteriorated infrastructure, but its efforts were widely hampered by an escalating insurgency involving a variety of groups comprising both Iraqis and non-Iraqi fighters from other Arab and Islāmic countries. Prominent among them were remnants of the former Ba'thist regime and a group under the control of Abū Mus'ab al-Zarqawi, a Jordanian-born terrorist linked to al-Qaeda. By July 2003 a provisional Iraqi Interim Governing Council (IGC) had been established under the direction of the CPA. In the months following Bush's declaration of an end to hostilities, attacks on coalition forces became bloodier and more frequent, often numbering more than 30 a day. Civilians and Iraqi police were also increasingly targeted by anti-coalition forces, and the UN and the International Committee of the Red Cross pulled out most of their staffs after fatal bomb attacks.

Following the collapse of the Ba'thist regime, Iraq's major cities erupted in a wave of looting that was directed mostly at government offices and other public institutions, and there were severe outbreaks of violence – both common criminal violence and acts of reprisal against the former ruling clique. Restoring law and order was one of the most arduous tasks for the occupying forces, one that was exacerbated by continued attacks against their troops that soon developed into full-scale guerrilla warfare; increasingly, the conflict came to be identified as a civil war.

After 35 years of Ba'thist rule, three major wars, and a dozen years of economic sanctions, the economy was in a shambles and only slowly began to recover. Moreover, the country remained saddled with a ponderous debt that vastly exceeded its annual gross domestic product, and oil production – the country's single greatest source of revenue – was badly hobbled. In the Shī'ite regions of southern Iraq, many of the local religious leaders who had fled Hussein's regime returned to the country, and Shī'ites from throughout the world were able to resume the pilgrimage to the holy cities of Al-Najaf and Karbala' that had been banned under Hussien. The sectarian violence that engulfed the country caused enormous chaos, however, with brutal killings by rival Shī'ite and Sunni militias. The militia group of Muqtada al-Sadr, a radical Shī'ite cleric, the Mahdi Army, was particularly deadly in its battle against Sunnis and U.S. and Iraqi forces and was considered a major destabilizing force in the country.

Although some European leaders voiced their conditional support for the war and none regretted the end of the violent Ba'thist regime, public opinion in Europe, the Middle East, and other parts of the world remained overwhelmingly against the war. Many viewed it as an act of aggression by the United States intended to secure American access to Iraq's oil resources, and most Arab leaders decried the occupation of a fellow Arab country by foreign troops.

Reaction to the war was initially mixed in the United States, but as violence continued and casualties mounted, more Americans began to criticize the Bush administration for what they perceived to be misleading statements about the threat posed by Iraq in the months leading up to the war, and the mishandling of the subsequent occupation of the country.

In 2004 the appearance in the news of photographs of U.S. soldiers abusing Iraqis at Abu Ghraib prison west of Baghdad – a facility notorious for brutality under the Ba'th regime – further damaged world opinion of the United States. The photographs and other evidence indicated that prisoners held by the U.S. at Abu Ghraib and various other locations had been beaten, sexually assaulted, deprived of sleep and medical attention, frightened by dogs, and subjected to other forms of intimidation, humiliation, and abuse. They were kept naked for days at a time, photographed in that state, and forced to pose in sexually explicit positions. These acts were part of interrogations, supposedly to get prisoners to reveal useful information about terrorist activities. The existence of "ghost detainees" – so called because their identities and locations were being kept secret, potentially in contravention of international law – was also reported.

This treatment violated international humanitarian law, specifically the Geneva Conventions, which prohibited the humiliating or degrading treatment of prisoners of war. According to investigators from the International Committee of the Red Cross, some of the abuses could be classified as torture and therefore violated not only the Geneva Conventions but also the International Covenant on Civil and Political Rights, the Convention Against Torture, and the Universal Declaration of Human Rights.

Several U.S. soldiers were to be jailed for their part in the incidents, and Brig. Gen. Janis Karpinski, the officer in charge of the prison, was suspended. Prisoner abuse scandals also rocked the British, Danish, and Polish contingents in Iraq.

Meanwhile, efforts to hand over control of the government

to the Iraqis continued. In June 2004 the CPA and the governing council were dissolved and political authority passed to an interim government headed by Ghazi al-Yawar. Subsequently Ayad 'Allawi was selected prime minister. On January 30 2005, despite the ongoing violence, general elections were successfully held for Iraq's new 275-member Transitional National Assembly. A draft constitution approved by a national referendum in October 2005 called for a new legislature, the members of which would largely be elected from constituent districts. Sunni Arabs voted overwhelmingly against the new constitution, fearing that it would make them a perpetual minority.

In a general election on December 15, the Shī'ite United Iraqi Alliance (UIA) gained the most seats but not enough to call a government. After four months of political wrangling, Nuri Kamal al-Maliki of the Shī'ite party Islāmic Da'awah formed a coalition government that included both Arabs and Kurds. Kurdish leader Jalal al-Talabani, who was re-elected as president in April 2006, nominated al-Maliki as head of the new government, which included Shī'ite, Sunni, and Kurdish ministers. Al-Maliki vowed to curb violence, restore law and order, and fight corruption in the country, stressing that he was the prime minister of all Iraqis. At the end of June, he presented an ambitious 24-point plan of national reconciliation. While the Kurds and most Shī'ites welcomed the plan, the Sunnis gave only conditional approval, and some Sunnis rejected it outright. They demanded that any such plan include unconditional amnesty for insurgents and a scheduled withdrawal of U.S. and other foreign troops from Iraq before negotiations for reconciliation began.

Political violence continued to grow, especially between Shī'ite and Sunni militia and terror groups and against coalition forces and the police, bringing the country to the brink of civil war and leading to the deaths of tens of thousands of people, including many civilians, on all sides of the struggle. Most of the killings were carried out by armed militias belonging to Muqtada al-Sadr's Shī‘ite Jaysh al-Mahdī and the Firqat-Badr militia of the Supreme Council for the Islāmic Revolution in Iraq. These two militias were able to infiltrate the police force and organize death squads, which carried out violence and retaliation against Sunnis. The Sunni militants were mainly armed terrorist Islāmic groups, such as al-Qaeda, which fought alongside secular Sunni nationalist contingents, such as former Ba'thists. Many Iraqis believed that some neighbouring countries were helping to fuel the violence. The Sunnis accused Iran of intervening to help the Shī‘ites, while the Shī‘ites accused Syria and some Arab Gulf countries of helping Sunni insurgents and Islāmists.

In October 2006, the National Assembly adopted by a very thin margin a law that would allow the establishment of federal regions in Iraq. While one of the major Shī‘ite parties and the Kurds supported this law, Sunni leaders and a number of Shī‘ite deputies opposed it bitterly, saying it would allow the establishment of a semi-autonomous Shī‘ite province in the south, which would lead to more violence in the country and weaken the authority of the central government. The Kurdish community in the north remained more peaceful than the rest of the country and began building up its own institutions and enacting legislation to create a semi-autonomous region.

Five years after the start of the Iraq War, the absence of a shared vision for the future of Iraq continued to be a major problem in achieving effective government in the country. Acts of violence by Sunni insurgents, al-Qaeda partisans, and Shī‘ite militias against the U.S. and Iraqi government forces continued throughout 2007, as did confrontations between Shīʿite militias in many parts of the country. After a confrontation, in August, between the Mahdi Army of Muqtada al-Sadr and forces belonging to the Islāmic Supreme Council of Iraq in Karbalāʾ, Sadr withdrew his group from the United Iraqi Alliance, the main Shīʿite bloc in the parliament. The action was the most dramatic sign of political transformation in Iraq, signalling the fraying of old alliances and the possibility of new groupings. The main Sunni group in the government, the Iraqi Accord Front, withdrew its six ministers to protest, among other things, an alleged "genocide campaign" against the Sunnis. Key legislation remained hostage to protracted negotiations in an unwieldy parliament that could barely muster a quorum.

By the end of 2007, ethnic and sectarian change in Baghdad had left eastern parts of the city with mainly Shīʿite inhabitants (with pockets of Sunni areas mainly in the north and downtown Baghdad). Iraqis (mostly Sunnis) continued to flee to neighbouring countries, mainly Syria and Jordan. In August Turkey and Iraq agreed to clear Turkish Kurdish rebels from northern Iraq, and Turkey threatened to halt cross-border guerrilla attacks by these Kurdish rebels by force if necessary. U.S. and Iraqi officials accused Iran of interfering in Iraq's internal affairs and attempting to destabilize the country by supplying arms and training to militias. In March 2007, talks were held between Iranian, U.S., and Iraqi officials, and the parties agreed to set up a committee to work on Iraq's stabilization.

In late 2006 the Iraq Study Group, an independent bipartisan panel co-chaired by former U.S. Secretary of State James A. Baker III and former U.S. Congressman Lee Hamilton, had issued a report that found the situation in Iraq to be "grave and deteriorating". It advocated region-wide diplomatic efforts to resolve the conflict and called for the U.S. military role to evolve into one that provided diminishing support for an Iraqi government that should assume responsibility for the country's security. In 2007, however, seeking to stabilize Iraq, Bush announced a controversial plan to increase the number of U.S. troops there. Some success was achieved in reducing violence in Al-Anbar province, where Sunni Arab tribes, supported by the United States, had formed a unified front called the Anbar Salvation Council to fight al-Qaeda, and in Diyala province, where the United States tried to bring about some reconciliation between Shī'ite and Sunni tribes, urging them to cooperate in the fight against insurgents and al-Qaeda groups. There was a decrease in the number of attacks and casualties in Baghdad and western Iraq.

In September 2007, however, the commander of the U.S. forces in Iraq told the U.S. Congress that he envisioned a gradual withdrawal of 30,000 troops from Iraq starting in the spring of 2008. The same month the British government reduced its troop levels and began to withdraw those that remained from the city of Basra to bases outside the city. These moves were aimed at paving the way for a complete withdrawal in the future. Iraqi security forces took over positions previously held by the British. The U.S. Senate also passed a non-binding resolution aimed at partitioning Iraq along ethnic and sectarian lines – Kurdish, Sunni, and Shī'ite; these units, however, would be kept inside Iraq in a loose federation. Though the Kurds welcomed the resolution, the plan was met with criticism by other Iraqis and by Arab countries.

Treatment of Suspected Terrorists and the Norms of International Law

The applicability of the accepted rules of war to the conflict in Afghanistan and to the war on terrorism generally came under special scrutiny. Once the invasion of Afghanistan began in October 2001, the Bush administration declared that captured members of the al-Qaeda terrorist organization were "unlawful combatants" who had no right to protection under international law. Furthermore, such persons could be held indefinitely without formal charges under powers that Congress granted the president to fight terrorism. The administration also said it would apply the Geneva Conventions to soldiers of Afghanistan's deposed Taliban regime but would not grant them status as prisoners of war.

In January 2002, as the pacification of Afghanistan continued, the United States began transferring captured Taliban fighters and suspected al-Qaeda members from Afghanistan to a special prison at the country's permament naval base in Guantánamo Bay, Cuba. Eventually hundreds of prisoners from more than 30 countries – including the United Kingdom, France, and Australia – were held at the facility without charge and without the legal means to challenge their detentions (habeas corpus).

Under the Geneva Conventions, parties to an armed conflict have the right to capture and intern enemy combatants as well as civilians who pose a danger to the security of the state. The detaining power has the right to punish enemy soldiers and civilians for crimes committed prior to their capture as well as during captivity, but only after a fair trial in accordance with applicable international law. The Geneva Conventions stipulate that prisoners of war should be tried in a military court unless the existing laws of the detaining power permit trials of its own military personnel in a civil court for the same offence. Prisoners of war have the right to defence by a qualified advocate or counsel of their own choice, to the calling of witnesses, and, if they deem it necessary, to the services of a competent interpreter. According to the International Committee of the Red Cross (ICRC), all detainees taken in war are protected by the Geneva Conventions, and violations of the accords may constitute either war crimes or crimes against humanity.

The prison at Guantánamo became the focus of international controversy in June 2004, after a confidential report by the ICRC found that significant numbers of prisoners had been interrogated by means of techniques that were "tantamount to torture". The leak of the report came just two months after the publication of the photographs of abusive treatment of prisoners by U.S. soldiers at Abu Ghraib. In response to the Abu Ghraib revelations, the U.S. Congress eventually passed the Detainee Treatment Act, which banned the "cruel, inhuman, or degrading" treatment of prisoners in U.S. military custody. Although the measure became law with Bush's signature in December 2005, he added a "signing statement" in which he reserved the right to set aside the law's restrictions if he deemed them inconsistent with his constitutional powers as commander-in-chief.

In June 2006 the U.S. Supreme Court declared that the system of military commissions that the administration had intended to use to try selected prisoners at Guantánamo on charges of war crimes was in violation of the Geneva Conventions and the Uniform Code of Military Justice, which governs American rules of courts martial. Later that year, Congress passed the Military Commissions Act, which gave the commissions the express statutory basis that the court had found lacking; the law also prevented enemy combatants who were not American citizens from challenging their detention in the federal courts.

In separate programmes run by the Central Intelligence Agency (CIA), dozens of individuals suspected of involvement in terrorism were abducted outside the United States and held in secret prisons in eastern Europe and elsewhere or transferred for interrogation to countries that routinely practised torture. Although such extrajudicial transfers, or "extraordinary renditions", had taken place during the Clinton administration, the Bush administration greatly expanded the practice after the September 11 attacks. Press reports of the renditions in 2005 sparked controversy in Europe and led to official investigations into whether some European governments had knowingly permitted rendition flights through their countries' territories, an apparent violation of the human rights law of the European Union.

In February 2005 the CIA confirmed that some individuals in its custody had been subjected to "enhanced interrogation techniques", including waterboarding (simulated drowning), which was generally regarded as a form of torture under international law. The CIA's position that waterboarding did not constitute torture had been based on the legal opinions of the Justice Department and specifically on a secret memo issued in 2002 that adopted an unconventionally narrow and legally questionable definition of torture. After the memo was leaked to the press in June 2004, the Justice Department rescinded its opinion. In 2005, however, the department issued new secret memos declaring the legality of enhanced interrogation techniques, including waterboarding. The new memos were revealed in news reports in 2007, prompting outrage from critics of the administration. In July 2007 Bush issued an executive order that prohibited the CIA from using torture or acts of cruel, inhuman, or degrading treatment, though the specific interrogation techniques it was allowed to use remained classified. In March 2008 Bush vetoed a bill directed specifically at the CIA that would have prevented the agency from using any interrogation technique, such as waterboarding, that was not included in the U.S. Army's field manual on interrogation.

Islāmic Republic of Afghanistan

Under the new constitution ratified on January 4 2004, Afghanistan was declared an Islāmic republic. The constitution prohibited laws that were contrary to the tenets of Islām, but it also promised that followers of other religions would be free to exercise their faiths and specified individual rights of the kind found in many Western democratic constitutions. It guaranteed women equal rights with men and made specific provision for women's education and social welfare. International reaction was generally positive; the U.S. ambassador to Afghanistan, Zalmay Khalilzad, called the results "one of the most enlightened constitutions in the Islāmic world."

Security fears and the threat of violence from terrorist groups, as well as armed disputes over regional and ethnic issues, posed a continuing problem, however. As elections approached, NATO pledged to increase its International Security Assistance Force (ISAF) to 8,500 troops. U.S.-led forces charged with hunting down the Taliban and capturing al-Qaeda leader Osama bin Laden were enlarged to 18,500, and their brief was expanded to include economic, political, and social development. U.S. military officials promised an expanded programme of "provincial reconstruction teams" to strengthen central and local government through village development.

Security fears and difficulties in registering Afghanistan's estimated 10 million voters forced a postponement of the elections until October 2004. The Pashtun Hamid Karzai won the election and was sworn in as president on December 7. His choice of running mates – Ahmad Zia Masoud, the brother of assassinated Tajik *mujahideen* hero Ahmad Shah Masoud, and Hazara leader Karim Khalili – demonstrated the importance of ethnic balance in the country's new democracy.

In 2005 Afghanistan appeared to move toward constitutional stability and economic growth, but widespread incidents of violence made it clear that the Taliban and other fundamentalist guerrillas remained a serious threat to Karzai's government. Violence by the Taliban escalated; in June a suicide bomber killed 20 people in Kandahar's main mosque, including Kabul's security chief, who was attending the funeral of an anti-Taliban cleric killed three days earlier. Anti-American demonstrations in several locations were stoked by press reports that claimed that U.S. authorities at the prison in Guantánamo Bay, Cuba, had desecrated the Qur'ān. At least 14 deaths were reported.

The process outlined in the Bonn agreement of December 2001, by which Afghanistan's state structure would be rebuilt, approached completion with the September 18 election of the Wolesi Jirga, the lower house of Afghanistan's National Assembly, and provincial and local councils across the country. The constitution required at least two female delegates from each of Afghanistan's 34 provinces, and election officials said that almost 350 of some 2,900 candidates were female. Though Taliban guerrillas had promised not to disrupt the polling, they carried out a deadly campaign of violence leading up to the elections and killed several candidates and election workers.

Afghanistan's economic progress was stymied by bad roads, land mines, lack of electricity, and a poor educational system, as well as security concerns and the weakness of the central government. The greatest threat to economic recovery, however, remained the nationwide economic dependence on opium production. Relations with neighbouring Pakistan were strained as Kabul officials continued to assert that *madrasah*s and camps in Pakistan were providing training and refuge for fighters carrying out anti-government attacks and killings inside Afghanistan. India, which had traditionally sought good relations with Afghanistan, directed its assistance at education, health care, power sectors, and training for civil servants and police. Besides seeking to moderate Pakistan's influence, India viewed Afghanistan as its gateway to trade and communication with Central Asia.

In 2006, five years after the overthrow of the Taliban, the government of President Karzai remained dependent upon international military assistance to face the threat of growing armed resistance. With no fighting force at his own command, Karzai was compelled to seek support from ethnic and provincial leaders supported by militias with little loyalty to the central government. A U.S.-trained Afghan National Army undertook its first serious engagement in the 2006 summer offensive, but its reliability remained uncertain. In addition to escalating violence, opium production, which had increased by 50 per cent since 2005, threatened to undermine the country's economy and reinforced local support for the Taliban.

By early spring it was obvious that Helmand province in the south had become an effective base of Taliban operations, with as many as 5,000 Taliban fighters in the area. In May, U.S. and NATO units together with the Afghan army opened a massive offensive, Operation Mountain Thrust, using armoured vehicles and air cover to back up a combined force of more than

10,000 fighters. Fighting continued throughout the summer, and hundreds of Taliban militants were reportedly killed. In July the command of this operation was transferred to ISAF.

President Karzai worked to extend the reach of government authority while balancing the need for international assistance against the appearance of favouring foreign interests over Afghan ones. Opponents who accused Karzai of cooperating with the enemies of Afghanistan and Islām gave support and sanctuary in the Pashtun tribal areas along the Afghanistan–Pakistan border to Taliban fundamentalists sympathetic to al-Qaeda and bin Laden. Heavy fighting continued in 2007, but by midsummer a new Taliban strategy was unfolding: suicide bombing, kidnapping, and other tactics similar to those used by al-Qaeda in Iraq were becoming typical of the resistance.

Many ordinary Afghans had become disillusioned when the hopeful optimism that followed the fall of the Taliban produced so little positive change in their lives. In an attempt to ease factionalism, the parliament passed, and in March 2007 Karzai approved, a controversial national reconciliation bill granting amnesty to all Afghans involved in the country's 25 years of occupation and conflict – Taliban as well as *mujahideen*. Critics of the bill feared that it would allow those responsible for war crimes to go unpunished, but others insisted that national reconciliation was necessary to secure the country's future.

Islām, Religious Pluralism, and the West

At the end of 2007, despite several years having passed since the wars in Afghanistan and Iraq, U.S. and coalition counter-insurgency forces remained in both countries, and anti-Western attacks, sometimes sparked by civilian casualties, continued. Since September 11 2001 there have been further attacks by Islāmist terrorists on the West. On October 12 2002, a massive bomb blast at a nightclub on the Indonesian island of Bali killed 184 people, the majority of whom were Western tourists. Under intense international pressure, the Megawati government of Indonesia supported a United Nations motion to ban the Jemaah Islāmiyah terrorist network and faced growing demands to act against radical Islāmist groups. On March 11 2004, Madrid suffered a devastating series of terrorist attacks when ten bombs, detonated by Islāmist militants, exploded on four trains at three different rail stations during rush hour. The attacks killed 191 people and injured some 1,800 others. Then on July 7 2005, London suffered a series of coordinated terrorist attacks, believed to have been carried out by Muslim extremists, on Underground trains and a double-decker bus, killing more than 50 people and injuring some 700 others.

There were also, however, efforts to reconcile Islām with secular societies and religious pluralism. In an unprecedented letter to world Christian leaders in October 2007, 138 Muslim scholars issued an appeal for peace and understanding between the two religions, saying that "the very survival of the world itself is perhaps at stake". Signers of the letter included the grand muftis of Egypt, Palestine, Oman, Jordan, Syria, Bosnia and Herzegovina, and Russia, as well as representatives of both Shī'ite and Sunni communities in Iraq. The message was addressed to Pope Benedict XVI, Orthodox Ecumenical Patriarch Bartholomew I, Anglican Archbishop Rowan Williams, Orthodox Christian patriarchs, and leaders of the World Council of Churches and the world alliances of the Lutheran, Methodist, Baptist, and Reformed churches. The appeal was welcomed in a response issued by Vatican Secretary of State Tarcisio Bertone on behalf of Pope Benedict, noting its "positive spirit" and praising its "call for a common commitment to promoting peace". The appeal was also praised in a response drafted by four scholars at Yale Divinity School and endorsed by nearly 300 Christian leaders.

In June 2007 the Los Angeles-based Muslim Public Affairs Council said that prejudice and discrimination against Muslims was a "root cause" of radicalism. The organization issued a report that called for "fighting bad theology with good theology" through such means as forming a U.S. government advisory board of young Muslims and placing Muslim chaplains on every American college campus. In an effort to improve intrafaith relations, Shī'ite and Sunni leaders in Costa Mesa, California, Detroit, Michigan, and Washington, D.C. signed a Muslim Code of Honour that denounced *takfir* – the labelling of another Muslim as a heretic – and hateful speech about the practices and leaders of other Muslim groups. The *Washington Post* newspaper reported in September that the U.S. military had created religious training programmes for Iraqi detainees, led by moderate Muslim clerics, to attempt to persuade them to adopt a moderate, non-violent form of Islām.

Meanwhile, outgoing Prime Minister Tony Blair announced that the British government had created a fund to help train Muslim *imām*s in British universities in an effort to reduce the reliance of mosques in the United Kingdom on religious leaders from abroad who might not understand British society. Islāmic studies were designated as "strategically important" to the British national interest. In May, security officials from countries in the European Union announced a plan to profile mosques on the continent and to identify extremist Muslim leaders.

Turkish Foreign Minister Abdullah Gul won parliamentary election as Turkey's president after having campaigned with the Islāmic-influenced Justice and Development Party. Gul affirmed Turkey's status as a secular democracy, and he pledged to "defend and strengthen" the country's values.

The early twenty-first century also saw renewed attempts at peace talks between Israel and the Palestinians, but despite the pull-out of Israeli soldiers and settlers from parts of the West Bank and from all of the Gaza Strip in 2005, tensions continued. In the wake of the war with Lebanon in 2006, Israeli Prime Minister Ehud Olmert, who had promised to pull back to permanent borders by 2010, announced that his plan for further withdrawals from the West Bank was "no longer relevant". On January 25 2006, in a major political upheaval, Hamas won a landslide victory in elections for the Palestinian Legislative Council. Although there was a renewal of the peace process between Israel and the Palestinians the following year, armed groups of Hamas and Fatah supporters within the Gaza Strip fought a series of internecine battles and the region continued to be an area of conflict.

Tensions between extremist factions and reformists or Westerners surfaced again in 2007. In Islāmabad, Pakistan, more than 100 people were killed during eight days of conflict that began with street battles between militants and security forces and ended with a raid on the compound of the Red Mosque. The mosque's leaders and the radical students who supported them wanted to impose Sharī'ah in the capital city. In August about 100 Muslim protesters disrupted a news conference in Hyderabad, India, and assaulted exiled Bangladeshi novelist Taslima Nasrin. Nasrin's writings accused Islām and other religions of denying women's rights and provoking conflict. Gillian Gibbons, a British teacher, was convicted in November in Khartoum, Sudan, of having insulted Islām by allowing her predominantly Muslim students to name a teddy bear Muḥammad. Sentenced to 15 days in prison, she was pardoned after two prominent British Muslims appealed to Sudan's president, Omar al-Bashir.

Despite continuing efforts to deter extremists and promote reconciliation, there is little to suggest that tensions between Islāmist fundamentalists and their perceived enemies will diminish. Rather, support for organisations such as al-Qaeda may have been strengthened among the many young Muslims who have been radicalised by U.S.-led military actions in Iraq and Afghanistan.

PART 4

THE ISLĀMIC ARTS

10

ARCHITECTURE

Early Mosques and Other Religious Buildings

Architecture is by far the most important expression of Islāmic art, particularly the architecture of mosques, or *masjid*s, which were created outside Arabia in every centre taken over by the new faith during its first decades. These were not simply or even primarily religious centres. They were rather the community centres of the faithful, in which all social, political, educational, and individual affairs were transacted.

As well as large mosques for the whole community, such as those erected at Kūfah and Basra in Iraq and at al-Fustat in Egypt, tribal mosques and mosques for various quarters of a town or city are also known. In older urban centres taken over by Muslims, there were two variants. In some places, such as Jerusalem and Damascus, and perhaps in most cities conquered through formal treaties, the Muslims took an available unused space and erected on it some shelter, usually a very primitive one. Alternatively, they forcibly transformed sanctuaries of older faiths into Muslim ones. This was the case at Hamah in Syria and at Yazd-e Khvast in Iran.

The new faith's requirement for centralization, or a space for a large and constantly growing community, seems to have demanded the creation of a new architectural type, developed in Iraq: the hypostyle mosque (a building with the roof resting on rows of columns). A hypostyle structure could be square or rectangular and could be increased or diminished in size by the addition or subtraction of columns. The single religious or symbolic feature was a *minbar* (pulpit) for the preacher, and the direction of prayer was indicated by the greater depth of the colonnade on one side of the structure.

During the rule of the Umayyad caliph al-Walīd I (705–15), a number of complex developments within the Muslim community were crystallized in the construction of three major mosques at Medina, Jerusalem, and Damascus. The very choice of these three cities is indicative: they comprise the city in which the Muslim state was formed and in which the Prophet was buried; the city held in common holiness by Jews, Christians, and Muslims, to which was rapidly accruing the mystical hagiography surrounding the Prophet's Nocturnal Ascent into heaven; and the ancient city that became the capital of the new Islāmic empire. Thus they were to symbolize the permanent establishment of the new faith and of the state that derived from it.

At first glance the three buildings appear in plan to be quite different from each other. The Medina mosque was essentially a large hypostyle with a courtyard, with colonnades on all four sides. Al-Aqsa Mosque in Jerusalem consisted of an undetermined number of parallel naves but no courtyard, because the rest of the huge esplanade of the former Jewish temple served as the open space in front of the building. The Umayyad Mosque of Damascus is a rectangle whose outer limits and three gates are parts of a Roman temple, with an interior consisting of an open space surrounded on three sides by a portico and a covered space of three equal long naves parallel to the *qiblah* wall (in the direction to which Muslims offer prayers), which are cut in the middle by a perpendicular nave.

The three buildings, however, share important characteristics. They are all large spaces with a multiplicity of internal supports; and although only the Medina mosque is a pure hypostyle, the Jerusalem and Damascus mosques have the flexibility and easy internal communication characteristic of a hypostyle building. All three exhibit a number of distinctive new practical elements and symbolic meanings. The *mihrab*, a heavily decorated niche in the *qiblah* wall, probably commemorates the symbolic presence of the Prophet as the first *imām*. It is in Damascus only that the ancient towers of the Roman building were first used as minarets to call the faithful to prayer and to indicate from afar the presence of Islām (initially minarets tended to exist only in predominantly non-Muslim cities). All three mosques are also provided with an axial nave, a wider aisle unit on the axis of the building, which served both as a formal axis for compositional purposes and as a ceremonial one for the prince's retinue. Finally, all three buildings were heavily decorated with marble, mosaics, and woodwork.

The hypostyle tradition was to dominate mosque architecture from 715 to the tenth century. As it occurs at Nishapur in north-eastern Iran, Siraf in southern Iran, al-Qayrawan (Kairouan) in Tunisia, and Córdoba in Spain, it can indeed be considered as the classic early Islāmic type. Its masterpieces occur in Iraq and in the West. The monumentalization of the early Iraqi hypostyle is illustrated by the two ruined structures in Samarra' and by the mosque of Ibn Tulun at Cairo (876–9).

In al-Qayrawan, the Great Mosque was built in stages between 836 and 866. Its most striking feature is the formal emphasis on the building's T-like axis punctuated by two domes, one of which hovers over the earliest preserved ensemble of *mihrab*, *minbar*, and *maqsurah* (arched facade). At Córdoba, the Great Mosque was built over two centuries from 785 to 988. It was enlarged twice in length – from 961 to 965 the celebrated *mihrab* and *maqsurah*, comprising one of the great architectural ensembles of early Islāmic art, were constructed – and then given an extension to the east. The extensive and heavily decorated *mihrab* area exemplifies a development that started with the Medina mosque and would continue: an emphasis on the *qiblah* wall.

Although the hypostyle mosque was the dominant plan, a fairly large number of others occur, most built in smaller urban locations or as secondary mosques in larger Muslim cities. Since a simple type of square subdivided by four piers into nine-domed units occurs at Balkh in Afghanistan, at Cairo, and at Toledo, it may be considered a pan-Islāmic type. Other types, a single square hall surrounded by an ambulatory, or a single long barrel-vault parallel or perpendicular to the *qiblah*, are rarer and should perhaps be considered as purely local.

Three other types of early Islāmic building can be defined architecturally, and a fourth one functionally. The first type, the Dome of the Rock in Jerusalem, completed in 691 and a masterwork of Islāmic architecture, is the earliest major Islāmic monument. Its octagonal plan, use of a high dome, and building techniques are hardly original, although its decoration is unique. Its purpose, however, is what is most remarkable. Since the middle of the eighth century, the Dome of the Rock has become the focal centre of the most mystical event in the life of the Prophet: his ascension into heaven from the rock around which the building was erected. According to an inscription preserved since the erection of the dome, however, it would seem that the building did not originally commemorate the Prophet's ascension but rather the Christology of Islām and its relationship to Judaism. It seems preferable, therefore, to interpret the Dome of the Rock as a victory monument of the new faith's ideological and religious claim on a holy city and on all the religious traditions attached to it.

The second distinctly Islāmic type of religious building is the *ribāṭ*. As early as in the eighth century, the Muslim empire entrusted the protection of its frontiers to warriors for the faith (*al-murābiṭūn*, "the people of the retreat") who lived in special institutions known as *ribāṭ*s. Evidence for these exist in Central Asia, Anatolia, and North Africa. The best preserved is at Susah, Tunisia: it consists of a square fortified building with a single fairly elaborate entrance and a central courtyard. It has two stories of private or communal rooms.

The last type of religious building to develop before the end of the tenth century is the mausoleum. Originally Islām was strongly opposed to any formal commemoration of the dead, but three factors slowly modified this attitude. First, the growth of the Shī'ite heterodoxy led to an actual cult of the descendants of the Prophet through his son-in-law 'Alī. Second, as Islām strengthened its hold on conquered lands, local practices and especially the worship of certain sacred places resulted in the Islāmization of ancient holy places by associating them with deceased Muslim heroes and holy men or with prophets. Third, as more or less independent local dynasties began to grow, they sought to commemorate themselves through mausoleums. The masterpieces of early funerary architecture occur in Central Asia, such as the royal mausoleum of the Samanids at Bukhara (before 942). For their

mausoleums the Muslims took over or rediscovered the ancient tradition of the centrally planned building as the characteristic commemorative structure.

The fourth kind of Muslim building is the *madrasah*, an
institution for religious training set up independently of mosques. It is known from texts that such privately endowed
schools existed in the north-eastern Iranian world as early
as in the ninth century, but no description exists of how they
were planned or looked.

Early Secular Architecture

With the disappearance of Sasanian kingship, the pre-Islāmic
Iranian imperial tradition ceased, and elsewhere conquered
minor kings and governors left their palaces and castles. A new
imperial power, first in Damascus, then briefly in the northern
Syrian town of al-Rusafah, and eventually in Baghdad and
Samarra' in Iraq, was accompanied by a new secular Muslim
architecture.

Three factors contributed to its evolution. One was that the
accumulation of an immense wealth of ideas, workers, and
money in the hands of the Muslim princes settled in Syria and
Iraq gave rise to a unique palace architecture. The second
factor was the impetus given to urban life and to trade. New
cities were founded from Sijilmassah on the edge of the
Moroccan Sahara to Nishapur in north-eastern Iran, and
ninth-century Arab merchants traded as far away as China.
The third factor is that, for the first time since Alexander the
Great, a world extending from the Mediterranean to India
became culturally unified. As a result, decorative motifs, design ideas, structural techniques, and artisans and architects
were available in the same places.

Early Islāmic princely architecture has become the best known and most original aspect of early Islāmic secular buildings. There are basically three kinds of these princely structures. The first type consists of ten large rural princely complexes found in Syria, Palestine, and Transjordan dating from around 710 to 750, erected by Umayyad princes. Private palaces were built, notably at al-Rusafah, Qasr al-Hayr West, Khirbat al-Mafjar, Qaṣr 'Amrah, and Mshatta. All of them derive their architectural vocabulary from that of pre-Islāmic times. Unique to the Umayyad dynasty in Syria and Palestine, they share a number of features that can best be illustrated by Khirbat al-Mafjar, the richest of them all.

Khirbat al-Mafjar contained a residential unit consisting of a square building with an elaborate entrance, a porticoed courtyard, and a number of rooms or halls arranged on two floors. Few of these rooms seem to have any identifiable function, although at Khirbat al-Mafjar a private oratory, a large meeting hall, and an anteroom leading to a cool underground pool have been identified. The main throne room was on the second floor above the entrance. Its plan is not known but probably resembled the preserved throne rooms or reception halls at Qaṣr 'Amrah and Mshatta, which consisted of a three-aisled hall ending in an apse.

Next to an official residence, there usually was a small mosque, generally a miniaturized hypostyle in plan. The most original feature of these establishments was the bath, which had its own elaborate entrance and contained a large hall that, at least in the instance of Khirbat al-Mafjar, was heavily decorated. It would appear that these halls were for pleasure – places for music, dancing, and probably occasional orgies. In some instances, as at Qaṣr 'Amrah, the same setting may have been used for both pleasure and formal receptions.

A second type of princely architecture – the urban palace – has been preserved only in texts or literary sources, with the exception of the palace at Kūfah in Iraq. Datable from the very end of the seventh century, it seems to have functioned both as a residence and as the *dār al-imārah*, or centre of government. This dual function is reflected in the use of separate building units and in the absence of much architectural decoration. The construction of smaller palaces, probably pavilions in the midst of gardens in or around major cities, seems to have begun with the 'Abbāsids during the last decades of the eighth century.

The third type of early Islāmic princely architecture is the palace-city. Several of these huge palaces are part of the enormous mass of ruins at Samarra', the temporary 'Abbāsid capital from 838 to 883. Jawsaq al-Khaqani, for instance, is a walled architectural complex of nearly one square mile that in reality is an entire city. It contains a formal succession of large gates and courts leading to a cross-shaped throne room, a group of smaller living units, basins and fountains, and even a racetrack. These structures may have been settings for the very elaborate ceremonies developed by the 'Abbāsid princes. When a Byzantine envoy arrived in 914, for instance, he was given a formal presentation (described in Khatib al-Baghdadi's *Ta'rikh Baghdad* [1071; "History of Baghdad"]) intended to impress the ambassador with the Muslim ruler's wealth and power. Treasures were laid down, thousands of soldiers and slaves in rich clothes guarded them, lions roared in the gardens, and on gilded artificial trees mechanical devices made silver birds chirp. These palace-cities with their walled enclosures, in which thousands lived a life unknown to others and into which simple mortals did not penetrate without bringing their own shroud, was transformed into the mysterious City of Brass of *The Thousand and One Nights*.

The systematic urbanization of early Muslim civilization was one of its most characteristic features. There does not seem to have been any idealized master plan for the internal arrangement of these urban sites, even mosques or palaces being often located eccentrically and not in the middle of the town. Extraordinary attention was paid to water distribution and conservation, as demonstrated by the magnificent ninth-century cisterns in Tunisia; the ninth-century Nilometer (a device to measure the Nile's level) in Cairo; and the elaborate dams, canals, and sluices of Qasr al-Hayr in Syria. The construction of commercial buildings on a monumental scale also occurred. The most spectacular example is the caravanserai of Qasr al-Hayr East, with its magnificent gate.

The concern for palaces and cities that characterized early Islāmic secular architecture shows itself most remarkably in the construction of Baghdad between 762 and 766/7 by the 'Abbāsid caliph al-Mansur. It was a walled round city whose circular shape served to demonstrate Baghdad's symbolic identity as the navel of the universe. A thick ring of residential quarters was separated by four axial, commercial streets entered through spectacular gates. In the centre of the city there was a large open space with a palace, a mosque, and a few administrative buildings. By its size and number of inhabitants, Baghdad was unquestionably a city; however, its plan so strongly emphasized the presence of the caliph that it was also a palace.

Early Materials and Decoration

The early Islāmic period, on the whole, did not innovate much in the realm of building materials and technology but utilized what it had inherited from older traditions. The most important novelty was the rapid development in Iraq of a baked brick architecture in the late eighth and ninth centuries, a method later used in Syria at al-Raqqah and Qasr al-Hayr East and in Egypt and Iran.

As supports for roofs and ceilings, early Islāmic architecture used walls and single supports. Most columns and capitals were either reused from pre-Islāmic buildings or were directly imitated from older models. In the ninth century in Iraq a brick pier was used, a form that spread to Iran and Egypt. Columns and piers were covered with arches. The most extraordinary technical development of arches occurs in the Great Mosque at Córdoba, where, in order to increase the height of the building in an area with only short columns, the architects created two rows of superimposed horseshoe arches. Almost immediately they realized that such a succession of superimposed arches constructed of alternating stone and brick could be modified to create a variety of patterns that would alleviate the inherent monotony of a hypostyle building.

The majority of early Islāmic ceilings were flat. Gabled wooden roofs, however, were erected in the Muslim world west of the Euphrates, and simple barrel vaults to the east. Vaulting, either in brick or in stone, was used, especially in secular architecture. Domes were employed frequently in mosques, consistently in mausoleums, and occasionally in secular buildings. Almost all domes are on squinches (supports carried across corners to act as structural transitions to a dome). The most extraordinary use of the squinch occurs in the mausoleum at Tim, where the surface of this structural device is broken into a series of smaller three-dimensional units rearranged into a sort of pyramidal pattern. This rearrangement is the earliest extant example of *muqarnas*, a stalactite-like decoration that would later be an important element of Islāmic architectural ornamentation.

Early Islāmic architecture is most original in its decoration. Mosaics and wall paintings followed the practices of antiquity and were primarily employed in Syria, Palestine, and Spain. Stone sculpture existed, but stucco sculpture, first limited to Iran, spread rapidly throughout the early Islāmic world. A variety of techniques borrowed from the industrial arts were used for architectural ornamentation. The *mihrab* wall of al-Qayrawan's Great Mosque, for example, was covered with ceramics, while fragments of decorative woodwork have been preserved in Jerusalem and Egypt.

The themes and motifs of early Islāmic decoration can be divided into three major groups. The first emphasizes the shape or contour of an architectural unit. The themes used were vegetal bands for vertical or horizontal elements, marble imitations for the lower parts of long walls, chevrons or other types of borders on floors and domes, and even whole trees on the spandrels or soffits (undersides) of arches, as in the Umayyad Mosque of Damascus or the Dome of the Rock; all these motifs tend to be quite traditional, being taken from the rich decorative vocabularies of pre-Islāmic Iran or of the ancient Mediterranean world.

The second group consists of decorative motifs for which a concrete iconographic meaning can be given. The huge architectural and vegetal decorative motifs at Damascus were meant to symbolize a sort of idealized paradise on earth, while the crowns of the Jerusalem sanctuary are thought to have been symbols of empires conquered by Islām. This use of visual forms in mosques for ideological and symbolic purposes was not easily accepted, however, and most later mosques are devoid of iconographically significant themes. The only exceptions fully visible are the Qur'ānic inscriptions in the mosque of Ibn Tulun at Cairo, which were used both as a reminder of the faith and as an ornamental device to emphasize the structural lines of the building.

Like religious architecture, secular buildings seem to have been less richly decorated at the end of the early Islāmic period than at the beginning. The paintings, sculptures, and mosaics of Qasr al-Hayr West, Khirbat al-Mafjar, Qaṣr 'Amrah, and Samarra' primarily illustrated the life of the prince. There were official iconographic compositions, such as the monarch enthroned, or ones of pleasure and luxury, such as hunting scenes or depictions of the prince surrounded by dancers, musicians, acrobats, and unclad women. Most of these subjects were not iconographic inventions of the Muslims but can be traced back to the classical world or to pre-Islāmic Iran and Central Asia.

The third type of architectural decoration consists of large ornamental panels, most often in stucco, for which no meaning or interpretation is yet known. The most important examples are at Mshatta and Samarra', although striking examples are also to be found at Khirbat al-Mafjar, Qasr al-Hayr East and West, al-Fustat, Siraf, and Nishapur. Two decorative motifs were predominately used on these panels: vegetal motifs and geometric forms. Copied consistently from Morocco to Central Asia, the aesthetic principles of this latter type of a complex overall design influenced the development of the principle of arabesque ornamentation.

Fatimid Architecture

The middle period in the development of Islāmic art extends roughly from the year 1000 to 1500, when a strong central power was replaced by a mosaic of overlapping dynasties. Turkish and Mongol invasions brought into the Muslim world new peoples and institutions; Berbers, Kurds, and Iranians began to play more effective cultural roles; and new Islāmic provinces were established in Anatolia and the Balkans, the Crimea, much of Central Asia and northern India, and parts of eastern Africa. The immense variety of impulses that affected the Muslim world during these five centuries was one of the causes of the artistic explosion among the various dynasties. The five divisions of Fatimid, Seljuq (the most important), Western Islāmic, Mamluk, and Mongol Iran (Il-Khanid and Timurid) art, however, are partly arbitary and to a large extent tentative.

The Fatimids (909–1171), an Arab dynasty professing with missionary zeal the beliefs of the Isma'iliyah sect of the Shī'ites, were established in Tunisia and Sicily in 909. In 969 they moved to Egypt and founded the city of Cairo. They soon controlled Syria and Palestine. During its heyday in the eleventh century, Cairo was the only wealthy Islāmic centre and could thus easily gather artisans and art objects from all over the world.

The great Fatimid mosques of Cairo – al-Azhar (started in 970) and al-Hakim (c. 1002–03) – were designed in the traditional hypostyle plan with axial cupolas. It is only in such architectural details as the elaborately composed facade of al-Hakim, with its corner towers and vaulted portal, that innovations appear. The originality of Fatimid architecture does not lie in works sponsored by the caliphs themselves but in the patronage of lower officials and of the bourgeoisie, if not even of the humbler classes, which was responsible for the most interesting Fatimid buildings. The mosques of al-Aqmar (1125) and of al-Salih (c. 1160) are among the first examples of monumental small mosques constructed to serve local needs. These mosques were elaborately decorated on the exterior, exhibiting a conspicuousness absent from large hypostyle mosques.

A second innovation in Fatimid architecture was the tremendous development of mausoleums. This may be explained partially by Shī'ism's emphasis on the succession of holy men, but the development of these buildings in terms of both quality and quantity indicates that other influential social and religious issues were also involved. Most of the mausoleums were simple square buildings surmounted by a dome. Many of these have survived in Cairo and Aswan. Only a few are somewhat more elaborate, with side rooms. The most original is the Juyushi Mosque (1085) overlooking the city of Cairo.

The Fatimids introduced, or developed, only two major constructional techniques: the systematization of the four-centred "keel" arch and the squinch. A peculiarly Egyptian development was the *muqarnas* squinch, which became an architectural element in itself used for windows; it consisted of four units: a niche bracketed by two niche segments, superimposed with an additional niche. Fatimid domes were smooth or ribbed and developed a characteristic "keel" profile.

Stone sculpture, stucco work, and carved wood were utilized for architectural decorations. The Fatimids also employed mosaicists, who mostly worked in places like Jerusalem, where they imitated or repaired earlier mosaic murals. Many fragments of Fatimid wall paintings have survived in Egypt. Most notable is the mid-twelfth-century Cappella Palatina at Palermo, built by the Norman kings of Sicily, where the facets in the *muqarnas* ceiling were painted with ornamental vegetal and zoomorphic designs but also with scenes of daily life and other subjects. Stylistically influenced by Iraqi 'Abbāsid art, these paintings are innovative in their more spatially aware representation of personages and of animals. Very similar tendencies appear also in the stucco and wood sculptures of Fatimid decoration. Another decorative trend is especially used on twelfth-century *mihrab*s:

explicitly complicated geometric patterns, usually based on stars, which in turn generate octagons, hexagons, triangles, and rectangles. Geometry becomes a sort of network in the midst of which small vegetal units continue to remain, often as inlaid pieces. Long inscriptions written in very elaborate calligraphies also became a typical form of architectural decoration on most of the major Fatimid buildings.

Seljuq Architecture

During the last decades of the tenth century, at the Central Asian frontiers of Islām, a migratory movement of Turkic peoples began that was to affect the whole Muslim world. The Seljuq empire consisted of a succession of dynasties, all but one of which (the Ayyubids of Syria, Egypt, and northern Mesopotamia) were Turkic and seem to have created a comparatively unified culture from India to Egypt. Cities were established or expanded, particularly in western Iran, Anatolia, and Syria. Militant Muslims, the Seljuqs also sought to revive Muslim orthodoxy.

The functions of monumental architecture in the Seljuq period were considerably modified. Large congregational mosques were still built. The earliest Seljuq examples occur in the two major new provinces of Islām – Anatolia and northwestern India – as well as in the established Muslim region of western Iran. In some areas, such as the Esfahan region, congregational mosques were rebuilt, while in other parts of Islām, such as Syria or Egypt, where there was no need for new large mosques, older ones were repaired and small ones were built. Minarets became extraordinarily plentiful, particularly in Iran, where dozens are preserved from the twelfth and thirteenth centuries.

Small or large, mausoleums increased in numbers and became at this time the ubiquitous monument they now appear to be. Most, such as the tomb tower of Abū Yazīd al-Bistami (died 874) at Bastam, were dedicated to holy men – both contemporary Muslim saints and all sorts of holy men dead for centuries. The most impressive mausoleums, however – like the one of Sanjar at Merv – were built for royalty. Pilgrimages were organized and, in many places hardly mentioned until then as holy places (e.g. Meshed, Bastam, Mosul, Aleppo), a whole monastic establishment serving as a centre for the distribution of alms was erected, with hostels and kitchens for the pilgrims.

Although enormously expanded, mosques, minarets, and mausoleums were not new types of Islāmic architecture. The *madrasah*, however, was a new building type. Although early examples have been discovered in Iran, such as the eleventh-century *madrasah* of Khargird and at Samarkand, it is from Anatolia, Syria, and Egypt that most of the information about the *madrasah* has been derived. In the latter regions it was usually a privately endowed establishment reserved for one or two of the schools of jurisprudence of orthodox Islām. Often the tomb of the founder was attached to the *madrasah*. Later *madrasah*s were built for two or three schools of jurisprudence, and the Mustansiriyah in Baghdad was erected in 1233 to be a sort of ecumenical *madrasah* for the whole of Sunni Islām. In the Seljuq period there occurred a revival of the *ribāt* inside cities. *Khānqāh*s (assembly halls), monasteries, and various establishments of learning other than formal *madrasah*s were also built.

The most impressive development of secular architecture of the time was the citadel, or urban fortress, through which the new princes controlled the usually alien city they held in fief. The largest citadels, like those of Cairo and Aleppo, were whole cities with palaces, mosques, sanctuaries, and baths. Others, like the Citadel of Damascus, were simpler constructions. Occasionally, as in the Euphrates valley, single castles were built, possibly in imitation of those constructed by the Christian Crusaders. Walls surrounded most cities, and all of them were built or rebuilt during the Seljuq period.

Little is known about Seljuq palaces or private residences in general. Anatolian palaces are on the whole rather small, villa-like establishments; but, in Afghanistan and Central Asia, excavations at Tirmidh, Lashkari Bazar, and Ghazni have brought to light a whole group of large royal palaces erected in the eleventh and early twelfth centuries.

Commercial architecture became very important. Individual princes and cities probably were trying to attract business by erecting elaborate caravanserais on the main trade routes such as Ribat-i Malik, built between Samarkand and Bukhara in Uzbekistan. The most spectacular caravanserais were built in the thirteenth century in Anatolia. Equally impressive, however, although less numerous, are the caravanserais erected in eastern Iran and northern Iraq. Bridges also were rebuilt and decorated, like the one at Cizre in Turkey.

The forms of architecture developed by the Seljuqs were remarkably numerous, and they varied considerably from region to region. The justly celebrated Great Mosque of Esfahan was one of the most influential of all early Seljuq religious structures. Probably completed around 1130 after a long and complicated history of rebuilding, it consisted of a large courtyard on which opened four large vaulted halls known as *eyvān*s. On the side of the *qiblah* the hall of the main *eyvān* was followed by a huge cupola. The area between *eyvān*s was subdivided into a large number of square bays covered by domes. The Esfahan mosque also had a unique feature: on the north side a single domed hall positioned on the main axis of the building was in all probability a formal hall for princes to change their clothes before entering into the sanctuary of the mosque.

The two features of the Great Mosque at Esfahan that became characteristic of Seljuq mosques were the *eyvān* and the dome. The *eyvān* was an architectural element known already in Sasanian architecture that had been used in residential buildings from Egypt to Central Asia before the eleventh century. In the mosques of the twelfth century, four *eyvān*s were used, with two principal effects. One was that the *eyvān*s centralized the visual effect of the mosque by making the courtyard the centre of the building. The *eyvān*s also broke up into four areas what had for centuries been a characteristic of the mosque: its single, unified space. Whether large or small, cupolas or domes were used in mosques, caravanserais, and palaces. They were the main architectural features of almost all mausoleums, where they were set over circular or polygonal rooms.

Two characteristic Iranian architectural forms are not present in the Great Mosque of Esfahan but occur elsewhere in the city. One is the tower. Those narrow and tall (up to about 150 feet [50 metres]) were minarets, of which several dozen have been preserved all over Iran and Central Asia (such as the one at Jam). Shorter and squatter towers were mausoleums. These were particularly typical of northern Iran. The other characteristic architectural type exists only in Esfahan in a much-damaged state. It is the *pishtaq*, or a formal gateway that served to emphasize a building's presence and importance.

Vaulting in baked brick became the main vehicle for monumental construction in the Seljuq period. A large octagonal base developed the *muqarnas* squinch from a purely ornamental feature into one wherein both structural and decorative functions combined. In some later buildings, such as the mausoleum of Sanjar at Merv, a system of ribs was used to vault an octagonal zone. Seljuq architects sought to make their domes visible from afar and for this reason invented the double dome, thus raising the exterior height without making the exterior dome too heavy. The outer shell was raised on a high drum, while the interior kept the traditional sequence: square base, zone of transition, and dome. Domes along the *eyvān*s and the construction of tall circular or polygonal minarets and high facades also enhanced visibility of a building from the exterior.

Architectural decoration was intimately tied to structure. Two mediums predominated. One was stucco, which continued to be used to cover large wall surfaces. The other was brick. Originating in the tenth-century architecture of northeastern Iran, brick came to be employed as a medium of construction as well as a medium of decoration. The complex decorative designs worked out in brick often had a rigidly geometric effect. Specially cut shapes of terracotta and brick, frequently produced in unusual sizes, served to soften these geometric patterns by modifying their tactile impact and by introducing additional curved or bevelled lines to the straight lines of geometry.

Paintings were used for architectural decoration, especially in palaces. From the second half of the twelfth century coloured tiles began to be utilized to emphasize the contour of a decorative area in a structural unit; tiles were not used, however, to cover whole walls. There are also examples of architectural sculpture of animals and people. Most of the decorative designs tended to be subordinated to geometry.

In Iraq, northern Mesopotamia, Syria, and Egypt (after 1171), the architectural monuments do not, on the whole, appear as overwhelmingly impressive as those of Iran, largely because the taste of Umayyad and 'Abbāsid times continued to

dominate mosque architecture. It is in the construction of new
building types, particularly the *madrasah*, that most originality
is apparent, while the use of *eyvān*s and the construction of the
many minarets found in Mosul or on the Euphrates certainly
attest to the influence of Iranian Seljuq design.

The main achievement of Ayyubid, Zangid, or Seljuq architecture in the Fertile Crescent, however, was the translating
into stone of new structural systems first developed in brick.
The most impressive instance of this lies in the technically
complex *muqarnas* domes and half domes or in the *muqarnas*
pendentives of Syrian buildings. Elaborate *mihrab*s were also
made of multicoloured stones that were carefully cut to create
impressive patterns.

In the new Islāmic province of Seljuq Anatolia, in the
thirteenth century, the assimilation of influences from
throughout the Muslim world – introduced by immigrants,
as well as from the several native Anatolian traditions of
Byzantine, Armenian, and Georgian architecture – resulted
in an overwhelmingly original architecture. Three uniquely
Anatolian architectural features can be distinguished. One was
limited to Konya at this time but would have an important
widespread development later on. As it appears in the Ince or
Karatay *madrasah*s, it consists of the transformation of the
central courtyard into a domed space while maintaining the
eyvān. Thus the centralized aspect of the *eyvān* plan becomes
architecturally explicit. The second feature is the creation of a
facade that usually consisted of a high central portal – often
framed by two minarets – with an elaborately sculpted decorative composition that extended to two corner towers. The
third feature is the complexity of the types of funerary monuments that were constructed.

Most Anatolian architecture is of stone. In Konya and a
number of eastern Anatolian instances, brick was used. Barrel

vaults, groin vaults, *muqarnas* vaults, squinch domes, pendentive domes, and the new pendentive known as "Turkish triangle" were all used by Anatolian builders, thereby initiating the great development of vault construction in Ottoman architecture (see below).

Architectural decoration consisted primarily in the stone sculpture found on the facades of religious and secular buildings. Although influenced by Iran and Syria in many details, most Anatolian themes were original. The exuberance of Anatolian architectural decoration can perhaps be best demonstrated in the facades of Sivas' Gök Medrese and of Konya's Ince Minare. In addition to the traditional geometric, epigraphic, and vegetal motifs, a decorative sculpture in the round or in high relief was created that included many representations of human figures and especially animals. There are few examples of wall painting from Anatolia. Especially in Konya, however, a major art of painted-tile decoration did evolve, possibly developed by Iranian artists who fled from the Mongol onslaught.

The Moorish Period

Two types of structures characterize the Almoravid (1056–1147) and Almohad (1130–1269) periods in Morocco and Spain. One comprises the large, severely designed Moroccan mosques such as those of Tinmel, of Hasan in Rabat, or of the Kutubiyyah (Koutoubia) in Marrakech. They are all austere hypostyles with tall, massive, square minarets. The other distinctive type of architecture was that built for military purposes, including fortifications and, especially, massive city gates with low-slung horseshoe arches, such as the Oudaia Gate at Rabat and the Rabat Gate at Marrakech (both twelfth century).

In North Africa the artistic milieu did not change much in the fourteenth and fifteenth centuries. Hypostyle mosques such as the Great Mosque of Algiers continued to be built, while *madrasah*s were constructed with more elaborate plans; the Bu 'Inaniyah *madrasah* at Fès is one of the few monumental buildings of the period. A few mausoleums were erected, such as the so-called Marinid tombs near Fès (second half of the fourteenth century) or the complex of Chella at Rabat (mostly fourteenth century). Architectural decoration in stucco or sculpted stone was usually limited to elaborate geometric patterns, epigraphic themes, and a few vegetal motifs.

A stunning exception to the austerity of North African architecture exists in Spain in the Alhambra palace complex at Granada, constructed in the fourteenth century by two successive princes, Yusuf I and Muḥammad V. Apart from a number of gates built like triumphal arches and several ruined forecourts, only three parts of the palace remain intact. First there is the long Court of the Myrtles leading to the huge Hall of Ambassadors located in one of the exterior towers. This was the part of the Alhambra built by Yusuf I. Then there is the Court of the Lions, with its celebrated lion fountain. Numerous rooms open off this court, including the elaborately decorated Hall of the Two Sisters and the Hall of the Abencerrajes. The third part, slightly earlier than the first two, is the Generalife; it is a summer residence built higher up the hill and surrounded by gardens with fountains, pavilions, and portico walks.

The Alhambra, one of the few palaces to have survived from medieval Islāmic times, illustrates superbly a number of architectural concerns documented in literary references: the contrast between an unassuming exterior and a richly decorated interior to achieve an effect of secluded or private brilliance;

the constant presence of water, either as a single, static basin or as a dynamic fountain; the inclusion of oratories and baths; and the lack of an overall plan (the units are simply attached to each other).

The architectural decoration of the Alhambra was mostly of stucco. Some of it is flat, but the extraordinarily complex cupolas of *muqarnas*, such as in the Hall of the Two Sisters, appear as huge multifaceted diadems. Much of the design and decoration of the Alhambra is symbolically oriented. The poems that adorn the Alhambra as calligraphic ornamentation celebrate its cupolas as domes of heaven rotating around the prince sitting under them.

Islāmic art as such ceased to be produced in Spain after 1492, when Granada, the last Moorish kingdom in Spain, fell to the Christians; but the Islāmic tradition continued in North Africa, which remained Muslim. In Morocco the so-called Sharifian dynasties from the sixteenth century onward developed ornamentally the artistic forms created in the fourteenth century.

Mamluk Architecture

The Mamluks were chiefly Turks and Circassians from the Caucasus and Central Asia who during the thirteenth century took over power as non-hereditary sultans in Syria and Egypt. They succeeded in arresting the Mongol onslaught in 1260 and managed to maintain themselves in power in Egypt, Palestine, and Syria until 1517.

During the Mamluk period, Egypt and Syria were rich commercial emporiums. This wealth explains the quality and quantity of Mamluk art. Most of the existing monuments in the old quarters of Cairo, Damascus, Tripoli, and Aleppo are Mamluk; in Jerusalem almost everything visible on the Haram al-Sharif, outside the Dome of the Rock, is Mamluk.

Driven in part by the desire of parvenu rulers and their cohorts to be remembered, architectural patronage flourished because of the institutionalization of the *waqf*, an economic system in which investments made for holy purposes were inalienable. This law allowed the wealthy to avoid confiscation of their properties at the whim of the caliph by investing their funds in religious institutions. In the Mamluk period, therefore, there was a multiplication of *madrasah*s, *khānqāh*s, *ribāt*s, and *masjid*s, often with tombs of founders attached to them. The Mamluk establishment also repaired and kept up all the institutions, religious or secular, that had been inherited by them, as can be demonstrated by the well-documented repairs carried on in Jerusalem and Damascus.

Nearly 3,000 major monuments have been preserved or are known from texts in cities from the Euphrates to Cairo. The hypostyle form continued to be used for mosques and oratories, as in the Cairene mosques of Baybars I (1262–3), Nasir (1335), and Mu'ayyad Shaykh (1415–20). *Madrasah*s used *eyvān*s, and the justly celebrated *madrasah* of Sultan Hasan in Cairo (1356–62) is one of the few perfect four-*eyvān madrasah*s in the Islāmic world. Mausoleums were squares or polygons covered with domes.

Characteristic of Mamluk buildings is the tendency to build structures of different functions in a complex or cluster. Thus the Qala'un mosque (1284–5) in Cairo has a mausoleum, a *madrasah*, and a hospital erected as one architectural unit. Mamluk patrons also tended to build their major monuments near each other, as in certain streets of Cairo, such as Bayn al-Qasrayn. From the second half of the fourteenth century onward, building space for mausoleums began to be limited in Cairo, and a vast complex of commemorative monuments was created in the city's western cemetery. In Aleppo and Damascus similar phenomena can be observed.

Originality is evident in the constructional systems used, although traditional structural features continued to be employed. The main innovations are of three kinds. First, minarets became particularly elaborate and, toward the end of the period, almost absurd in their ornamentation. Facades were huge, with overwhelming portals 25 to 35 feet high. A second characteristically Mamluk feature was technical virtuosity in stone construction. At times this led to a superb purity of form, as in the Gate of the Cotton Merchants in Jerusalem or the complex of the Barquq mosque in Cairo. At other times, as in the Mamluk architecture of Baybars and Qa'it Bay, there was an almost wild playfulness with forms. Another aspect of Mamluk masonry was the alternation of stones of different colours to provide variations on the surfaces of buildings. The third element of change in Mamluk art was perhaps the most important: almost all formal artistic achievements rapidly became part of the common vocabulary of the whole culture, thus ensuring high quality of construction and decorative technique throughout the period.

With the exception of portals and *qiblah* walls, architectural decoration was usually subordinated to the architectural elements of the design. Generally the material of construction (usually stone) was carved with ornamental motifs. Stucco decoration was primarily used in early Mamluk architecture, while coloured tile was a late decorative device that was rarely employed.

Mongol Iran: Il-Khanid and Timurid Periods

As the Mongol army swept through Iran in the thirteenth century, such cities as Balkh, Nishapur, and Rayy, which had been centres of Islāmic culture for nearly six centuries, were eradicated. The turning point toward some sort of stability took place in 1295 with the accession of Mahmud Ghazan to the Mongol throne. Under him and his successors (the Il-Khanid Dynasty), order was re-established throughout Iran, and cities in north-eastern Iran, especially Tabriz and Soltaniyeh, became the main creative centres of the new Mongol regime.

Stylistically, Il-Khanid architecture is defined best by buildings such as the mosque of Varamin (1322–6) and the mausoleums at Sarakhs, Merv, Rad-Kan, and Maragheh. Elements of architectural composition, decoration, and construction that had been developed earlier were refined by Il-Khanid architects. *Eyvān*s were shallower but better integrated with the courts, facades were more thoughtfully composed, the *muqarnas* became more linear and varied, and coloured tiles were used to enhance the building's character.

The architectural masterpiece of the Il-Khanid period is the mausoleum of Öljeitü at Soltaniyeh. With its double system of galleries, eight minarets, large blue-tiled dome, and an interior measuring 80 feet (25 metres), it is clear that the building was intended to be imposing. Il-Khanid attention to impressiveness of scale also accounted for the 'Alī Shah mosque in Tabriz, whose *eyvān* measuring 150 by 80 by 100 feet (45 by 25 by 30 metres) was meant to be the largest ever built. In the regions of Esfahan and Yazd numerous smaller mosques (often with unusual plans) and less pretentious mausoleums, as well as palaces with elaborate gardens, were built in the fourteenth century.

The Timurid period began architecturally in 1390 with the sanctuary of Ahmad Yasavi in Turkistan. Between 1390 and the last works of Sultan Husayn Bayqara almost a century later, hundreds of buildings were constructed at Herat. The most spectacular examples of Timurid architecture are found in Samarkand, Herat, Meshed, Khargird, Tayabad, Baku, and Tabriz, although important Timurid structures were also erected in southern Iran.

Architectural projects were well patronized by the Timurids as a means to commemorate their respective reigns. Every ruler or local governor constructed his own sanctuaries, mosques, and, especially, memorial buildings dedicated to holy men of the past. While the Shah-e Zendah in Samarkand – a long street of mausoleums comparable to the Mamluk cemetery of Cairo – is perhaps the most accessible of the sites of Timurid commemorative architecture, more spectacular ones are to be seen at Meshed, Torbat-e Sheykh Jam, and Mazar-e Sharif. The Timurid princes also erected mausoleums for themselves, such as the Gur-e Amir and the 'Ishrat-Khaneh in Samarkand.

Major Timurid buildings, such as the so-called mosque of Bibi Khanom, the Gur-e Amir mausoleum, the mosque of Gowhar Shad in Meshed, and the *madrasah*s at Khargird and Herat, are characterized by strong axial symmetry. Often the facade on the inner court repeats the design of the outer facade, and minarets are used to frame the composition. Changes took place in the technique of dome construction. The *muqarnas* was not entirely abandoned but was often replaced by a geometrically rigorous net of intersecting arches that could be adapted to various shapes by modifying the width or span of the dome. The Khargird *madrasah* and the 'Ishrat-Khaneh mausoleum in Samarkand are particularly striking examples of this structural development. The Timurids also made use of double domes on high drums.

In the Timurid period the use of colour in architecture reached a high point. Every architectural unit was divided, on both the exterior and interior, into panels of brilliantly coloured tiles that sometimes were mixed with stucco or terracotta architectural decorations.

Ottoman Architecture

Originally one of the small Turkmen principalities (*beylik*s) that sprang up in Anatolia after the collapse of Seljuq rule, by 1520 the Ottomans had taken control of almost the whole of the Arab world. The grand tradition of Ottoman architecture, established in the sixteenth century, was derived from two main sources. One was the rather complex development of new architectural forms that occurred all over Anatolia in the fourteenth and early fifteenth centuries. In addition to the usual mosques, mausoleums, and *madrasah*s, a number of buildings called *tekke*s were constructed to house dervishes and other holy men. The *tekke* (or *zāwiyah*) was often joined to a mosque or mausoleum. The entire complex was then called a *külliye*. All these buildings continued to develop the domed, central-plan structure, constructed by the Seljuqs in Anatolia.

The other source of Ottoman architecture is Byzantine, especially as embodied in Hagia Sophia. Byzantine influence appears in such features as stone and brick used together or in the use of pendentive dome construction. Also influential were the contacts that the early Ottomans had with Italy: in several mosques at Bursa in Turkey there are stylistic parallels in the designs of the exterior facade and of windows, gates, and roofs to features found in Italian architecture.

The apogee of Ottoman architecture was achieved in the great series of *külliye*s and mosques that still dominate the Istanbul skyline: the Fatih *külliye* (1463–70), the Bayezid Mosque (after 1491), the Selim Mosque (1522), the Sehzade *külliye* (1548), and the Süleyman *külliye* (after 1550). The Sehzade and Süleyman *külliye*s were built by Sinan, the greatest Ottoman architect, whose masterpiece is the Selim Mosque at Edirne, Turkey (1569–75). All of these buildings exhibit total clarity and logic in both plan and elevation; such simplicity of design is often attributed to the fact that Sinan and many Ottoman architects were first trained as military engineers. In these buildings descending half domes, vaults, and buttresses and minarets lead the eye up the exterior to an imposing central dome.

Ottoman architecture never managed to renew its sixteenth-century brilliance, and throughout the eighteenth and nineteenth centuries, a consistent Europeanization occurred. Later buildings, such as the impressive Sultan Ahmed mosque in Istanbul, were mostly variations on Sinan's architecture, and sometimes there were revivals of older building types, especially in the provinces. Occasionally, as in the early eighteenth-century Nûruosman mosque in Istanbul, interesting new variants appear, illustrating the little-known Turkish Baroque style.

While mosques and *külliye*s are the most characteristic monuments of Ottoman architecture, important secular buildings were also built: baths, caravanserais, and especially the huge palace complex of Topkapi Saray at Istanbul, in which 300 years of royal architecture are preserved in its elaborate pavilions, halls, and fountains.

Architectural decoration was generally subordinated to the structural forms or architectonic features of the building. A wide variety of themes and techniques originating from many different sources was used. The Ottoman version of colour-tile decoration deserves particular mention, for it succeeds in transforming smaller buildings such as the mosque of Rüstem Pasa in Istanbul into a visual spectacle of brilliant colours.

Safavid Architecture

The art of the Safavid Dynasty reached its zenith during the reigns of Tahmasp (1524–76) and of 'Abbās I (1588–1629) and represented the last significant development of Islāmic architecture in Iran. The Safavid period, like the Ottoman era, was an imperial age, and therefore there is hardly a part of Iran where either Safavid buildings or major Safavid restorations cannot be found. The main centres were Tabriz and Ardabil in the north-west, Kazvin in the central region, and, especially, Esfahan in the west, where the best known Safavid monuments are located. There 'Abbās I built a whole new city. According to one description, it contained 162 mosques, 48 *madrasah*s, 1,802 commercial buildings, and 283 baths. What remains constitutes some of the finest monuments of Islāmic architecture.

At the centre of Esfahan is the Meydan-e Shah, a large open space, about 1,670 by 520 feet (510 by 158 metres), originally surrounded by trees. Used for polo games and parades, it could be illuminated with 50,000 lamps. Each side of the *meydan* was provided with the monumental facade of a building. On one of the smaller sides was the entrance to the celebrated Masjed-e Shah mosque. On the other side was the entrance into the bazaar or marketplace. On the longer sides were the small funerary mosque of Sheykh Lotfollah and, facing it, the 'Alī Qapu, the "high gate", the first unit of a succession of palaces and gardens that extended beyond the *meydan*, most of which have now disappeared except for the Chehel Sotun, the palace of the "Forty Columns". The 'Alī Qapu was, in its lower floors, a semi-public place to which petitions could be brought, while its upper floors are a world of pure fantasy – a succession of rooms, halls, and balconies overlooking the city, which were purely for the prince's pleasure.

The Meydan-e Shah unites in a single composition all the concerns of medieval Islāmic architecture: prayer, commemoration, princely pleasure, trade, and spatial effect. No other remaining Safavid monument can match its historical importance, and in it are found the major traits of Safavid construction and decoration. The forms are traditional, for the most part, and even in vaulting techniques and the use of coloured tiles it is to Timurid art that the Safavids looked for their models. The Persian architects of the early seventeenth century sought to achieve a monumentality in exterior spatial composition; a logical precision in vaulting, and a colouristic brilliance that has made the domes and portals of Esfahan justly famous.

Mughal Architecture

Like Ottoman art, the art of the Mughals was a late imperial art of Muslim princes. It successfully fused Persian, Indian, and various provincial influences to produce works of unusual refinement and quality. From the thirteenth century onward there can be seen an adaptation of Islāmic functions to indigenous forms. The earliest Islāmic tomb to survive is the Sultan Ghari, built in 1231, but the finest is the tomb of Iltutmish, who ruled from 1211 to 1236. The interior, covered with Arabic inscriptions, in its richness displays a strong Indian quality.

It was in the fourteenth-century architecture of South Asian sites such as Tughluqabad, Gaur, and Ahmadabad that a uniquely Indian type of Islāmic hypostyle mosque was created, with a triple axial nave, corner towers, axial minarets, and cupolas. In Ahmadabad the Jāmi' Masjid (c. 1424) is a masterly exposition of the style, while dating from the second half of the fifteenth century are the small but exquisite mosques of Muhafiz Khan (1492) and Rani Sabra'i (1514).

It was also during these centuries that the first mausoleums set in scenically spectacular locations were built. By then the conquering Muslims had fully learned how to utilize local methods of construction, and they adapted South Asian decorative techniques and motifs. At Bijapur is the Dol Gunbad (built by Muhammad 'Ādil Shāh), a tomb of exceptional grandeur, with one of the largest domes in existence.

What Mughal architecture brought to the Islāmic tradition (other than traditional Indian themes, especially in decoration) was technical perfection in the use of red sandstone or marble as building and decorative materials. The mausoleum of Humayun in Delhi (1565–9) is built entirely of sandstone and red marble; the city of Fatehpur Sikri (from 1569 onward) and the Taj Mahal at Agra (1631–53) summarize the development of Mughal architecture.

At Akbar's Fatehpur Sikri is the Jāmi' Masjid (1571), with its colossal gateway, one of the finest mosques of the Mughal period and one that served as a model for later congregational mosques; other notable buildings on the site are the exquisitely carved Turkish Sultana's house; the Panch-Mahal; the Dīvān-e Khāss and the so-called hall of private audience.

Shah Jahan (1628–58) built the Taj Mahal as a tomb for his wife, Queen Mumtaz Mahal. The five principal elements of the complex – main gateway; garden set out along classical

Mughal lines (a square quartered by long watercourses, with paths, fountains, and ornamental trees); mosque; *jawāb* (literally "answer"; a building mirroring the mosque); and mausoleum (including its four minarets) – were conceived and designed as a unified entity according to the tenets of Mughal building practice, which allowed no subsequent addition or alteration. The marble mausoleum rises up from a tall terrace (at the four corners of which are elegant minarets) and is crowned by a graceful dome. The southern end of the complex is graced by a wide red sandstone gateway with a recessed central arch inlaid with black Qur'ānic lettering and floral designs. Two notable decorative features are repeated throughout the complex: pietra dura and Qur'ānic verses in Arabic calligraphy. One of the inscriptions in the gateway invites the faithful to enter paradise.

Later architectural monuments, during the reign of Aurangzeb, represent a distinct decline. The tomb of Safdar Jang at Delhi (*c.* 1754) was among the last important works to be produced under the Mughal dynasty and had already lost the coherence and balance characteristic of mature Mughal architecture.

European Influence and Contemporary Trends

Much of the Muslim world was first introduced to "modern" European architecture through its adaptation in Istanbul or in other major Ottoman cities like Smyrna or Alexandria. Nineteenth-century European engineers and architects adapted modern structural technology and decorative styles to local Islāmic needs or idioms: the Suq al-Hamidiyah bazaar in Damascus was built with steel roofing; the Hejaz railway station at Damascus was decorated in a sort of Oriental Art

Nouveau style. Much of the Europeanized architecture, however, was drab and pretentious.

In the 1940s and 1950s, extensive planning programmes
and building projects were undertaken in even the poorest
countries, and the wealthy Arab states, as well as pre-
revolutionary Iran, transformed their traditional cities and
countryside with spectacular modern complexes ranging from
housing projects to universities. Many of these buildings were
planned and constructed by Western firms and architects, and
some are mere copies of European and American models, ill-
adapted to the physical conditions and visual traditions of the
Muslim world. Others are interesting and even sensitive
projects: spectacular and technically innovative, such as the
Intercontinental Hotel in Mecca (Frei and Otto) and the Haj
Terminal of the King Abdul Aziz International Airport at
Jidda, Saudi Arabia (the U.S. firm of Skidmore, Owings &
Merrill); or intelligent and imaginative, such as the govern-
ment buildings of Dhaka, Bangladesh (designed by the late
Louis Kahn of the United States) or the numerous buildings
designed by the Frenchman André Ravereau in Mali or
Algeria.

In the early twenty-first century, virtually all six Gulf Cooperation Council (GCC) countries – Bahrain, Kuwait, Oman,
Qatar, Saudi Arabia, and the United Arab Emirates (U.A.E.) –
showcased levels of economic development and infrastructure
expansion not seen since the 1970s oil boom. At this time a
range of transportation and construction projects was underway in Dubai, including light- and urban-rail systems, a sports
complex, luxury hotels, and island developments. In 2007 the
mixed-use Burj ("Tower") Dubai, the final height of which
was expected to exceed 2,640 feet (800 metres), was officially
designated the world's tallest structure, despite the fact that it
was still under construction.

Led by an increase in the number of foreign firms in the region and the profusion of world-class banking institutions, together with a great concentration of Arab investment capital and liquidity, infrastructure projects were being financed on a scale not hitherto experienced. Nakheel ("The Palms"), a Dubai property-development company with government ties, claimed to have some $30 billion in projects under way in 2007, most notably a trilogy of palm-shaped man-made archipelagoes, to include residences for more than 250,000 people, and the World, which comprised some 300 small man-made islands arranged to look from the air like a map of the world. Saadiyat Island, just off the coast of Abu Dhabi, was at the centre of a reclamation project that would expand a natural island half the size of Bermuda into a much larger complex of hotels, golf courses, marinas, and private resi-dences. It was expected to house as many as 150,000 full-time residents, as well as a 670-acre (270-hectare) cultural district. Bahrain, Oman, and Qatar had similar islands under con-struction or in the planning stages.

On the tourism front, in addition to the dozens of luxury hotels planned for the new islands, hotels containing more than 7,000 rooms and suites opened in 2007, with plans to double the hotel "bed stock" in Dubai alone to at least 80,000 within a decade. Dubai already boasted the Burj Al Arab, a $1 billion, 1,052-foot (321-metre) sail-shaped "seven-star" hotel, and the $500 million Hydropolis, the region's first under-water hotel. Not to be outdone, Abu Dhabi welcomed guests to its $3 billion Emirates Palace Hotel. Local and foreign demands have also spurred an expansion of spas and swimming pools, ice-skating rinks, and golf courses, as well as expanded facilities for camel and horse racing (in Dubai construction began on the 76 million square-foot [7.1 million square-metre] Meydan racecourse complex). One of the most remarkable projects was Dubailand, a massive complex of entertainment and tourist amenities that included the Mall of Emirates (the largest indoor shopping mall outside North America) and a 1 square-mile (2.25 square-kilometre), 25-storey indoor ski resort. Ski Dubai, which opened in late 2005, was a winter wonderland in the desert, with "real" man-made snow, ski slopes of varying difficulty, a snowboard quarterpipe, and other facilities.

The arts were not ignored, especially in Abu Dhabi, which announced that the cultural district on Saadiyat Island would include a performing arts centre by Iraqi-born London-based architect Zaha Hadid and two art museums: a Frank Gehry-designed Guggenheim Museum, and Louvre Abu Dhabi, the Paris icon's first international outpost.

Zaha Hadid, known for her radical deconstructivist designs characterized by a sense of fragmentation, instability, and movement, in 2004 became the first woman to be awarded the Pritzker Architecture Prize. Her previous work included the Vitra Fire Station (1989–93) in Weil am Rhein, Germany, composed of a series of sharply angled planes and resembling a bird in flight, and the Lois & Richard Rosenthal Center for Contemporary Art in Cincinnati, the first American museum designed by a woman.

Within the Islāmic world emerged several schools of architects that adopted modes of an international language to suit local conditions. The oldest of these schools were in Turkey, where architects such as Eldhem and Cansever, among many others, built highly successful works of art. Other major Muslim contributors to a contemporary Islāmic architecture were the Iranians Nader Ardalan and Kemzan Diba, the Iraqis Rifat Chaderji and Muḥammad Makkiya, the Jordanian Rassem Badran, and the Bangladeshi Mazhar ul-Islām. Finally, a unique message was being transmitted by the visionary Egyptian architect Hassan Fathy, who, in eloquent and prophetic terms, urged that the traditional forms and techniques of vernacular architecture be studied and adapted to contemporary needs. Directly or indirectly, his work inspired many young architects in the Muslim world and led to a host of fascinating private houses, mosques, and educational facilities. The Aga Khan Award for Architecture was instituted to encourage genuine and contemporary architectural innovation in Islāmic lands.

11

VISUAL AND DECORATIVE ARTS

From the very beginning of Islām there occurred a major art of trade and of the city. More than any other culture and certainly earlier than any other, the Islāmic world created a number of secular tastes and sponsored techniques of secular beautification. This gave an impetus to techniques of ceramics, textiles, and metalwork, raising the quality of all decorative arts. This particular feature of the Islāmic tradition survived all political misfortunes. Remarkably beautiful objects were made as late as the early nineteenth century, and the techniques and traditions were often revived in the twentieth century with considerable success. New techniques in the decorative arts were invented and spread throughout the Muslim world. The amount and intensity of creative energies spent on them transformed the decorative arts into major artistic forms of Islāmic culture.

The emphasis has always been on artists' technical skill, on their ability to do visual tricks, or on the speed and efficiency with which they created. The artist was regarded not as a prophet or a genius but as a technically equipped individual who succeeds in beautifying the surroundings of all people. There is a hedonistic element in Islāmic art, therefore, but this hedonism is intellectually and emotionally mitigated by the conscious knowledge of the perishable character of all things human. Islāmic art is thus a curious paradox, for as it softened and embellished life's activities, it was created with destructible materials, thereby reiterating Islām's conviction that only God remains.

Although Islāmic art is strictly aniconic, and Muslims are not permitted to make images of God or of the Prophet, many forms of Islāmic art celebrate Muḥammad's name and presence. There are calligraphic representations of his various names, especially Muḥammad, found everywhere in the Islāmic world and preserved in many mosques, especially those of the Ottoman Empire, in which they held a prominent position. There are also many Persian, Turkish, and Mughal miniatures in which his figure is represented in a stylized fashion, though his face is usually hidden or effaced. Miniatures of the Mi'rāj (Nocturnal Ascent) represent some of the greatest masterpieces of this genre of painting.

The Islāmic visual arts were created by the confluence of two phenomena: a number of earlier artistic traditions and a new faith. Technically, as well as ideologically, the Islāmic world took over an extremely sophisticated system of visual forms, but remained resistant to influences from Arabia itself. The pre-Islāmic sources of Islāmic art are thus entirely extraneous to the milieu in which the new faith was created. In this respect the visual arts differ considerably from most other aspects of Islāmic culture.

What did happen during early Islāmic times, however, was the establishment of a dominant new taste. It occurred first in Syria and Iraq, the two areas with the largest influx of Muslims and with the two successive capitals of the empire, Damascus under the Umayyads – who ruled from 661 to 750 – and Baghdad under the early 'Abbāsids – whose rule extended as late as 1258 but whose princes ceased to be a significant cultural factor after the second decade of the tenth century. From Syria and Iraq this new taste spread in all directions and adapted itself to local conditions and local materials, thus creating considerable regional and chronological variations in early Islāmic art.

Early Decorative Arts

Very little is known about early Islāmic gold and silver objects, although their existence is mentioned in many texts as well as suggested by the wealth of the Muslim princes. Except for a large number of silver plates and ewers, probably made for Umayyad and 'Abbāsid princes and belonging to the Sasanian tradition, nothing has remained. Dating from the tenth century are a large number of Buyid silks, a group of funerary textiles with plant and animal motifs as well as poetic texts. One of the characteristic features of early Islāmic textiles is their use of writing for identifying and decorative purposes.

The most important medium of early Islāmic decorative arts is pottery. Initially Muslims continued to sponsor whatever varieties of ceramics had existed before their arrival. Probably in the last quarter of the eighth century new and more elaborate types of glazed pottery were produced. The area of initial technical innovation seems to have been Iraq. Trade with Central Asia brought Chinese ceramics to Mesopotamia, and Islāmic ceramicists sought to imitate them. It is probably in Iraq, therefore, that the technique of lustre glazing was first developed in the Islāmic world. Egypt also played a leading part in the creation of the new ceramics; a glass goblet is the earliest datable lustre object. Early pottery was also produced in north-eastern Iran, where excavations at Samarkand and Nishapur have brought to light a new art of painted under-glaze pottery. Its real novelty lay, however, in the variety of subjects employed.

While new ceramic techniques may have been sought to imitate other mediums (mostly metal) or other styles of pottery (mostly Chinese), the decorative devices rapidly became purely and unmistakably Islāmic in style. A wide variety of motifs were combined: vegetal arabesques or single flowers and trees; inscriptions, usually legible and consisting of proverbs or of good wishes; animals that were usually birds drawn from the vast folkloric past of the Middle East; occasionally human figures drawn in a strikingly abstract fashion; geometric des-igns; all-over abstract patterns; single motifs on empty fields; and simple splashes of colour, with or without underglaze sgraffito designs (i.e. designs incised or sketched on the body or the slip of the object).

Crafts in other mediums also developed. Glass was as important as pottery, but examples have been less well pre-served. A tradition of ivory carving developed in Spain, and the objects dating from the last third of the tenth century onward attest to the high quality of this uniquely Iberian art. Many of these carved ivories certainly were made for princes; their decorative themes were drawn from the whole vocabu-lary of princely art known through Umayyad painting and sculpture of the early eighth century. These ivory carvings are also important in that they exemplify the fact that an art of sculpture in the round never totally disappeared in the Islāmic world – at least in small objects.

Fatimid Arts

The middle period (1000–1500) was a time of expansion,
when the art of various dynasties becomes evident. The
Fatimid caliphs (909–1171) both sought and produced decorative arts within their empire. Little has been preserved of
the former, notably a small number of superb ewers in rock
crystal. A text has survived, however, that describes the imperial treasures looted in the middle of the eleventh century by
dissatisfied mercenary troops. It lists gold, silver, enamel, and
porcelain objects that have all been lost, as well as textiles
(perhaps the cape of the Norman king Roger II is an example
of the kind of textiles found in this treasure). The inventory
also records that the Fatimids had in their possession many
works of Byzantine, Chinese, and even Greco-Roman provenance. Altogether, then, it seems that the imperial art of the
Fatimids was part of a sort of international royal taste that
downplayed cultural or political differences.

Ceramics, on the other hand, were primarily produced by
local urban schools and were not an imperial art. The most
celebrated type of Fatimid wares were lustre-painted ceramics
from Egypt itself. A large number of artisans' names have been
preserved, thereby indicating the growing prestige of these
craftsmen and the aesthetic importance of their pottery. Most
of the surviving lustre ceramics are plates on which the
decoration of the main surface has been emphasized. The
decorative themes used were quite varied and included all
the traditional Islāmic ones – e.g. calligraphy, vegetal and
animal motifs, and arabesques. The most distinguishing feature of these Fatimid ceramics, however, is the representation
of the human figure. Some of these ceramics have been
decorated with simplified copies of illustrations of the princely
themes, but others have depictions of scenes of Egyptian daily

life. The style in which these themes have been represented is simultaneously the hieratic, ornamental manner traditional to Islāmic painting combined with what can almost be called spatial illusionism. Wheel-cut rock crystal, glass, and bronze objects, especially animal-shaped aquamaniles (a type of water vessel) and ewers, are also attributed to the Fatimids.

Manifestations of non-princely Fatimid art include the art of book illustration. The few remaining fragments illustrate that probably after the middle of the eleventh century there developed an art of representation other than the style used to illustrate princely themes. This was a more illusionistic style that still accompanied the traditional ornamental one in the same manner as in the paintings on ceramics.

Seljuq Arts

The arts of the Seljuq period demonstrate an extraordinary artistic energy, a widening of the social patronage of the arts, and a hitherto unknown variety of topics and modes of expression. Glass and textiles continued to be major mediums during the Seljuq period. Ceramics underwent many changes, especially in Iran, where lustre painting became widespread and where new techniques were developed for colouring pottery. The growth of tile decoration created a new dimension for the art of ceramics. Inlaid metalwork became an important technique. First produced at Herat in Iran (now in Afghanistan) in the middle of the twelfth century, this type of decoration spread westward, and a series of local schools were established in various regions of the Seljuq domain. In this technique, the surfaces of utilitarian metallic objects (candlesticks, ewers, basins, kettles, and so forth) were engraved, and then silver was inlaid in the cut-out areas to make the decorative design more clearly visible. Manuscript illustration also became an important art. Scientific books, including the medical manuals of Dioscorides and of Galen, or literary texts such as the picaresque adventures of a verbal genius known as the *Maqamat*, were produced with narrative illustrations throughout the text.

All of the technical novelties of the Seljuqs seem to have had one main purpose: to animate objects and books and to provide them with clearly visible and identifiable images. Even the austere art of calligraphy became occasionally animated with letters ending in human figures. The main centres for producing these arts were located in Iran and the Fertile Crescent. It would seem from a large number of art objects whose patrons are known that the main market for these works of art was the mercantile bourgeoisie of the big cities. Thus the decorative arts and book illustration reflect an urban taste.

The themes and motifs used were particularly numerous. In books they tend to be illustrations of the text, even if a manuscript such as the Schefer *Maqamat* (1237) sought to combine a strict narrative with a fairly naturalistic panorama of contemporary life. Narrative scenes taken from books or reflecting folk stories are also common on Persian ceramics. In all mediums, however, the predominant vocabulary of images is the one provided by the older art of princes; however, its meaning is no longer that of illustrating the actual life of princes but rather that of symbolizing a good and happy life. Next to princely and narrative themes, there are depictions of scenes of daily life, astronomical motifs, and myriad topics that can be described but not understood.

While it is possible within certain limits to generalize about the subject matter of Seljuq art, regional stylistic definitions tend to be more valid. Thus the bronzes produced in northeastern Iran in the twelfth century are characterized by simple decorative compositions rather than by the very elaborate ones created by the so-called school of Mosul in Iraq during the thirteenth century. In general, the art of metalwork exhibits a consistently growing intricacy in composition and in details to the point that individual subjects are at times lost in over-lapping planes of arabesques.

Ceramic pieces from Iran have usually been classified accord-ing to a more or less fictitious provenance. Kashan ware exhibits a perfection of line in the depiction of moon-faced personages with heavily patterned clothes, while Rayy ceramic work is less sophisticated in design and execution but more vividly co-loured. Saveh and Gurgan are still other Iranian varieties of pottery. In Syria, Raqqah pottery imitated Iranian ceramic wares but with a far more limited vocabulary of designs.

The main identifiable group of miniature painters was the so-called Baghdad school of the first half of the thirteenth century. The miniatures painted by these artists are character-ized by the colourful and often humorous way in which the urbanized Arab is depicted. The compositions are documen-tary caricatures in which the artist has recorded the telling and recognizable gesture or a known and common setting or activity. In many images or compositional devices one can recognize the impact of the richer Christian Mediterranean tradition of manuscript illumination. A greater attention to aesthetic considerations is apparent in the illustrated manu-script of the Persian epic *Varqeh o-Golshah*, unique in the Seljuq period.

Western Islāmic Arts

Although a very original calligraphy was developed, the other western Islāmic arts cannot be compared in wealth and importance either with what occurred elsewhere in Islām at the same time or with earlier objects created in Spain. There are some important examples of metalwork, wood inlaid with ivory, and a lustre-glaze pottery known as Hispano-Moresque ware. The fact that the latter was made in Valencia or Málaga after the termination of Muslim rule demonstrates that Islāmic traditions in the decorative arts continued to be adhered to. The term Mudéjar, therefore, is used to refer to all the things made in a Muslim style but under Christian rule. Numerous examples of Mudéjar art exist in ceramics and textiles.

Mudéjar art must be carefully distinguished from Mozarabic art: the art of Christians under Muslim rule. Mozarabic art primarily flourished in Spain during the earlier periods of Muslim rule. Its major manifestations are architectural decorations, decorative objects, and illuminated manuscripts. Dating mostly from the tenth and eleventh centuries, the celebrated illuminations for the commentary on the Revelation to John by an eighth-century Spanish abbot, Beatus of Liébana, are purely Christian subjects treated in styles possibly influenced by Muslim miniature painting or book illustration. The most celebrated example, known as the "Saint-Sever Apocalypse", is in the collection of the Bibliothèque Nationale in Paris.

Mamluk Arts

Egypt and Syria were wealthy during the Mamluk period and museum collections of Islāmic art generally abound with Mamluk metalwork and glass. Some of the oldest remaining carpets are Mamluk. The arts of the Mamluk period achieved a high level of technical perfection but were often lacking in originality, however. The so-called "Baptistère de Saint Louis" (*c.* 1310) is the most impressive example of inlaid metalwork preserved from this period. Several Mamluk illustrated manuscripts, such as the *Maqamat* (1334) in the Nationalbibliothek, Vienna, display an amazing ornamental sense in the use of colour on gold backgrounds. Mamluk mosque lamps provide some of the finest examples of medieval glass. The wooden objects made by Mamluk craftsmen were widely celebrated for the quality of their painted, inlaid, or carved designs. And the bold inscriptions that decorate the hundreds of remaining bronzes testify to the Mamluks' mastery of calligraphy.

Persian Painting

A new period of Persian painting began in the Mongol era, and, even though here and there one can recognize the impact of Seljuq painting, on the whole it is a limited one. Although the new style was primarily expressed in miniature painting, it is known from literary sources that mural painting flourished as well. Masterpieces of Persian literature were illustrated: first the *Shāh-nāmeh* (*Book of Kings*) by the eleventh-century poet Ferdowsi and then, from the second half of the fourteenth century, lyrical and mystical works, primarily those by the twelfth-century poet Nezami. Historical texts or chronicles such as the *Jāmiʿ al-tawarikh* (*Universal History of Rashid al-Din*) were also illustrated, especially in the early Mongol period.

The first major monument of Persian painting in the Mongol period is a group of manuscripts of the *Jāmiʿ al-tawarikh*. The miniatures are historical narrative scenes. Stylistically they are related to Chinese painting – an influence introduced by the Mongols during the Il-Khanid period. Chinese influence can still be discovered in the masterpiece of fourteenth-century

Persian painting, the so-called Demotte *Shāh-nāmeh*, illustrated between 1320 and 1360, with its 56 preserved miniatures. The compositional complexity of these paintings can be attributed to the fact that several painters probably were involved and that the artists drew from a wide variety of different stylistic sources (e.g. Chinese, European, and local Iranian traditions). It is the earliest known illustrative work that sought to depict in a strikingly dramatic fashion the meaning of the Iranian epic. Its battle scenes, its descriptions of fights with monsters, and its enthronement scenes are all powerful representations of the colourful and often cruel legend of Iranian kingship. The artists also tried to express the powerlessness of humanity confronted by fate in a series of mourning and death scenes.

The Demotte *Shāh-nāmeh* is but the most remarkable of a whole series of fourteenth-century manuscripts, all of which suggest an art of painting in search of a coherent style. At the very end of the period a manuscript such as that of the poems of Sultan Aḥmad still exhibits an effective variety of established themes, while some of the miniatures in the Deutsche Staatsbibliothek, Berlin, and in the Topkapi Saray, Istanbul, illustrate the astounding variety of styles studied or copied by Persian masters.

A more organized and stylistically coherent period in Persian painting began around 1396 with the Khwaju Kermani manuscript and culminated between 1420 and 1440 in the paintings produced by the Herat school, where the emperor Baysunqur created an academy in which classical Iranian literature was codified, copied, and illustrated. Although several *Shāh-nāmeh*s are known from this time, the mood of these manuscripts is no longer epic but lyrical. Puppet-like figures almost unemotionally engage in a variety of activities always set in an idealized garden or palace depicted against a rich gold background. It is a world of sensuous pleasure that also embodies the themes of a mystically interpreted lyrical poetry, for what is represented is not the real world but a divine paradise in the guise of a royal palace or garden. At its best, as in the Metropolitan Museum Nezami, this style of Persian painting succeeds in defining something more than mere ornamental colourfulness. It expresses in its controlled lyricism a fascinating search for the divine, similar to the search of such epic characters as Nezami, Rumi, or Hafezt; at times earthly and vulgar, at other times quite ambiguous and hermetic, but often providing a language for the ways in which human beings can talk about God.

Another major change in Persian painting occurred during the second half of the fifteenth century at Herat under Husayn Bayqara. This change is associated with the first major painter of Islãmic art, Behzad and his school. In the Garrett *Zafarnameh* (*c.* 1490), the Egyptian Cairo National Library's Bustan (1488), or the British Museum's Nezami (1493–4), the stereotyped formulas of the earlier lyric style were endowed with new vitality. Behzad's interest in observing his environment resulted in the introduction of more realistic poses and numerous details of daily life or genre elements. His works also reflect a concern for a psychological interpretation of the scenes and events depicted. It is thus not by chance that portraits have been attributed to Behzad.

Ottoman Arts

During the late period of Islãmic art, Ottoman., Safavid, and Mughal painters moved from one empire to the other, especially from Iran to India, and there is some interplay between the work of the three empires.

There are several distinctive Ottoman schools of pottery: Iznik, Rhodian, and Damascus ware. Their development is intimately tied to that of architectural ceramic decoration, such as that which transformed Istanbul's Rüstem Paşa mosque. Both in technique and in design, Ottoman ceramics are the only major examples of pottery produced in the late Islāmic period.

Ottoman miniature painting does not compare in quality with Persian painting, which originally influenced the Turkish school. Yet Ottoman miniatures do have a character of their own, either in the almost folk-art effect of religious images or in the precise depictions of such daily events as military expeditions or great festivals. Among the finest examples of the latter is the manuscript *Surname-i Vehbi,* painted by Abdülcelil Levnî in the early eighteenth century.

The production of metalwork, wood inlaid with ivory, Usak carpets, and textiles flourished under the Ottomans, both in Istanbul workshops sponsored by the sultan and in numerous provincial centres.

Safavid Painting

The Safavid period marks the last significant development of Islāmic art in Iran, for after the middle of the seventeenth century original creativity disappeared in all mediums. Rugs and objects in silver, gold, and enamel continued to be made and exhibited a considerable technical virtuosity, even when they were lacking in inventiveness.

In the sixteenth and seventeenth centuries, possibly for the first time in Islāmic art, painters were conscious of historical styles. Miniatures from the past were collected, copied, and imitated. Patronage, however, was fickle. A royal whim would gather painters together or exile them. Many names of painters have been preserved, and there is little doubt that the whim of patrons was being countered by the artists' will to be socially and economically independent as well as individually recognized for their artistic talents.

Three major painting styles, or schools (excluding a number of interesting provincial schools), existed in the Safavid period. One school of miniature painting is exemplified by such masterpieces as the Houghton *Shāh-nāmeh* (completed in 1537), the Jāmi' *Haft owrang* (1556–1665), or the illustrations to stories from Hafez. These large, colourful miniatures were all executed in a grand manner. Their compositions are complex; individual faces appear in crowded masses; there is much diversification in landscape; and, despite a few ferocious details of monsters or of strongly caricaturized poses and expressions, these book illustrations are concerned with an idealized vision of life. The sources of this school lie with the Timurid academy. Behzad, Sultan Muhammad, Sheykhzadeh, Mir Sayyid 'Alī, Aqa Mirak, and Mahmud Musavvir continued and modified, each in his own way, the ideal of a balance between an overall composition and precise rendering of details.

The miniatures of the second tradition of Safavid painting seem at first to be like a detail out of the work of the previous school. The same purity of colour, elegance of poses, interest in details, and assertion of the individual figure is found. Aqa Reza and Reza 'Abbasi (both active around 1600) excelled in extraordinary portrayals of poets, musicians, courtiers, and aristocratic life in general.

In both traditions of painting, the beautiful personages depicted frequently are satirized; this note of satirical criticism is even more pronounced in portraiture of the time. But it is in pen or brush drawings, mostly dating from the seventeenth century, that the third aspect of Safavid painting appeared: an interest in the depiction of minor events of daily life. With stunning precision Safavid artists showed a whole society falling apart with a cruel sympathy totally absent from the literary documents of the time.

While architecture and painting were the main artistic vehicles of the Safavids, the making of textiles and carpets was also of great importance. It is in the sixteenth century that a hitherto primarily nomadic and folk medium of the decorative arts was transformed into an expression of royal and urban tasks by the creation of court workshops. The predominantly geometric themes of earlier Iranian carpets were not abandoned entirely but tended to be replaced by vegetal, animal, and even occasional human motifs. Great schools of carpet-making developed particularly at Tabriz, Kashan, and Kerman.

Mughal Arts

Mughal art was in continuous contact with Iran or, rather, with the Timurid world of the second half of the fifteenth century. The models and the memories were in Herat or Samarkand, but the artists were raided from Safavid Iran, and the continuous flow of painters from Iran to the Mughal Empire is a key factor in understanding Mughal painting. There appears to have developed what can only be called an Indo-Persian style, based essentially on the schools of Iran but affected by the individual tastes of the Indian rulers and by local styles.

The kind of subject that tended to be illustrated was remarkably close to those used in Safavid history books – legendary stories, local events, portraits, and genre scenes.

What evolved quickly was a new manner of execution, and this style can be seen as early as about 1567, when the celebrated manuscript *Dastan-e Amir Hamzeh* (*Stories of Amir Hamzeh*) was painted (some 200 miniatures remain and are found in most major collections of Indian miniatures). Also notable are the *Khamseh* (*Quintet*) of Amir Khosrow of Delhi, and a manuscript of the *Ne'mat-nameh* (*Book of Ne'mat*) painted for a sultan of Malwa in the opening years of the sixteenth century. Its illustrations are derived from the Turkmen style of Shiraz but show clear Indian features adapted from the local version of the western Indian style.

Traditional Iranian themes – battles, receptions, and feasts – acquired monumentality, not only because of the inordinate size of the images but also because almost all of the objects and figures depicted were seen in terms of mass rather than line. Something of the colourfulness of Iranian painting was lost, but instead images acquired a greater expressive power. Mughal portraiture gave more of a sense of the individual than did the portraits of the Safavids. As in a celebrated representation of a dying courtier, Mughal drawings could be poignantly naturalistic. Mood was important to the Mughal artist – in many paintings of animals there is a playful mood; a sensuous mood is evident in the first Muslim images to glorify the female body and the erotic.

By the opening years of the sixteenth century, a new and vigorous style had come into being. Among the finest examples of this are a series illustrating the *Bhagavata-Purana* and the *Caurapañcasika* of Bilhana. A technically more refined variant of this style, preferring the pale, cool colours of Persian derivation, a fine line, and meticulous ornamentation, is best illustrated by a manuscript of the ballad *Candamyana* by Mulla Daud (*c.* first half of the sixteenth century).

Although the Mughal dynasty came to power in India with Babur's great victory at Panipat in 1526, the Mughal style was almost exclusively the creation of Akbar (1556–1605), who created a large *atelier* which he staffed with artists recruited from all parts of India. The work covered a wide variety of subjects: histories, romances, poetic works, myths, legends, and fables, of both Indian and Persian origin. The earliest paintings (*c.* 1560–70) are illustrations of *Tuti-nameh* (*Parrot Book*) and the *Dastan-e Amir Hamzeh*. The *Tuti-nameh* shows the Mughal style in the process of formation: the hand of artists belonging to the various non-Mughal traditions is clearly recognizable, but the style also reveals an intense effort to cope with the demands of a new patron. The transition is achieved in the *Dastan-e Amir Hamzeh*, quite unlike Persian work in its leaning toward naturalism and filled with swift, vigorous movement and bold colour. The forms are individually modelled; the figures are superbly interrelated in closely unified compositions, in which depth is indicated by a preference for diagonals; and much attention is paid to the expression of emotion.

Immediately following were some very important historical manuscripts, including the *Tarikh-e Khandan-e Timur-iyeh* (*History of the House of Timur, c.* 1580–85) and other works concerned with the affairs of the Timurid dynasty, to which the Mughals belonged. Each of these contains several hundred illustrations, and the painter provides a picture of contemporary life and of the rich fauna and flora of India. It was in the illustrations to Persian translations of the Hindu epics the *Mahabharata* and the *Ramayana* that the Mughal painter revealed to the full the richness of his imagination, and the *Razm-nameh*, as the *Mahabharata* is known in Persian, is one of the outstanding masterpieces of the age.

In addition to such large manuscripts, books, generally poetic works, with a smaller number of illustrations done by a single master artist were produced. In style the works tend to be finely detailed and exquisitely coloured. Representing some of the most delicate and refined works of the reign of Akbar are the *Baharistan* of Jāmi' (1595), a *Khamseh* of Nezami (1593), a *Khamseh* of Amir Khosrow (1598), and an *Anwar-e Suhayli* (1595–6).

Among the most elaborate works of the emperor Jehangir (1605–27), who preferred portraiture to books, are the great court scenes showing him surrounded by courtiers. The compositions have lost the bustle and movement so evident in the works of Akbar's reign; the figures are more formally ordered, their comportment in keeping with the strict rules of etiquette of the Mughal court. Though many have magnificent borders decorated with a wide variety of floral and geometrical designs, the colours are subdued and harmonious, the bright glowing palette of the Akbari artist having been abandoned. Jahangir honoured his painters, designating his favourite Abū al-Hasan Nadir-uz-Zaman ("Wonder of the Age"); among his works is a perceptive study of Jahangir looking at a portrait of his father. Ustad Mansur, designated Nadir-ul-'Asr ("Wonder of the Time"), produced studies of birds and animals which are unparalleled.

Under Shah Jahan (1628–58), the style becomes noticeably rigid. The best work is found in the *Shahjahannameh* (*History of Shah Jahan*) and in several albums assembled for the emperor. Subjects include genre scenes, showing gatherings of ascetics and holy men, lovers in a garden or on a terrace, musical parties, and carousals. From the reign of Aurangzeb (1659–1707), the standard of workmanship declined, however, and Mughal painting essentially came to an end during the reign of Shah 'Alam II (1759–1806).

Traditions of craftsmanship established in the decorative arts came to full flower during the Mughal dynasty, the finest objects being made in the imperial workshops. An important contribution to carpet weaving was the landscape carpet that reproduced pictorial themes inspired by miniature painting. Metal objects of sumptuous quality were also made, a unique example of which is a splendid, elaborately chiselled sixteenth-century cup. Jade or jadeite was used together with crystal to make precious vessels as well as sword and dagger hilts. The greatest period for jade carving seems to have been the seventeenth century; a few outstanding examples associated with the emperors Jahangir and Shah Jahan are of singular delicacy and perfection. The practice of inlaying jade, and also stone, with precious or semi-precious stones became more popular with the reign of Shah Jahan.

The range of ornamental patterns used reflected architectural decoration. They consisted mainly of arabesques and varied geometric patterns together with floral scrolls and other designs adapted from Indian traditions. From the seventeenth century, a type of floral spray became the most favoured motif and was found on almost every decorated object.

European Influence and the Modern Period

There had been European influence prior to European occupation: in Mughal India, European landscapes and Western spatial concerns influenced painting in the eighteenth century; and Persian painting has exhibited constant Western influence since the seventeenth century. During European occupation of Muslim territory, there was a conscious revival of traditional decorative arts, but new techniques were often employed. This especially occurred in India and Morocco, where the retail success of an art object depended less on the local tradition than on the taste of the Europeans. Traditional techniques and designs of the decorative arts often had to be maintained artificially through government subsidies, for the local market, except in Morocco or India, was more easily seduced by second-rate European objects.

During the period of occupation it was questioned whether alien techniques necessarily brought with them new forms. As various schools based on the École des Beaux-Arts in Paris were formed, however, the faculties and the students suffered from constant uncertainty as to whether they should preserve an art that was mostly artisanal or revolutionize it altogether. The results of dozens of new art schools and of a more enlightened patronage than during the nineteenth century are less than spectacular, however, especially in painting. In spite of several interesting attempts to deal with calligraphy, with geometric designs, or with local folk arts, successes so far have not been clearly identified. But Turkey, Jordan, Egypt, Morocco, Iraq, Pakistan, and Indonesia have all produced talented artists.

12

LITERATURE

Islāmic literatures exist over a vast geographical and linguistic area, for they were produced wherever the Muslims went. This chapter focuses on the literatures of Iran (Persia), a major centre of Islām; Turkey and the Turkic-speaking peoples of Central Asia; and Arabic, the language of the Qur'ān. Many Indian vernaculars nevertheless contain almost exclusively Islāmic literary subjects; a number of classical themes in Islāmic lore were elaborated in Kashmiri lyric and epic poetry, and Muslim India can boast a fine heritage of Arabic poetry and prose. Some fine Muslim short stories have been produced in modern Malayalam. There is also an Islāmic content in the literature of Malaysia and in that of some East African languages, including Swahili, while in modern times the diaspora of Muslims has seen Islāmic literatures produced widely throughout the world.

Arabic Poetry

The tradition of Arabic literature stretches back some 16 centuries in the Arabian Peninsula and began within the context of a tribal, nomadic culture. With the advent and spread of Islām, that tradition was carried far and wide during the course of the seventh to the tenth century. It initially sought to preserve the values of chivalry and hospitality while expressing a love of animals and describing the stark realities of nature, but it proceeded to absorb cultural influences from every region brought within the fold of Dar al-Islām, or the Islāmic world.

Arabic script was used by all who followed Islām. The Qur'ān was considered to be the highest manifestation of literary beauty, and its imagery permeates all Islāmic poetry and prose. During his lifetime, the revelations to Muḥammad were memorized and recorded in written form, but it was only during the reign of the third caliph to rule after Muḥammad's death, 'Uthmān ibn 'Affan, that the Muslim community established a canonical version of the Qur'ān. Within the realm of Arabic literature, the Qur'ān has played a foundational role and continues to serve as the major stylistic yardstick for literary expression in the Arabic language.

From the very earliest stages in the Arabic literary tradition, the role of the poet has been of major significance. In the pre-Islāmic period the tribal poet's performances of his odes were a powerful tool, arousing the group's heroes to battle, extolling the chivalry and generosity of its men and the beauty of its women, and pouring scorn on the foibles of opposing tribes. Fallen heroes were commemorated in the *marthiyyah*, or elegy, and it is in this role that the voice of the female poet is prominently heard, as, for example, in the verses of the seventh-century poets al-Khansa' and Layla al-Akhyaliyyah.

In contrast to the tribal poets were the *su'luk* ("brigand") poets, who were depicted as living a life of solitude and hardship in the desert, such as Ta'abbata Sharran ("He Who Has Put Evil in His Armpit") and al-Shanfara.

This tradition of poetry emerged in the seventh century as the primary linguistic precedent to the Arabic of the newly recorded text of the Qur'ān. Thereafter, poetry came to occupy a central place within the courts of the caliph and of the sultans, emirs, governors, and other potentates who ruled over the Islāmic world, often being commissioned by the ruling authorities for public recitation on "state occasions" (especially panegyrics).

The earliest-known Arabic poetry reveals a variety of types of poem marked by particular patterns of rhyme and syllabic pulse. The *qit'ah* ("segment") was a relatively short poem devoted to a single theme or else composed and performed for a particular occasion; the *marthiyyah* is an example of such a poem. While many *qit'ah*s are complete in and of themselves, the structure of others suggests they are segments from lengthier poetic performances. That lengthier type is the *qasidah*, a polythematic poem with a tripartite structure that might extend to 100 lines or more. It constitutes an elaborate celebration of the tribe and its way of life. In the opening *nasib*, the poem's speaker comes across a deserted encampment and muses nostalgically about times past and his absent beloved. A second section (the *rahil*) recounts a desert journey, thus affording the opportunity for descriptions of animals that are among the most famous and beloved within the entire tradition of Arabic poetry. A section in praise of the tribe (the *madih*) comes third, in which one of several possible "purposes" is proclaimed: boasts concerning the heroism and endurance of the tribe's fighters, the generosity and hospitality of its people, the beauty of its women, or the feats of its animals. Descriptions of wine drinking, gambling, jousts, and horse races all contribute to the overall picture through which the performance of the *qasidah* presents a ritualized liturgy in praise of community.

Initially seven and later ten of the longer examples of the *qasidah* were recognized as outstanding representatives of the large corpus of longer poems that had been recorded in written form. They were collected as *Al-Mu'allaqat* (also known variously as the seven (or ten) "long poems" and the Seven Long Odes). The opening of the *mu'allaqah* of sixth-century poet Imru' al-Qays is probably the most famous line of poetry in Arabic: "Halt, you two companions, and let us weep for the memory of a beloved and an abode mid the sand-dunes between Al-Dakhul and Hawmal."

These *qit'ah* and the *qasidah* were the predominant forms of Arabic poetry but not the only ones. The *rajaz* served several functions, for example, as camel drivers' songs, known as *al-hida'*. The *urjuzah* (a poem composed in *rajaz*) was also utilized for verbal display and other types of didactic and even obscene poetry. Some poetic forms utilized the colloquial form of the Arabic language (the *quma*, for example, and the *kan wa kan*). In the Iberian Peninsula, the *zajal* and the *muwashshah* provide a wonderfully accurate picture of Al-Andalus during the Islāmic period (eighth–fifteenth centuries), and, following their migration across North Africa to the Mashriq, contributed significantly to both the elite and popular traditions of Arabic poetry.

A major change in the form of the Arabic poem occurred in the late 1940s, when two Iraqi poets, Nazik al-Mala'ikah and Badr Shakir al-Sayyab, adopted a poetic system that used variable line length and patterns of assonance and repetition in place of end rhyme. They ushered in a new era of the prose poem and other experiments in form and poetic discourse.

However, the traditional form of the *qasidah* continued at the hands of certain poets – among them Al-Akhtal al-Saghir (the pen name of Bishara al-Khuri), Badawi al-Jabal (the pen name of Muhammad al-Ahmad), and Muhammad al-Jawahiri – to hold an important place in the hearts of many Arabs.

In genre, there were three types of public performance poetry: panegyric (*madh*), the praise of the tribe and its elders, a genre that was to become the primary mode of poetic expression during the Islāmic period; the lampoon (*hija'*), whereby the poet takes verbal aim at the community's enemies and impugns their honour (most often at the expense of women); and praise of the dead, or elegy (*ritha'*).

The great master of the panegyric, and arguably Arabic's most illustrious poet, is al-Mutanabbi ("He Who Claimed to Be a Prophet"), who composed a famous ode in praise of the great tenth-century ruler of Aleppo, Sayf al-Dawlah. Panegyric was adopted immediately in the cause of Islām. The sixth- and seventh-century poet Hassan ibn Thabit, often referred to as "the Prophet's poet", composed panegyrics in praise of Muhammad, initiating a tradition of poems in praise of the Prophet that continued throughout the ensuing centuries.

With the first dynasty of caliphs, the Umayyads, panegyric became a major propaganda device. The public performance of poems that record the policies and victories of rulers continued into the 'Abbāsid period. With Abū Tammam the panegyric became the supreme manifestation of a trend in poetic creativity toward elaboration in imagery and diction that was subsumed under the heading of *badi'* (innovative use of figurative language). As an important source of patronage, the panegyric – now extolling both the state of the people ruled and the glory of the ruler's own personage – became the major mode of expression in *qasidah* form until the twentieth century.

The themes of *hija'* ("lampooning") and *fakhr* ("boasting") often occur together. Al-Mutanabbi is also famous for his withering attacks on Abū al-Misk Kafur, the Ethiopian slave who was regent in Egypt in the tenth century. While defeat in battle is, of course, a primary focus of derision in this type of poetry, the honour of the community and the family has resided to a major extent in the protection of its women, and they were also thus impugned. The *Al-Naqa'id* (*Flytings*), which record poetic jousts between poets in Al-Mirbad, the central square of the city Al-Basrah (Basra), during the Umayyad caliphate, took the level of invective to new heights (or depths): "Al-Farazdaq's mother gave birth to a fornicator; what she produced/Was a pygmy with stubby legs." The instinct for lampoon found no shortage of targets in the ensuing centuries. The great poet Abū Nuwas even teases the caliph Harun al-Rashid over a scandal concerning the caliph's sister. The realities of life in the Arabic-speaking world from the twentieth century, however, rendered most attempts at lampoon dangerous, though this did not prevent the Iraqi poet Muzaffar al-Nawwab from taking pot shots at the rulers of Saudi Arabia: "The son of Ka'bah is having sex./The world's prices are on hold."

The celebration of the life and courage of a tribal comrade fallen in battle is the occasion for the earliest elegies in Arabic. The elegy also became a means of public affirmation of the strength of Islām and its rulers. A particular topic of communal mourning is the fall of an entire city to enemy forces, such as the renowned elegy of the ninth-century poet Ibn al-Rumi on the fall of Al-Basrah to an army of slave labourers. Through the twentieth century and into the twenty-first, the elegy continued to fulfil its purpose as an expression of personal sorrow and broader communal grief and steadfastness; "Wa-'ada . . . fi kafan" (1964; "And He Came Home . . .

in a Shroud"), by the Palestinian poet Mahmud Darwish, is a modern example.

To these three poetic genres was added at an early stage a very vigorous Arabic poetic tradition: description (*wasf*). Its emphasis was on how poets depicted animals and other aspects of nature and often indulged in complex patterns of imagery that likened attributes of one animal to those of another. The images of camels and horses of the pre-Islāmic poets, such as Imru' al-Qays, are justifiably well known. The strong link in Islām between the garden and paradise ensured that elaborate descriptions of attempts by temporal rulers to replicate within their own palaces the pleasures of the life to come would become, and remain, a prominent theme of Arabic poetry. The theme and the imagery were later adopted by the romantic poets of the twentieth century, as in 'Alī Mahmud Taha's poem *Ughniyah rifiyyah* (*Rustic Song*).

As the ceremonial *qasidah* during the Islāmic centuries became more and more the realm of panegyric, other themes within the pre-Islāmic tradition – wine, hunting, love, and maxims – emerged as separate genres in their own right. Although the Qur'ān made injunctions against wine drinking, the sheer number of poetic divans (collected works) that contain sections devoted to *khamriyyat* (wine poetry) illustrates the extent to which poetry could be used to confront religious orthodoxy. This reached its height with Abū Nuwas: "Ho, pour me a glass of wine, and confirm that it's wine!/Do not do it in secret, when it can be done in the open." The imagery of the wine poem also provides the framework for the poetry of the Sufi (mystical) poets, such as that of the Egyptian Ibn al-Farid. His mystical *khamriyyah* mentions not only wine (now acting as a symbol for the achievement of a transcendent state) but also the ancient theme of the absent beloved.

A separate type of hunt poem (*tardiyyah*) also emerged, to be taken up enthusiastically by the Umayyad and 'Abbāsid caliphs. In these poems the scene of the morning departure is still present, having been carried over from the opening section (*nasib*) of the *qasidah*, and the speaker's companions are the saker falcon (*saqr*) and the hunting dog. Abū Nuwas's divan contains many examples of this category, and a noted practitioner was the caliph, poet, and critic Ibn al-Mu'tazz.

The proclivity often indulged in by the Arab poet for homiletic advice and contemplation found a fruitful source in not only the Qur'ān's pointed comments on the ephemerality of this life in comparison with the next, but also in the Islāmic community's quest for a more individual mode of access to the transcendent. While many poets contributed to the genre, it is Abū al-'Atāhiyah whose name is most closely associated with the ascetic poem (*zuhdiyyah*). In poem after poem he concentrates on the mortality of humanity, asking what has happened to the great historical figures of yesteryear and pointing to their common abode in the grave: "Note well! All of us are dust. Who among humanity is immortal?" With the poetry of al-Ma'arri, the homiletic aspect is blended with philosophical contemplation and pessimism: for him life is an experience of sheer misery.

The theme of love has been present in the Arabic poetic tradition since the earliest poems committed to written form. The desert environment, the nomadic lifestyle, and the need for constant travel all contribute to a poetic vision that focuses on absence, departure, lack, and nostalgia. During the Islāmic period, this desert-inspired approach to love was adapted and transformed into a strand of love poetry called 'Udhrī, named for the tribe to which the poet Jamil, one of its best-known practitioners, belonged. In these poems the lover spends a lifetime of absence and longing, pining for the beloved, who is tyrannical and cruel (aiming arrows at the heart and eye) and yet remains the object of worship and adoration. The early centuries of recorded Arabic poetry are replete with collections of poetry written by 'Udhrī poets, all of whom are known by a name that incorporates their beloved's: Jamil Buthaynah, Majnun Layla, Kuthayyir 'Azzah.

Another strand of love poetry, 'Umarī, named for the poet 'Umar ibn Abi Rabi'ah – whose poems reveal much closer contact with the beloved and reflect a strongly narcissistic attitude on the part of the poem's speaker – emerged in Arabia's urban centres early in the Islāmic era. With the passage of time, elements from these two strands were blended into a unified tradition of the Arabic love poem (*ghazal*). Al-Bashshar ibn Burd's divan contains love poems of both types, while Abū Nuwas composes verses involving homosexual and bisexual relationships. The genres of *zajal* and *muwashshah* that originated in Muslim Spain blended 'Umarī and 'Udhrī themes with songs and popular poems in Romance dialects. The *ghazal* has remained popular into the modern period.

The twentieth century produced significant change in Arabic love poetry. The Syrian diplomat and poet Nizar Qabbani managed in a single career to become the Arab world's primary love poet and a commentator on political controversies: "Ah, my love!/What is this nation of ours that can treat love like a policeman?" New initiatives in imagery and mood were fostered by romantic poets such as Khalil Jubran (more commonly known in the West as Khalil Gibran), Iliyya Abū Madi, Abū al-Qāsim al-Shabbi, and 'Alī Mahmud Taha.

The major break with tradition came in the aftermath of the Second World War. The metrical experiments undertaken by the Iraqi poets Nazik al-Mala'ikah and Badr Shakir al-Sayyab in the 1940s, the translation into Arabic of the Middle Eastern segments of Sir James Frazer's *The Golden Bough: A Study in*

Comparative Religion (1890) and T.S. Eliot's poem *The Waste Land* (1922), and political events, especially regarding Israel and Palestine, stimulated the development of an entirely new outlook on the form and content of the poem and the role of the poet. Tawfiq Zayyad, Fadwa Tuqan, Samih al-Qāsim, and Rashid Husayn all addressed themselves to the injustices they saw in Palestinian daily life, while Mahmud Darwish's work encapsulated the fate of his fellow Palestinians through vivid depictions of their losses, their defiance, and their aspirations. Other poets, such as the Iraqi 'Abd al-Wahhab al-Bayati, expressed their commitment to the cause of revolutionary change on a broader canvas.

Beirut in the 1950s witnessed the creation of the poetry group Shi'r ("Poetry"). At its core were Yusuf al-Khal and Adonis (the pen name of 'Alī Ahmad Sa'id), arguably the most influential figure in modern Arabic poetry. In its radical approach to poetic form (including the prose poem) and its experiments with language and imagery, this group was emblematic of the many new directions that Arabic poetry was to follow. Poets such as the Lebanese Khalil Hawi and the Egyptian Salah 'Abd al-Sabur left behind them divans that are already acknowledged as twentieth-century classics of Arabic poetry. Among the notable poets taking poetry in new directions at the turn of the twenty-first century were the Syrian Muhammad al-Maghut, the Moroccan Muhammad Bannis, the Iraqi Sa'di Yusuf, and the Egyptians Muhammad 'Afifi Matar and Amal Dunqul.

Arabic Prose Literature and Drama

The emergence of Arabic prose literature began in the eighth century. Some of the earliest extant Arabic materials consist of the utterances of soothsayers (*kuhhan*), which are in the characteristic form of a pre-Islāmic discourse known as *saj'* (usually translated as "rhyming prose" but almost certainly a very early form of poetic expression) also used in the Qur'ān. There were also accounts of the pre-Islāmic peninsular tribes and their great battles, the so-called Ayyām al-'Arab ("Battle Days of the Arabs"), characteristic of the genre of the *khabar* ("report"). Along with the collections known as Hadith (accounts of the Prophet's sayings and actions) and Sahih (the second most important source of Islāmic law and practice after the Qur'ān itself), these reports also became part of the collections of *maghāzi* (accounts of the Prophet's raids during his lifetime) and *sirah* (biographies of the Prophet).

A major feature of premodern prose literature in Arabic was *adab*, a term that in modern usage is translated as "literature" but which also implies a close linkage between the act of writing and the manners and norms of a community. In the case of Arabic, that community consisted of functionaries of the Islāmic court, especially bureaucrats and chancery officials. With the elaboration of caliphal and other varieties of court life, the *adib* ("litterateur"), the practitioner of *adab*, joined forces with the *nadim* ("boon companion") and the *zarif* ("arbiter of taste and fashion") in providing both enlightenment and entertainment for the ruler. The *adab* prepared codes of conduct and practice for the secretariat, which was growing in conjunction with the administrative needs of the ever-expanding Islāmic dominions, and produced useful (and often diverting) materials.

The arts and subgenres of *adab* were brought to new levels of sophistication in the ninth century by one of Arabic literature's greatest figures, 'Amr ibn Bahr, whose physical ugliness led him to be forever known by the nickname al-Jahiz ("The Man with Boggling Eyes"); and during the tenth and eleventh centuries by Abū Hayyan al-Tawhidi, one of Arabic's greatest stylists. A prodigious polymath, al-Jahiz compiled anthologies of poetry and anecdote about animals (*Kitab al-hayawan*) and misers (*Kitab al-bukhala'*), wrote essays (*rasa'il*) on every conceivable topic, and produced a highly influential work of criticism, *Kitab al-bayan wa al-tabyin* (*Book of Clarity and Clarification*). What sets his work apart is his total mastery of a clear and concise Arabic style and his great predilection for digression. Abū Hayyan al-Tawhidi wrote a renowned anthology of anecdotes, *Kitab al-imta' wa al-mu'anasah* (*Book of Enjoyment and Bonhomie*), and an often scurrilous commentary on cultural and political infighting, *Kitab mathalib al-wazirayn* (*Book on the Foibles of the Two Ministers*).

Many other court officials, bureaucrats, and arbiters of public discourse also contributed to a continuing process whereby information, opinion, and entertainment – manuals, discourses on the Qur'ān, collections of anecdotes and poetry, and essays on specialist topics – were placed at the disposal of the educated elite of the courts within the Islāmic dominions. Ibn Qutaybah's *Kitab 'uyun al-akhbar* (*Book of Springs of Information*, or *Book of Choice Narratives*), which made available to its readers information and anecdote on a wide variety of topics (eloquence, friendship, asceticism, and a final section on women), is one of the earliest examples of the curious yet engaging variety of materials that was characteristic of the court's literary salons (*majalis*). The *Kitab al-aghani* (*Books of Songs*) of Abū al-Faraj al-Isbahani (al-Isfahani), was a major source on Arabic poetry and poets as well as performance practice. Among the *rasa'il* (essays) devoted to particular topics were al-Jahiz's *Risalat al-qiyan* (*The Epistle on Singing-Girls of Jahiz*) and *Dhamm al-hawa* (*Condemnation of Passion*), a preacher's warning concerning the perils of passion – the theme of love was especially popular. Sheikh al-Nafzawi's *Al-Rawd al-'atir fi nuzhat al-khatir* (*The Perfumed Garden Concerning the Heart's Delights*) is, thanks to the interest of Sir Richard Burton (who translated it under the title *The Perfumed Garden of the Cheikh Nefzaoui*), widely known in the English-speaking world as a classic among sex manuals.

Speakers and writers of other languages who became Muslims and worked in the various offices of the court also translated works into Arabic. The eighth-century Persian scholar Ruzbih, who adopted the Arabic name Ibn al-Muqaffa', translated a collection of animal fables about kingship, *Kalilah wa Dimnah* (*Kalilah and Dimnah*). Much of the Hellenistic heritage was also translated from Greek into Arabic and stored in the great Baghdad library Bayt al-Hikmah ("House of Wisdom"). There was also a tradition of historical and geographical writing. Especially notable is al-Mas'udi's *Muruj al-dhahab wa ma'adin al-jawahir* (*The Meadows of Gold and Mines of Gems*), in which he traces the history of the world up to his own time. The tradition of writing histories of enormous scope continued throughout the ensuing centuries, with famous contributions by Ibn Miskawayh, Ibn al-Athir, Ibn Kathir, and Ibn Khaldun, whose introduction to his history *Al-Muqaddimah*, which sought to explain the basic factors in the historical development of the Islāmic countries, is generally acknowledged as a major milestone in historical studies.

The *hajj* has been the inspiration for a school of travel narrative, a genre for which the Arabs are well known (and of which the series of tales recounted by Sindbad the Sailor, a late addition to *The Thousand and One Nights*, is an apt reflection). Some of the best known are Ibn Jubayr's *Rihlah* (*Travels*), a somewhat hyperbolic account of the curiosities he encountered on his journey from Grenada to Mecca, and Ibn

Battūtah's narrative of his travels from Tangier to Mecca and on to China and back, *Tuhfat al-nuzzar fi ghara'ib al- amṣār wa 'aja'ib al-asfar* (*Beholder's Delight Concerning Strange Cities and Incredible Travels*). Others composed narratives involving travel into the worlds of the imagination. The eleventh-century Andalusian poet Ibn Shuhayd, for example, utilized his *Risalat al-tawabi' wa al-zawabi'* (*Epistle on Familiar Spirits and Demons*) to converse with the spirits of his poetic forebears.

One genre that is specific to the Arabic literary tradition is the *maqamah*, a form of narrative that emerged during the tenth century out of several already existing trends. It was a visitor to the court of Rayy in Iran, al-Hamadhani, who managed to combine the new aesthetics of style – especially the adoption of *saj'* – with attractive vignettes of social and intellectual life into a totally new genre. Developed by his great successor al-Hariri into a vehicle for tremendous feats of stylistic virtuosity, the *maqamah* genre was a much-favoured mode of prose expression for the intellectual elite of the Arabic-speaking world until the latter half of the twentieth century.

Attitudes within Arab societies toward appropriateness of language use and performance mode long excluded popular narrative from the Arabic literary canon. Until the advent of broadcast media, the *hakawati* (storyteller), who would recite episodes from some of the great sagas of Arab lore (in Arabic, *siyar sha'biyyah*), remained a major fixture of Arabic-speaking countries. These included the exploits of the legendary poet-cavalier 'Antar, the much-travelled tribal confederacy of the Banū Hilal, the warrior-princess Dhat al-Himmah, and the wily 'Alī Zaybaq. These types of story have served as inspiration and as models not only for writers of modern fiction but also for numerous experiments in drama.

The development of modern Arabic fiction took place within a cultural context in which two major forces were in play: an interest in the products and critical methods of Western literary traditions and a search for inspiration in the Arabic literary heritage. The short story was the first to adapt itself. Early Egyptian pioneers such as 'Abd Allāh Nadim and Mustafa Lutfi al-Manfaluti published vignettes that cast a critical eye on the habits and foibles of their fellow countrymen, while in Lebanon Khalil Jubran (Khalil Gibran) and later Mikha'il Nu'aymah analyzed the problems of family life and broader societal issues, such as the role of the clergy and problems of emigration. A major advance in short-story writing occurred in the early and mid-twentieth century with a group of Egyptian writers, the Jama'at al-Madrasah Hadithah ("New School Group"), of whom Yahya Haqqi and Mahmud Tahir Lashin were the most accomplished.

Writers in other regions developed their own local traditions; these include the Palestinian Khalil Baydas, the Tunisian 'Alī al-Du'aji, the Iraqi Dhu al-Nun Ayyub, and the Lebanese Tawfiq Yusuf 'Awwad. Women writers also began to contribute short stories that provided new insights into issues of family and society; among such pioneers were Suhayr al-Qalamawi of Egypt, Ulfat Idilbi of Syria, and Samirah 'Azzam of Palestine.

Two writers, by their concentration on the art of the short story, came to be widely acknowledged as masters of the craft: Yusuf Idris of Egypt and Zakariyya Tamir of Syria. Beginning a writing career in the 1950s, Idris recounted the realities of the life of the poor and, as political oppression grew, added symbolic portrayals of oppression and alienation that encapsulated an entire era in contemporary Arab societies. Zakariyya Tamir's contributions to the genre tended to be concerned with a highly terse and symbolic representation of the callous indifference of authority and bureaucracy, often expressed through nightmarish visions of violence.

At the beginning of the twenty-first century, the short story was by far the most popular literary genre in the Arab world. It was also frequently adapted for film and television. Distinguished contributors to the genre included Ahmad Buzufur (Buzfur) of Morocco, Hasan Nasr of Tunisia, Haydar Haydar of Syria, Fu'ad al-Tikirli and Muhammad Khudayyir of Iraq, Layla al-'Uthmān of Kuwait, and Yahya al-Tahir 'Abdallah, Muhammad al-Bisati, Salwa Bakr, and Ibrahim Aslan of Egypt.

Through the popularity of early translations into Arabic of works of European fiction and imitations of them by Arab writers, the novel rapidly established a place for itself in the Islāmic world. Among the earliest examples in Arabic were *Ghabat al-haqq* (1865; *Forest of Truth*), an idealistic allegory about freedom, and *Al-Huyam fi jinan al-sham* (1870; *Passion in Syrian Gardens*), a work set during the seventh-century Islāmic conquest of Syria, by Salim al-Bustani. The latter work appeared in serial form in the Bustani family's journal, *Al-Jinan*, and this publication mode established a pattern that was to be followed by writers of Arabic fiction for many decades. Premodern history also came to be frequently invoked in the Arabic novel. Jurji Zaydan's series of novels, for example, set key events in Islāmic history against local backgrounds.

At the same time, a neoclassical strand became evident that focused in particular on the classical genre of the *maqamah*. Nasif al-Yaziji's *Majma' al-Bahrayn* (1856; *The Meeting Place of the Two Seas*) is a conscious revival of the style, while Ahmad Faris al-Shidyaq's *Al-Saq 'ala al-saq fi ma huwa al-Faryaq* (1855; *One Leg over Another* [or *The Pigeon on the Tree Branch*], *Concerning al-Faryaq* [*Faris al-Shidyaq*]), which contains a set of *maqamat*, looks to the future in its use of the autobiographical travel narrative as a means to compare and criticize contemporary societies. Those critical features are even more marked in Muḥammad al-Muwayliḥi's *Hadith 'Isa ibn Hisham* (1907; *Isa ibn Hisham's Tale*), a highly sarcastic account of turn-of-the-century Egypt under British occupation.

The novel in Arabic developed at a different pace in different regions. An important moment in the Egyptian tradition was the 1913 novel *Zaynab* by "a peasant Egyptian". It presents the reader with a nostalgic picture of the Egyptian countryside, which serves as the backdrop for the fervent advocacy of the need for women's education. The author, Muḥammad Husayn Haykal, wrote the work while studying in France, and the influence of European Romantic narrative traditions is clear. Elsewhere, novel writing was initiated at a later date: in Iraq by Mahmud Aḥmad al-Sayyid with *Fi sabil al-zawaj* (1921; *On the Marriage Path*); in Algeria by Aḥmad Rida Huhu with *Ghadat umm al-qura* (1947; *Maid of the City*); and in Morocco by 'Abd al-Majid ibn Jallun with *Fi al-tufulah* (1957; *In Childhood*).

The development of nationalism coupled with developments in education and interest in other literary traditions spurred the novel's development during the 1930s. Early publications were Taha Husayn's fictionalized autobiography, *Al-Ayyam* (3 parts, 1929–67; *The Days*), and the republication of Haykal's *Zaynab* in 1929. The following decade saw the appearance of works by Tawfiq al-Hakim (notably *'Awdat al-ruh* [1933; *Return of the Spirit*] and *Yawmiyyat na'ib fi al-aryaf* [1937; *Diary of a Country Prosecutor*; English translation. *The Maze of Justice*]), Ibrahim al-Mazini, 'Abbās Maḥmūd al-'Aqqād, Mahmud Taymur, and Mahmud Tahir Lashin. Much influenced by these important literary figures, a young philosophy graduate from Cairo University began to explore the novel genre, and in 1939 the first novel of Naguib Mahfouz (Najib Mahfuz) appeared: *'Abath al-aqdar* (*Fates' Mockery*).

Mahfouz, who in 1988 became the first Arab writer to win the Nobel Prize for Literature, is acknowledged as the writer who brought the Arabic novel to a stage of complete maturity and acceptance within the Arabic-speaking world. The social realism of his early "quarters" novels, each one set in a different section (quarter) of the old city of Cairo, culminated in the justly famous *Cairo Trilogy* (1956–7). He then turned to a more symbolic mode (with examples such as *Al-Liss wa al-kilab* [1961; *The Thief and The Dogs*] and *Thartharah fawq al-Nil* [1966; *Chatter on the Nile*]). Thereafter he participated with the members of a younger novelistic generation in a variety of explorations of newer modes and styles, while still casting a critical eye on developments in his homeland and reflecting on the major issues confronting the citizens of the developing world. Today, the novel genre flourishes throughout the Arab world; indeed, to the Egyptian critic Jabir 'Usfur, the beginning of the twenty-first century marked "the era of the novel", to cite the title of his book *Zaman al-riwayah* (1999).

The dramatic tradition in Arabic began with the *hakawati* (storytellers) and enactments of shadow plays (*khayal al-zill*) in cafes and other venues, which regularly poked fun at the foibles of politicians and bureaucrats. Written texts for some thirteenth-century bawdy farces by the Egyptian oculist Ibn Daniyal also provide evidence that a performance tradition had been in existence for some time. The 1847 Syrian production by Marun al-Naqqash of *Al-Bakhil*, a play inspired by Molière's drama *L'Avare* (1669; *The Miser*), is generally regarded as the beginning of the modern Arabic tradition of staged drama. When the Syrian civil war erupted in the 1860s, many theatre troupes moved to Egypt, where the theatrical scene was lively and varied. Drama spread to other regions through the visits of troupes from both Western countries and Egypt itself. Slapstick and singing and dancing were popular, but there were few plays of a more literary or textual aspect. The Egyptian writer Tawfiq al-Hakim, who published his earliest plays under the pseudonym Husayn Tawfiq, answered this need, publishing a series of lengthy plays based on themes culled from Greek legend, the Qur'ān, and Middle Eastern history in the 1930s.

The first of the plays was *Ahl al-kahf* (English translation *Tawfiq al-Hakim's The People of the Cave*), based on the legend of the Seven Sleepers of Ephesus, who emerge from a prolonged period of sleep to find themselves living in the Christian era. *Ahl al-kahf* is probably based on the interpretation of this story in the Qur'ān. Attempts to perform this play revealed at once a tension between a quest for a "literary" tradition of Arabic drama based on the form of the language that is standard throughout the Arab world, and the natural desire to employ colloquial dialects and portray the immediate and pressing social and political issues of the day – a tension that has continued to dog Arabic drama ever since. As al-Hakim's career proceeded, he undertook a number of experiments in an attempt to reconcile these tensions. His most memorable experiment was his attempt to forge what he termed a "third language", which achieved a cleverly crafted level between the literary and the colloquial through the use of syntactic and lexical elements common to both. The result allowed a play to be read on the page as a literary text and to be acted on stage as a somewhat lofty version of the colloquial.

Al-Hakim was one of the favourite authors of Egyptian President Gamal Abdel Nasser, and the two decades after 1952, when Nasser came to power, have come to be regarded as a kind of "golden era" for not merely Egyptian drama but Arabic drama as a whole. Beginning in the 1950s and 1960s with Nu'mān 'Āshūr, who presented the Egyptian public with insightful analyses of its class structure and values, a series of dramatists, among them Sa'd al-Din Wahbah, Mahmud Diyab, and 'Alī Salim, penned in the colloquial dialect of Cairo dramatic texts that were highly successful on stage. Another contributor in this period was Yusuf Idris, whose celebrated play *Al-Farafir* (1964; *The Farfoors*, or *The Flipflap*) combined elements of traditional comic forms of dramatic presentation with such Brechtian effects as the presence of an "author" as a stage character and the use of theatre-in-the-round staging. Alfred Faraj took a somewhat different course, invoking tales and incidents from history and folklore (and especially from *The Thousand and One Nights*) in order to illustrate contemporary political and social realities. His works, in a more literary Arabic than that adopted by his fellow dramatists, gained a broad audience throughout the Arabic-speaking world. Even within the less-fertile environment of the 1980s and 1990s, a younger generation of Egyptian dramatists made notable contributions to the genre, among them Muhammad Salmawi and Lenin al-Ramli.

These patterns of development were echoed elsewhere in the Arab world. In Syria the leading dramatist was Sa'dallah Wannus, whose works made important contributions to the development of experimental theatre in the Arab world, in particular the relationship of stage to audience. Staged in the aftermath of the Arab–Israeli Six-Day War of June 1967, *Haflat samar min ajl al-khamis min Huzayran* (1968; *Soirée for the Fifth of June*) was a devastating commentary on the Arab defeat. *Mughamarat ra's al-mamluk Jabir* (1971; *The Adventure of Mamluk Jabir's Head*) and *Al-Malik huwa al-malik* (1977; *The King's the King*) continued his ongoing experiments with theatre dynamics through what he termed *masrah al-tasyis* ("theatre of politicization").

In Palestine, there were plays that reflected the trials and conflicts that were part of daily life, such as Mu'in Basisu's *Thawrat al-Zanj* (1970; *The Zanj Revolt*) and the poet Samih al-Qāsim's *Qaraqash* (1970). The tightly controlled circumstances in which the Palestinians lived also led to the appearance of the Hakawati theatre troupe, which toured villages and performed its own plays in a variety of public spaces through the turn of the twenty-first century. The Tunisian writer 'Izz al-Dīn al-Madani, one of the most fruitful contributors to the history of modern Arabic drama during the twentieth century, composed a series of plays that were both experimental and popular; they included *Thawrat sahib al-himar* (1971; *The Donkey Owner's Revolt*) and *Diwan al-Zanj* (1973; *The Zanj Collection*). Moroccan theatre was represented at the turn of the twenty-first century primarily by the multi-talented al-Tayyib al-Siddiqi, who adapted textual materials culled from the heritage of the past, as in *Diwan Sidi 'Abd al-Rahman al-Majdhub* (1966; *The Collection of Sidi 'Abd al-Rahman al-Majdhub*).

Most prominent among twentieth-century Iraqi playwrights was Yusuf al-'Ani, whose *Ana ummak ya Shakir* (1955; *Shakir, I'm Your Mother*) graphically portrays the misery of the Iraqi people in the period before the downfall of the monarchy in the revolution of 1958. Elsewhere in the Arabian Gulf, theatre remained, where it existed at all, a very young cultural phenomenon. Arabic drama seems likely to remain a problematic genre in the twenty-first century, but one fulfilling an important cultural function.

Persian Poetry

In 641 the Muslims entered Iran, and Persian influence on literary taste becomes apparent in Arabic literature from the mid-eighth century onward. Soon Iran could boast a large literature in its own tongue. Persian literature was more varied in its forms and content than that written in classical Arabic, and new genres, including epic poetry, were introduced. The lyric reached its finest expression in the Persian language.

During the 'Abbāsid period, a distinct Modern Persian literature came into existence in north-eastern Iran. The first famous representative of this new literature was the poet Rudaki (died 940/41), of whose *qasidah*s only a few have survived. He also worked on a Persian version of *Kalilah wa Dimnah*, and on a version of the *Sendbad-nameh*. Rudaki's poetry points ahead to many of the characteristic features of later Persian poetry. The imagery in particular is sophisticated.

From the tenth century onward, Persian poems were written at almost every court in the Iranian areas, sometimes in dialectical variants. The first important centre of Persian literature existed at the court of Mahmud of Ghazna (died 1030) and his successors, who eventually extended their empire to north-western India. Himself an orthodox warrior, Mahmud in later love poetry was transformed into a symbol of "a slave of his slave" because of his love for a Turkmen officer, Ayaz. Under the Ghaznavids, lyric and epic poetry both developed, as did the panegyric. Classical Iranian topics became the themes, resulting in such diverse works as the love story of Vameq and 'Azra (possibly of Greek origin) and the *Shāh-nāmeh* (*Book of Kings*). A number of gifted poets praised Mahmud and his successors, among them Farrokhi of Seistan (died 1037), the author of a powerful elegy on Mahmud's death.

The main literary achievement of the Ghaznavid period, however, was that of Ferdowsi (died 1020). He compiled the inherited tales and legends about the Persian kings in the epic *Shāh-nāmeh*, which deals with the history of Iran from its beginnings and contains between 35,000 and 60,000 verses in short rhyming couplets. A large part of the work centres on tales of the hero Rostam and the struggle between Iran and Turan (the central Asian steppes). The poem is often considered the masterpiece of Persian national literature. Numerous attempts have been made to emulate it in Iran, India, and Turkey.

Other epic poems, on a variety of subjects, were composed during the eleventh century. The tales of Alexander the Great and his journeys and poetical romances were popular themes. These were soon superseded, however, by the great romantic epics of Nezami of Ganja (died *c.* 1209), in Caucasia. The first work of his *Khamseh* (*Quintet*), *Makhzan ol-asrar* (*Treasury of Mysteries*), is didactic in intention; the subjects of the following three poems are traditional love stories. The last part of the *Khamseh* is *Eskandar-nameh*, which relates the adventures of Alexander in Africa and Asia, as well as his discussions with the wise philosophers. Nezami's ability to present a picture of life through highly refined language and a wholly apt choice of images is quite extraordinary. Unsurprisingly, Nezami's work inspired countless poets' imitations in different languages – including Turkish, Kurdish, and Urdu – while painters constantly illustrated his stories for centuries afterward.

In addition to epic poetry, the lesser forms, such as the *qasidah* and *ghazal*, developed during the eleventh and twelfth centuries. Many poets wrote at the courts of the Seljuqs and also at the Ghaznavid court in Lahore, where the poet Mas'ud-e Sa'd-e Salman (died 1121) composed a number of heartfelt *qasidah*s during his political imprisonment. They are outstanding examples of the category of *habsiyah* (prison poem). Other famous examples include those written by the Arab knight Abū Firas (died 968) in a Byzantine prison; and in modern times, those by the Urdu poets Ghalib in the nineteenth century and Faiz in the twentieth century, and by the contemporary Turkish poet Nazim Hikmet (died 1963).

The most complicated forms were mastered by poets of the very early period, the limits of artificiality being reached in Azerbaijani *qasidah*s by the poet Qatran (died 1072). Anvari (died *c.* 1189), whose patrons were the Seljuqs, is considered the most accomplished writer of panegyrics in the Persian tongue. His *Tears of Khorāsān*, mourning the passing of Seljuq glory, is among the best known of Persian *qasidah*s. In the west of Iran, Anvari's contemporary Khaqani (died *c.* 1190), who wrote mainly at the court of the Shirvan-Shahs of Transcaucasia, is the outstanding master of the hyperbolic style, best known perhaps for his verses on the ruined Taq Kisra at Ctesiphon on the Tigris. His *qasidah*s on the pilgrimage to Mecca, which also inspired his *masnavi* ("the doubled one", or rhyming couplet, and by extension a poem consisting of a series of such couplets) *Tuhfat al-'Iraqayn ol-'Eraqeyn* (*Gift of the Two Iraqs'*), translate most eloquently the feelings of a Muslim at the festive occasion.

The Ghaznavid and Seljuq periods also produced first-rate scholars. Naser-e Khosrow (died 1087/8), who acted for a time as a missionary for the Isma'ili branch of Shī'ite Islām, wrote a book about his journey to Egypt, *Safar-nameh*. The work done in mathematics by early Arabic scholars was continued by Omar Khayyam (died 1122). But Omar has become famous in the West through the free adaptations by Edward FitzGerald of his *roba'iyat*, which has been translated into almost every known language.

From the eleventh century onward what was to be one of the most common types of Persian literature came into existence: the mystical poem. Sana'i (died 1131?), at one time a court poet of the Ghaznavids, composed the first mystical epic, the didactic *Hadiqat al-haqiqat wa shari 'at-aṭarīqah* (*The Garden of Truth and the Law of the Path*), which has some 10,000 verses. In this poem, the pattern for all later mystical *masnavi*s is established: wisdom is embodied in stories and anecdotes; parables and proverbs are woven into the texture of the story. Among Sana'i's smaller *masnavi*s, *Sayr al-'ibad ila al-ma'ad* (*The Journey of the Servants to the Place of Return*) deserves special mention. Its theme is the journey of the spirit through the spheres, a subject dear to the mystics and still employed in modern times as, for example, by Iqbal in his Persian *Javid-nameh* (1932). Sana'i's epic endeavours were continued by one of the most prolific writers in the Persian tongue, Farīd od-Dīn 'Aṭṭār (died *c.* 1220). The most famous among his *masnavi*s is the *Mantiq ut-tayr* (*The Conference of the Birds*), the story of 30 birds who, in search of their spiritual king, journey through seven valleys.

The most famous of the Persian mystical *masnavi*s is by Mawlana ("Our Lord") Jalal ad-Din ar-Rumi (died 1273) and is known simply as the *Masnavi*. It comprises some 26,000 verses and is a complete encyclopaedia of all the mystical thought, theories, and images known in the thirteenth century. It is regarded by most of the Persian-reading orders of Sufis as second in importance only to the Qur'ān. Jalal ad-Din was also the author of love lyrics – inspired by love for the wandering mystic, Shams ad-Din of Tabriz – whose beauty surpasses even that of the tales in the *Masnavi*. His dithyrambic lyrics, whose vocabulary and imagery are taken directly from everyday life, are vivid, fresh, and convincing, and the sincerity of his love and longing is never overshadowed, nor is his personality veiled. In these respects he is unique in Persian literature.

During the thirteenth century, when Islāmic literatures reached their zenith, Mosleh od-Din Sa'di (died 1292) returned in about 1256 to his birthplace, Shiraz, after years of journeying; his *Bustan* (*The Orchard*) and *Golestan* (*Rose Garden*) have been popular ever since. The *Bustan* is a didactic poem written in polished, easy-flowing style and a simple metre; the *Golestan*, completed one year later, in 1258, and dealing with different aspects of human life and behaviour, has been judged "the finest flower that could blossom in a Sultan's garden" (Johann Gottfried von Herder). Sa'di may also have been the first writer in Iran to compose the sort of love poetry that is now thought of as characteristic of the *ghazal*.

The influence of mysticism, on the one hand, and of the elaborate Persian poetical tradition, on the other, is apparent during the later decades of the thirteenth century, both in Anatolia and in Muslim India. The Persian mystic Fakhr-ud-Din 'Iraqi (died 1289), a master of delightful love lyrics, lived for almost 25 years in Multan (in present-day Pakistan), where his lively *ghazal*s are still sung. While in Multan he may have met the young Amir Khosrow of Delhi (died 1325), who was one of the most versatile authors to write in Persian, not only in India but in the entire realm of Persian culture. Khosrow wrote panegyrics of seven successive kings of Delhi and, imitating Nezami's *Khamseh*, introduced a novelistic strain into the *masnavi* by recounting certain events of his own time in poetical form. His *ghazal*s contain many of the elements that in the sixteenth and seventeenth centuries were to become characteristic of the "Indian" style. Khosrow's poetry surprises the reader in its use of unexpected forms and unusual images, complicated constructions and verbal plays, all handled fluently and presented in technically perfect language.

Epics, panegyrics, and mystico-didactical poetry had all reached their finest hour by the end of the thirteenth century; the one genre to attain perfection slightly later was the *ghazal*, of which Mohammad Shams od-Din Hafez (died 1389/90) is the incontestable master. Hafez lived in Shiraz, and his small collection of work – his divan contains about 400 *ghazal*s – was soon acclaimed as the finest lyrical poetry ever written in Persian. He is an outstanding exponent of the ambiguous and oscillating style that makes Persian poetry so attractive. The different levels of experience are all expressed through the same images and symbols: the beloved is always cruel, whether a chaste virgin or a professional courtesan, or (as in most cases) a handsome young boy, or God himself – or even, on the political plane, the remote despot. The human beloved could effortlessly be regarded as God's manifestation; the rose became a symbol of highest divine beauty and glory; the nightingale represented the yearning and complaining soul; wine, cup, and cupbearer became the embodiment of enrapturing divine love. No other Persian poet has used such complex imagery on so many different levels with such harmonious and well-balanced lucidity.

Hafez's contemporary in Shiraz was the satirist 'Obeyd-e Zakani (died 1371), noted for his obscene verses and for his short *masnavi* called *Mush o-gorbeh* (*Mouse and Cat*), an amusing political satire. With few new forms or means of expression open to them, 'Obeyd and other poets began ridiculing the classic models of literature: thus, Boshaq (died *c.* 1426) composed odes and *ghazal*s exclusively on the subject of food.

The last great centre of Islāmic art in the region of Iran was the Timurid court of Herat, where Dowlatshah (died 1494) composed his much-quoted biographical work on Persian poets. The leading figure in this circle was 'Abd or-Rahman Jami (died 1492), who wrote an excellent imitation of Nezami's *Khamseh*, enlarging it by the addition of two mystical *masnavi*s into a septet called *Haft owrang* (*The Seven Thrones*, or *Ursa Major*). Among his other works are biographies of the Sufi saints and, in imitation of Sa'di, the *Baharestan* (*Orchard of Spring*), written in prose interspersed with verses. Jami also wrote treatises about literary riddles and various kinds of intellectual games, of which Muslim society in the late fifteenth century was very fond and which remain a feature of erudite Persian and Turkish poetry. His influence on the work of later poets, especially in Ottoman Turkey, was very powerful.

During the first five centuries of Modern Persian literary life, a multitude of prose works were written. Among them, the "Mirror for Princes" deserves special mention. This genre, introduced from Persian into Arabic as early as the eighth century, flourished once more in Iran during the late eleventh century. One important example is the *Qabus-nameh* by the Zeyarid prince 'Onsor ol-Ma'ali Keykavus (died 1098), which presents "a miscellany of Islāmic culture in pre-Mongol times." At the same time, Nizam al-Mulk (died 1092), the grand vizier of the Seljuqs, composed his *Seyasat-nameh* (*Book of Government*), a good introduction to the statesman's craft according to medieval Islāmic standards. In the same period and environment, even a mystic like al-Ghazālī felt disposed to write a *Nasihat al-muluk* (*Counsel for Kings*). Others, especially in India, exhorted rulers in their writings.

Belles lettres proper found a fertile soil in Iran. The fables of *Kalilah wa Dimnah*, for example, were retold several times in Persian. The most famous version, called *Anvar-e soheyli* (*Lights of Canopus*), was composed by a famous mystic, Hoseyn Wa'ez-e Kashefi of Herat (died 1504). The "cyclic story" form (in which several unconnected tales are held together by a common framework or narrator device), inherited from India, became as popular in Iran as it had been in the Arabic-speaking countries. The *Sendbad-nameh* and the *Tutinameh* (*Parrot Book*), which is based on Indian tales, are both good examples. The first comprehensive collection of entertaining prose is *Jawami' al-hikayat* (*Collections of Stories*), by 'Owfi (died *c.* 1230).

Anecdotes were an important feature of the biographical literature that became popular in Iran and Muslim India. Biographies of the poets of a certain age or of a specified area were collected together. One of the most remarkable works in this field is *Chahar maqaleh* (*Four Treatises*) by Nezami-ye 'Aruzi, a writer from eastern Iran. Written in about 1156, this little book is an excellent introduction to the ideals of Persian literature and its writers, discussing in detail what is required to make a perfect poet. This tendency toward "anecdotal" writing can also be observed in the cosmographical books and in some of the historical books produced in medieval Iran. The cosmography *Nuzhat al-qulub* (*Pleasure of the Hearts*), by Hamdollah Mostowfi (died after 1340), underlined the mysterious aspects of the marvels of creation and mixed folkloristic and scientific material.

Historical writing proper had been begun by the Persians as early as the late tenth century, with Bal'ami's abridged translation of the vast Arabic chronicle by at-Tabarī (died 923). Its heyday in Iran, however, was the Il-Khanid period (mid-thirteenth to mid-fourteenth century). Iran was then ruled by the successors of Genghis Khan, spurring interest in the history of pre-Islāmic Central Asia, whence the rulers had come. *Tarikh-e jehan-goshay* (*History of the World Conqueror*), by 'Ata Malek Joveynī (died 1283), and *Jami' at-tawarikh* (*Collector of Chronicles*), by the physician and vizier Rashid ad-Din (executed 1318), are outstanding examples of histories filled with valuable information.

In addition to poetry and serious prose work, Islāmic literature also contains a great quantity of popular literature, of which the most famous expression is *Alf laylah wa laylah* (*The Thousand and One Nights*), first translated into Persian as *Hazar afsanak* (*Thousand Tales*). These fanciful fairy tales were later expanded with stories and anecdotes from Baghdad. Subsequently, some tales about rogues, tricksters, and vagabonds were added in Egypt. Independent series of stories, such as that of Sindbad the Sailor, were also included.

From pre-Islāmic times the Arabs had recounted tales of the *ayyām al-ʿArab* ("Days of the Arabs"), which concerned their tribal wars, and had dwelt upon tales of the heroic deeds of certain of their brave warriors. In Iran, many of the historical legends and myths had been borrowed and turned into high literature by Ferdowsi. Accounts of the glorious adventures of heroes from early Islāmic times were afterwards retold throughout Iran, India, and Turkey. Thus, the *Dastan-e Amir Hamzeh*, a story of Muḥammad's uncle Hamzah ibn ʿAbd al-Muṭṭalib, was slowly enlarged by the addition of more and more fantastic details. The epics of Köroglu are common to both Iranian and Turkish tradition; he was a noble warrior-robber who became one of the central figures in folk literature from Central Asia to Anatolia.

Some popular epics were composed in the late Middle Ages, having as their basis local traditions. One such epic was based on the Turco-Iranian legend of an eighth-century hero, Abū Muslim. Apart from heroic figures, the Muslim peoples further share a comic character – basically a type of low-class theologian, called Nasreddin Hoca in Turkish, Juha in Arabic, and Mushfiqi in Tadzhik.

Shortly after the introduction of the printing press, Turkey and Iran began to produce cheap books, sometimes illustrated, containing popular romantic love stories or fairy tales. According to Persian tradition, the last classic author in literature was Jami, who died in 1492. The beginning of the sixteenth century was crucial in the history of the Muslim East. In 1501, the young Isma'il I founded the Safavid rule in Iran, and the Shī'ite persuasion of Islām was declared the state religion. Safavid Iran lost most of its artists and poets to the neighbouring countries: there were no great masters of poetry in Iran between the sixteenth and eighteenth centuries. While the Persian Shah Isma'il wrote Turkish mystical verses, his contemporary and enemy, Sultan Selim I of Turkey (died 1520), composed quite elegant Persian *ghazal*s. And while some accomplished poets were to be found writing in Persian in Mughal India in this period, Babur (died 1530) composed his autobiography in Eastern Turkic.

For Islāmic countries, the nineteenth century marked the beginning of a new epoch. While the last "classical" poet, Qa'ani (died 1854), had been displaying the traditional glamorous artistry, his contemporary, the satirist Yaghma (died 1859), had been using popular and comprehensible language to make coarse criticisms of contemporary society. As in the other Islāmic countries, a move toward simplicity is discernible during the last decades of the nineteenth century. The members of the polytechnic college Dar ol-Fonun (founded 1851), led by its erudite principal Reza Qoli Khan Hedayat, helped to shape the "new" style by making translations from European languages. Shah Naser od-Din himself described his journeys to Europe in the late 1870s in a simple, unassuming style and in so doing set an example to future prose writers.

At the turn of the twentieth century, literature became for many younger writers an instrument of modernization and of revolution in the largest sense of the word. The feelings and situation of women were stated and interpreted; their oppression, their problems, and their grievances were a major theme of literature in the first decades of the twentieth century. The works of the "King of Poets", Bahar (died 1951), though highly classical in form, were of great influence; they dealt with contemporary events and appealed to a wide public.

One branch of modern Persian literature is closely connected with a group of Persian authors who lived in Berlin after the First World War. There they established the Kaviani Press, and among the poems they printed were several by 'Aref Qazvini (died 1934), one of the first genuinely modern writers. They also published the first short stories of Mohammad 'Alī Jamalzadeh, whose outspoken social criticism and complete break with the traditional inflated and pompous prose style inaugurated a new era of modern Persian prose. Many young writers adopted this new form, among them Sadeq Hedayat (died 1951), whose stories – which describe the distress and anxiety of a hopeless youth, and are written in a direct, everyday language – have been translated into many languages.

As in neighbouring countries, women played a considerable role in the development of modern Persian literature. The lyrics of Parvin E'tesami (died 1940) are regarded as near classics, despite a trace of sentimentality in their sympathetic treatment of the poor. Some Persian writers whose left-wing political ideas brought them into conflict with the government left for the Soviet Union. Of these, the gifted poet Lahuti (died 1957) is the most important representative.

The new attitudes that have informed literature are even more conspicuous in poetry, where there has been a loosening of tradition, and imagery has been used in new ways. One notable poet was Forugh Farrokhzad, who wrote powerful yet very feminine poetry. Her free verses, interpreting the insecurities of the age, are full of longing. Poems by such critically minded writers as Seyavush Kasra'i also borrow the classical heritage of poetic imagery, transforming it into expressions that win a response from modern readers.

Turkish Literature

The earliest Turkish literature was produced in Mongol-controlled Anatolia during the later thirteenth century. From the fourteenth century, writing in Turkish flourished in the Ottoman Empire. The oldest genre of Turkish literature is the heroic epic, of which the prime example is the *Kitab-i Dede Korkut* (*The Book of My Grandfather Korkut*; English translation *The Book of Dede Korkut*); sources suggest that the tales date from the ninth and tenth centuries. Originally created by an oral bard, or *ozan*, there is no overall narrative framework, but most of the 12 tales revolve around legendary Oghuz heroes. Much of the style of the *Korkut* predates the heroic tradition of the Oghuz Turkish poet-musician known as the *âsik*, who emerged in the sixteenth century in Anatolia, Iran, and the southern Caucasus. The classical *âsik* of the Anatolian Turkmen tribes was Karacaoglan, who flourished in the later sixteenth century or possibly the mid-seventeenth century. His poetry is closely related to folk verse, and he generally treats lyrical themes without the mystical subtext that was common in courtly verse of the period.

During the seventeenth century the popular urban song (*sarki*) was taken up by court poets and musicians. The great seventeenth-century poet Nâ'ilî was the first to include such songs in his divan, a practice that reached its culmination in the following century with Ahmed Nedim. The outstanding *âsik* of the later seventeenth century was Âsik Ömer, who wrote both folkloric *qosma* poems and courtly lyrics, or *gazel*s (Persian: *ghazal*s).

By the middle of the thirteenth century, mystical (Sufi) poetry had become a major branch of Turkish literature, with Sufi poets working primarily in Anatolian Turkish. One of the two well-known poets of the thirteenth and fourteenth centuries was Âsik Pasa, author of the *Garibnameh* (*The Book of the Stranger*), a didactic poem of some 11,000 couplets that explores philosophical and moral themes. It is considered among the finest *mesnevî*s (Persian: *masnavi*s) of the era. Yunus Emre, author of a divan and of the didactic *mesnevî Risâlet'ün nushiyye* (*Treatise of Counsel*), was the period's other well-known poet.

Later in the thirteenth century Seyid Imadeddin Nesimi, probably of south-east Anatolia, created brilliant Sufi verse in Persian and in a form of Turkish rather closer to Azerbaijani. The fifteenth century saw a split between heterodox Sufi tendencies, as seen in the verse of Kaygusuz Abdal, and the orthodox Sufism of Esrefoglu Rumi, whose verse, like that of Emre, communicates his sacerdotal authority to his disciples. By the early sixteenth century, this style of poetry, generally known as *ilâhî* ("divine"), was practised by such sheikh-poets as Ibrahim Gülseni and his son Gülsenîzâde Hayali. The growth during the sixteenth and seventeenth centuries of this type of poetry, which was intended to be sung in the *dhikr* ceremony, was a function of the monopoly over mysticism held by the Sufi brotherhoods of that era. The most outstanding representative of this tradition is Niyazi Misri, a seventeenth-century poet of the Halvetiye *tarikat*.

The forms, genres, and themes of pre-Ottoman and Ottoman Turkish poetry – those works written between about 1300 and 1839 – were generally derived from those of Persian literature. The dominant forms were the *gazel* and the *kasîde* (originally from the Arabic *qasidah*). The images of the *gazel* cast the poet as the lover singing to his beloved – that is, as the nightingale singing to the rose. The speaker, addressee, and theme might change from couplet to couplet. Originally, it was mainly religious *gazel*s that retained a single speaker and theme, but by the mid-seventeenth century, with the work of poets Cevri, Nâ'ilî, Fehim, and Nesatî, *gazel*s of all sorts became largely monothematic.

The *kasîde* was an encomium whose object was to praise its subject, and could be secular or religious. The religious *kasîde* had as its ostensible subject God, the Prophet Muḥammad, or ʿAlī, Muḥammad's son-in-law and the fourth caliph. Secular *kasîde*s usually took as their subject individuals – a sultan, a vizier, a pasha, or a high member of the secular bureaucracy – or specific events, such as a military victory.

The Ottomans' principal narrative poetic form, the *mesnevî*, was also made up of couplets. During the late fourteenth and early fifteenth centuries, Ottoman writers achieved distinction by writing original *mesnevî*s, such as the *Çengname* (*Tale of the Harp*), a mystical allegory by Ahmed-i Dâi, and the satirical *Harname* (*Tale of the Donkey*), by Sinan Seyhi. A century later, Lâmiî Çelebi of Bursa, influenced by the fifteenth-century Persian scholar and poet Jami, initiated translations of the major Persian *mesnevî*s into Turkish. The acknowledged Ottoman master of the genre in the late fifteenth and early sixteenth centuries, however, was Nev'î-zade Atâyî, who broke up the narrative into small unconnected tales. Also notable is the *Leyla ü Mecnun* (*Leyla and Mejnun*) of Mehmed bin Süleyman Fuzuli, written in the sixteenth century.

By the seventeenth century both the Persian and the Chagatai *mesnevî* forms had gone into decline, and Ottoman writers generally ceased to treat the genre as one of first-rate literary significance. Nevertheless, the final two major works of Ottoman literature were written in the *mesnevî* form: *Hüsn ü ask* (1782; *Beauty and Love*), a mystical allegory by Seyh Galib, and *Mihnetkesan* (1822; *The Sufferers*), a self-satirizing autobiography by Keçecizade Izzet Molla.

While the *gazel* was the Ottoman lyric form par excellence, stanzaic forms, including the elaborate *tercibend* and *terkibbend*, were also in limited use. Poems that use these forms are frequently elegies, in which case they are called *mersiyes*. A masterpiece of the *terkibbend* genre is the elegy for Sultan Süleyman I written by Bâkî in the sixteenth century. Other Ottoman stanzaic forms utilize varying numbers of couplets, such as the *müseddes*, which has three, exemplified by the fine *Müseddes der ahvâl-i hod* (*Six-Line Poem on His Own State*), by Nâ'ilî.

Patronage for Ottoman poets in the classical age varied: poets were attached to the imperial household in Bursa or, later, Istanbul, or they were supported at the provincial Anatolian courts of the Ottoman princes. Aside from the sultan, the leading ministers of state might also contribute toward the upkeep of poets. A major basis for this structure of poetic patronage was the bureaucratization of the *ulema* (the Turkish spelling of *'ulama'*). A talented poet who was a graduate of a *madrese* (*madrasah*) could expect an appointment first as a *mülâzim* (assistant professor) and eventually as a *müderris* (professor).

From the beginning of the reign of Sultan Selim I in 1512 until the 1539 reorganization of the bureaucracy (following the execution of Ibrahim Pasa in 1536), the Ottoman state seemed able to support leading poets. But after this time the state began to view its bureaucratic and fiscal needs as holding priority over its literary ones. The real and apparently inexorable decline in state patronage for poetry set in with the accession of Murad III as sultan in 1574.

Ottoman poetry of the later fifteenth and sixteenth centuries represents a mature synthesis of the three major Islāmic languages – Turkish, Persian, and Arabic – within a secure matrix of Turkish syntax. The literary production of the Ottoman court, however, remained predominantly Turkish. Stylistically, the sixteenth century was marked by two major trends: further elaboration of the Turkish courtly style of the later fifteenth century and the creation of a new synthesis of Sufi and secular concerns. The foremost representative of the former movement was Bâkî; the latter was Hayali Bey.

In the second half of the sixteenth century, the courtly style asserted itself by way of the brilliant poetry of Bâkî, a ranking member of the *ulema*, and in the first half of the seventeenth century by Yahya Efendi, who rose to the position of *seyhü- lislâm*, the highest rank within the *ulema*. However, this style was challenged by Nef'i, an aristocrat from the eastern Ana- tolian provinces and a master of the *kasîde*, who emphasized his outsider identity by perfecting his satirical verse (*hiciv*; Arabic: *hija'*) and by adopting features of the new Indo– Persian style of the Mughal court. In doing so, he initiated a major stylistic movement in Ottoman poetry. The principal poets of this school were Cevri, Nâ'ilî, Fehim, and Nesatî, all of whom wrote some of the very finest verse in Ottoman Turkish.

In the seventeenth century this newer style of poetry was termed *tâze-gû'î* ("fresh speech") or *tarz-i nev* ("new style"). (By the early twentieth century it had come to be known as poetry of the Indian school, or Sabk-i Hindi.) This period also saw Persian poets such as Kalîm Kâshânî and Saib-i Tabrizi, encouraged by the Mughal court, develop their meditations on the poetic imagination. Much of this new philosophy of literature and poetic style influenced an important group of seventeenth-century Ottoman poets. The Mawlawiyah (Turkish: Mevleviyah), an order of dervishes who were followers of the thirteenth-century Sufi mystic and poet Rumi, exerted a major influence on poetry. Cevri and Nesatî are the prime examples of leaders of the "fresh speech" who were committed Mawlawiyah. In the Ottoman capital the order began to create an alternative structure of literary evaluation that was independent of the courtly tradition, which had by this time become largely dominated by the higher *ulema*. The leading poet of the later seventeenth century was Nâbî, whose fame rests mainly on his didactic *mesnevî Hayrîyye*, which contains moral maxims for his son.

The eighteenth century witnessed significant changes in style and genre that led ultimately to the dissolution of the classic form of Ottoman poetry. The first third of the eighteenth century was dominated by Ahmed Nedim, who rose to prominence under the grand vizier Damad Ibrahim Pasa between 1718 and 1730. Nedim's fame rests largely on his *kasîde*s, and on his work in two lesser genres. Nedim's *tarîh*s (chronograms) display an entirely new awareness of the physical characteristics of the buildings being praised and thus mark a shift from formal, highly stylized techniques of literary representation to ones based partly on observation of worldly phenomena. Similarly, his *sarki*s (a form of urban popular song) revel in the physical surroundings of the pleasure grounds of Sa'adabad Palace in Tehran.

The leading poet of the middle of the eighteenth century was Koca Ragib Pasa, whose *gazel*s shows a happy synthesis of the canonical tradition of Bâkî with the "fresh" (or "Indian") style of Nâ'ilî. In the last third of the eighteenth century poets turned from lyricism toward colloquial speech, sometimes also embracing a new form of poetic subversion by which the praise characterizing the traditional lyric was replaced by its traditional opposite – *hiciv*, the poetry of satire. Fazil Enderunî went even further in his *sehrengiz* (city-description) genres, of which *Hubanname* (*The Book of Beauties*), *Zenanname* (*The Book of Women*), and *Çengîname* (*The Book of Dancing Boys*) were part. All of these are replete with dialogue and descriptions that are both satirical and vulgar. These tendencies took a more mature form in the *Mihnetkesan* (1823–4) of Keçecizade Izzet Molla, who wrote a humorous autobiographical *mesnevî* of his trials and misfortunes as he was sent into exile from the capital which has been hailed by some as the first work of modern Ottoman literature.

One of the most important Ottoman literary classics was created at the end of the eighteenth century, when Seyh Galib, a sheikh of the Galata Mawlawiyah dervishes, wrote his highly Persianate language *mesnevî Hüsn ü ask* (1782; *Beauty and Love*), an allegorical narrative poem, which is perhaps the greatest *mesnevî* ever written by an Ottoman poet. The last chapter of traditional Ottoman verse was written in the mid- and late nineteenth century within a bureaucratic circle, the Encüman-i Suarâ ("Council of Poets") group of Leskofçali Galib Bey, which also included Arif Hikmet Bey and Yenisehirli Avnî Bey. The Indian-style poets of the mid-seventeenth century, especially Nâ'ilî, Nesatî, and Fehim, furnished the models for these late Ottoman poets, who rejected the type of change that began engulfing Ottoman literature in the 1840s.

The lack of faith in traditional literary models that had emerged during the later eighteenth century took a drastic new turn for the generation that experienced the Tanzimat reforms which began in 1839, aimed at modernizing the Ottoman state. The most radical new voice was that of Ibrahim Sinasi, who started the newspaper *Tasvir-i Efkar* (*Description of Ideas*). He subsequently became the first modern Ottoman playwright with his *Sair evlenmesi* (1859; *The Wedding of a Poet*). At mid-century Sinasi succeeded in winning both Ziya Pasa and Namik Kemal over from Leskofçali Galib Bey's group to the cause of modernization. In exile in Geneva in 1870, Ziya Pasa wrote the *Zafername* (*The Book of Victory*) as a satire on the grand vizier Mehmed Emin Âli Pasa and as a general attack on the state of the empire; it was a far-reaching modern development of the type of satire used by Vasif Enderunî in the previous generation. Namik Kemal in the late 1860s left Turkey for London, where he devoted himself to poetry and theatre that carried a strong nationalist and modernizing message. His most famous play was *Vatan; yahut, Silistre* (1873; *The Motherland; or, Silistria*). After the accession of Abdülhamid II as sultan in 1876, the increasingly strict censorship, which lasted until the revolution of the Young Turks in 1908, limited the possibilities for the development of new Ottoman literature.

The novel made its appearance in Turkish in the late nineteenth century, most notably with the works of Ahmet Mithat, who published prolifically between 1875 and 1910. During Mithat's lifetime, both the novel and poetry assumed a strongly public, didactic orientation that would prove highly influential among many writers well into the twentieth century. Tevfik Fikret became a major literary voice of the late Ottoman era through his editorship of the literary journal *Servet-i fünun* (1896–1901; *The Wealth of Knowledge*) and his leadership of the literary circle of the same name. His poetry displays a shift from the romanticism of his early works (such as *Rübab-i sikeste* [1900; *The Broken Viol*]) to social and political criticism after 1901.

Despite the numerous political problems of the Young Turk era (1908–18), the easing of censorship allowed writers a greater freedom of expression. Refik Halid Karay became one of the leading short-story writers in Turkey, his work characterized by a highly nuanced ear for the local speech of various social groups and a keen eye for detail in locations within Istanbul. Among his best short stories are *Seftali bahçeleri* (1919; *The Peach Orchards*), a half-ironic description of the placid lives of an earlier generation of provincial bureaucrats, and *Saka* (1913; *The Joke*), a more jaundiced view of the same class during his own time.

Other writers who emerged during the early twentieth century, such as Memduh Sevket Esendal, Omer Seyfeddin, Yakup Kadri Karaosmanoglu, and Resat Nuri Güntekin, employed the short story mostly as a vehicle for social edification and commentary. One of the period's more striking figures was Halide Edib Adivar, who wrote some of her best-known works in English and was the first Turkish female writer to attain widespread recognition. Among her works are *The Clown and His Daughter* (1935), which later became a bestseller in Turkish as *Sinekli bakkal*. Sevket Süreyya Aydemir's autobiographical novel *Suyu arayan adam* (1961; *The Man in Search of Water*) displays a brilliant style and reveals a deep search for a personal and national self that was rare in Turkish prose.

In poetry the outstanding figure of that generation was Yahya Kemal Beyatli. Although he supported republican principles, much of Beyatli's poetry glorifies the Ottoman past. His lasting artistic achievement was his synthesis of classical Ottoman and contemporary French poetry. One of the most multifaceted figures of twentieth-century Turkish literature was Ahmed Hamdi Tanpinar, who wrote scholarly works on modern Turkish literature, short stories, lyrical poetry and novels – the last giving him a reputation as the founder of modernist fiction in Turkey. *Saatleri ayarlama enstitüsü* (serialized 1954, published in book form 1961; *The Time*

Regulation Institute), the most complex novel written in Turkish until the 1980s and 1990s, was his most important; it is the autobiography of Hayri Irdal, a poorly educated petit bourgeois born in Istanbul in the 1890s.

Most poets of the 1930s and 1940s rejected Beyatli's neo-Ottomanism and preferred a much simpler style reminiscent of folk poetry. The outstanding figure of the era was the communist Nazim Hikmet. Much influenced by the modernist style of the Russian poets Aleksandr Blok and Vladimir Mayakovsky, his *Seyh Bedreddin destani* (1936; *The Epic of Sheikh Bedreddin*) is an unprecedented work that blends a folk ballad style with poetic modernism. A political prisoner for long periods in Turkey, Hikmet's later poetry was not published in Turkey until 1965 and so affected only a much younger generation. He went on to become the most widely known and translated Turkish poet of the twentieth century. His major works include *Moskova senfonisi* (1952; *The Moscow Symphony*) and *Memleketimden insan manzaralari* (1966–7; *Human Landscapes from My Country*).

In 1941 three poets – Orhan Veli Kanik, Oktay Rifat, and Melih Cevdet Anday – initiated the Garip ("Strange") movement with publication of a volume of poetry by the same name. In it they emphasized simplified language, folkloric poetic forms, and themes of alienation in the modern urban environment. Later, Anday broke with this style, treating philosophical and aesthetic issues in his poetry in a more complex manner. One of his best-known collections is *Göçebe denizin üstünde* (1970; *On the Nomad Sea*). The Garip group had immense influence on Turkish poetry.

Behçet Necatigil chose a distinct poetic path, eventually creating poems that are models of brevity and wit. *Sevgilerde* (1976; *Among the Beloveds*) is a collection of his earlier poetry. Fazil Hüsnü Daglarca, who wrote modernist poetry, became one of Turkey's most influential poets during the post-Second World War era. Choosing a simplified and modernist literary form, Necip Fazil Kisakürek turned his critique of the alienation of the individual in modern society into a conservative Islāmist political message. Collections of his poetry include *Sonsuzluk kervani* (1955; *The Caravan of Eternity*) and *Siirlerim* (1969; *My Poems*).

The two outstanding short-story writers of the mid-twentieth century were Sait Faik Abasiyanik and Sabahattin Alī. Abasiyanik revolutionized the Turkish short story by choosing a stream-of-consciousness style in which plot is de-emphasized. His many collections of short stories include *Semaver* (1936; *The Samovar*) and *Mahkeme kapisi* (*The Court-House Gate*), published posthumously in 1956. Sabahattin Alī addressed social themes. His short story *Ses* (1937; *The Voice*) is representative of his thematic concerns: it describes an encounter between two educated urbanites and a village troubadour, through which Sabahattin Alī points toward the incompatibility of the aesthetic ideals of the West and those of a Turkish village.

As literacy spread to the countryside after the founding of the Turkish republic in 1923 and the output of urban writers became more varied, Turkish writers expanded their thematic horizons. Among the most influential novelists of the generation born in the 1920s is Yashar Kemal, who in 1955 published the novella *Teneke* (*The Tin Pan*) and his first full-length novel, *Ince Memed* (*Thin Memed*; English translation *Memed, My Hawk*), both of which brought him immediate recognition. The latter, later made into a film, is set in the rural eastern Anatolia of his youth and portrays the glaring social contradictions there, often aggravated by the process of modernization under the capitalist system. Kemal subsequently published novels at frequent intervals, including *Yer demir gök bakir*

(1963; *Iron Earth, Copper Sky*), *Binbogalar efsanesi* (1971; *The Legend of a Thousand Bulls*), and *Demirciler çarsisi cinayeti* (1974; *Murder in the Ironsmiths Market*), as well as highly acclaimed collections of short stories.

Adalet Agaoglu portrayed life from a more personal and introverted perspective. Her novels deal with a broad spectrum of the social changes and repression that occurred within the Turkish republic, and she was among the first Turkish writers to treat sexual themes in depth. Her first novel, *Ölmeye yatmak* (1973; *Lying Down to Die*), brought her considerable success. Another writer who treated sexual issues was the promising young novelist Sevgi Soysal, whose career was cut short by her death in 1976. Her first novel, *Yürümek* (1970; *To Walk*), features a stream-of-consciousness narrative and a keen ear for local dialogue.

Although he wrote prolifically in every genre, Necati Cumali is known primarily as a short-story writer; he explored the end of Turkish life in the Balkans in his collection *Makedonya 1900* (1976; *Macedonia 1900*). The poet Attilâ Ilhan also wrote several successful novels. His poems on the Balkan Wars focus on the political catastrophes that led to the fall of the Ottoman Empire and the emergence of modern Turkey, a theme that he also developed in several of his novels, including *Dersaadette sabah ezanlari* (1982; *Morning Calls to Prayers at the Sublime Port*).

Among the poets of the latter half of the twentieth century, Sezai Karakoç blended European and Ottoman sensibilities with a right-wing Islāmist perspective. His poetry collections include *Körfez* (1959; *The Gulf*) and *Siirler VI* (1980; *Poems VI*). The poet Ismet Özel began his career as a Marxist, but by the 1980s his writing had become strongly Islāmist. Özel's volumes of poetry include *Evet isyan* (1969; *Yes, Rebellion*) and *Celladima gülümserken* (1984; *While Smiling at My*

Executioner). Ataol Behramoglu merged political themes and folkloric forms in his poetry, volumes of which include *Kusatmada* (1978; *During the Siege*) and *Türkiye üzgün yurdum, güzel yurdum* (1985; *Turkey My Sad Home, My Beautiful Home*). In Hilmi Yavuz's poems the aesthetics of Ottoman civilization become the object of deep, at times nostalgic, reflection within a thoroughly modernist framework. His volumes of poetry include *Dogu siirleri* (1977; *Poems of the East*); *Seasons of the Word* (2007) is a collection of his poetry in English translation.

The two best-known novelists in Turkey at the turn of the twenty-first century were Orhan Pamuk and Latife Tekin. In very distinct ways, both expanded the scope of the novel in Turkish and opened up modern Turkish literature to readers in Europe and North America. Pamuk gained international fame with *Beyaz kale* (1985; *The White Castle*), the first of his novels to be translated into English. This work, set in the mid-seventeenth century, is a meditation on the oppositions between East and West. He returned to these themes in his subsequent novels, including *Kara kitap* (1990; *The Black Book*) – which, set in contemporary Istanbul, alludes to Ottoman mystical literature while playfully deconstructing the Turkish cultural present – and *Kar* (2002; *Snow*). Pamuk won the Nobel Prize for Literature in 2006.

Tekin's first novel, *Sevgili arsiz ölüm* (1983; *Dear Shameless Death*), depicts many of her own experiences as a displaced villager from Anatolia in the metropolis of Istanbul. *Berci Kristin çöp masallari* (1984; *Berji Kristin: Tales from the Garbage Hills*) focuses on female characters living in a new shanty town. Tekin's deconstruction of narrative duplicates the deconstruction of every element of the life of the former villagers, which does not spare any part of their former religious and social belief system. The manner in which her novels use the Turkish language sets her critique of modernity apart from and beyond earlier attempts to treat similar themes in Turkish literature.

The works of Pamuk and Tekin mirrored Turkey's identity at the turn of the twenty-first century, when the country was the heir to, on the one hand, a sophisticated urban civilization with a history of both confronting the West and desiring to assimilate its values and, on the other hand, a rural culture that remained embedded in the developing world and vulnerable to a predatory modernity.

PART 5

PLACES – THE ISLĀMIC WORLD TODAY

Islāmic Secularism and Nationalism

In 2007, 1,387,454,500 people practised Islām in 210 countries throughout the world. The majority were in Asia (961,961,000) and Africa (378,135,700), with large populations in the Middle East, India and Malaysia, and a significant diaspora throughout Europe (39,691,800). North America had 5,450,600 Muslims, Latin America 1,777,000, and Oceania just 438,400. The sections on regions and countries of the world below focuses on places where there is a significant presence of Muslims or a Muslim state.

While some modern states, such as Turkey, have taken a secular route, separating religion from government (see Chapter 6; Secular Nationalism in the Twentieth Century, for the history of the Turkish secular state), others, such as Iran and Saudi Arabia, have adopted an Islāmic state, supporting Sharī'ah law (see Chapter 6; Islāmic nationalism, for the formation of Saudi Arabia as an Islāmic state).

More than nine-tenths of the population in **Turkey** is Muslim. In 1928 Islām ceased to be the official state religion, and since that time the state has found itself periodically at odds with religion. Turkey's strong secularism has resulted in what have been perceived by some as strictures on the freedom

of religion: for example, the headscarf has long been prohibited in a number of public venues. In addition, the armed forces
have maintained a vigilant watch over Turkey's political
secularism, which they affirm to be a keystone among Turkey's
founding principles. The military has not left the maintenance
of a secular political process to chance, however, and has
intervened in politics on a number of occasions. The harshness
of Turkey's penal code, particularly article 301, which pun-
ishes insults to the Turkish state and Turkish identity, was also
seen as an obstacle to the country joining the European Union
(EU).

In 1995, the Welfare Party, an Islāmic party, polled a
majority in national elections but was unable to find a coalition partner; the following year it formed a short-lived coalition government. Six years later, in 2002, the Justice and
Development Party (Adalet ve Kalkinma Partisi; AKP), a party
with Islāmist roots, swept to power. Galvanized by an amendment to Turkey's constitution eliminating a ban on wearing
the headscarf on university campuses in February 2008, opponents of the AKP renewed charges that the party's Islāmist
agenda threatened Turkish secular order. In March 2008 the
constitutional court voted unanimously to hear a case that
called for the disbanding of the AKP and a five-year ban of its
leader, Recep Tayyip Erdogan, and dozens of other party
members from Turkish politics.

Saudi Arabia, the birthplace of Islām, adheres to the ideology of Wahhābīsm, an austere form of Islām that was embraced by early Sa'ud family leaders and that became the state
creed. Most Saudi Arabians are adherents of the majority
Sunni branch of Islām. In modern times, the Wahhābī interpretation of Sunni Islām has been especially influential, and the
views of important members of the 'ulama' (religious scholars)
are important in government. The current government of

Saudi Arabia has largely relied on religion – including its close and continuing ties to Wahhābīsm and its status as the custodian of Mecca and Medina, the two holy cities of Islām – to bolster its political legitimacy. The king is supposed to uphold Islām and apply its precepts and, in turn, is subject to its constraints.

Shī'ites make up a small portion of the population and are found mostly in the oases of Al-Hasa and Al-Qatif in the eastern part of the country. Most are Ithnā 'Asharīyah, although there remain small numbers of Isma'ilis. Public worship and display by non-Muslim faiths is prohibited. Public displays by non-Wahhābī Muslim groups, including by other Sunni sects, have been limited and even banned by the government. Sufism, for instance, is not openly practised, nor is celebration of the Prophet's birthday (*mawlid*). Shī'ites have suffered the greatest persecution.

Most Saudis continue to dress in a traditional fashion. In public women are expected to be fully veiled, and a long black cloak known as an '*abayah* is worn. A veil called a *hijab* covers the head, and another known as a *niqab* covers the face. In accordance with the Wahhābī interpretation of Islām, only two religious holidays are publicly recognized, 'Īd al-Fitr and 'Īd al-Adhā. The celebration of other Islāmic holidays, such as *mawlid* and 'Ashura' – an important holiday to Shī'ites – are tolerated only when celebrated on a small scale at the local level but are otherwise condemned as dangerous innovations. Public observance of non-Islāmic religious holidays is prohibited, with the exception of September 23, which celebrates the unification of the kingdom.

The country's international trade and its willingness to purchase arms from the West (in 2007 it was the largest purchaser in a $20 billion arms deal between the Gulf states and the United States) may enable it to combat extremism. In

2006 there were clashes between the government and Islāmic extremists, and a half dozen al-Qaeda operatives were killed. Some Islāmists were unhappy about Riyadh's proclamation that it would make major changes to the educational system in an effort to emphasize the spirit of modernity, non-violence, and cooperation with non-Muslims that was dictated by Islāmic teachings. The following year liberals welcomed a royal decree overhauling the kingdom's judicial system. The reforms would preserve the centrality of Sharī'ah but would take away many powers exercised by the Supreme Judicial Council, which was controlled by conservative clerics. In late September Saudi Arabia's grand mufti, Sheikh 'Abd al-'Azīz al-Sheikh, issued a *fatwa* prohibiting Saudi youth from travelling abroad under the pretext of *jihad*.

The Sunni–Shī'ite Division Within Islām

The division of Islām into two major groups, Sunni and Shī'ite, has its origins in the struggles over the proper line of succession to the Prophet Muḥammad (for the history of the schism and their beliefs, see Chapter 3). The Sunnis constitute approximately nine-tenths of the worldwide Muslim population. Empire builders from the beginning, their first caliph, Abū Bakr, ensured that Islām would be a religion of conquest as he extended the Muslim state's sway over all of Syria and eroded the power of the Byzantines. The Ottoman Empire, defeated in the First World War, was the last great Sunni stronghold. In the early 1990s Osama bin Laden, the leader of al-Qaeda, launched a *jihad* against what he saw as the insidious forces of secularism, including Europe and the United States, which he held responsible for subjecting and humiliating the once-proud Sunni Muslims.

The Shī'ites live mostly in Iran, southern Iraq, Lebanon, and Bahrain. For Shī'ites perhaps the most significant leader in modern times was Ayatollah Ruhollah Khomeini, whose supporters overthrew the Shah of Iran in 1979 and ushered in the reign of the supreme ayatollah and the Islāmic Republic of Iran. A powerful, charismatic leader who exercised extraordinary political as well as spiritual power, Khomeini was referred to by Iranians as well as Shī'ites worldwide as "the Imām".

Relations between Sunni and Shī'ite Muslims fell to a low point in Iraq in 2003 after the U.S.-led invasion and occupation of the country. When elections were held in 2005, Sunni parties boycotted them, and the Shī'ite parties won overwhelmingly, gaining control of the government after more than a millennium of perceived oppression by the Sunni majority. For their part, the Sunni majority resented what it perceived to be the arrogant policies of the Shī'ites in power and worried about revenge against their ranks.

The Shī'ites filled posts within the police and military, raising accusations from Sunni neighbourhoods of abuses of power and of killings. Some Sunnis, including those displaced from jobs in the security forces and police, responded by forming militias. Attacks took the form of bombings; one group in 2006 blew up a Shī'ite mosque and holy place at Samarra'. The repercussions for Sunnis were bloody. The two groups continued to exchange violent attacks in 2007. In the broader Middle East, ethnic tensions rose as Arab leaders from nearby states saw Shī'ite Iran as having the ambition to control Iraq and gain wider influence over the Middle East.

The Middle East

Islām originated in Saudi Arabia and it was with conquest of the surrounding states that the faith spread. The dominance of the religion varies, as indicated above with regard to Saudi Arabia and Turkey, and is also influenced by the history and ethnicity of the communities.

In **Cyprus**, Turkish Cypriots – roughly one-fifth of the population descendants of the soldiers of the Ottoman army that conquered the island in 1571 and of immigrants from Anatolia brought in by the sultan's government – are Sunni Muslims. The remainder of the population are Greek Cypriots, primarily Eastern Orthodox Christians. In 1974 Turkey invaded the island, defeating Greek forces, and established an independent Turkish Federated State of Cyprus in the north. Since then additional immigrants from Turkey, brought in to work vacant land and increase the total labour force, and more recently refugees from Lebanon, have increased Muslim representation. In May 1983 Rauf Denktash, president of the new state, broke off all intercommunal talks, and in November he proclaimed the Turkish Republic of Northern Cyprus (TRNC); the republic's independence was recognized only by Turkey.

The culture of Cyprus is divided between the northern Turkish and the southern Greek sections of the country. The Turkish community in northern Cyprus has promoted its own Turkish and Islāmic culture, supporting its own newspapers and periodicals and changing many place names to Turkish. The anniversary of the proclamation of the TRNC (November 15) is celebrated in the north, as are traditional Muslim holidays.

The **Syrian** people have a long and varied history but are predominantly Arab in character. In the first half of the

seventh century, Syria was absorbed into the Muslim caliphate.

After the First World War and the collapse of the Ottoman
empire, Syria became a French mandated territory, along with
Lebanon. A treaty establishing its independence was signed in
1936, but the country did not gain complete self-determination
until 1946.

Some ethnic groups have been partially assimilated by the
Arab majority, which includes the Bedouins. Second in
number to the Arabs are the Kurds. The Armenians may
be divided into two groups – the early settlers, who have
been more or less Arabized, and the later immigrants, who
arrived after the First World War and retain their identity
and language. Islām is practiced by a majority of the population. The Sunni sect accounts for about three-quarters of the
Muslim population and is in the majority everywhere except
in as-Suwayda' *muhafazah* (governorate) in the south and the
Latakia *muhafazah* in the north. The 'Alawites (an extreme
Shī'ite subsect) are the next largest group, and most live in
the Latakia *muhafazah* or in the *muhafazat* of Hims and
Hamah. Most of the Druzes, the third largest group, live in
as-Suwayda' *muhafazah*; the rest in Damascus, Aleppo, and
al-Qunaytirah.

The constitution of 1973 declares that Syria constitutes an
integral part of the Arab homeland, that all legislative power
lies with the people, and that freedom of expression and
equality before the law are guaranteed. However, the enforcement of these principles has not been thorough: especially from
the late 1970s, constitutionally guaranteed rights were increasingly suppressed under President Assad's rule. The regional
(Syrian) leadership of the Arab Socialist Ba'th (Renaissance)
Party elects the head of state, who must be a Muslim. The
principles of Syrian law and equity derive basically from

Islãmic jurisprudence and secondarily from the French civil code.

In March 2006, Najah al-Attar was appointed a vice president, the first woman and first non-Ba'th Party member to hold the post. The following year, a prominent figure in Syria's Islãmist movement, Sheikh Mahmoud Qul Aghasi, known as Abū al-Qa'qa, was assassinated. He had urged his followers, the Strange Ones of Syria, to fight against U.S. intervention in the Muslim world.

The Arab republic of **Lebanon** came into being in 1920, when France, which administered Lebanon as a League of Nations mandate, established the state of Greater Lebanon. Lebanon then became a republic in 1926 and achieved independence in 1943. It had to struggle to define its position in relation to Israel, to its Arab neighbours, and to Palestinian refugees living in Lebanon. The Lebanese pluralistic communal structure eventually collapsed under the pressures of this struggle.

Lebanon has a heterogeneous society composed of numerous ethnic, religious, and kinship groups. Since the seventh century it has served as a refuge for persecuted Christian and Muslim sects. The population is estimated to consist of a majority of Muslims and a large minority of Christians. Shī'ite Muslims are the most numerous group, followed closely by the Sunnis; the Druzes constitute a small percentage.

Modern Lebanon is a republic with a parliamentary system of government. Its constitution provides for a unicameral National Assembly elected for a term of four years by universal adult suffrage. According to the 1989 Tā'if agreement, parliamentary seats are apportioned equally between Christian and Muslim sects. This sectarian distribution is also to be observed in appointments to public office. By an unwritten convention, the president must be a Maronite Christian, the premier a Sunni Muslim, and the speaker of the National Assembly a Shī'ite. The president, in consultation with the speaker of the National Assembly and the parliamentary deputies, invites a Sunni Muslim to form a Cabinet, and the Cabinet members' portfolios are organized to reflect the sectarian balance.

The main problem for Lebanon was to implement the unwritten power-sharing National Pact of 1943 between the Christians and Muslims. A second factor, the role of Lebanon in the Arab world, was also a complex issue. Many Syrians still felt that the French decision to separate Lebanon from Syria in 1920 was invalid; many in Lebanon agreed. Lebanon's non-involvement in the Arab–Israeli wars of 1967 and 1973, its strong and often heavy-handed security policies, and rumours of its secret understandings with Israel all directed attention to this issue. After the ruinous Jordanian campaign against Palestinian militias in September 1970, Palestinians thought of Lebanon as their last refuge, and by 1973 roughly one-tenth of the population of Lebanon was Palestinian.

Under an agreement announced in Cairo on November 3 1969, the Lebanese government gave the Palestinians virtually a free hand in the refugee camps and at forward posts in the south along the Israeli frontier. In return, the PLO promised not to intervene in Lebanese politics. By 1975 the mostly Muslim Lebanese National Movement led by Kamal Jumblatt sought political reform and support for the Palestinian guerrillas. Into this arena stepped the relatively deprived Shī'ite Muslims, by now the most numerous religious community in Lebanon. Maronite Christians, intent on preserving their concept of Lebanon, frantically sought to keep their political dominance by crushing the power of the Lebanese leftists and particularly the Palestine Liberation Organization (PLO), whose actions seemed (from the perspective of many

Maronites) to threaten the unity and safety of the nation. In the civil war that began in April 1975 the country was torn apart, and the central government virtually ceased to exist. On October 22 1988, most members of the Lebanese parliament (last elected in 1972) met in Tā'if, Saudi Arabia, and accepted a constitutional compromise that adjusted the parliament, presidency, and cabinet so that Christian and Muslim representatives would share power equally.

The war that had engulfed the Lebanese exposed the vulnerability of the political system. Control of the official central government is precarious; sectarian militias and foreign countries exert great influence. Hezbollah replaced the PLO as Israel's principal antagonist in southern Lebanon, waging a vigorous war against the Jewish state even after that country's final withdrawal from Lebanon in mid-2000. In 2006 Hezbollah launched a military operation against Israel, and the UN brokered a ceasefire in August. The following year, the Lebanese army seized full control of the Nahr al-Bared Palestinian refugee camp after 105 days of fighting the extremist organization Fatah al-Islām.

Iraq, Iran, and Palestine have been, and remain, some of the most contested areas in the world in the late twentieth and early twenty-first centuries (for the history of the wars in these regions see Chapters 7 and 9; for the creation of Palestine, see Chapter 6).

Palestine, also known as the Holy Land, is held sacred among Jews, Christians, and Muslims. Since the twentieth century it has been the object of conflicting claims of Jewish and Arab national movements, and the conflict has led to prolonged violence and, in several instances, open warfare.

In the early twenty-first century, Israeli Jews constituted roughly half of the population west of the Jordan River, while Arabs – Muslim, Christian, and Druze – and other smaller minorities accounted for the rest. The Arab population is descended from Arabs who lived in the area during the mandate period and, in most cases, for centuries before that time. Palestinian nationalists usually emphasize that their shared identity as Arabs transcends the religious diversity of their community: thus, both Muslim Arabs, constituting about 16 per cent of the Israeli population, and Christian Arabs, about 2 per cent, identify themselves in the first instance as Arabs.

Baghdad became the capital of the ʿAbbāsid Caliphate in the eighth century. The modern nation-state of **Iraq** was created following the First World War (1914–18) and gained independence in 1932. Roughly two-thirds of Iraq's people are Arabs, about one-fourth are Kurds, and the remainder consists of small minority groups. Iraq is predominantly a Muslim country, in which the two major sects of Islām are represented more equally than in any other state. Shīʿites are almost exclusively Arab (with some Turkmen and Kurds), while Sunnis are divided mainly between Arabs and Kurds but include other, smaller groups, such as Azerbaijanis and Turkmen.

Since the inception of the Iraqi state in 1920 the ruling elites have consisted mainly of minority Sunni Arabs. Iraq's Shīʿites, like their co-religionists in Iran, follow the Ithnā ʿAsharīyah, or Twelver, rite, and, despite the pre-eminence of Iran as a Shīʿite Islāmic republic, Iraq has traditionally been the physical and spiritual centre of Shīʿism in the Islāmic world. Shīʿism's two most important holy cities, Al-Najaf and Karbalaʾ, are located in southern Iraq, as is Al-Kūfah, sanctified as the site of the assassination of ʿAlī, the fourth caliph, in the seventh century. Samarraʾ, near Baghdad, is also of great cultural and religious significance to Shīʿites as the site of the life and disappearance of the twelfth, and eponymous, *imām*, Muḥammad al-Mahdīal-Hujjah. In premodern times southern and eastern Iraq formed a cultural and religious meeting place between the Arab and Persian Shīʿite worlds, and until relatively recent times, large numbers of notable Iranian scholars could be found studying or teaching in the great *madrasah*s in Al-Najaf and Karbalaʾ.

The fundamental cultural milieu of Iraq is both Islāmic and Arab. Over the course of the twentieth century, rapid urban growth accelerated social change, as a higher proportion of the population was exposed to modern, largely Westernized, life-styles. Alcoholic beverages and Western-style entertainment became freely available, a circumstance much deplored by devout Muslims. Although the number of Muslims in Iraq embracing a fundamentalist interpretation of Islām grew, Islāmic extremism did not present a major social or political problem until the start of the Iraq War in 2003. The role of women gradually changed, with a higher proportion partici-pating in the labour force in spite of encouragement from the government to stay at home and raise large families.

Although Iraqis generally are a religious and conservative people, there are strong secular tendencies. This is reflected in the dress, which, while conservative by Western standards, is quite relaxed by the standards of the region, particularly compared with neighbouring Saudi Arabia and the Persian Gulf states. Men will frequently wear Western-style suits or, in more casual surroundings, the long shirtlike *thawb*. The traditional chador and veil, the *hijab*, is common among conservative women, but Western attire is also common.

Iran – traditionally known as Persia – which has been influenced by waves of indigenous and foreign conquerors and immigrants, was conquered by the Muslim Arabs in the seventh century. The region fell under the sway of successive waves of Persian, Turkish, and Mongol conquerors until the rise of the Safavids, who introduced Ithnā ʿAsharīyah Shīʾism as the official creed in the early sixteenth century. Over the following centuries, with the state-fostered rise of a Persian-based Shī'ite clergy, a synthesis was formed between Persian culture and Shī'ite Islām. The rise of the Qajar line in 1796 was marked by the growing influence of the European powers in Iran's internal affairs, and by the growing power of the Shī'ite clergy in social and political issues.

The country's difficulties led to the ascension in 1925 of the Pahlavi line, whose ill-planned efforts to modernize Iran led to widespread dissatisfaction and the dynasty's subsequent over-throw in the revolution of 1979 (see Chapter 7). This revolution brought a regime to power that uniquely combined elements of a parliamentary democracy with an Islāmic theocracy run by the country's clergy. At the head of both the state and oversight institutions is the leader, or *rahbar*, a ranking cleric whose duties and authority are those usually equated with a head of state. Reformist elements rose within the government during the last decade of the twentieth century, opposed both to the ongoing rule of the clergy and to Iran's continued political and economic isolation from the international community.

The vast majority of Iranians are Muslims of the Ithnā 'Asharīyah, or Twelver, Shī'ite branch, which is the official state religion. The Kurds and Turkmen are predominantly Sunni Muslims, but Iran's Arabs are both Sunni and Shī'ite. Religious toleration, one of the characteristics of Iran during the Pahlavi monarchy, came to an end with the Islāmic revolution in 1978–9. Participation in sports was also restricted as the government regarded the sports stadium as a rival to the mosque. Since the 1990s there has been a revival of athletics in Iran, including women's activities. Sports have become inextricably bound up with demands for political liberalization, and nearly every major event has become an occasion for massive public celebrations by young men and women expressing their desire for reform and for more amicable relations with the West.

Despite constitutional guarantees of freedom of the press, censorship by conservative elements within the government is widespread.

Part of the Ottoman Empire until 1918 and later a mandate of the United Kingdom, **Jordan** has been an independent kingdom since 1946. It is among the most politically liberal countries of the Arab world. Amman is one of the region's principal commercial and transportation centres as well as one of the Arab world's major cultural capitals.

The overwhelming majority of the people are Arabs, principally Jordanians and Palestinians; there is also a significant minority of Bedouin. Although the Palestinian population is often critical of the monarchy, Jordan is the only Arab country to grant wide-scale citizenship to Palestinian refugees. Other minorities include a number of Iraqis who fled to Jordan as a result of the Persian Gulf War and Iraq War. Islām is the official religion, and Jordan is declared to be part of the Arab *ummah* ("nation"). The king remains the country's ultimate authority and wields power over the executive, legislative, and judicial branches. As well as regular courts, Sharī'ah (Islāmic) courts and other religious courts for non-Muslims exercise jurisdiction over matters of personal status.

Political parties were banned before the elections in 1963. Between 1971 and 1976, when it was abolished, the Arab National Union was the only political organization allowed. Although not a political party, the transnational Muslim Brotherhood continued, with the tacit approval of the government, to engage in socially active functions, and it captured over one-fourth of the lower house in the 1989 election. In 1992 political parties were legalized – as long as they acknowledged the legitimacy of the monarchy. Since then, the Brotherhood has maintained a significant minority presence in Jordanian politics through its political arm, the Islāmic Action Front.

In 1993, King Hussein expressed public reservations over a PLO–Israeli accord but nonetheless stated his willingness to support the Palestinian people. One year later, Jordan and Israel signed a peace treaty in which Hussein was recognized as the custodian of the Muslim holy sites in East Jerusalem. In January 1995 Hussein signed accords with the PLO pledging support for Palestinian autonomy and the establishment of a Palestinian state that included East Jerusalem. He also played a central role in brokering a deal between Israel and the PLO regarding Israeli withdrawal from Hebron in the West Bank in early 1997, and subsequently acted as a mediator between the Israelis and Palestinians.

His son and successor, King 'Abdullah II, continued his father's political policies and economic reforms as well as improving the status of women. In recent years, Jordan has struggled to contain the growing political influence of Islāmist groups and to address issues sparked by the war in neighbouring Iraq.

Egypt was part of the Roman Republic and Empire and then the Byzantine Empire, until its conquest by Arab Muslim armies in AD 639–42. Under the Fatimid dynasty (969– 1171) it espoused the official doctrine of Isma'ili Shī'ism but Saladin, who founded the Ayyubid dynasty, restored Egypt to Sunni rule in 1171. In 1517 the Ottoman Empire established control over Egypt; French control followed and then that of the United Kingdom. In 1952 a military coup installed a revolutionary regime that promoted a combination of socialism and pan-Arab nationalism. During the Cold War, Egypt's central role in the Arabic-speaking world increased its geopolitical importance as Arab nationalism and inter-Arab relations became powerful and emotional political forces in the Middle East and North Africa. Egypt led the Arab states in a series of wars against Israel but was the first of those states to make peace with the Jewish state, which it did in 1979.

The population of the Nile valley and the delta, which are home to the overwhelming majority of Egyptians, derives from the indigenous African population and those of Arab ancestry. The inhabitants of the Sinai and the northern section of the Eastern Desert are all fairly recent immigrants from Arabia. The inhabitants of the Western Desert, outside the oases, are of mixed Arab and Amazigh (Berber) descent. In addition to the indigenous groups, there are in Egypt a number of small foreign ethnic groups, the largest community being the Greeks, followed by the Italians, British, and French.

Following the Muslim conquest, urban and rural culture began to adopt elements of Arab culture. Since that time, Egypt's history has been part of the broader Islāmic world, and the country's cultural milieu remains predominantly Arab. Lifestyles in the larger cities are, in many ways, akin to patterns found in urban culture worldwide. Although modesty is maintained in urban modes of dress – particularly given the tendency from the early 1980s onward for women to return to wearing the *hijab* – urban clothing styles differ only marginally from those found in many European cities. In rural areas life is more traditional; women over age 16 do not work in the field, and seldom appear in public except with a *hijab*.

Islām is the official religion of Egypt, and most Egyptians adhere to its Sunni branch. The country has long been a centre of Islāmic scholarship, and al-Azhar University in Cairo is widely considered the world's pre-eminent institution of Islāmic learning. Likewise, many Muslims, even those outside Egypt, consider al-Azhar's sheikhs to be among the highest religious authorities in the Sunni world. The Muslim Brotherhood, a transnational religio-political organization that seeks to expand conservative Muslim values, was founded in Egypt in 1928. Sufism is also widely practised.

Egypt has operated under several constitutions, both as a monarchy and, after 1952, as a republic. At the heart of the post-revolutionary regime was a commitment to pan-Arabism, and during the following decades Egypt engaged in several abortive attempts to forge transnational unions with other Arab countries. In 1977, however, deteriorating relations between Egypt and other Arab states over Egypt's peace negotiations with Israel led to Egypt's suspension from the Arab League, a regional organization of which it had been a founding member. The current constitution, of 1971, proclaimed the Arab Republic of Egypt to be "a democratic, socialist state", with Islām as its state religion and Arabic as its national language. Egypt was the first Arab country to abolish the Sharī'ah court system (1956). The civil and penal codes as well as court procedure are based on French law, but these are influenced by Sharī'ah.

Since the 1990s, under President Hosni Mubarak the regime has been increasingly authoritarian. While the pre-revolutionary Wafd Party has been re-formed, and the moderate religious groups have established an Islāmic Alliance, the Muslim Brotherhood is banned. However, dozens of candidates who were elected as "independents" in the 2005 election for People's Assembly were actually members of the Muslim Brotherhood. There has been growing censorship by the Islāmic courts, and the rector of al-Azhar University tempered freedom of speech and the press. In its struggle against Islāmist terrorism, the regime resorted to preventive detention and, allegedly, torture. As Muslim fundamentalism was allowed to flourish, tensions between Egypt's Christian Coptic and Muslim populations increased.

In 2007, the government intensified its campaign to contain political dissent led by the banned Muslim Brotherhood, the largest opposition group in the parliament, and initiated a series of arrests and a freeze on the group's funding sources. In March President Mubarak passed a referendum to amend 34 articles of the constitution. The controversial amendments included a new anti-terrorism law, which would provide the police with increased powers of arrest and surveillance, and a ban on the creation of political parties based on religion (widely viewed as aimed at the Muslim Brotherhood).

Among the various states of Arabia proper, Islām dominates in Yemen, Kuwait, Oman, Bahrain, Qatar, and the United Arab Emirates. The present Republic of **Yemen** came into being in May 1990, when the Yemen Arab Republic (North Yemen) merged with the People's Democratic Republic of Yemen (South Yemen). The people overwhelmingly consider themselves Arabs; Yemenis of northern origin are said to be descended from Mesopotamians who entered the region in the first millennium BC, and they claim ancestry of the biblical figure Isma'il (Ishmael). The southern group, which represents the old South Arabian stock, claims descent from Qahtan, the biblical Joktan.

Throughout Yemeni society, the broadest distinctions between population groups are based not on ethnicity but on religious affiliation. Islām is the state religion, and the Sunni branch of Islām, represented by the Shafi'i school, predominates. The Shī'ite minority comprises the Zaydi school (see below), which has long been politically dominant in the mountainous highlands of the north, and the Isma'ilis, now a relatively small group found in the Haraz region of northern Yemen and in Jabal Manakhah, the mountainous area west of Sanaa.

Under the constitution, Sharī'ah is the source of all legislation. The composition and membership of political parties are regulated by law. Parties based on such factors as regional, tribal, sectarian, or ethnic persuasion are expressly prohibited. Both the major Muslim sects operate religious institutes for the preparation of judges and other religious personnel. By the early twenty-first century the number of small religious schools associated with foreign Islâmic groups had proliferated. Several thousand small religious academies were closed in 2005, and all non-Yemenis matriculating in unregistered schools were asked to leave the country for fear such institutions were involved in religious extremism.

Islâm spread readily and quickly in Yemen after its introduction in the seventh century. For the history of Yemen, however, the most important event after the triumph of Islâm was the introduction in the ninth century of the Zaydi sect from Iraq – a group of Shī'ites who accepted Zayd ibn 'Alī, a direct descendant of Muḥammad, as the last legitimate successor to the Prophet. Much of Yemeni culture and civilization for the next 1,000 years was to bear the stamp of Zaydi Islâm. That same span of time was host to a confusing series of factional, dynastic, local, and imperial rulers contesting against one another and against the Zaydis for control of Yemen.

From the fifteenth century Yemen and the Red Sea became an arena of conflict between the Egyptians, the Ottomans, and various European powers seeking control over the emerging market for *Coffea arabica* (a species of coffee) as well as over the long-standing trade in condiments and spices from the East. The British took over Aden in 1839, and in the mid-nineteenth century the Ottoman Empire moved back into North Yemen, from which it had been driven by the Yemenis two centuries earlier. The north became independent at the end of the First World War in 1918; the *imām* of the Zaydis, Yahya Mahmud al-Mutawwakil, became the de facto ruler. The British retained control of the south until 1967.

In the north, the Yemen Arab Republic (North Yemen) was declard by the *imām* Muḥammad al-Bahr in 1962. The new government in Aden in the south renamed the country the People's Republic of South Yemen. The two parts were united after political and armed struggle between various factions in 1990. Disagreement between the two political regions escalated into armed conflict in the spring of 1994. The Yemeni civil war resulted in the defeat of the southern armed forces and the flight into exile of most of the Yemen Socialist Party (YSP) leaders and other southern secessionists. Control of the state in united Yemen lay in the hands of a General People's Congress (GPC)–Islah coalition dominated by 'Alī 'Abd Allāh Salih. The political conflict and unrest that accompanied and followed the civil war led to a revival of the power of the security forces and to the curtailment of the freedom of opposition parties, the media, and non-governmental organizations, although, by the turn of the twenty-first century, democracy and human rights were more secure than they had been in either of the two Yemens.

During the 1990s, Sunni Islāmist groups gravitated to Yemen, and preaching and teaching at many Yemeni mosques and *madrasah*s took on a clearly anti-American tone. In 2000 Muslim militants associated with al-Qaeda bombed the U.S. warship *Cole* in Aden's harbour. The group, whose leader, Osama bin Laden, was of Yemeni ancestry, enjoyed substantial support among Yemeni Islāmists. Following the September 11 attacks on the United States in 2001, the Salih government moved against al-Qaeda by arresting dozens of militants and freezing assets of those believed to have supported the organization. In 2004 a Zaydi rebellion protesting the government's close ties with the United States erupted in extreme north-western Yemen. The rebels sought a return of the imamate, and, although their leader, Husayn al-Hawthi, was killed at the end of the year, the rebellion continued. The country continues to be subject to terrorist attacks. In 2007 two foreign students were killed by Shī'ite rebels in an attack on a religious school, and a suicide bomber attacked a convoy of Spanish tourists in Mar'ib.

In the eighteenth century, Bedouin from the interior founded a trading post at **Kuwait** Bay; the emirate's ruling family, the Al Sabah, formally established a sheikhdom in 1756. In time and with accumulated wealth, the small fort grew to become Kuwait City, which now contains most of the country's population. A British protectorate from 1899 until 1961, Kuwait drew world attention in 1990 when Iraqi forces invaded and attempted to annex it. A military coalition led by the United States drove Iraq's army out of Kuwait within days of launching an offensive in February 1991.

Nearly two-thirds of the population are expatriate workers, formerly from other Arab states but now largely from South and South-east Asia. Arabs – either Bedouin, sedentary, or descendants of immigrants from elsewhere in the region – constitute the largest ethnic group, and a small number of ethnic Persians have resided in the country for centuries. Kuwaiti citizens are almost entirely Muslim, and a law passed in 1981 limits citizenship to Muslims. The majority are Sunni, but about one-third are Shī'ite. Both the Iranian revolution of 1979 and the Kuwaiti government's subsequent discrimination against Shī'ites fostered a heightened sense of community among the country's Shī'ite population in the 1980s and 1990s, and this led to political tension between the two groups. Personal and civil law (roughly, family law and probate law) are based largely on Sharī'ah.

The country remains culturally conservative and its Arab–
Islāmic heritage permeates daily life. The rise of Islāmic
fundamentalism in the 1970s and 1980s was reflected in a
general return to traditional customs, as seen in the public
dress of women, who began wearing the *hijab*, or veil, far more
than in the past. The right of women to drive cars and to work
outside the home is generally accepted and has not been a
matter of public debate, yet the question of granting women
the right to vote – women were not enfranchised until 2005 –
has divided Islāmists, some of whom seek to enforce even more
conservative Islāmic standards such as those found in neighbouring Saudi Arabia.

In recent years, clashes between the parliament and the
cabinet have increased. In May 2006, the emir dissolved the
parliament before its term expired and called for new elections
after demands from lawmakers for democratic reforms and
electoral re-districting. After an intense campaign, the Islāmist
and reformist candidates (that is, the opposition) won 33 of
the 50 elected seats.

Renowned in ancient times for its frankincense and metal-
working, **Oman** occupies a strategically important location,
for which it has long been a prize for empire builders. During
the eighteenth century the Al Bu Sa'id dynasty expelled a
Persian occupation and established Omani control over much
of the Persian Gulf. The Al Bu Sa'id weathered much political
turbulence but preserved its hold on power into the twenty-
first century.

More than half of Oman's population is Arab and the
overwhelming majority are Muslims. The Ibadi branch of
Islām, a moderate Kharijite group, claims the most adherents.
In belief and ritual, Ibadism is close to Sunni Islām, differing in
its emphasis on an elected, rather than a hereditary, *imām* as
the spiritual and temporal leader of the Ibadi community.

Non-Ibadi Arabs and the Baloch are mostly Sunnis. Those in the South Asian communities are mainly Shī'ite, although a few are Hindus.

Oman has Islāmic courts, based on the Ibadi interpretation of the Sharī'ah, which handle personal status cases. Its predominantly Ibadi Muslim population observes social customs that – though still conservative by Western standards – are markedly less strict than those of neighbouring Saudi Arabia. Women in particular have enjoyed relatively more freedom in Oman than elsewhere on the Arabian Peninsula.

Bahrain Island has been settled and colonized by various groups, including the Khalifah family (Al Khalifah), a native Arab dynasty that has ruled Bahrain since the late eighteenth century. It was a British protectorate from 1861 to independence in 1971. After independence, tensions mounted between the predominantly Shī'ite population and Sunni leadership – especially following the 1979 revolution in Iran.

Roughly two-thirds of the population is Arab. More than four-fifths is Muslim and includes both the Sunni and Shī'ite sects, with the latter in the majority. The ruling family and many of the wealthier and more influential Bahrainis are Sunni, and this difference has been an underlying cause of local tension, particularly during and after the Iran–Iraq War (1980–88). In 2006 conflict arose between Islāmic conservatives and liberals over the realm of personal freedoms. Liberal intellectuals, professional associations, and women's groups denounced efforts by Islāmic conservatives in the parliament to pass legislation aimed at enforcing strict Sharī'ah rules, such as the imposition on society of a "morals police" and the segregation of the sexes at the university and in commercial stores.

In 2002, the emir, Hamad ibn 'Isa Al Khalifah, who had succeeded his father in 1999, brought in a new constitution. This established a constitutional monarchy, called for equality between Sunnis and Shī'ites, and guaranteed civil and property rights to all citizens. The executive is composed of a prime minister, who is head of government, and a council of ministers, all of whom are appointed by the king. Bahrain's legal system is based on Sharī'ah and English common law. There are separate courts for members of Sunni and Shī'ite sects. Although still at heart an Arab-Islāmic country, Bahrain has been more accepting of modernization and Westernization than many of its neighbours and Western-style clothing is common.

Both Qatar and the United Arab Emirates are states where the Arab population is in the minority because of the presence of foreign workers. Following the rise of Islām, **Qatar** became subject to the Islāmic caliphate; it was later ruled by a number of local and foreign dynasties before falling under the control of the Al Thani (Thani dynasty) in the nineteenth century. The Al Thani sought British patronage against competing tribal groups and against the Ottoman Empire, and in exchange Britain controlled Qatar's foreign policy until the latter's independence in 1971. Thereafter, the monarchy continued to nurture close ties with Western powers. The country's daily life is thoroughly modern, and its rulers have sought to enhance civil liberties.

Qatar was originally settled by Bedouin nomads from the central part of the Arabian Peninsula. Qatari citizens, however, constitute only one-seventh of the total population today, the remainder being foreign workers – mostly from Pakistan, India, and Iran. Islām is the official religion, and Qataris are largely Sunni Muslims. There is a small Shī'ite minority. The ruling Al Thani adheres to the same Wahhābī interpretation of Islām as the rulers of Saudi Arabia, though not as strictly. Women, for example, have greater freedom in Qatar than in Saudi Arabia. Personal status law is governed largely by the

Sharī'ah. Qatari society tends to be conservative in most respects and is heavily influenced by Islāmic customs. The press is among the freest in the region, and though they are religious and traditional, Qataris pride themselves on their tolerance for the cultures and beliefs of others.

Historically the domain of individual Arab clans and families, the **United Arab Emirates** is a federation of seven emirates along the eastern coast of the Arabian Peninsula. Following a series of truces with Britain in the nineteenth century, the emirates united to form the Trucial States. The states gained autonomy following the Second World War (1939–45), when the trucial states of Bahrain and Qatar declared independent statehood; the rest were formally united in 1971.

Only about one-fifth of the residents are citizens. The remainder are mostly foreign workers and their dependants, with South Asians constituting the largest of these groups. Arabs from countries other than the United Arab Emirates and Iranians account for another significant portion. About three-fourths of the population is Muslim, of which roughly four-fifths belong to the Sunni branch of Islām; Shī'ite minorities exist in Dubayy and Al-Shariqah. The constitution calls for a legal code based on Sharī'ah, but in practice the judiciary blends Western and Islāmic legal principles. The cultural traditions of the United Arab Emirates are rooted in Islām, though changes in attitudes toward marriage and the employment of women are discernible.

Indonesia

Indonesia is the fourth most populous country in the world. The majority of Indonesians are related to the peoples of eastern Asia, although over the centuries there has also been considerable mixing with Arabs, Indians, and Europeans; 88 per cent of citizens are Muslim, according to the most recent census. Formerly known as the Dutch East Indies (or Netherlands East Indies), after a period of occupation by the Japanese (1942–5) during the Second World War Indonesia declared its independence from The Netherlands in 1945. It was not until the United Nations acknowledged the western segment of New Guinea as part of Indonesia in 1969 that the country took on its present form. The former Portuguese territory of East Timor was incorporated into Indonesia in 1976, but following a UN-organized referendum in 1999, it declared its independence and became fully sovereign in 2002.

The major religions of Indonesia were all introduced on the coast and, except in such open areas as Java and southern Sumatra (which were free of natural impediments), penetrated slowly inland. The early Indonesian states that centred on Java or Sumatra evolved through many forms of Hinduism and Buddhism. In the fourteenth century Islām, brought by Muslim traders primarily from South Asia, emerged as the dominant religion along the coasts of Java and Sumatra. By the fifteenth century, Islām had gained a firm footing in coastal areas of other islands of the archipelago as well. Aceh became a self-consciously Muslim state by the sixteenth century, with contacts with Muslim India and its own heterodox school of Muslim mysticism. With the spread of Islām came an expansion of its power structure. Mataram, the great Muslim kingdom of seventeenth-century Java, lashed out against the princes and Muslim notables of the northern coast.

The fall of Malacca (now Melaka) on the Malay Peninsula to the Portuguese in 1511 was a turning point in Indonesian history. By the end of the century, the level of Muslim Indonesian trade with the Middle East, and thence with Europe, was the greatest it had ever been. Dutch and British interests in the region increased: in 1602 the Dutch East India Company received its charter, two years after the formation of the English East India Company. All sought commercial monopoly and a period of colonial rule followed.

The Islām that came to Indonesia from India, perhaps from southern India, brought the heterodox mystic sects of Sufism, the character of which was probably not foreign to the Javanese ascetics. Both a Sufi "saint" (walī) and a Javanese guru likely understood and respected each other's yearning for personal union with God. The Javanese tradition, by which small groups of disciples were initiated by a teacher into higher wisdom, was paralleled in the Sufi teaching methods. For Muslim theologian and Javanese scholar alike, the concern was always less with the nature of the divine than with skills for communicating with God. Arabic texts, moreover, tended eventually to be recited as meditative aids, just as the Tantric mantras had been.

Throughout all the religious changes on the court level, the common people adopted part of each new religion as an additional layer on top of their traditional local beliefs. Consequently, Islām is expressed differently in Indonesia from the way it is in the Middle East. The religion is most strictly practised in Aceh, western Sumatra, western Java, south-eastern Kalimantan, and some of the Lesser Sunda Islands. On Java, Muslims who follow orthodox practices are referred to as the *santri*. By contrast, the *abangan* adhere to a more syncretic tradition, strongly influenced by ancestral beliefs and practices. With the growth of a more religion-conscious middle class, especially since the late twentieth century, the *abangan* way of believing has been in retreat, while more-orthodox Muslim practices have been on the rise. However, the many local rituals connected with birth, death, and marriage are carefully observed by people at all levels, and ceremonies (*selamatan*) are held on all special occasions. Muslims may choose to use Islāmic law in some civil cases; since the mid-1970s religious law has applied to all civil matters dealing with marriage.

In the late 1990s inter-ethnic conflicts, which up to that point had been suppressed successfully, began to resurface. These conflicts, too, manifested to some degree along political lines. Large-scale deadly uprisings broke out in Sanggau Ledo, in West Kalimantan, and the unrest spread to other parts of the province just prior to the May 1997 general election. The violence erupted between the local Dayak groups, who generally supported the non-Muslim PDI, and the Madurese, who mostly belonged to the Muslim PPP. This agitation in West Kalimantan soon triggered uprisings in other regions, most notably in West Java. The decline of the economy also precipitated public unrest accompanied by violence and riots.

The country also came under the international spotlight for the activities of terrorists in its domains. In 2002, U.S. officials as well as the Singaporean and Malaysian governments claimed that Indonesia had become a major regional base for international terrorist groups. Particular attention was given to the leadership role that a small number of Indonesians had played in the Jemaah Islāmiyah network. Initially the government of Megawati Sukarnoputri was criticized for being tardy in acting against terrorism, but Indonesian officials in 2002 were cooperating closely with the CIA and other regional intelligence forces in investigating and apprehending suspected terrorists. Events took a dramatic and tragic turn on October 12, when a massive bomb blast at a nightclub on the resort island of Bali killed 184 people, the majority of whom were Western tourists. This was the worst terrorist attack since September 11 2001. The Indonesian government allowed several hundred foreign police and intelligence officials to join the investigation into the bombing. The clandestine al-Qaeda-linked Jemaah Islāmiyah movement was quickly identified as having carried out the bombing, and more than 80 members were subsequently arrested. Several of the key figures were tried and sentenced to death. Although the Megawati government supported a UN motion to ban Jemaah Islāmiyah, it gave little leadership in the public debate over Islāmic radicalism. Megawati repeatedly maintained that responsibility for combating terrorist ideology rested with Islāmic leaders rather than with the government. Jemaah Islāmiyah and other extremist groups remained a significant threat and other bombings followed.

In 2007 the issue of the role of Islāmic law came to the fore. In recent years, there had been a growing trend in some strongly Islāmic regions to introduce more comprehensive Sharī'ah-inspired regulations, such as dress codes, bans on alcohol and gambling, and mandatory Islāmic knowledge requirements for officials. At least 22 districts had such regulations, even though control of religious affairs rested with the central government. Many women's groups and non-Muslims objected to these regulations on the grounds of discrimination and the undermining of human rights. The Sharī'ah issue became even more controversial when Islāmic parties introduced in the parliament an anti-pornography bill that, in addition to outlawing sexually explicit materials, also sought to proscribe a wide range of social and personal activities, including kissing in public, homosexuality, and cultural performances in which artists were not fully clothed. The bill drew a storm of protest from cultural groups, regions with traditions of semi-naked performance (Bali and Papua were such areas), and secular nationalists and liberal Muslims who claimed that Islāmists were instituting Sharī'ah by stealth. Islāmic parties responded that the bill was primarily concerned with public morality rather than religion, but they nonetheless agreed to withdraw the legislation. The revised bill had most of the contentious clauses removed, and secularists claimed this as a defeat for Islāmism and a reassertion of Indonesia's religiously neutral traditions.

Malaysia

Malaysia, composed of Malaya (now Peninsular Malaysia), Singapore, Sarawak, and Sabah, was established on September 16 1963. In August 1965 Singapore seceded from the federation and became an independent republic. Although the Malaysian constitution established a secular state, it recognizes Islām as the official religion.

The Malay Peninsula, situated at one of the great maritime crossroads of the world, contains the Orang Asli (aborigines), Malays, Chinese, and South Asians. In addition, there are small numbers of Europeans, Americans, Eurasians, Arabs, and Thai. The Orang Asli are primarily adherents of traditional religions, but a number have been converted to Islām. The Malays constitute about two-thirds of the population and adherence to Islām is regarded as one of the most important factors distinguishing them from a non-Malay; the number of Malays who are not Muslim is negligible. The Chinese make up about one-third of the peninsular population. The peoples from South Asia – Indians, Pakistanis, and Tamils from Sri Lanka – constitute about 10 per cent of the population of Peninsular Malaysia. Most of the Indians and Sri Lankans are Hindu, while the Pakistanis are predominantly Muslim. The Sikhs, from the Punjab, adhere to their own religion, Sikhism.

The main ethnic groups in Sarawak are the Chinese and the Iban. The Malays of Sarawak, although ethnically diverse, are culturally homogeneous, speaking a common language and practising Islām. The Bidayuh live in hill country, and the majority practise traditional religions, but Christian missionaries have made some converts among them.

The great majority of Melanau are Muslim, with the rest (except for a small number of Christians) following traditional religions. Sabah also has a kaleidoscopic mixture of peoples. The largest groups are the Kadazan (of whom a small number are Muslim), Chinese, Bajau (most of whom are Muslim), and Murut.

The introduction of Western cultural influences in the nineteenth century affected many aspects of Malaysian life. Contemporary Malaysian culture is thus multifaceted, consisting of many strands – animistic, early Hindu, early and modern Islāmic, and, especially in the cities, Western – and the collective pattern is distinct from other cultures and recognizably Malaysian. The state legislatures retain responsibility for issues pertaining to Islāmic law and for matters regarding personal and family laws affecting Muslims, as well as for land laws. Malaysian political life is dominated by the National Front (Barisan Nasional), a broad coalition of ethnically oriented parties that long has been controlled by the United Malays National Organization. The main opposition parties are the Democratic Action Party (consisting primarily of Chinese), the Muslim Unity Movement (a coalition of pro-Islāmic parties), and the Sabah People's Union.

Islām, introduced to Malacca (now Melaka) in the fifteenth century by Arab and Indian merchants, soon became the dominant religion of the Malays. From the thirteenth the seventeenth century, Sunni Islām spread widely, coming from the Middle East via India. The spread of Islām was intimately linked to the florescence of the great Indian Ocean maritime trading routes that connected China through the Strait of Malacca to India, the Middle East, and East Africa. The arrival of Islām coincided with the rise of the great port of Malacca. The Indianized king converted to Islām, becoming a "sultan" and hence attracting Muslim merchants. Soon Malacca became South-east Asia's major trading entrepôt, while at the same time it gained suzerainty over much of coastal Malaya and eastern Sumatra. Malacca served as the main centre for the propagation of Islām as well as the eastern terminus of the Indian Ocean trading network. Malacca's political and religious influence reached its height under Tun Perak, who served as prime minister (1456–98) after defeating the expanding Thai in a fierce naval battle; during his service Islām became well entrenched in such districts (and subsidiary sultanates) as Johor, Kedah, Perak, Pahang, and Terengganu.

The mostly Islāmicized people of the Malacca area began calling themselves "Malays" (a likely elite reference to earlier Srivijayan origins). Thereafter the term Malay applied to those who practised Islām and spoke a version of the Malay language. Over time a loose cultural designation became a coherent ethnic group spread throughout Malaya, northern and western Borneo, eastern Sumatra, and the smaller islands in between, a region that can be termed the "Malay world". Islām, however, came to overlay the earlier beliefs so that, before the rise of religious reform movements in the nineteenth century, few Malays were orthodox Muslims. Hindu-influenced ritual remained important for the elite, and animist spirits were richly incorporated into Islāmic folk beliefs. Islām reached Sarawak and Sabah in the fifteenth and sixteenth centuries; many coastal peoples converted, but the interior remained largely animist until the twentieth century.

In the sixteenth century the region came under European control. The Portuguese arrived at Malacca in 1509, capturing it two years later. Since fewer merchants chose to endure the high taxes and the conquerors' intolerance of Islām, Malacca languished under Portuguese control. The Dutch seized Malacca in 1641. In 1786 the English East India Company acquired Penang (or Pinang) Island, off Malaya's north-west coast. By 1824 it had acquired interests in Singapore Island and Malacca. The British Colonial Office took direct control in 1867. By 1914 the British had achieved formal or informal colonial control over nine sultanates, but pledged not to interfere in matters of religion, customs, and the symbolic political role of the sultans. The various states were increasingly integrated to form British Malaya. Sabah (North Borneo) was the last region to be brought under British control.

Post-war negotiations resulted in the creation in 1948 of the Federation of Malaya, and on August 31 1957 it achieved independence (*merdeka*). Singapore, with its predominantly Chinese population, remained outside the federation as a British crown colony. Beginning in the late 1970s, an Islāmic fundamentalist revival, or *dakwah* movement, increasingly attracted the support of young Malays who had become alienated by the growth of a Westernized, materialistic society.

Long considered a model of ethnic and religious tolerance, Malaysia showed signs in 2006 that its carefully maintained social fabric was beginning to fray as tensions mounted between conservative Muslims and their non-Muslim countrymen. Some local governments enacted bans on couples kissing and holding hands in public and on owning dogs (considered unclean by conservative Muslims). A coalition of non-governmental groups known as Article 11 called on the government to enforce constitutional guarantees of religious equality and freedom of worship against creeping Islāmization, but the prime minister instead accused Article 11 of endangering Malaysia's social harmony by focusing attention on sensitive issues. Critics warned that the government's weak response to the encroachments of Islāmic fundamentalism might lead to the further erosion of religious freedom and inter-ethnic harmony in Malaysia. The following year, Malaysia's Federal Court ruled that only the Islāmic Sharī'ah court had the power to rule on a woman's petition to have her religious designation changed from Muslim to Christian on her government identity card; the ruling was effectively a final refusal, since a request before the Sharī'ah court to leave Islām would be equivalent to admitting apostasy, an offence punishable by fine or imprisonment.

India, Pakistan, and Afghanistan

India's Muslim population is greater than that found in any country of the Middle East and is only exceeded by that of Indonesia and, slightly, by that of Pakistan or Bangladesh.

In Islāmic India, Sunni Muslims are the majority sect almost everywhere. There are, however, influential Shī'ite minorities in Gujarat, especially among such Muslim trading communities as the Khojas and Bohras, and in large cities, such as Lucknow and Hyderabad, that were former capitals of pre-independence Muslim states in which much of the gentry was of Persian origin. In 1947, with the partition of the subcontinent, perhaps ten million Muslims left for Pakistan. Muslims, however, are still the largest single minority faith (more than one-ninth of the total population), with large concentrations in many areas of the country, including Jammu and Kashmir, where Muslims represent two-fifths of the population and outnumber Hindus, western Uttar Pradesh, West Bengal, Kerala, and many cities.

India is a diverse, multi-ethnic country that is home to

thousands of small ethnic and tribal groups. This complexity developed from a lengthy and involved process of migration and intermarriage. Throughout its history, India was intermittently disturbed by incursions from beyond its northern mountain wall. Islām was brought from the north-west by Arab, Turkish, Persian, and other raiders beginning early in the eighth century AD. The significant and permanent military movement of Muslims into northern India, however, dates from the late twelfth century and was carried out by a Turkish dynasty that arose indirectly from the ruins of the 'Abbāsid caliphate. Sultan Mahmud of Ghazna (now Ghazni, Afghanistan) conducted more than 20 raids into north India between 1001 and 1027 and established in the Punjab the easternmost province of his large but short-lived empire.

By 1186 the Ghurids had destroyed the remnants of Ghaznavid power in the north-west and moved against the northern Indian Rajput powers. By the thirteenth century they had established the foundation of an Indian Muslim state. Delhi, no longer subordinate to Ghazna, was to become a proud centre of Muslim power and culture in India. Nevertheless Sultan Shams al-Din Iltutmish (reigned 1211–36) made clear to what extent Islām and Sharī'ah could determine the contour of politics and culture in the overwhelmingly non-Muslim Indian environment. Early in his reign, a party of theologians approached him with the plea that the infidel Hindus be forced, in accordance with Islāmic law, to accept Islām or face death. On behalf of the sultan, his *wazir* (vizier) told the divines that this was impractical, since the Muslims were as few as grains of salt in a dish of food.

The Muslim sultans continued to rule through the following centuries, Muḥammad ibn Tughluq bringing the south under direct control in the fourteenth century. By then a theory of Islāmic power, different from the universal Islāmic theory of

state, had also begun to emerge. The Turkish state was, in a
formal sense, Islāmic. The sultans could not allow open
violation of Sharī'ah. They appointed Muslim divines ('ulama') to profitable offices and granted revenue-free lands to
many of them. But the policy of the state was based increasingly upon the opinion of the sultans and their advisers and not
on any religious texts as interpreted by the 'ulama'. In view of
practical needs and worldly considerations (jahandari), the
sultans supplemented Sharī'ah by framing their own state laws
(thawabit). These regulations in cases of conflict overrode the
universal Muslim law.

By 1388, when Firuz Tughluq died, the decline of the
sultanate was imminent; the ensuing struggle for the throne
rapidly diminished the authority of Delhi and provided op-
portunities for Muslim nobles and Hindu chiefs to enhance
their autonomy. Rebellions by Hindu chiefs saw the formation
of several Hindu states, most notably the Vijayanagar, and in
1398 the invasion of Timur provoked the collapse of the
dynasty and the rise of regional states, with no overall control.

In the sixteenth century, Babur inaugurated the Mughal
Empire (1526–1761) in India. Mughal culture blended Perso-
Islāmic and regional Indian elements into a distinctive but
variegated whole. It flourished especially under Babur's grandson, Akbar (ruled 1556–1605) and his successors, who promoted a tolerant regime. Under Akbar, Central Asians
(Turanis), Iranians (Iranis), Afghans, Indian Muslims of diverse subgroups, and Rajputs were integrated into a single
imperial service. The emperor saw to it that no single ethnic or
religious group was large enough to challenge his supreme
authority. To legitimize his non-sectarian policies, he issued in
1579 a public edict (mahzar) declaring his right to be the
supreme arbiter in Muslim religious matters – above the body
of Muslim religious scholars and jurists. With the accession of

Aurangzeb (ruled 1659–1707), a stricter communalism that imposed penalties on protected non-Muslims and stressed the shah's role as leader of the Muslim community, by virtue of his enforcing the Sharī'ah, emerged.

By the beginning of the eighteenth century, however, the empire had begun to disintegrate. The decline of the ruling Muslim elite and the expansion of European interests culminated in the absorption of the subcontinent within the British Empire. Direct administration by the British, which began in 1858, effected a political and economic unification of the subcontinent. With the loss of political power during the period of Western colonialism in the nineteenth and twentieth centuries, the concept of the Islāmic community (*ummah*), instead of weakening, became stronger.

One of the most significant risings of Muslims came with the Indian Mutiny of 1857. The immediate cause of military disaffection was the deployment of the new breech-loading Enfield rifle, the cartridge of which was purportedly greased with pork and beef fat. Bengali troops refusing to use the ammunition were placed in irons, but their comrades soon came to their rescue, shot the British officers and made for Delhi, where there were no British troops. The Indian garrison at Delhi joined them, and by the next nightfall they had secured the city and Mughal fort, proclaiming the aged titular Mughal emperor, Bahadur Shah II, as their leader. There at a stroke was an army, a cause, and a national leader – the only Muslim who appealed to both Hindus and Muslims. The British retaliated, and on August 2 1858, less than a month after the Governor Lord Canning proclaimed the victory of British arms, Parliament passed the Government of India Act, transferring British power over India from the East India Company, whose ineptitude was primarily blamed for the mutiny, to the crown.

In the years leading up to independence in 1947, Islāmic nationalism increased, alongside other nationalist expression. Sir Sayyid Aḥmad Khan (1817–98), India's greatest nineteenth-century Muslim leader, had founded India's first centre of Islāmic and Western higher education, the Anglo-Mohammedan Oriental College (now Aligarh Muslim University), at Aligarh in 1875. In 1906, the first meeting of the Muslim League was held, at which the Aga Khan's deputation issued an expanded call "to protect and advance the political rights and interests of Mussalmans of India". In 1916 the Indian National Congress and the Muslim League, under Mohammad Alī Jinnah, agreed to a pact to progress a joint programme of independence. The Muslim quarter of India's population became increasingly wary of the Congress's promises, however, Hindu–Muslim riots spread, and by 1930 Indian Muslims had begun to think in terms of separate statehood for their minority community.

When Jawaharlal Nehru refused to permit the League to form coalition ministries with the Congress majority after the 1937 elections, the League hope for future joint government virtually disappeared. The years from 1937 to 1939, when the Congress actually ran most of British India's provincial governments, became the seed period for the Muslim League's growth in popularity and power within the entire Muslim community. After the Second World War, however, it proved impossible to found a constitution based on shared powers, and Jinnah instead called upon the "Muslim Nation" to launch "direct action". India's bloodiest year of civil war since the mutiny followed.

The Indian Independence Act, ordering the demarcation of the dominions of India and Pakistan by midnight of August 14–15 1947, was passed in July. Racing the deadline, two boundary commissions worked desperately to partition Punjab and Bengal in such a way as to leave the maximum practical number of Muslims to the west of the former's new boundary and to the east of the latter's, but, as soon as the new borders were known, roughly 15 million Hindus, Muslims, and Sikhs fled from their homes on one side of the newly demarcated borders to what they thought would be "shelter" on the other. As many as a million people were slaughtered in communal massacres in the process.

Since independence, the legacy of partition has been felt, not only in continuing conflict with Pakistan but also in sectarian disturbances within India itself. The territory of Jammu and Kashmir has been disputed between Pakistan and India, the two countries going to war over the territory three times. In India itself, in 1992 an army of Hindu protestors tore down the 464-year-old Babri Masjid Mosque, which Muslims considered one of their oldest and most sacred places. Its destruction ignited the country's worst inter-religious rioting since partition and set the stage for severe clashes between Hindu and Muslim extremists during the rest of the decade. In the early twenty-first century there was a resurgence of *jihad* terrorism. Terrorist attacks were staged in various parts of the country: in 2002 in Gujarat some 1,000 Muslims died in sectarian violence and in Mumbai, in July 2006, bomb attacks on suburban trains claimed nearly 200 lives and injured at least 800. While the BJP has tried to whip up nationalist sentiment among Hindu groups, the government has endeavoured, not always successfully, to prevent such incidents from igniting a communal conflagration.

In the Islāmic Republic of **Pakistan**, almost all the people are Muslims. Following the exodus of Muslims from India after partition, a second major wave of Muslim immigration began when thousands of refugees started to flee Afghanistan, occupied by the Soviet Union in 1979, to live in camps and settlements along the Pakistani border. By the close of the 1980s, as many as 3.5 million Afghan refugees had arrived in the country.

Most Muslims belong to the Sunni sect, with a significant representation among the Shī'ite branch. There is also a very small, though influential, sect called Ahmadiyah, or Qadianis, which does not regard the prophet Muhammad as the final prophet. A 1974 constitutional amendment declared the Ahmadiyah community to be non-Muslims. Since then the community has experienced considerable persecution, particularly during the administration of Zia ul-Haq (1977–88). The majority of Pakistani Sunnis belong to the orthodox Hanafi school. Shī'ites are divided into numerous subsects; among them are Isma'ilis (the followers of the Aga Khan), as well as the Twelvers (Ithnā 'Asharīyah) and Bohras, which are prominent communities in commerce and industry. The principal business communities among Sunnis are Gujarati Memons and Chiniotis from Punjab.

With the exception of some sects, such as Dawoodi Bohras, there is generally no ordained priesthood among Pakistan's Muslims. Anyone who leads prayers in mosques may be appointed *imām*. Those who are trained in theology are given the title of mullah or *mawlana* or, collectively, *'ulama'*. There are powerful hereditary networks of "holy men" called *pir*s, who receive great reverence, as well as gifts in cash or kind, from a multitude of followers. An established *pir* may pass on his spiritual powers and sanctified authority to one or more of his *murid*s ("disciples"), who may then operate as *pir*s in their own right. There are also many self-appointed *pir*s who practise locally without being properly inducted into one of the four Sufi orders. *Pir*s who occupy high positions in the *pir* hierarchy wield great power and play an influential role in public affairs.

The amended 1972 constitution provides for a president as

head of state and a prime minister as head of government; both must be Muslims. The National Assembly has 237 seats. Of these, 217 are filled by direct popular election; 207 are for Muslim candidates and 10 for non-Muslims. The remaining 20 seats are reserved for women who are chosen by the elected members. The role of Islām in the political and cultural unification of Pakistan has, however, been controversial. The Pakistan People's Party (PPP) was formed in 1968 by Zulfikar Alī Bhutto, working with a number of socialists who wanted Pakistan to disregard the idiom of religion in politics in favour of a programme of rapid modernization of the country and the introduction of a socialist economy. In 1962 the Muslim League splintered into two parts, the Pakistan Muslim League and the Council Muslim League. In the elections of 1970 it almost disappeared as a political party, but it was resurrected in 1985 and became the most important component of the Islāmic Democratic Alliance, which took over Punjab's administration in 1988. The Islāmic Assembly, founded in 1941, commands a great deal of support among the urban lower-middle classes. Two other religious parties, the Assembly of Islāmic Clergy and the Assembly of Pakistani Clergy, have strong centres of support, the former in Karachi and the latter in the rural areas of the North-West Frontier Province.

The constitution of 1956 declared Pakistan to be an Islāmic republic, but Pakistani politics soon began to dissolve into factionalism, regionalism, and sectarianism. A period of martial law and later civil war followed, and in 1972 the establishment of Bangladesh. Bhutto became the undisputed leader of former West Pakistan, declaring a policy of Islāmic socialism. General Mohammad Zia ul-Haq took over as chief administrator of martial law on July 5 1977, and introduced a full Islāmic code of laws; on September 16 1978, he was proclaimed president of Pakistan. In response to the Afghanistan war and the revolution in Iran, President Zia extended his Islāmization programme. In addition to Islāmic criminal laws, this included interest-free banking and other measures in keeping with traditional Islāmic economic practice. In December 1988, following elections after Zia's death, Benazir Bhutto became the first woman to lead a modern Islāmic state.

From the 1990s, violence by Islāmic extremist groups directed against the nation's small Christian community and the heterodox Ahmadiyah sect rose throughout the country. In the twenty-first century, Pakistan's alleged support for Islāmic insurgents in the disputed Kashmir region frequently strained relations with India. Yet, in late 2001 President Pervez Musharraf's government cooperated with U.S. forces attempting to uproot Islāmic extremists in Afghanistan, which led to acts of violence by Pakistani supporters of that country's ruling Taliban regime – a group Pakistan had theretofore supported. The fighting in Afghanistan threatened to spill over into Pakistan, and Musharraf's regime was faced with the possibility that it might be toppled by extremists, who claimed numerous supporters in the government, military, and intelligence services.

Musharraf's grip on power appeared to be diminished by Islāmabad's failure to root out renascent al-Qaeda and Taliban forces in the frontier area, and sectarian conflict has been a continuing problem in recent years. The suicide bombing of a Shī'ite procession south of Islāmabad in 2006 caused some 30 deaths and scores of injuries and the killing of Shī'ite leader Allama Hassan Turabi precipitated riots in Karachi. In December 2007 Pakistan's first reported woman suicide bomber blew herself up at a military checkpoint in Peshawar, while another suicide bomber detonated a device in a nearby mosque, killing more than 50. Earlier, in an audio recording, Osama bin Laden called rebellion against Musharraf an act of faith. In spring 2007, religious militants seized control of the Lal Masjid mosque in Islāmabad and ordered students from nearby religious schools to attack public and commercial outlets. More than 100 died in the summer when Special Forces forcibly took control of the complex, prompting numerous suicide bombings in different parts of the country. At the end of the year, Benazir Bhutto, who had returned to Pakistan to campaign in the upcoming parliamentary elections scheduled for early January 2008, was assassinated at a political rally in Rawalpindi.

Islāmic armies first entered the **Afghan** area in the seventh century, and the ninth and tenth centuries witnessed the rise of numerous local Islāmic dynasties. In the eleventh century Mahmud of Ghazna carried Islām into India from Afghanistan. Later came conquest by the Mongols and Timur, and then division between the Mughals of India and the Safavids of Persia. The modern boundaries of Afghanistan were established in the late nineteenth century in the context of a rivalry between imperial Britain and tsarist Russia. Modern Afghanistan became a pawn in struggles over political ideology and commercial influence. In the last quarter of the twentieth century, Afghanistan suffered the ruinous effects of civil war greatly exacerbated by a military invasion and occupation by the Soviet Union (1979–89). In subsequent armed struggles, a surviving Afghan communist regime held out against Islāmic insurgents (1989–92), and, following a brief rule by *mujahid-een* groups, the Taliban rose up against the country's governing parties and warlords and established a theocratic regime (1996–2001) that soon fell under the influence of a group of well-funded Islāmists led by Osama bin Laden (see Chapters 8 and 9). The Taliban regime collapsed in December 2001 in the wake of a sustained U.S.-dominated military campaign aimed at the Taliban and fighters of bin Laden's al-Qaeda organization. Soon thereafter, anti-Taliban forces agreed to a period of transitional leadership and an administration that would lead to a new constitution and the establishment of a democratically elected government.

Virtually all the people of Afghanistan are Muslims, of whom some three-quarters are Sunnis of the Hanafi branch. The others, particularly the Hazara and Kizilbash, follow either Ithnā 'Asharīyah or Isma'ili Shī'ite Islām. Sufism is practised widely. The Nuristani are descendants of a large ethnic group, the Kafir, who were forcibly converted to Islām in 1895; the name of their region was then changed from Kafiristan ("Land of the Infidels") to Nurestan ("Land of Light"). There are also a few thousand Hindus and Sikhs.

Religion has long played a paramount role in the daily life and social customs of Afghanistan. Even under the *mujahideen* leaders, Afghanistan appeared to be on a course of Islāmization: the sale of alcohol was banned, and women were pressured to cover their heads in public and adopt traditional Muslim dress. But far more stringent practices were imposed as the Taliban enforced its Islāmic code in areas under its control. These measures included banning television sets and most other forms of entertainment. Men who failed to grow beards and leave them untrimmed were fined and jailed – full beardedness being perceived by extremists as the mark of a Muslim – and little mercy was shown to convicted criminals. Authorities closed down girls' schools and forced women to give up employment in nearly all occupations. Strong penalties were applied against women who were not fully covered in the streets or who were found in the company of males unrelated to them.

Today, the ban enforced by the Taliban on most forms of entertainment has been lifted, and the social atmosphere has become more relaxed. Afghans are again enjoying activities from kite flying to football, and photography is no longer prohibited. Though facilities are minimal, schools have been reopened – including those for girls – and women are once again entering the workforce. However, urban women have continued to wear the chador (or *chadri*, in Afghanistan), the full body covering mandated by the Taliban. Some men have shaved or trimmed their beards, but, aside from disregarding the style of turban associated with the Taliban, most have continued to dress traditionally.

Africa

The majority of Africa's peoples are indigenous; European colonial settlers constitute the largest majority of new peoples, with substantial numbers in Kenya, South Africa, Zimbabwe, Zambia, Namibia, and Mozambique. The vast majority arrived after the 1885 Berlin West Africa Conference and the resulting "scramble for Africa", during which European leaders carved out spheres of influence. Much earlier, in several waves of migrations beginning in the seventh century, Arabs spread across northern Africa and, to a lesser extent, into West Africa, bringing a new religion (Islām) and a new language (Arabic), along with some new cultural and political institutions. They also spread Islām southward along the east coast, largely through trading and kinship relationships.

Africa north of the Sahara is differentiated from the rest of the continent by its long history of political and cultural contacts with peoples outside of Africa. Among its inhabitants are the Berbers of Morocco, Algeria, and Tunisia. Northern Africa is predominantly Islāmic and southern Africa largely Christian, although their distributions are not discrete. For example, the Coptic church is found in Egypt and Ethiopia, and Islām is common along the coast of eastern Africa and is expanding southward in western Africa. Many of the Sudanic peoples – such as the Malinke, Hausa, Songhai, and Bornu – are Islāmized, and the religion has also achieved substantial gains among such Guinea Coast people as the Yoruba of Nigeria and the Temne of Sierra Leone. Much conversion to Christianity also has occurred, most notably in the coastal regions of sub-Saharan Africa. In most of the rest of sub-Saharan Africa the people practise a variety of traditional religions.

A distinctive **North African** facet of Islāmic tradition, stemming from Islāmic folk practices and Sufi teaching, is the important role played by *marabout*s. These saintly individuals were widely held to possess special powers and were venerated locally as teachers, healers, and spiritual leaders. *Marabout*s frequently formed extensive brotherhoods and at various times would take up the sword in defence of their religion and country. In more peaceful times these local religious icons would practise a type of Islām that stressed local custom and direct spiritual insight as much as Qur'ānic teachings. Their independence was often perceived as a threat to established authority, and Islāmic reformers and state bodies have historically sought to restrict the growth of *marabout* influence.

North Africa, comprising the modern countries of Morocco, Algeria, Tunisia, and Libya, began to be invaded by the Arabs after their conquest of Egypt in 642. They started to raid the Berber (Amazigh) territory to its west, which they called Bilad al-Maghrib ("Lands of the West") or simply the Maghrib. In 705 this region became a province of the Muslim empire then ruled from Damascus by the Umayyad caliphs (661–750). By the eleventh century the Berbers had become Islāmized and in part also Arabized. The rule of the caliphs was now replaced by four separate Muslim states dominated by dynasties that either nominally recognized caliphal authority, as was the case with the Aghlabids, or totally rejected it, as was the case with the three other states.

The fragmentation of political life in the Maghrib, following both Arab invasion and a general decline in the authority of the Fatimids, was arrested by the Almoravids in the mid-eleventh century. By 1082 Almoravid rule extended as far east as Algiers; by 1110, the Almoravids had become masters of the whole of Muslim Spain. They were the founders of the first of two empires that unified the Maghrib under Berber Islāmic rule.

After the collapse of the Almoravids' successors, the Almohads, the Maghrib became divided into three Muslim states, each ruled by a Berber dynasty. The Maghribi rulers legitimized their authority by cultivating relations of trust and cooperation with the leading religious scholars of the time. Their capital cities became, consequently, the foremost centres of learning in their realms and were adorned not only with exquisite mosques but also with sumptuous *madrasah*s, residential colleges built and financed by the rulers.

Between 1471 and 1510 the line of confrontation between the Muslims of the Maghrib and the Christians of the Iberian Peninsula shifted from Spain to the Maghrib itself. The Portuguese occupied a number of positions on the Moroccan coast between 1471 and 1505. The Spaniards conquered Granada, the last Muslim stronghold on the peninsula, in 1492, and between 1505 and 1510 they began establishing garrison posts along the Maghribi coast. The strong religious reaction in the Maghrib to Christian colonial intrusion enabled the Sa'di dynasty of *sharīf*s to capture power in Morocco in 1549 and paved the way for Ottoman rule to be established.

When Europe began its colonial expansion in the Maghrib – starting with the French occupation of Algiers in 1830 – the region was divided into four political entities. Morocco, ruled by the 'Alawite dynasty, was a sovereign country. Algeria, Tunisia, and Libya were autonomous states that recognized the religious authority of the Ottoman sultan. The Moroccan protectorate was established in 1912, and Libya was invaded by Italy in 1911. In both countries there was resistance by nationalists, but by 1939 the colonization of Morocco, Tunisia, and Libya by French and Italian settlers was well advanced.

The Second World War brought major changes to North Africa, promoting the cause of national independence. The Sanusi leader Sidi Muḥammad Idris al-Mahdī al-Sanusi was restored to power and became King Idris I of a united Libya in 1951. The French conceded independence to Tunisia and Morocco in 1956 and a "savage war of peace" led to Algerian independence in 1962. The Libyan monarchy was overthrown by a military coup in 1969 and replaced by the popular republicanism of Colonel Muammar al-Qaddafi.

The new regime of **Libya** was passionately pan-Arab, and maintained a strong interventionist orientation on the Palestine issue and in support of other guerrilla and revolutionary organizations in Africa and the Middle East. In July–August 1977 hostilities broke out between Libya and Egypt, and, in spite of expressed concern for Arab unity, the regime's relations with most Arab countries were poor. On March 2 1977, the General People's Congress declared that Libya was to be known as the People's Socialist Libyan Arab Jamahiriyyah ("government through the masses"). By 1981, however, a drop in the demand and price for oil was slowing Libya's economy, and there were signs of domestic discontent. Libyan opposition movements launched sporadic attacks against Qaddafi and his military supporters but met with arrest and execution. In recent years, relationships with the West have been restored.

Almost all Libyans speak Arabic, the country's official language, and adhere to the Sunni branch of Islām. They claim descent from the Bedouin Arab tribes of the Banū Hilal and the Banū Sulaym, who invaded the Maghrib in the eleventh century. In the eastern region the influence of the Sanusiyah remains strong. By the twentieth century about 97 per cent of Libya's inhabitants were Arabic-speaking Muslims of mixed Arab and Berber descent. Among other social groups are the *sharīf*s (holy tribes), who came originally from the Fezzan; the *marabout*s (dervishes who are credited with supernatural powers), who infiltrated from Saguia el Hamra in what is now Western Sahara; and the Koulouglis, who are descended from the Janissaries (elite Turkish soldiers). The *sharīf*s claim direct descent from the Prophet Muḥammad. Their alleged blood relationship with the Prophet gives them a powerful standing in Muslim society, where they are looked upon as holy men with divine powers of foresight. *Marabout* tribes are descended from holy men who also claimed relation to Muhammad. They founded their religious devotions upon an ascetic life manifested in their existence as hermits.

In **Algeria** the Algerian War of Independence, which would begin nearly a decade later, was set in motion by events in May 1945, when a display of Algerian nationalist flags at Sétif prompted French authorities to fire on demonstrators. An unorganized uprising ensued, in which 84 European settlers were massacred. The violence and suppression that followed resulted in the death of about 8,000 Muslims (according to French sources) or as many as 45,000 (according to Algerian sources). The war began on October 31 1954. The movement, led by the newly formed National Liberation Front (Front de Libération Nationale; FLN), stated that its aim was to restore a sovereign Algerian state. It advocated social democracy within an Islāmic framework and equal citizenship for any resident in

Algeria. Two weapons would be used: guerrilla warfare at
home and diplomatic activity abroad, particularly at the
United Nations (UN). In 1962, after a referendum, France
granted Algeria independence, and most Europeans left the
country.

Since independence the country has consistently sought to
regain its Arab and Islāmic heritage. Internal tensions have
continued, and the revolution in Iran in 1979 and the war in
Afghanistan spurred a rise in Islāmic militancy and direct action.
The breakdown of the socialist system contributed even further
to the rise of Islamists. The emergence of ā myriad parties mainly
benefited the Islāmic Salvation Front (Front Islāmique du Salut;
FIS), which built on the population's resentment of the incompetence and corruption of the regime and captured clear majo-
rities in the provincial and municipal councils in 1990. Relations
between the Islāmists and the army remained strained and in
1992 the army cancelled the elections as violence increased and
the country moved toward civil war. In 1995 General Liamine
Zeroual attempted to legitimize his position by holding presi-
dential elections. From the mid-1990s several discussions were
held between the government and other parties.

In 2005, a referendum on a plan for national reconciliation
received 97 per cent support from the 79 per cent of the
electorate who voted. The legislation for reconcilation, which
came into effect in 2006, provided for a six-month amnesty
period for those not directly engaged in violence and a partial
amnesty for those dissidents who were involved. On the other
hand, it gave a blanket immunity to the security forces, making
it an offence to question this or other governmental decisions
in this respect – a provision that caused considerable protest.
The effect of the charter was limited.

Political violence has also increased, owing to youth radi-
calization and attacks by the Salafist Group for Preaching and

Combat (GSPC), which claimed to have joined al-Qaeda in September 2006.

Most Algerians, both Arab and Amazigh, are Sunni Muslims of the Maliki rite. While Algeria's post-independence governments have confirmed the country's Islāmic heritage, their policies have often encouraged secular developments. Islāmic fundamentalism has been increasing in strength since the late 1970s in reaction to this. Muslim extremist groups periodically have clashed with both left-wing students and emancipated women's groups, while fundamentalist *imāms* (prayer leaders) have gained influence in many of the country's major mosques. The daily life of the average Algerian is permeated with the atmosphere of Islām, which has become identified with the concept of an autonomous Algerian people and of resistance to what many Algerians perceive as a continued Western imperialism.

Morocco is composed mainly of Arabs and Imazighen or an admixture of the two. Islām is the official state religion, and the vast majority of Moroccans are Sunni Muslims of the Maliki rite. The royal house, the 'Alawite dynasty, has ruled since the seventeenth century, basing its claim to legitimacy on descent from the Prophet Muḥammad. The royal family is revered by Moroccan Muslims because of its prophetic lineage. As in many Islāmic countries, Sufism claims adherents, and forms of popular religion – including the veneration of saints and the visitation of tombs – are widely practised.

In theory, the Qur'ān is still the source of law. It is, in effect, exercised by the *qāḍī*s (Muslim religious judges) and is limited to matters relating to the personal status of Muslims. The legal system, however, has not been immune to pressures for reform. Moroccan women, in particular, have sought reforms in the *Mudawwanah*, or code of personal status and family law, in an effort to change inequities in inheritance, divorce, and other matters that have traditionally favoured men. In 2004 parliament issued a new, more liberal, personal status code.

Following independence, political support has been divided between more traditional elements, represented by Hizb al-Istiqlal (Independence Party), the National Union of Popular Forces (Union Nationale des Forces Populaires, or UNFP), which favoured socialism with republican leanings, and the Front for the Defence of Constitutional Institutions, which supported the king. Elections have been widely regarded as fraudulent and there have been periods of political repression to maintain royal control. By the early 1980s, several bad harvests, a sluggish economy, and the continued financial drain of the war in Western Sahara increased domestic strains, of which violent riots in Casablanca in June 1981 were symptomatic.

The threat of an Algerian-style insurrection fuelled by a radical Islāmic opposition worried the political leadership throughout the 1990s and into the early twenty-first century. Amnesties for political prisoners long held in remote regions of the country signalled a new attention to human rights, while much-publicized curbs on the power of the police and security forces suggested closer adherence to the rule of law. Government vigilance over threats to the political system was underlined in September 2006 with the arrest of 56 people, including five soldiers and two policemen, all members of Jama'at al-Ansar al-Mahdī, a clandestine pro-al-Qaeda group.

The population of **Tunisia** is essentially Arab Berber, though there have been Arab immigrants and Muslim refugees from Sicily and Spain over the centuries. Virtually the entire population is Muslim, and Islām, in its Maliki Sunni form, is the state religion. The president must be a Muslim. A prominent feature of social policy has been the effort to improve the status and lives of women. Compared with their counterparts in other Arab countries, women in Tunisia have enjoyed greater equality before the law.

After independence was granted, the Neo-Destour Party ensured that Tunisia moved quickly with reforms, most notably in the areas of education, the liberation of women, and legal reforms. Economic development was slower, but the government paid considerable attention to the more impoverished parts of the country. In the early 1980s, an Islāmist opposition developed around the Islāmic Tendency Movement (Mouvement de la Tendance Islāmique [MTI]) against the increasingly autocratic rule of Bourguiba. In 1987, after his removal from office, some reforms occured, but future governments became increasingly authoritarian. Following early local electoral victories by Algerian Islāmists in 1990 and Islāmist opposition to the Persian Gulf War (1990–91), the government began to crack down on Islāmist political activity. In 2007, the regime continued its repressive policies and targeted persons whom the government suspected of having sympathies for political Islām as well as those who sought to create awareness of human rights abuses.

The Sudan, in north-eastern Africa, has been an arena for interaction between the cultural traditions of Africa and those of the Mediterranean world since ancient times. A major cleavage exists between the northern and the southern parts of the country. The north is dominated by Muslims, most of whom speak Arabic and identify themselves as "Arabs", while the people of the south are "Africans" (i.e. blacks) who for the most part follow traditional African religions, though there are also some Christians among them. Those who identify themselves as Arabs were estimated at 39 per cent of the total population in 1956. Besides Arabs, there are several Muslim but non-Arab groups in the north, the most notable of whom are the Nubians. The Humr Baqqarah and Fur peoples adhere to Islāmic beliefs and practices, which came to them through Arab influence, and traditional local practices coexist with Islāmic beliefs.

It is estimated that more than half of the population of The Sudan is Muslim. Ninety percent of Muslims live in the northern two-thirds of the country. The Muslims of The Sudan belong overwhelmingly to the Sunni sect. Sunni Islām in The Sudan, as in much of the rest of Africa, has been characterized by the formation of *ṭarīqa*s, or Muslim religious brotherhoods. The oldest of these *ṭarīqa*s is the Qādīriyah, which was introduced to the Sudan from the Middle East in the sixteenth century. Another major *ṭarīqa* is the Khatmiyah, or Mirgha-niyah, which was founded by Muḥammad 'Uthmān al-Mir-ghani in the early nineteenth century. Perhaps the most powerful and best organized *ṭarīqa* is the Mahdiyah; its followers led a successful revolt against the Turco–Egyptian regime (1821–85) and established an independent state in the Sudan that lasted from 1884 to 1898. The Mahdiyah and Khatmiyah *ṭarīqa*s formed the basis for the political parties that emerged in the Sudan in the 1940s and have continued to play a dominant role in the nation's politics in the post-independence period.

The country has had numerous regime changes, including military coups in 1985 and 1989, since independence in 1956. Successive regimes found it difficult to win general acceptance from the country's diverse political constituencies. An early conflict arose between those northern leaders who hoped to impose unity upon the nation through the vigorous extension of Islāmic law and culture to all parts of the country and those who opposed this policy. From independence until 1972 there prevailed a costly and divisive civil war. The Addis Ababa Agreement of 1972 ended the conflict only temporarily, and in 1983 the civil war resumed. A peace agreement was signed in

2005. The African Union maintains a peacekeeping force but conflict with rebel forces in Darfur continues. Relations between northern and southern Sudan remain divisive. On October 11 2007 the Sudan People's Liberation Movement, the ruling party in southern Sudan, suspended its participation in the Government of National Unity (GNU), claiming that its partner in the GNU (the Northern Sudan's National Congress Party) was failing to fulfil the terms of the internationally supervised Comprehensive Peace Agreement of 2005. Little progress has been made toward defining the boundary between north and south.

The Sudan's constitution calls for Sharī'ah to be the basis for the country's laws and regulations. Muslims remain subject to Islāmic law, as do constituents in northern states of the country regardless of their religious belief. Southern states – with a primarily animist-Christian population – are exempt from much, but not all, of Islāmic law.

Western Africa is divided between the western Sudan, where Islām has spread widely and between 60 and 70 per cent of the people are nominally Muslim, and the Guinea Coast, where Islām has been slow to penetrate. In the western Sudan wherever Islām is the dominant faith, Muslim religious teachers have taken over the role of traditional diviners in determining the causes of troubles, and they provide remedies in conformity with Islāmic patterns. The traditional ritual dances and masked performances are gradually disappearing or have been greatly modified as a result of opposition from Muslim teachers. In the Guinea Coast region, sometimes traditional religions have been blended into complex new sects with Christian and Muslim elements, as in the Yoruba-centred Church of the Cherubim and Seraphim.

In the fifteenth century **central Africa** opened direct relations both with the Mediterranean world of Islām and with the

Atlantic world of Christendom. Islāmic contacts remained limited until the nineteenth century, however. In Burundi Muslims constitute about one-tenth of the population. There is a growing number of Sunni Muslims in the Central African Republic. In the Republic of the Congo (Brazzaville), most of the small Muslim community is made up of foreigners who reside in Brazzaville or Pointe-Noire; there are also small expatriate Muslim communities in the Democratic Republic of the Congo and Gabon.

In **southern Africa**, populations are predominantly Christian and other religions. There are small expatriate Muslim communities in Botswana, Lesotho, Zambia (among the Asians), and in South Africa, where Islām is practised among many Indians and Malays. A sizeable community of Muslims is also found in north-west Madagascar, where Afro-Arabs spread Islām in the sixteenth century. In Malawi Muslims constitute almost one-fifth of the population. Islām spread into Malawi from the east coast. It was first introduced at Nkhotakota by the ruling Swahili-speaking slave traders, the Jumbe, in the 1860s. Traders returning from the coast in the 1870s and 1880s brought Islām to the Yao of the Shire Highlands. In Mozambique, fewer than one-fifth are Muslims. Although Islāmic communities are found in most of Mozambique's cities, Muslims constitute the majority in only the northern coastal region between the Lúrio and Rovuma rivers.

Eastern Africa is divided between The Horn of Africa and East Africa, both of which have long been in contact with the Arabian Peninsula and south-western Asia. In the Horn of Africa, Islām and Christianity are of ancient standing. Both assimilate the many local cultures of the region, and in turn many elements from the local cultures find their way into the world view of the two major religions. On the Muslim side the cult of saints is well developed and the Islāmic cosmology coincides to a remarkable degree with that of the Amhara Christians. Thus, among the Somali, who posthumously canonize their own lineage ancestors, saints are petitioned to remedy every distress and anxiety and are venerated as essential mediators between man and the Prophet Muḥammad and God. In the case of the Arusi Oromo, the Prophet himself and numerous other Muslim saints are assimilated to traditional spirits and ultimately to Waqa.

In East Africa by the late nineteenth century both Islãm and Christianity were becoming widely known. But even before that time, most of the East African peoples took for granted a metaphysical model in which a supreme deity created and maintained the universe, and in which the spirits of dead ancestors watched over the prosperity and morals of each community and punished any offenders.

The Muslim Diaspora: Communities in the West

There are now significant numbers of Muslims in the West. By 2000 substantial numbers of recent immigrants had increased the Muslim presence in the **United States** to about four million. Islãm was brought to the United States by African Muslim slaves, and it retained a real if minuscule presence in the country throughout the nineteenth century. It re-emerged at the beginning of the twentieth century as a result of the efforts of the Ahmadiyah movement, an unorthodox sect founded in India by Mirza Ghulam Aḥmad (c. 1839–1908), and of Shaikh Ahmed Faisal (1891–1980), the Moroccan-born leader of an independent Black Muslim movement.

In 1930, an Islãmic movement arose among blacks in the United States; members called themselves the Nation of

Islām, but they were popularly known as Black Muslims. Although they adopted some Islāmic social practices, the group was in large part a black separatist and social protest movement. Their leader, Elijah Muḥammad, who claimed to be an inspired prophet, interpreted the doctrine of Resurrection in an unorthodox sense as the revival of oppressed ("dead") peoples. The popular leader and spokesman Malcolm X (el-Hajj Malik el-Shabazz) broke with Elijah Muḥammad and adopted more orthodox Islāmic views. He was assassinated in 1965.

After the death of Elijah Muḥammad in 1975, the group was renamed World Community of Islām in the West and officially abandoned its separatist aims. The name was again changed in the late 1970s, to American Muslim Mission. The changes culminated in 1985 with the resignation of Elijah's son Wallace as head of the American Muslim Mission and his dissolution of the organization. The majority of former members followed him into the larger Muslim community. The move toward orthodoxy was, however, rejected by some former members, and two new organizations, both called the Nation of Islām, were formed.

Louis Farrakhan (originally Louis Eugene Wolcott), the successor of Malcolm X as leader of the New York Temple and the Nation's most prominent spokesman at the time of Elijah Muḥammad's death, left to found a third Nation of Islām. Farrakhan began his organization with only a few thousand adherents but soon re-established a national movement. He published Elijah Muḥammad's books, started a periodical, *The Final Call*, and eventually purchased Elijah Muḥammad's former mosque in Chicago and refurbished it as the new headquarters of the Nation of Islām. He also expanded the movement internationally, opening centres in England and Ghana. By the 1990s he had emerged as a prominent African-American leader. An estimated 10,000 to 50,000 people are members of the Nation of Islām.

Since the 1950s, immigrants began to introduce a great variety of religious beliefs to the **United Kingdom,** and in the first decade of the twenty-first century there are large and growing communities that practise Islām. The largest number of Muslims came from Pakistan and Bangladesh, with sizeable groups from India, Cyprus, the Arab world, Malaysia, and parts of Africa. Though Britain's 1.6 million Muslims make up a smaller part of the national population than their counterparts in France, Germany, and the Benelux countries, they have captured and remained in the international spotlight owing to the July 7 2005 suicide bombings in London. The perpetrators of the attacks were three British-born Muslims and a Jamaican-born Muslim living in Aylesbury. The 2006 Pew global attitudes survey found that a significant majority of British Muslims viewed Western populations as selfish, arrogant, and immoral, and attitudes among British Muslims were more similar to public opinion in Islāmic countries than elsewhere in Europe.

Britain's Muslims have a number of distinctive features that place them apart from their west European counterparts. Though French Muslims come predominately from North Africa and German Muslims originate in south-eastern Europe and Turkey, most British arrivals come from tight-knit communities in northern Pakistan, with smaller percentages originating from Bangladesh and India. They maintain strong links with their former homelands, a factor that can have a radicalizing effect. After decades of conflict in Afghanistan, hundreds of young British Muslims joined al-Qaeda training camps before the fall of the Taliban regime there in 2001.

Cohesive Muslim communities emerged in Britain in the 1950s owing to labour shortages in many of its industrial centres. State efforts to combat racism extended to an acceptance of immigrants' rights to preserve a distinctive identity, usually based around the practice of their religion. The rise of the fashionable doctrine of multiculturalism contributed to a more fragmented society in which separate communities developed. Familiarity with the national language was not yet a requirement for citizenship, and Muslims huddled in closed communities.

Some 70 per cent of British Muslims are under 40 years of age, and a significant minority are repelled by Britain's hedonism and what appears to them to be a lack of any spiritual dimension. Their idealism and piety are frequently blocked by the parochial nature of British Islām. *Imām*s may speak little or no English. Mosque committees are often dominated by factions pursuing sectarian rivalries that have South Asian origins. In the wider community, clans known as *biraderi* try to preserve a rural tribal outlook and prevent talented younger people from obtaining positions of responsibility. Not surprisingly, radical voices that insist that loyalty to a global Islāmic faith takes precedence over allegiance to the British state enjoy growing appeal. They depict the Anglo-American confrontation with Iraq over its invasion of Kuwait in 1990 and the persecution of Muslims in Bosnia and Herzegovina as a Western assault on the Islāmic world.

In the spring and summer of 2001, young Muslims were prominently involved in some of the worst riots seen in Britain in many years. Government inquiries emphasized the economic marginality of Muslim communities. The Blair government's handling of Muslim issues came under careful scrutiny after the 2005 London bombings. In particular, there was deep concern about the policy of granting refuge to radical Islāmic clergymen and agitators from the Middle East, many of whom in the 1980s had acquired a following among young people attracted by their revolutionary message; some of the youths went to Afghanistan and Kashmir to take up arms. Abu Hamza, the best known of the clerics extolling a violent *jihad*, was sentenced to seven years in prison in 2006 for inciting murder and racial hatred.

There was also sharp criticism of the Foreign Office's courtship of reactionary figures among British-based Muslims linked to the Muslim Brotherhood, which, though radical in its objectives, usually operates through political means. These reactionaries were given funding, political honours, and official platforms in the hope that they could prevent further acts of terrorism. In return, they demanded a range of privileges, including a right of oversight of foreign policy issues that were sensitive to British Muslims. Many were close to the dogmatic Wahhābī strand of Islām dominant in Saudi Arabia. Some feared that the South Asian forms of Islām prevalent in Britain might succumb to a form of Arabization. Moderates representing the contemplative Sufi tradition, who claim the adherence of a majority of British Muslims, complained about being overlooked by British officials who believed that it was only through cooperation with radicals that further violence could be prevented.

Fearing fresh violence, the government is trying to reach out beyond clerical figures who have hitherto been the main beneficiaries of its patronage. Progress depends on the emergence of articulate leaders among young Muslims who care about bridging the wide generational and gender gaps in Muslim communities, as well as promoting economic and educational achievement in a minority where both have been conspicuously lacking. A struggle is afoot to ensure that an emerging British Islāmic identity is not shaped around the separatist agenda of radicals but has characteristics that preserve religious integrity while allowing successful engagement with a secular society.

Islām has a long history elsewhere in Europe. Islāmic incursions into the Iberian and Balkan peninsulas have been influential in the cultures of those regions. Muslim communities still exist in several parts of the Balkans, including European Turkey (see above), Albania, Bosnia and Herzegovina, and north-eastern Bulgaria. Muslims are more numerous in European Russia, including the Kazan Tatars and Bashkirs in the Volga–Ural region, and in the Caucasus region, including the Azerbaijani and other groups.

Albania is Europe's only predominantly Muslim country – a legacy of nearly five centuries of Ottoman rule. At the end of the Second World War some 70 per cent of the population was Muslim. Most of them were traditional Sunnis, but about one-quarter were members of the liberal, pantheistic Bektashi sect, which for a time had its headquarters in Tiranë. The communist government, during its 45 years of absolute rule, engaged in large-scale persecution of believers and in 1967 it officially proclaimed Albania an atheistic country, closing all churches and mosques, confiscating property, and banning religious observances. Since this policy was abandoned in 1990 and freedom of worship guaranteed, churches and mosques have reopened all over the country.

Bosnia and Herzegovina is home to numerous ethnic groups, the largest being the Bosniacs, Serbs, and Croats, who constitute about two-fifths, one-third, and one-fifth, respectively, of the population. Culturally the major difference between them is that of religious origin and affiliation. Serbs belong to the Serbian Orthodox tradition, Croats to the Roman Catholic, and Bosniacs to the Islāmic. The resulting tensions between the communities, who identified their nationalism with their religious identity, ultimately resulted in the 1992–5 war in which nearly 100,000 were killed.

In the late fifteenth century Bosnia and Herzegovina fell to the Ottoman Turks and Bosnia was rapidly absorbed into the Ottoman Empire, under whose rule it remained until 1878 when Austria-Hungary took control. During the Ottoman period a large part of the native population converted to Islām. This was a gradual development; it took more than a hundred years for Muslims to become an absolute majority. At the end of the First World War the Kingdom of Serbs, Croats and Slovenes was created. In 1946 the Socialist Republic of Bosnia and Herzegovina became one of the constituent republics of the Federal People's Republic of Yugoslavia.

Life in Bosnia underwent all the social, economic, and political changes that were imposed on the whole of Yugoslavia by its new communist government, but Bosnia was particularly affected by the abolition of many traditional Muslim institutions, such as Qur'ānic primary schools, rich charitable foundations, and dervish religious orders. However, a change of official policy in the 1960s led to the acceptance of "Muslim" as a term denoting a national identity. By 1971 Muslims formed the largest single component of the Bosnian population. During the next 20 years the Serb and Croat populations fell in absolute terms as many Serbs and Croats emigrated. In the 1991 census Muslims made up more than two-fifths of the Bosnian population, while Serbs made up slightly less than one-third and Croats one-sixth. From the mid-1990s, the term "Bosniac" had replaced Muslim as the name for this group. The demise of communism brought religious revival within all three populations, partly in response to the end of official disapproval and partly in assertion of national identity.

In the 1980s the rapid decline of the Yugoslav economy led to widespread public dissatisfaction and this, together with the manipulation of nationalist feelings by politicians, destabilized Yugoslav politics. Independent political parties appeared in 1988. A tripartite coalition government was formed in 1990, but growing tensions both inside and outside Bosnia made cooperation with the Serbian Democratic Party, led by Radovan Karadzic, increasingly difficult.

In 1991 several self-styled "Serb Autonomous Regions" were declared in areas of Bosnia with large Serb populations and a "Serb National Assembly" was set up. By then full-scale war had broken out in Croatia, and the break-up of Yugoslavia was under way. The possibility of partitioning Bosnia had been discussed during talks between the Croatian president, Franjo Tudjman, and the Serbian president, Slobodan Milosevic, and two Croat "communities" in northern and southwestern Bosnia were proclaimed in November 1991. When the European Community (EC; now European Union) recognized the independence of Croatia and Slovenia, it invited Bosnia to apply for recognition also. Following a referendum, independence was officially proclaimed on March 3 1992.

When Bosnia's independence was recognized by the United States and the EC on April 7, Serbian paramilitary forces immediately began firing on Sarajevo, and the bombardment of the city by heavy artillery began soon thereafter. Much of the violence in the ensuing war had the aim of creating ethnic purity in areas that once had a mixture of peoples. In addition to killing thousands, this "ethnic cleansing" displaced more than one-third of the population of Bosnia and Herzegovina either within its borders or abroad. Several peace proposals failed, largely because the Serbs refused to concede any territory (they controlled about 70 per cent of land by 1994).

U.S.-sponsored peace talks in Dayton, Ohio, in November 1995 led to an agreement for a federalized Bosnia in which 51 per cent of the land would constitute a Croat–Bosniac federation and 49 per cent a Serb republic.

An election in September 1996 produced a tripartite national presidency chaired by Izetbegovic but including Croat and Serbian representatives. The two parts of the republic were largely autonomous, each having its own president and assembly. By the early twenty-first century, projects funded by the World Bank had succeeded in reconstructing much of the country's infrastructure, and some political and economic reforms were implemented. Nevertheless, ethnic tensions continued to flare, and the long-term future of the Republic of Bosnia and Herzegovina was questionable, as a vast majority of Croats and Serbs believed their future lay in independence or with Croatia and Serbia, respectively, rather than with the republic.

Prior to the 1950s there were few ethnic minorities in **Germany**; of the so-called "guest workers" (*Gastarbeiter*) and their families who immigrated to Germany beginning in the mid-1950s, the largest group is of Turkish ancestry. Distinct both culturally and religiously, they are scattered throughout German cities. Muslims now account for some 5 per cent of the total population.

For centuries migrants travelling by way of the Mediterranean from the Middle East and Africa, and through Europe from Central Asia and the Nordic lands, settled permanently in **France**. France was, in the nineteenth and especially in the twentieth century, the prime recipient of foreign immigration into Europe, adding still other mixtures to the ethnic melting pot.

Reflecting the presence of immigrants from North Africa, Algeria, and Morocco, France has one of Europe's largest Muslim populations: more than 4,000,000 Muslims, a sizeable percentage of them living in and around Marseille in the south-east, as well as in Paris and Lyon. In 2004 the government banned headscarves (used by Muslims) and other religious symbols in state schools.

In **Spain**, there are now hundreds of thousands of adherents of Islām, whose numbers have grown rapidly because of immigration. In 711 Muslim Arabs invaded Spain from North Africa and quickly conquered almost the entire peninsula, establishing Muslim states in Spain that were to last until 1492. In the 1980s Spain's new position as a highly industrialized and relatively prosperous country made it attractive to people from the developing world. For the first time since the Middle Ages, Spain received large numbers of immigrants. By the early twenty-first century there were several million legal foreign residents and illegal immigrants in Spain, the latter concentrated mainly in Andalusia (Andalucía), in metropolitan Madrid and Barcelona, and in the Balearic and Canary islands. Many arrived from Morocco and from sub-Saharan Africa; there also are significant numbers of Asians and Europeans from non-EU countries. In 2005 legislation legalized the status of many immigrant workers and gave immigrants most of the same rights as Spanish citizens (except the right to vote).

GLOSSARY

adab Islāmic concept that became a literary genre distinguished by its broad humanitarian concerns; it developed during the brilliant height of 'Abbāsid culture in the ninth century and continued through the Muslim Middle Ages.

Allāh The one and only God in the religion of **Islām**. Etymologically, the name Allāh is probably a contraction of the Arabic *al-Ilāh,* "the God". Allāh is the pivot of the **Muslim** faith. The Muslim holy scripture, the **Qur'ān,** constantly preaches Allāh's reality, his inaccessible mystery, his various names, and his actions on behalf of his creatures.

amīr (emir) A military commander, governor of a province, or a high military official.

fitnah A heretical uprising, especially the first major internal struggle within the Muslim community (AD 656–661), which resulted in both civil war and religious schism between the **Sunnis** and **Shī'ites.**

ghazal A genre of lyric poem in Islāmic literature, generally short and graceful in form and typically dealing with themes of love.

Ḥadīth Record of the traditions or sayings of the Prophet Muḥammad, revered and received as a major source of religious law and moral guidance, second only to the authority of the **Qur'ān,** or scripture of **Islām.**

hajj The pilgrimage to the holy city of Mecca in Saudi Arabia, which every adult **Muslim** of either sex must make at least once in his or her lifetime.

ijmā' The universal and infallible agreement ("consensus") of the **Muslim** community, especially of Muslim scholars on any Islāmic principle, at any time.

imām The head or "leader" of the Muslim community; the title is used in the **Qur'ān** several times to refer to leaders and to Abraham.

intifādah In Arabic, literally, "shaking off". Has come to be synonymous with mass popular rebellion, typically by Palestinian Arabs in Israeli occupied areas such as the West Bank and the Gaza Strip.

Islām Major world religion belonging to the Semitic family; it was promulgated by the Prophet Muḥammad in Arabia in the seventh century AD. The Arabic term *islām*, literally "surrender", illuminates the fundamental religious idea of Islām – that the believer (called a **Muslim**, from the active particle of *islām*) accepts "surrender to the will of **Allāh** (God)".

jihad "Struggle", or "battle". Jihad is a religious duty imposed on **Muslims** to spread Islām by waging war; jihad has come to denote any conflict waged for principle or belief and is often translated to mean "holy war".

jizyah Head or poll tax that early Islāmic rulers demanded from their non-Muslim subjects.

madrasah An institution of higher education in Muslim countries. The madrasah functioned until the twentieth century as a theological seminary and law school, with a curriculum centred on the **Qur'ān**.

mahdī In Islāmic eschatology a messianic deliverer ("divinely guided one") who will fill the Earth with justice and equity, restore true religion, and usher in a short golden age lasting seven, eight, or nine years before the end of time. Many orthodox Sunnī theologians question Mahdist beliefs because the Qur'ān does not mention him nor does nearly any reliable ḥadīth, but these beliefs form an integral part of Shī'i doctrine.

masjid (mosque) Any house or open area of prayer in **Islām**. The Arabic word *masjid* means "a place of prostration" to God.

mihrab A prayer niche in the *qiblah* wall (facing Mecca) of a **mosque**.

mi'rāj In Islamic legend, the ascension of the Prophet Muḥammad into heaven.

mu'adhdhin (muezzin) The official who proclaims the call to prayer (*adhān*) on Friday for the public worship and the call to the daily prayer (*ṣalāt*) five times a day.

mujahideen "Those who engage in **jihad**".

mujtahid In the early Muslim community every adequately qualified jurist had the right to exercise *ijtihad*, the independent or original interpretation of problems not precisely covered by the **Qur'ān**, **Ḥadīth**, and *ijmā'*. Those who did so were termed *mujtahid*s. This tradition now only persists within the minority **Shī'ite** branch of **Islām**.

Muslim A follower of **Islām**, from the active participle of the Arabic *islām*, meaning "surrender".

qāḍī A Muslim judge who renders decisions according to the **Sharī'ah**, the canon law of **Islām**.

qasidah Poetic form developed in pre-Islāmic Arabia and perpetuated throughout Islāmic literary history into the present. It is a laudatory, elegiac, or satiric poem of 60 to 100 lines, maintaining a single end rhyme that runs through the entire piece.

qiblah The direction of the sacred shrine of the Ka'bah in Mecca, Saudi Arabia, towards which Muslims turn five times each day when performing the ṣalāt (daily ritual prayer).

qit'ah Poetic genre in which the first hemistich (half-line of verse) does not rhyme, and the effect is as though the poem had been "cut out" of a longer one (hence its name). The *qit'ah* is a light-hearted literary form used to deal with aspects of everyday life; it served mainly for occasional poems, satire, jokes, word games, and chronograms.

Qu'rān The sacred scripture of **Islām** and, for all **Muslims**, the very word of God, revealed through the agency of the archangel Gabriel to the Prophet Muḥammad.

Sharī'ah The fundamental religious concept of **Islām**, namely its law, systematized during the second and third centuries of the **Muslim** era (eight–ninth centuries AD). Total and unqualified submission to the will of **Allāh** is the fundamental tenet of Islām: Islāmic law is therefore the expression of Allāh's command for Muslim society and, in application, constitutes a system of duties that are incumbent upon Muslims by virtue of their religious belief.

sharīf Arabic title of respect, restricted, after the advent of **Islām**, to members of Muḥammad's clan of Hāshim.

Shī'ite (Shī'a) Member of the smaller of the two major branches of **Islām**, distinguished from the majority **Sunnis**. The Shī'ites believe that **Muslim** leadership belonged to Muḥammad's son-in-law, 'Alī, and his descendants alone.

sunnah The body of traditional social and legal custom and practice ("habitual practice") of the **Muslim** community.

Sunnite (Sunni) Member of one of the two major branches of **Islām**, the branch that consists of the majority of that religion's adherents. Sunni **Muslims** regard their sect as the mainstream and traditionalist branch of Islām, as distinguished from the minority sect, the **Shī'ites**. The Sunnites recognize the first four caliphs as Muḥammad's rightful successors.

tarīqah The Muslim spiritual path toward direct knowledge (*ma'rifah*) of God or Reality (*ḥaqq*).

'ulama' The learned of **Islām**, those who possess the quality of *'ilm* or "learning", in its widest sense.

'umrah The "minor pilgrimage" undertaken by **Muslims** whenever they enter Mecca.

ummah "Community" or "community of [Muslim] believers".

zakat An obligatory tax required of **Muslims**, one of the five Pillars of Islam.

INDEX

Note: Where more than one page number is listed against a heading, page numbers in bold indicate significant treatment of a subject.

Abasiyanik, Sait Faik 342
'Abbās I 142–3, 272
Abbas, Mahmoud 202
'Abbāsids 93, 94, 95, 96, **97–9**
  architecture 250, 251, 256, 261–2
  arts and culture 66, 282
'Abd Allāh ibn Yasin 131
'Abd al-Azīz I (ibn Sa'ud) 157
'Abd al-Malik ibn Marwān 89–90
'Abd al-Qādir al-Jilani 36, 120
'Abd ar-Rahman III 108
'Abd ar-Rāuf ofSingkel 148
'Abd ibn-Muttalib 8
'Abduh, Muhammad 53–5, 153
Abū al-Faraj al-Isbahani 311
Abū Bakr 11, 12, 14, 38, 40, 82–3, 352
Abū Bakr ibn 'Umar 132
Abu Ghraib Prison (Baghdad) 224, 230
Abu Hamza 409
Abū Hayyan al-Tawhidi 311
Abū'l-Fazl 145
Abū Nuwas 305, 306, 307, 308

Abū Tālib (uncle of Mohammad) 8, 11, 12
Abū Tamman 304
Abyssinia 11
Adawiyah, Rabīah al- 113
adhān (call to prayer) 4
Adivar, Halide Edib 340
Adonis ('Alī Ahmad Sa'id) 309
adultery 59
Afghan National Army 234
Afghani, Jamal ad-Din al- 53–5, 153
Afghanistan **214–18**, 232–5, 387, 391–3
  Al-Qaeda 205–6, 211, 229
  Soviet invasion 176
  Taliban 207–8, 390
Africa 61, 66, 89, 108, 109, 135, 151, 264, **393–405**
Aga Khan Award for Architecture 279
Aga Khan IV 170
Agaoglu, Adalet 343
Aghasi, Sheikh Mahmoud Qul (Abū al Qa'qa) 356

Aghlab, Ibrāhīm ibn al- 98
Ahl al-kahf ("The People of the Cave")
    (Hakim) 318–19
Ahl al-Kitāb (People of the Book) 18,
    19, 25, 90
Ahmad, Mirza Ghulam 405
Ahmadiyah (Qadianis) 388
Ahmad Sirhindi, Shaykh 145
'Ā'ishah (w. of Muḥammad) 12, 39,
    88
Akbar 144–5, 274, 296–7, 384
Al-Qaeda ("the Base") 182, **205–6**,
    211, 222, 226, 235, 391
  and British Muslims 407
  and Iraq 218, 220
  links to other "terrorist"
    groups 377, 398–9, 400
  Osama bin Laden 200, 208, 209,
    352–3
  September 11 attacks 195, 206,
    208, **209–14**, 368
  and United States 213, 214, 215,
    228, 229, 232, 239
'Alawites 355
Albania 410
alcohol 65, 392
Alexandria Protocol 165
Algeria 195, 199, 397–9
Alhambra palace complex 264–5
'Alī Muḥammad of Shiraz 44
Aligarh Muslim University
    (Delhi) 58
Allāh (God) 27–8, 80, 87
'Allawi, Ayad 225
Almohads (al-Muwahhidun) 133–4,
    263
Almoravids (al-Murabitun) 131,
    134, 263, 395
American Muslim Mission (Nation of
    Islām) 170, 405–6
American States, Organization
    of 211
Āminah (mother of Muḥammad) 6,
    7, 8
Amir Khosrow 295, 325–6
Anatolia 262–3, 270, 354
Anbar Salavation Council 228
Andalusia 134

Anday, Melih Cevdat 341
Anglo-Mohammedan Oriental College
    (Aligarh Muslim
    University) 386
'Ani, Yusuf al- 320
animal flesh 65
al-ansār ("helpers") 15, 19, 82, 133
Al-Aqsa Mosque (Jerusalem) 244
Arab Deterrent Force (ADF) 184
Arab Executive 162
Arab High Committee 163, 164
Arab Higher Executive for Palestine
    (Arab Higher Committee) 165–6
Arab League (League of Arab
    States) 165–6, 180, 181, 365
Arab Liberation Front 183
Arab Palestine 159–69
Arab Revolt (1936–9) 163–4
Arab-Israeli Wars 176–9, 198
'Arabi, Ibn al- 51, 52, 134
Arabic language 60, 71, 84, 90, 127,
    130, 155, 156
Arabic literature 301–20
Arabs and Arabic culture 75–6, 77,
    78, 84, 87, 90, 108, 122, **130–4**,
    159
'Arafāt, Yāsir 169, 178, 185–6, 188,
    202
arches 246, 252, 256, 263
architecture 128, 243–79
  building materials/
    decoration 251–4, 274, 288
'Aruzi, Nezami-ye 328
Al-Ash'arī 112
Ash'arites 133
Ash'arjya 42–3
ashrāf ("noblemen") 61
Āsik Pasa 333
Assembly of Islāmic Clergy 389
Assembly of Pakistani Clergy 389
Atatürk, Kemal 155
'Aṭṭār, Farīd od-Dīn 324
Attar, Najah al- 356
Aurangzeb 145–6, 275, 297, 384–5
Australia 211, 213–14
Averroës (ibn Rushd) 49, 134
Avicenna 47–8, 52, 115
Axial Age 75–6

Ayyubids 123
Azhar University (Cairo), al- 57–8, 110, 182, 364, 365

Ba'th Party (Iraq) 219, 221, 222
Babak 103
Babri Masjid Mosque 387
Babur 144, 330, 384
Badr, Battle of 16–17
Baghdādī, Abū al-Barakāt al- 50
Baghdad 36, 57, 98, 103, 107, 118, 119, 124, 221, 251
Bahadur Shah II 385
Baha'i faith 44, 153
Bahar ("King of Poets") 331
Bahrain 371–2
Bajjah, Ibn 48–9
baked brick architecture 252, 260–1, 262–3
Bakhtiar, Shahpur 190
Baladhuri, al- 104
Balfour Declaration (1917) 160, 161
Bali October 12 2002 attacks 214, 236, 376–7
Bani-Sadr, Abolhasan 191
Barakat, Sidi 146
al-bay'ah (allegiance) 18
Baybars I 124
Baysunqur 290
Bazargan, Mehdi 191
Bedouins 19, 77, 130, 355
Behzad 291
Ben-Gurion, David 162
Berbers 93, 108, 109, 130–4, 255
Beyatli, Yahya Kemal 340
Bhutto, Benazir 390, 391
Bhutto, Zulfikar Alī 389
bin Laden, Osama 212, 214, 215, 233, 390
  and al-Qaeda 205–6, 209
  anti-American stance 200, 206, 211, 352–3
  and the Taliban 208
Biruni, al- 116
Bistami, Abū Yazīd 104
Black Muslim Movement 405
Black Stone (Hajar al-Aswad) 35
Bolivia 212

Bosnia and Herzegovina 410–13
Brethren of Purity 43–4
Bukhari, al- 104
Bū'l-Fazl-i Bayhaqi, 116
Burj Al Arab Hotel 277
Burj Dubai 276
Bush, George W. 212, 213, 219, 220, 221, 222, 223, 228, 229, 230, 231–2
  and al-Qaeda 229
  approach to foreign affairs 212, 213
  Iraq 219, 220, 221, 222, 223, 228
  "prisoners of war" 230, 231–2
Buyids (Buwayhids) 113–14
Byzantine 84, 89, 110, 118, 270
Cairo (al-Qahirah) 110, 127, 255, 256, 266–7
calendar (Muslim) 37, 85, 155
calligraphy 284, 286, 287–8, 289, 299
Camp David Accords 180
caravanserai 251, 259, 271
carpet weaving 294, 298
celibacy 58
Central Africa 403–4
Central Intelligence Agency (CIA) 190, 231–2, 376
ceramics 282–3, 284, 285, 286, 287, 288, 292
chastity (ihsan) 59
China 25, 86, 98–9, 148, 212, 289–90
Christianity 20, 25, 50, 87, 90, 98, 129, 162, 183, 236, 356, 394, 404
  and Africa 394, 404
  and Islām 20, 25, 98, 129, 236
  and Jerusalem 90
  and Lebanon 183–4, 356
CIA (Central Intelligence Agency) 190, 231–2, 376
citadels (urban fortresses) 258–9
cities, premodern 105–7
Coalition Provisional Authority (CPA) 222, 225
Committee for the Defence of Legitimate Rights (CDLR) 197
competitive regions, rise of 107–11

Constitution of Medina 15
Council Muslim League 389
Crusades 121–3, 259
cultural diversity 25–6, 60–5
Cumali, Necati 343
Cyprus 354

Daglarca, Fazil Hüsnü 341–2
Damascus 244–5, 253, 275–6
Dandanqan, Battle of 117
Dar ol-Fonun college 330
Dara Shikoh 145
Darwish, Mahmud 306, 309
decorative arts
  architectural 90, 253, 254, 256,
    261–8, 267–8, 270–2, 274–5
  visual 280–99
dervishes (turuq) 64, 128, 155
Detainee Treatment Act (2004)
  (US) 230
dhimmī (unconverted protected
  groups) 90, 92, 93
dietary laws 65
Ditch (al-Khandaq), Battle of the 17
divorce 58
doctrinal views, sources of 26–33
Dome of the Rock (Jerusalem) 90,
  246–7, 253, 266
domes 252, 256, 260, 261, 262, 269,
  270
Dowlatshah 326–7
drama and plays 317–20
dress codes 155, 194, 360, 377
  religious 62–5, 190
  women 351, 364, 370
Druzes 111, 355, 356
Dubailand 278

Eastern Africa 404–5
education 55–8
Egypt 57, 107, 110, 123, 139, 154–
  5, 158, 171, 177
  war with Israel 176, 179–82
Emirates Palace Hotel 277
Enderunī, Fazil 338
Esfahan 272–3
Eshkol, Levi 178
Eskandri, Parvaneh 193

European influences in the arts 150,
  275–9, 298–9
extremism 181, 193, 198–9, 237,
  360, 367, 390, 392
  and terrorism 182, 197, 201, 203,
    206
eyvān (vaulted hall) 259, 260, 261,
  262, 266, 268

Fārābī, al- 46–7, 111
Fātimah (d. of Muḥammad) 8, 9
Faisal, Shaikh Ahmed 405
fakhr ("boasting") 305
Fakhr ad-Din al-Rāzī 50
falsafah 127, 134, 136, 143
family 58–60
Faraj, Alfred 319
Farouhar, Dariyush 193
Farrakhan, Louis (Louis Eugene
  Wolcott) 406–7
Farrokhzad, Forugh 331–2
Farwardīn, Bih'āfrīd ibn 97
Fatah (Palestine National Liberation
  Movement) 169, 182, 202, 358
Fatehpur Sikri 274
Fathy, Hassan 278–9
Fatimid dynasty 43, 57, 110, 254–7,
  284–5, 395
Faysal I 159, 160
Ferdowsi 115, 289, 322, 329
Fertile Crescent 262
Firqat-Badr 226
fitnahs 88–93, 93–5, 101–4
Five Pillars of Islām 34–6, 90
Fivers (Zaydis) 96
France 177, 220, 355, 356, 413–14
Front for the Popular Palestinian
  Struggle 183
fundamentalism 171, 195–208, 365,
  370
fuṣḥā (literary Arabic) 155
futuwah ("young men") 114

Garip ("Strange") poetry
  movement 341
Gaza Strip 168–9, 186, 188, 202,
  238
Germany 214, 413

Ghazālī, al- 48, 49, 52, 120, 132, 327
ghazal/gazel (love poetry) 308, 322, 325, 326, 330, 334, 337
Ghazan, Mahmud 126, 268
Ghazi al-Yawar 225
Ghaznavid dynasty 114–17
Gibbons, Gillian 238–9
glassware 283, 285, 288, 289
God (Allāh) 27–8, 80, 87
Great Britain 158–62, 163–5, 166–7, 177, 236, 237
Iraq War 218–28
Great Mosque (al-Qayrawan/ Kairouan) 246, 253
Great Mosque (Córdoba) 246, 252
Great Mosque (Esfahan) 259–60
Green Book (al-Qaddafi) 176
Guantánamo Bay (Cuba) 229, 230, 233
Gul, Abdullah 237–8
Gulf Co-operation Council (GCC) 276
Gulf War *see* Persian Gulf War

habsiyah (prison poems) 323
Hadid, Zaha 278
Hadith 7, 22, 26, 39, 41, 57, 91, 100, 102, 104, 150, 310
Hafez, Mohammad Shams od-Din 326
Haifa Congress 161
hajj ("pilgrimage") 20, 35–6, 64, 79, 131, 132, 258, 312–13
hakawati (storyteller) 313, 317
Hakawati theatre troupe 320
Hakim, al- 111
Hakim, Tawfiq al- 318
Halīmah 7, 8
al-Hallāj (mystic) 70, 113
Hamadhani, al- 313
Hamas 186, 188, 197, 200–2, 238
Hamdanid 111
Hanbal, Ahmad ibn 102
Harakat al-Muqawamah al-Islāmiyyah ("Islamic Resistance Movement") *see* Hamas
Hariri, al- 313

Hārūn ar-Rāshid 98, 101
hashishiyah (assassins) 119
Hāshim ibn Hākim (al-Muqanna'/ "Veiled One") 97–8
Hasan al-Banna' 158, 202
Hasan al-Basrī, al- 113
Hassan ibn Thabit ("the Prophet's poet") 304
Haykal, Muhammad Husayn 316
Hezbollah (Hizb Allāh) 193, 197, 199, 203–5, 358
hija' (lampoon) 304, 305, 336
Hijrah (emigration) 196
hikma (wisdom) 49–50
Hikmet, Nazim 341
Hilalian invasion 130
Hindus 25, 61, 145
Hishām, 'Amr ibn (Abū Jahl) 11
Homeland Security Act (2002) (US) 213
Hülegü 124
Husayn I 143–4
Husayn (s. of 'Alī) 36, 63, 69, 70, 142
Husayni, Amin al- 162, 166
Hussein, Saddam 187, 192, 219, 220, 221
Hydropolis (hotel) 277
hypostyle mosques **244, 245**, 249, 252, 255, 263, 264, 266, 274

Ibn al-Muqaffa' 312
Ibn al-Rumi 305, 337
Ibn an-Nafis 127
Ibn Battūtah 135
Ibn Khaldun 136–7, 312
Ibn Khallikan 127
Ibn Sa'ud ('Abd al-'Aziz I) 157
Ibn Tufayl 134
Ibn Tumart 132–3
Ibn Taymiyah 49, 127
Ibrahim, Yahya ibn 131
'īds (festivals) 35
Idris, Yusuf 314–15, 319
ihsan (chastity) 59
ijmā ("consensus") 26, 27, 43, 49

ijtihād ("individual thought") 26, 27, 100

Il-Khanid dynasty 268

ilāhī ("divine") poetry 333

Ilhan, Attilā 343

illustrations, book/manuscript 285, 286, 287, 288, 289, 290, 292, 294–6

*imām*s (spiritual/temporal leaders) 26, 37, 42, 43, 94, 237, 388, 408

Imami Shī'ites 113, 142

iman (faithfulness) 80, 85

Imru' al-Qays 303, 306

India 53, 61, 65, 66, 115, 126, 144, 158, 234, 382–7

Indian Independence Act (1947) 386–7

Indian Mutiny (1857) 385

Indian Ocean 139, 147–8, 152

Indonesia 25, 61–2, 214, 236, 373–8

infrastructure 276–7

international law and terrorism 229–32

International Security Assistance Force (ISAF) 215–16, 217, 232

intifadāh ("shaking off"/rebellion) 186, 188

Iqbal, Muhammad 53–5, 153–4

Iran 36, 98, 103, 115–6, 149, 154, 199, 360–2

  literature 69

  revolution (1978–9) 176, 189–94, 198, 361

  Shī'ites 153, 226, 353

Iran–Iraq war 192

Iraq 107, 159, 200, 359–60

  Baghdad 98, 103, 107, 124

  flourishing of 111–14

  architecture 251, 252

  War (1991–2) 218–22

  government and insurgency 222–8, 353

Iraq Study Group 227–8

Iraq Survey Group 221

Iraqi Accord Front 227

'Iraqi, Fakhr-ud-Din 325

ISAF (International Security Assistance Force) 215–16, 217, 232

Iskander Muda 148

Islām

  definition 3–4, 80, 196, 197

  early history 24–6

  statistics 3, 349

  and the West 235–9

Islāmic Assembly 389

Islāmic Conference, Organization of the 171

Islāmic Da'awah party 225

Islāmic Group (al-Jamā'a al-Islāmiyah) 181, 182, 199, 206

Islāmic Jihad (al-Jihad al-Islāmi) 181, 182, 199, 201, 206

Islāmic Liberation Front 199

Islāmic Salvation Front 199

Islāmic Tendency Movement (Mouvement de la Tendance Islāmique (MTI)) 401

Ismāil I 141–2

Ismaili/Ismāiliyah Shī'ites (Sab'iyah/Seveners) 43–4, 47, 97, 109, 115, 119, 170, 255, 351, 388

Israel, State of 167, 183–8, 200, 201, 202, 204, 238, 363

  war with Arab States 176–82

Ithna 'Asharīyah (Twelver Shī'ites) 42, 52, 53, 54, 97, 351, 359, 360–1, 388

'Izz al-Dīn al-Qassam Forces 201

jāhiliyyah, al- ("the age of ignorance") 20

Jahiz, al- 104, 310–11

al-Jamā'ah al-Islāmiyah (Islāmic Group) 181, 197

Jama'at al-Ansar al-Mahdī 400

Jama'at al-Madrasah Hadithah ("New School Group") 314

Jama'at-i-Islāmi (Islāmic Society) 175

Jami 327, 330

Japan 214

Jawsaq al-Khaqani palace city 250

Jaysh al-Mahdī 226

Jemaah Islāmiyah 236, 376, 377
Jerusalem 13, 36, 90, 121, 123, 177, 178
 architecture 243, 244, 245, 246–7
Jews and Judaism 20, 25, 90, 98, 159–69, 178, 247
Jiddah, Treaty of 157
jihad ("holy war/struggle") 24–5, 33, 35, 40, 151, 176, 181, 197, 201, 352, 387
 against the West 153, 195, 206
jizyah (religious taxes) 18, 25
Jordan 158, 167, 168, 178, 183, 362–3
Joveynī, 'Ata Malek 125
Jumblatt, Kamal 357
Justice and Development Party (Adalet ve Kalkinma Partisi/AKP) 350

Ka'bah 6, 11, 18, 19, 21, 34, 35, 36, 79, 82
Kalām ("speech") 39
Kamil, Mustafa 154
Karacaoglan 332
Karakoç, Sezai 343
Karay, Refik Halid 339–40
Karbala' (Iraq) 36, 63, 70, 223, 227, 359–360
Karim Khan Zand 149
Karzai, Hamid 215–16, 218, 233, 234, 235
Kaviani Press 331
Kemal, Yashar 342–3
Keykavus, 'Onsor ol-Ma'ali 327
Khadījah bint al-Khuwaylid (w. of Muhammad) 8–9, 10, 11–12, 80
Kharijites 40, 93, 103, 109
Khāwarijites ("seceders") 88–9
khabar ("report") 310
Khal, Yusuf al- 309
Khalifah, Hamad ibn 'Isa Al 371–2
Khalili, Karim 233
Khalilzad, Zalmay 232
Khamenei, Ayatollah 192, 193
khamriyyat (wine poetry) 306
Khan, Sir Sayyid Ahmad 386
Khartoum Arab Summit 179

Khatami, Mohammad 192–3, 194
khatib (sermon/khutbah giver) 37
khayal al-zill (shadow plays) 317
Khayyam, Omar 323
Khirbat al-Mafjar palace 249
Khomeini, Ayatollah Ruhollah 176, 189, 190–2, 353
Khwarizmi, al- 99
Kindī, Ya'qub ibn Ishaq as-Sabah al- 45–6, 104
Kizilbash ("Red Heads") 141
Koran see Qur'ān
Kücük Kaynarca, Treaty of (1774) 150
kufr (denial of God) 83
kuhhan (soothsayers) 310
külliye (building complexes) 270, 271
Kurds 219, 225, 226, 227, 228, 255, 355
Kuwait 369–70

languages 99, 115, 139, 300
 Arabic 60, 90, 127, 130, 155, 156
 New Persian 107, 116
Laylat al-Isra' wa'l-Mi'raj (Noctural Ascent of M.) 12–13, 21, 37, 90, 244, 246–7, 281
Laylat al-Qadr ("Night of Determination") 37
League of Arab States (Arab League) 165–6
Lebanon 158, 159, 168, 176, 181, 182, 183–4, 185, 203–5, 204, 356–8
Libya 176, 396–7
literature 67, 128, 155, 300–45
London, July 7 2005 attacks 236, 407, 408
love poetry 307, 308, 322, 325, 326, 330, 334, 337
lustre glazing 282–3, 284, 285, 288

Madani, 'Izz al-Din al- 320
madh (panegyric poetry) 304, 306, 323, 325
madrasah (buildings) 248, 258, 262, 264, 266, 395

madrasah (religious schools) **56–7,** **119–20,** 140, 189, 248, 335, 360
and extremists 189, 207, 234
Madrid, March 11 2004 attacks 236
maghāzi (accounts of M.) 310
Mahdī, al- 99
Mahdi Army 223, 227
Mahfouz, Naguib (Najib Mahfuz) 317
Majlisi, Moḥammad Baqir 144
Makassar (Macassar) 148
Mala'ikah, Nazik al- 303
Malaysia 25, 148, 378–82
Malcolm X (el-Hajj Malik el-Shabazz) 406
Maliki, Nuri Kamal al- 225
Mamluks 265–7, 288–9
Ma'mun, al- 101–2
Mansa Musa 135
Mansur, Ustad (Nadir-ul-'Asr) ("Wonder of the Time") 297
maqamah (narrative) 313, 315–16
Maqamat 286, 289
maqsurah (arched façade) 246
marabouts (saintly individuals) 394, 397
marriage 58–9
marsiyehs (elegies) 69
marthiyyah (elegies) 301, 302
martyrdom 64, 190
Marwān id Maghrib 92–3
Masjid al-Nabī (Mosque of the Prophet) 14
masjids (mosques) 36–7, 63, 85, 90, 237, **243–8,** 263–4, 266, 268, 274
masnavis/mesnevîs (rhyming couplet) 323, 324–5, 333, 334, 338
Masoud, Aḥmad Zia 233
Mas'ud I 116–17
mausoleums 247–8, 256, 258, 262, 264, 266, 268, 269, 274
Mawardi, al- 117
Mawdūdī, Mawlana Abū'l-Alā' 158
Mawlawiyah (Whirling/Dancing Dervishes) 64, 128, 155, 337

Mecca 8, 19, 21, 35–6, 62, 78–9, 81, 103, 110, 176, 351
Medina (Yathrib) 13–14, 19, 21, 22, 24, 36, 62, 78, 80, 81, 110, 351
Mehmed II 139
Meshed (Iran) 36
metalwork 285–6, 288, 292, 298, 370
Meydan racecourse complex 277
Meydan-e Shah 272–3
Middle East 354–73
mihrab (decorative niche) 245, 246, 253, 256, 262
Military Commissions Act (2006) (US) 230–1
Mina 35
minarets 245, 257, 260, 261, 263, 267, 269
miniature painters 287, 292, 293, 295
"Mirror for Princes" literary genre 327
Misri, Abū'l Fayd Dhu'n-Nun al- 104
modern art 298–9
Mohammad Reza Shah Pahlavi 154, 189, 190
Molla, Keçecizade Izzet 338
Möngke 124
Mongols 123–30, 268–70
Moorish architecture 263–5
Morocco 139, 146, 399–400
Mosque of the Prophet (Masjid al-Nabī) 14
mosques (masjids) 36–7, 63, 85, 90, 237, **243–8,** 255, 263–4, 266, 268, 271, 274
Mostowfi, Hamdollah 328
Mount Marwa 35
Mount Zafa 35
Mountain of Light (Jabal al-Nūr) 9
Al-Mu'allaqat ("long poems") 303
Mu'āwiyah 88
mubalaghah (hyperbole) 67
Mubarak, Hosni (Husni) 181–2, 365, 366
Mudéjar decorative style 288
muezzin (prayer-time announcer) 37
Mughals 139, 144–6

architecture 273–5
arts 294–8
al-muhājirūn ("fellow
 emigrants") 15, 19, 82, 133
Muhammad 3–23, 79, 80–2, 91, 92,
 133, 281, 334
 Advent of revelation 10–13
 and Islāmic piety 21–3
 and mythology 68, 70
 early life 6–9
 Mecca period 13–14
 Medinan period 15–16
 names and titles 4–5
 physical description 8
 Quraysh 16–21
Muhammad, Elijah 406
Muhammad I Askia 147
Muhammad ibn Sa'ud 151, 156
Muhammad ibn Tughluq 126, 383
Muhammad V 264
Muharram 37
Mu'in al-Din Chisti 36
mujahideen ("holy warriors") 176,
 207, 215, 391, 392
mujtahids (Shī'ite jurists) 42–3, 142,
 143
Mulaydah, Battle of al- 157
Muqaddimah (Ibn Khaldun) 136–7
muqarnas (decoration) 252, 256,
 260, 262, 265, 268, 269
muqātilah (fighters) 85–6
al-murabitun (Almoravids/"the people
 of the retreat") 131, 134, 247
Murad I 129
Murad III 336
Murad IV, Sultan 141
Mūsā al-Kāzim 96
Musharraf, Pervez 390
music 66–7
Muslim Brotherhood (Al-ikhwan Al-
 muslimun) 158, 171, 175, 181,
 182, 201, 202–3, 362, 364–5,
 366, 409
Muslim Code of Honour 237
Muslim ibn al-Hajjaj 104
Muslim League 386, 389
Muslim Lebanese National
 Movement 357

Muslim Public Affairs Council 237
Muslim World League 171
muslims, definition 80–1, 197
al-Mutanabbi ("He Who Claimed to
 Be a Prophet") 111, 304, 305
Mu'tasim 102
Mutawwakil, Yahya Mahmud al-
 367–8 42, 52, 54, 55, 102
Mu'tazilah ("those who stand
 apart") 41, 42, 52, 54, 55,
 102
al-Muwahhidun (Almohads) 133–4
myths and legends 67, 68–72

Nābī 337
Nader Shah (Nader Qoli Beg) 149
Nadir-ul-Zaman, Abū al-Hasan
 ("Wonder of the Age") 297
Nāfi, 'Uqbah ibn (Sidi 'Uqbah) 89
Nā'ilī 332, 335
Nakheel ("The Palms") 277
Nasrallah, Hassan 205
Nasrin, Taslima 238
Nasser, Gamal Abdel 177, 178–9,
 181, 203, 318
Nation of Islām (American Muslim
 Mission) 170, 405–6
National Commission on Terrorist
 Attacks Upon the United States
 (9/11 Commission) 221–2
National Security Agency (NSA)
 (US) 213
National Security Strategy of the
 United States of America
 (2002) 213
nationalism 152, 154–9, 316–17,
 385, 410
NATO (North Atlantic Treaty
 Organization) 211, 232, 234–5
Nawwab, Muzaffar al- 305
Nedim, Ahmed 337
Nef'i 336
Nesimi, Seyid Imadeddin 333
New Order (Nizam-i Cedid) 150
New Persian language 107, 116
9/11 Commission (National
 Commission on Terrorist Attacks
 Upon the United States) 221–2

Niyazi Misri 333
Nizam al-Mulk 118–20, 327
Nizamiyahs 119, 120
Nizari Isma'ilis 119, 122
Nobel Prize for Literature 317, 344
Nocturnal Ascent (Laylat al-
    Isre') 12–13, 21, 90, 244, 246–
    7, 281
North Africa 66, 89, 135, 264, 393,
    394–6
North Atlantic Treaty Organization
    (NATO) 211, 232, 234–5
Northern Alliance 214
numbers, mystical value 71
Nureddin (Nur ad-Din) 122–3

'Obeyd-e Zakani 326
Olmert, Ehud 238
Oman 370–1
Omar, Mullah Moḥammad 207
Ömer, Āsik 333
Operation Desert Fox (1998) 219
Operation Enduring Freedom 214–
    15
Operation Iraqi Freedom 220–1
Operation Mountain Thrust 234–5
opium production 234
Organization of American States
    211
Organization of the Islāmic
    Conference 171
Oslo Accords 188
Ottoman Empire 53, 128, 138, 139–
    41, 149–50, 352
    architecture 270–2
    arts and culture 281, 291–2,
    334–41
Özel, Ismet 343–4

Pakistan 61, 158, 176, 195, 207,
    208, 218, 234, 238, 382, 387–
    91, 407
Pakistan Muslim League 389
Pakistan People's Party (PPP) 389
palace-cities 250, 259, 261, 271
Palestine 159–69, 178–9, 200–2,
    212, 238, 357, 358–9, 363
Palestine Arab Congress 162

Palestine Liberation Organisation
    (PLO) 169, 182–8, 200, 357,
    363
Palestine National Council
    (PNC) 186
Palestine National Liberation
    Movement (Fatah) 169, 182,
    202
Palestinian Authority (PA) 188,
    202
Pamuk, Orhan 344–5
Parvin E'tesami 331
Pasa, Koca Ragib 337
Pashtuns 215–16, 233
Passfield White Paper 162, 163
Peel Commission (1937) 164
Pentagon (September 11
    attacks) 209, 210
People of the Book (Ahl al-Kītab) 18,
    19, 25, 90
Peres, Shimon 188
Persia 53, 60, 115, 127, 139, 289–
    91, 321–32
Persian Gulf War (1990–1) 187,
    200, 205, 219, 401
petroleum industry 171, 182, 198,
    200, 223
PFLP-General Command (PFLP-
    GC) 183
philiosophy 44–55
pishtaq (gateway) 260
PLO (Palestine Liberation
    Organization) 169, 182–8,
    200, 357
pluralism, religious and the
    West 235–9
poetry 53, 67, 69, 128, 301–9, 321–
    32, 341–2
Political Action Front 203
Popular Front for the Liberation of
    Palestine (PFLP) 183
pre-Muḥammadan society 75–9
premodern Islāmic society 105–7
princely architecture 249–51
"prisoners of war", treatment
    of 224, 229–31
prophets 4, 30–1
purdah 62

Qaddafi, Muammar al- 176, 396
Qadir, Haji Abdul 216
Qādiriyah 120, 402
qadis (judges) 91, 136, 399
al-Qalqashandi 127
Qarmatians 109
qasidah (liturgy) 303, 304, 306, 307, 322, 323
Qatar 372-3
qiblah 15, 36, 246
qit'ah ("segment"/poem) 302, 303
Qur'ān (Koran) 3-4, 10, 22, 26, 27-33, 68, 87, 197, 301, 399
Quraysh 6, 11, 14, 16-21, 79, 81
Qurayzah (jewish tribe) 17-18
qussas (storytellers) 68
Qutaybah, ibn 311
Qutb, Sayyid 158, 181

Rabbani, Burhaneddin 216
Rabī 'al-Awwal 21
Rabin, Yitzhak 188
Rafsanjani, Hojatoleslam 'Alī Akbar Hashemi 192
rajaz (poem) 303
Ramadan 35, 37
Rashid ad-Din 126
Razi, Abū Bakr ar- 46, 50, 115
reconstructionists 153-4
Red Cross, International Committee of the 222, 224, 230
religious buildings 243-8
rendition flights 231-2
representation of living creatures 66, 281
"Resolution 242", 179, 187
"Resolution 338", 187
"Resolution 425", 184
revivalism 171, 175-94
Revolutionary Guards (Iran) 190-1
ribāt (building) 247, 258, 266
riddah (secession) 83
Rio Treaty 211
ritha' (elegy) 304, 305
Rumfa, Muhammad 147
Rumi, Mawlana Jalal ad-Din ar- 67, 128, 324-5
Rushd, Ibn (Averroës) 49, 134

Russia 211, 213, 220 see also Soviet Union

Saadiyat Island 277
Sab'iyah (Seveners) 43-4, 47, 97
Sabk-i Hindi school of poetry 336-7
Sacred Mosque (Mecca) 35
sacred places and days 36-7
Sadat, Anwar el- 176, 180, 181
Sa'di, Mosleh od-Din 325
Ṣādiq, Ja'far aṣ- 96
Sadr, Muqtada al- 223, 226, 227
Safavid dynasty 53, 139, 141-4, 272-3, 292-4
Safi od-Din 141
Sahih 310
saj' ("rhyming prose") 310, 313
Saladin (Salah ad-Din Yusuf ibn Ayyub) 123
Salafist Group for Preaching and Combat (GSPC) 398-9
Salafiyah ("pious ancestors") 154
ṣalāt (daily worship) 85-6
Salih, 'Alī 'Abd Allāh 368
Salman, Mas'ud-e Sa'd-e 322
Samanid dynasty 114-17, 247-8
Samarra' 103
Sana'i 324
Sanhajah 131
sarki (urban song) 332-3
Sasanian Empire 77-8, 84, 86, 282
Saudi Arabia, Kingdom of 151, 157, 158, 200, 205, 207, 208, 210, 350-2
Sayyab, Badr Shakir al- 303
sculpture 253, 256
Sebüktigin 115
Selim III 150
Seljuq Turks 57, 117-21, 257-63, 285-7, 289
September 11 attacks 195, 206, 208, 209-14, 368
Seveners (Sab'iyah) 43-4, 47, 97
Seyh Galib 338
Shafi'i, Abū 'Abd Allāh ash- 99-100
Shah Jahan 145, 274-5, 297
shahādah (profession of faith) 34
Shamir, Yitzhak 187

Shams al-Din Iltutmish 383
Sharī'ah 62, **99–101**, 127, 140, 196, 366, 369
  legal system 362, 365, 371, 372, 376, 403
  and *madrasah* 56
  and nationalism 170
  and Sufism 126
  waqf 106
  and women 60, 377, 382
sharīf 63, 133, 146, 265, 395, 397
Sharon, Ariel 202
Sheikh, Sheikh 'Abd al-'Aziz al- 352
Shī'ite Muslims 9, 20, 26, **39–40**, 56, 60, 69, **95–7**, 139, 153, 247
  dress code 63
  imāms 42–3
  Iran 189, 190–2
  Iraq 223, 225, 226
  Lebanon 204
  sacred places and days 36, 37
  and Sunnīsm 352–3, 359
    see also Imami Shī'ites; Ismāili/
      Ismāiliyah Shī'ites
      Ithna 'Asharīyah (Twelver
        Shī'ites)
      Sab'iyah (Seveners)
Shī'i, Abū 'Abd Allāh ash- 109
Shi'r ("Poetry") group 309
short stories 314–15, 340, 342, 343
Siddiqi, al-Tayyib al- 320
Siffin, Battle of 88
Sinan (architect) 271
Sinasi, Ibrahim 338–9
sirah (biographies of M.) 310
Six-Day War (1967) 177–8
siyar sha'biyyah (Arab lore) 313
social service, doctrine of 32
social views, Islamic 26–33
Songhai 146
Soroush, Abdolkarim 192
Southern Africa 393, 404
Soviet Union 176, 185, 191, 387, 391 *see also* Russia
Spain 236, 283, 288, 395, 414
squinches (architectural supports) 252, 256, 260
Strange Ones of Syria 356

Sudan 108, 139, **146–7**, 199, 238–9, 394, **401–3**
Suez Crisis (1956) 177
Sufism 5, 25, 42, **44**, **60–1**, 126, **150**
  art and culture 14, 66–7, 128, 306, 333
  family life 58
  Indonesia 375
  philosophy 113
Suhrawardi al-Maqtul 68
Suhrawardi, as- 51, 52
sujūd (prostrations) 85
Sukarnoputri, Megawati 367, 377
Süleyman I the Lawgiver 140
Su'luk ("brigand") poets 302
sunnah ("traditions") 22, 26, 40, 85
Sunnī Muslims 26, 27, 41, 42, **100**, **114–5**, 119, 379
  dress code 63
  education 55–6, 57, 258
  Iraq 225, 226, 227, 228
  Saudi Arabia 350–1
  and Shī'ite Muslims 20, 39, 43, 47, **95–7**, 139, 223, 352–3
  United States 237
Supreme Council for the Islāmic Revolution in Iraq 226, 227
Supreme Muslim Council 162, 164
Suyuti, as- 147
Sykes-Picot Agreement 160
Syria 111, 122, 123, 160, 226, **354–6**
  and Israel 177–9, 180, 185

Taha Hussein 154–5
Tabarī, at- (Abu Ja'far Muḥammad ibn Jarir) 112
Tahmasp 142
Taj Mahal 274–5
al-Takfir wa al-Hijrah ("Identification of Unbelief and Flight from Evil") 181
Talabani, Jalal al- 225
Talas, Battle of 99
Taliban ("Students") 197, **207–8**, 218, 233, **391–2**, 393
  and al-Qaeda 209, 211, 213, 407
  and Pakistan 390

and United States 206, **214–15**,
    216, 217, 229, 232, **234–5**
Tamir, Zakariyya 314–15
Tanpinar, Ahmed Hamdi 340–1
Tanzimat 152–3
tarbush (hat) 63
tardiyyah (hunt poem) 307
ṭarīqah (fellowships) 120–1, 128,
    145, 402
tawḥīd (oneness of God) 197–8
Ta'ziyas ("passion-plays") 69
Tekin, Latife 344–5
tekkes (buildings) 270
terrorism 197, 222, 369
    against the West 204, **205–6, 209–
    14**, 217, 236
    India 387
    Indonesia 376–7
    and International Law **229–32**
    Iraq 220, 226, 353
    in the Middle East 181, 182, 193,
    201–2, 203
    Pakistan 218, 390–1
    September 11 attacks 232
    treatment of prisoners 231
Tevfik Fikret 339
theology, Islāmic 39–44
Timur (Tamerlane) 129–30
Toghrïl Beg 118
tourism 277–8
trade and spread of Islām 25, 75,
    103–4, 107–8, 110, 114, 135,
    149, 259, 282, 351–2, 404
Trans-Saharan Islām 146–7
Tunisia 109, 199, 400–1
Turkey 57, 64, 155, 158, 195, 227,
    237–8, 270, **349–50**
    literature 332–45
Turki 157
Twelver Shī'ites (Ithnā
    'Asharīyah) 42, 52, 53, 54, 97,
    359, 360– 1, 388

'Ubayd Allāh 109
'Udhri (love poetry) 307–8
Uhud, Battle of 17
'ulama'/ulema ("the learned") 56, 62,
    63, 91, 119, 140, 146, 196, 388

'Umar I 84–5
'Umari (love poetry) 308
Umayyads 89, 91, 94, 108, 244–5,
    249, 253, 261–2, 282, 283, 304
ummah (concept of community) 26,
    32–3, 81, 84–5, 87, 91, 94, 362,
    385
'umrah' ("lesser pilgrimage") 18, 36
Unified National Command of the
    Uprising 186
United Arab Emirates 208, 373
United Iraq Alliance (UIA) 225
United Kingdom 407–10
United Nations (UN) 176–7, 184,
    219, 222, 358, 368, 377
    Relief and Works Agency for
    Palestine Refugees in the Near
    East (UNRWA) 168
    Special Committee on Palestine
    (UNSCOP) 167
United States 170, 185, 200, 206,
    208, 229, **230–2**, 237, 239,
    405–7
    Afghanistan 215–16, 217, 232,
    233, 234–5
    Iran 190, 191
    Iraq War 218–28
    Operation Enduring
    Freedom 214–15
    September 11 attacks 195, 206,
    208, 209–14
universe (Qur'ānic view of) 28–9
urban palaces 250
urjuzah (poem) 303
Usman dan Fodio 151
'Uthmān ibn 'Affān 86
Uzbekistan 212

vaulting 252, 259, 260–1, 263
vilayat-e faqih ("guardianship of the
    jurist") 192
visual arts 280–99

Wahhab, Muḥammad ibn 'Abd al-
    128, 150, 156, 157, 350
Wali Allāh, Shah 152
Walīd I, al- 244
Wannus, Sa'dallah 319–20

waqf (funding)   106, 266
wasf (descriptive poem)   306
weapons of mass destruction   218, 219, 220, 221
Weizmann, Chaim   162
Welfare Party (WP)   156, 350
West Bank   168, 184, 188, 212, 238
West and Islām   152, 166–7, 185, 351, **405–14**, 372
  anti-Western feeling   191, 194, 200, 239
  influence in the arts   271, **275–9**, 287–8, 298–9, 314, 379
  rejection of Western values   196, 198, 203, 360, 407, 408
  terrorism   204, 206, **209–14**, 235–6, 238, 368
Western Africa   403
Whirling Dervishes (Mawlawiyah)   64, 128
women   **59–60**, 190, 199, 208, 238, 372–3, 382, 399, 400–1
  Afghanistan   199, 208, 232, 233, 392, 393
  dress codes   62, 64, 100, 360, 364, 370
  education   57, 58
  and literature   301, 314, 331–2, 340, 343, 344–5
  politics   156, 218, 356, 370, 390
  sport   361–2
World project, the (Dubai)   277

World Zionist Organization   162

Yasin, Shaykh Aḥmad 201
Yathrib (Medina)   13–14, 21, 22, 24, 36, 62
Yazīd I   89
Yemen 366–9
Yishuv (Palestinian Jews)   166
Yom Kippur War (1973)   176, 179
Yunus Emre   333
Yusuf I   264
Yusuf ibn Tashufin   132

Zahir, Shah, Mohammad   216
zakat ("purification")   34–5, 81
zalet (prayers)   34
Zangi   122
Zarqawi, Abū Mus'ab al-   222
Zawahiri, Ayman al-   182
zawm (fasting)   35, 35
Zayd ibn al-Harith (cousin in law of Muhammad   8, 9, 11, 14, 18, 20, 21, 40, 70, 88, 94, 96, 247
Zaydis   367
zaydīyah (Zaydis/Fivers)   96
Zeroual, General Liamine   398
Zia-ul-Haq, General Mohammad   176, 389–90
Zionism   159, 162, 163, 165
Zirids   130
Zoroastrians   25, 51, 78
zuhdiyyah (ascetic poem)   307

ENCYCLOPÆDIA
Britannica®

Since its birth in the Scottish Enlightenment Britannica's commitment to educated, reasoned, current, humane, and popular scholarship has never wavered. In 2008, Britannica celebrated its 240th anniversary.

Throughout its history, owners and users of *Encyclopædia Britannica* have drawn upon it for knowledge, understanding, answers, and inspiration. In the Internet age, Britannica, the first online encyclopedia, continues to deliver that fundamental requirement of reference, information, and educational publishing – confidence in the material we read in it.

Readers of Britannica Guides are invited to take a FREE trial of Britannica's huge online database. Visit

www.britannicaguides.com

to find out more about this title and others in the series.